Essays on Indian Society

History and Culture Series

ESSAYS ON INDIAN SOCIETY

Edited by
Dr. Raj Kumar

DISCOVERY PUBLISHING HOUSE
NEW DELHI-110002

First Published-2003
Reprinted: 2013
ISBN 81-7141-710-8

Published by

DISCOVERY PUBLISHING HOUSE
4831/24, Ansari Road, Prahlad Street,
Darya Ganj, New Delhi-110002 (India)
Phone: 23279245 • Fax: 91-11-23253475
E-mail:dphtemp@indiatimes.com

Printed at: Dynamic printers, Delhi

CONTENTS

CONTENTS

Preface

Essays on Indian society have been presented to our readers with two fold objectives.

(a) To understand changing social trends through the ages.

(b) To stimulate thinking in the right direction so as to avoid stressful behaviours and way of life, in order to achieve happiness and peace.

We hope our readers will enjoy reading it. We shall feel amply rewarded if readers find it satisfying.

Raj Kumar

Acknowledgement

In preparation of this work I am professedly influenced by writings of Professors G.C. Pande, Ravinder Kumar, D.N. Dhanagre, S. Kadhirvel, T.K. Ravindren, Rajni Kuthari and S.P. Gupta.

Works of Annei Besant has always formed a part of my thought process on this subject. I cannot adequately express my gratitude.

Some of the universities, research institutions, their librarians and staff members have been kind and helpful, I and grateful to them.

To my colleagues and fellow delegates during seminars and conferences, I am beholden for their patience and kind suggestions.

My publisher and his staff have worked hard who deserve my readers love and kindness.

Raj Kumar

Introduction

An interesting characteristic of Indian social engineering was the evolution of a social organism for preserving and protecting the heritage, adapting it to new conditions and transmitting it to posterity.

The factors of this organism were bound to each other by the one consideration of service and self sacrifice.

The fighting classes ensured the defence of the cultural citadel of Dharma, developed their resources in its behalf and shed their blood in its defence.

The vast multitude tilled the soil conducted the trade and shaped nature's materials to subserve the ends of man.

Their daily life, communal and domestic ceremonies, and social institutions catered for a harmonious healthy and happy social life.

They co-operated in the building of the cultural edifice by sacrificing part of their material resources for the common weal, so as to relieve from working for daily bread the class of people consecrated to culture, to lead humanity to spiritual altitudes.

This class of the Brahamana, was indebted to the other classes for the opportunities to put its mental resources to the best uses and dedicating them to the service of humanity.

The masses and the menials yielded obedience, as their lot was made bearable by their being relieved of the restrictions which the higher classes were bound under, in the interest of society. If they had less of rights they also had less of the duties which made life less pleasant if more useful.

There was no cleavage of classes in early times, where rights were carefully linked to duties, and society knew no steep gradients.

Hence a hypothesis of social tyranny is out of accord with the spirit of Indian society.

India no doubt because independent in 1947. We have come a long way. We have many amazing success stories. But it is now high time to think about the Indian social order which gave to us health, prosperity and peace?

Main Characteristics of the Social Order

1. An elaborate educational organization by which highest results were made accessible to the humblest members of social organization.
2. There was the evolution of forces of polity and the working of pólitical institutions in accordance with the spirit of Indian without sacrificing local needs or curbing the native instincts of various groups and communities.
3. There was the creation of immortal forms of art, in architecture, sculpture, painting and iconography.
4. The production of literary masterpieces, technique of science and grammar, art and poetries, prosody and music, dramaturgy and aesthetes.
5. There were industrial arts and metallurgy.
6. The scientific background of sociology.
7. Foundations of philosophical systems and schools of thoughts.
8. There is the history of human attempts, many sided and of various values to clutch at infinity in all its aspects to caystatlize the results by building up systems of dogma, metaphysics, spiritual culture and religious realization to sense the self as co-extensive and co-existent with the universal, infinite in space and eternal in line, out side of which nothing could ever be , and inside v hich everything is but an aspect of the one indivisible and ever-present entity.

Hence it is obvious that philosophy of Indian social order is not like similar social orders else where turning themselves into machines of economic production alone.

Raj Kumar

CHAPTER - I

CULTURE AND SOCIETY

When Matthew Arnold spoke of the barbarian, the philistine, and the populace, and divided the English society of his time into these three classes, he was looking for signs and traces of culture with a great deal of scepticism and frustration. The rich man who does not care for culture; the middle class man who is satisfied with his narrow successes, and thinks, in his self-importance, that there is nothing else worth acquiring; and the populace which is struggling all the time for mere subsistence, having hardly any time for the finer things of life: if these are the persons that constitute the society, how can there be any scope for culture? The dissemination or diffusion of culture presupposes that man is above want; that he has not to struggle for food and shelter; and that the prevalence of law and the dispensation of justice in society are assured. It is difficult for culture to flourish, if we have to fight for our daily bread. Any cultural system that does not satisfy these requirements is bound to be partial or fragmentary. The culture of ancient India, Greece, and Rome was a partial culture. It was restricted, in many ways, to one class of people. One can say about their culture what Tennyson said about Sir Lancelot:

> ***His honour rooted in dishonour stood***
> ***And faith unfaithful kept him falsely true***

The French and Russian revolutions were upsurges against the fragmentariness and exclusiveness of a culture of this kind. The scene in India is changing today for similar reasons. The struggle for power, the bid for white-collar jobs, and the frantic pursuit of security are all off-shoots of this desire for a universal diffusion of culture. The struggle for wealth and power is relentless because it is assumed that cultured life is impossible without such a foundation.

How then shall we make sure that a universal diffusion of culture becomes possible? In the first place, each individual has to be assured of his absolute security and his full dignity in the society he lives in. This means that an egalitarian society, whether it is made possible through a capitalist, socialist or Marxist initiative, comes into being. Secondly, the security and comfort of an affluent society should not send a person to sleep. Leisure has no value for one who does not know how to use it. The pursuit of culture depends on the availability of leisure. But it also presupposes an intense desire for culture, a passion for perfection. If the common man in Japan spends his spare time on *pachungo* and the aristocrat on playing bridge, there can be no hope for culture. Leisure is bound to be misused by the common man if a deep and steady aspiration for the finer things of life is not implanted in him right from the beginning. This means that our educational system must be overhauled so as to promote the cultural urge in each pupil at home and school. In saying this, we assume that there is an atmosphere of culture in the family and that teachers are available who can inspire in the young this passion for perfection from their childhood. The whole question then turns upon the action of individuals, the individuals that compose a family or run a school.

The attempt of diffuse culture on a universal scale is a long and arduous undertaking. Perhaps the Indian sages were right when they assumed that all human beings could not be said to have reached the same stage of evolution. There are manifold evolutionary steps. For one reason or the other, any by virtue of the temperament with which they are endowed, human beings move at different stages of the journey. The idea of the four *varnas* or categories of human beings was therefore conceived as a code of conduct for each one of these categories. Duties were prescribed according to the capacities and inclinations of each category within a religious framework. It is tragic that the principle of heredity gradually distorted and falsified this idea.

A great deal of bitterness has been caused in recent times by the very mention of the phrase *chatur varnas*. The petrification of the *varnas* into a system of castes and creeds and the recognition of social rank and position according to birth cannot be condemned to severely. But the four *varnas* or types characterize human society in all parts of the world. The thinker, the warrior, the purveyor, and the worker typify four kinds or levels of human activity and all of them are essential for the maintenance of society. A progressive society gives equal opportunities to all to prove their worth and aptitude and assigns to each individual the vocation for which he is fitted. We have yet to realize the value of this great truth in a caste-ridden society like ours. Mere variety, without the controlling principle of unity, results in chaos. Almost every religious revival in India vivisected the country further by adding one more sect to the numerous castes and creeds that already existed. Sectarianism could know no end when the living centre of national consciousness was itself dormant.

Unless there is a background of social and cultural unity to this diversity of castes and creeds and even of political parties in the nation, a structural disintegration may confront our society. The nation must be held together socially and culturally, if it is to be called upon to preserve the multitude of castes and creeds and judge a variety of political issues and programmes. Indian culture has always been instinct with this sense of unity. This sense of unity has to be disengaged from ancient, medieval and modern accretions and reasserted in the midst of a changing world order.

We live in a chaotic age that is full of contradictions and confusions. We struggle to survive in an era of strikes and other forms of labour unrest when capitalism itself has hardly been able to fulfil the constructive role which Marx assigned to it in *Das Capital.* The advanced countries tend to dominate developing countries, directly or indirectly. Several forms of human misery have been eliminated from some parts of the world. But other forms of it have cropped up in our pushbutton era. In an age pulsating with contradictory ideologies, it has become very difficult for a person to choose his own path of evolution.

The message of the Buddha bears a great relevance to these problems of our contemporary world. The Buddha preached the gospel of liberty, equality, and fraternity far more meaningfully than the French Revolution did. Though he was not sure of the complete elimination of human misery in the foreseeable future, he advocated compassion which can at least do a great deal to relieve it. Wherever he saw an open conflict between reason and religion, he stressed the need for a scientific and open-eyed approach to spiritual fulfillment. He stood for liberty in the highest sense of the term so that an individual could rise to his own highest stature, going beyond the life of the senses and intellect and climbing into an ineffable transcendence. As for the gospel of equality, he turned his back on the seventh heaven itself and affirmed that he would have nothing to do with it till the last human being was saved from ignorance and bondage. The world was, for the Buddha, a *sangha*, a fraternity, whose sovereignty the individual had to accept if he aspired to exceed himself.

India is now overhauling the structure of its society in order to remould it in the light of such an ideal. From this point of view, the secularism, which India has adopted as the sheet-anchor of its social and cultural policy, is indeed a significant philosophy. Secularism can be described as a religion without any religiosity in it. While permitting every individual perfect freedom of belief and conviction, it requires him, as a social unit, to fulfil certain obligations towards the society of which he is a member. Birth is no criterion of worth. He alone is competent who proves his competence by what he thinks, says, or does. No one has the right to inflict injury on others. The *dhoti* and the *pyjama*, the long coat and the short coat, not to speak of the petticoat, have all of them, their equal rights before the law, provided the minimum decency is observed. Each man is free to elect his own mode of worship and living.

The factors which foment social differences in India are now being opposed. Each religion has been assured proper protection while no religion can afford to be aggressive. Each language can grow to its full stature on the lines determined by its own genius. But no single language can strangle or overwhelm another. The liquidation of the zamindari system and of the feudal order of princes and the shift of emphasis, with regard to government servants, on their work as servants of the public as distinguished from their position as bureaucrats, are sure to take us a long way on the road to equality and liberty. The real challenge to our democracy today is casteism and communalism. But with the rapid spread of education, this too may be a discarded shibboleth.

The social reformer, who is at work in our midst, sometimes proposes drastic remedies which are worse than the disease itself. Intercommunal marriage is thus frequently upheld as the one panacea for all communal differences. A kind of social regimentation is sought to be imposed upor what is essentially the problem of the individual. Marriage is an intensely personal affair. The fact that man is the architect of his own fortune or misfortune is nowhere better borne out than with regard to marriage. The alliances which used to be arranged in the past between royal families on political grounds deserve as much to be condemned as the marriages which are sought to be promoted today for reasons of social unity. If a love marriage is intercommunal, a progressive society is bound to welcome it. But to arrange a marriage on intercommunal lines as a weapon against communalism is to exploit the individual in the interest of an irrelevant social idea. Such a step can hardly have the desired effect. Instead of promoting social reconciliation, it may as well pave the way for another irreconcilable community.

The real basis of reconciliation lies in the core of human kindliness and tolerance. It has only to be awakened in order to be brought to the forefront. Even today, in the villages, the Hindus and the Muslims live together in perfect amity and respect each other's religion and religious habits, without the Hindu becoming a Muslim or the Muslim a Hindu. We frequently find in our towns and villages families belonging to different communities living on the friendliest terms, without discarding their own habits and customs. A day may come when the barriers between communities will fall and all will adopt a universal code of conduct. But it is certain that any compulsion or regimentation towards hastening the dawn of such a day will only end in delaying it further. The great and sure remedy lies not in converting the other man to our fold, caste or creed. It does not also consist in a drastic negation of all such differences. It lies in revolutionizing our own outlook, in changing vision, and in seeing the other man as we see ourselves. Man has to take his stand, not on his egoistic self, but on his psyche which makes the whole world kin. He will then be able to feel the pulse of humanity and see steadily and whole, approaching the essential human values which lie masked under the heavy weight of custom and communal habit.

Seen in this light, secularism is what Tagore called "The Religion of Man". It is the credo of Sri Aurobindo's *vishwa manava*.

At a time when there is a wrong insistence on religion, caste, and creed, secularism, which is only a negative attitude, assumes positive significance. It is the stream of clear reason which washes away all impurities of mind and heart. Later, secularism has to be supplemented by innate psychic insight, by that primal human sympathy of which Wordsworth spoke. When we have assimilated the lower aspects of secularism, we shall be ripe for the next transformation. Secularism is thus the great healer of social differences. It is the integral approach that reconciles opposites.

When the social structure of our national life is founded on this basis, it will be possible to project this attitude actively on the international plane. I remember an amusing incident about an Indian couple who went to Germany for a holiday. They did not know a word of German. But a German couple that met them smiled to them in a kindly way and spoke to them through man's first language—the language of gestures. They signalled to the Indian couple as if to ask them whether they were husband and wife. On receiving a nod in the affirmative, the German couple pointed to the Indians' fingers and asked them why they did not have the marriage ring. The Indians did not have the marriage rings on at that time. They admitted as much. Then the German gentleman pointed to the heart suggesting that, when hearts were one, marriage rings did not matter at all.

This incident, I venture to think, brings us to the heart of the matter. It is the heart that matters and not the ring, the language, the creed, or the community which belongs to one or to which one belongs. Belongings are mere trappings. It is the soul of man that makes him nobly human. We have seen how soldiers fighting on opposite sides, when the two World Wars were on, felt towards each other like brothers, while lying wounded side by side. In the communal riots that followed in the wake of August 1947, we have known of Hindu families harbouring Muslim refugees at great risk to themselves and vice versa. The greater the difficulty, the greater is the spirit that man displays. One can only hope that a well-planned system of national education will awaken the soul in every individual and build here a new society on imperishable foundations.

I cannot do better than conclude this chapter with a few lines from Sri Aurobindo. These lines are to be found in Canto I, Book XI, of *Savitri*:

Then in the process of evolving Time
All shall be drawn into a single plan,
A divine harmony shall be earth's law,
Beauty and Joy remould her way to live....
The Spirit shall be the master of this world
Lurking no more in form's obscurity
And Nature shall reverse her action's rule,
The outward world disclose the Truth it veils.
Even should a hostile force cling to its reign
And claim its right's perpetual sovereignty
And man refuse his high spiritual fate,
Yet shall the secret Truth in things prevail.
For in the march of all-fulfilling Time
The hour must come of the Transcendent's will:
All turns and winds towards His predestined ends
In nature's fixed inevitable course
Decreed since the beginning of the worlds
In the deep essence of created things.

Chapter - II

OUR SOCIAL DILEMMA

Often I ask myself: What is India? What is the essence of India? What are the forces that have gone to make India and how are they related to the major dominating influences of the world in the past and in the present?

The subject is a vast one and covers the entire field of human activity, not only in India but elsewhere, and I suppose no single person can do justice to it. But we can take up some particular aspects of it and try to understand them. We can at least try to understand our India, although that understanding will be limited if we do not have the wider picture of the world before us.

What is culture? I look it up in the dictionary and I find a variety of definitions. One great writer has called it "the acquainting ourselves with the best that has been known and said in the world". Another definition says that it is "the training, development, or strengthening of the powers, mental or physical, or the condition thus produced; improvement or refinement of mind, morals, or tastes; enlightenment of civilisation." Culture, in this sense, is something basic and international. Then there are the national aspects of culture and there can be no doubt that many nations have each developed a certain genius and individuality.

Where does India fit in? Some people have talked of Hindu culture and Muslim culture and Christian culture. I do not understand these terms, although it is true that the great religious movements have influenced the culture of a race or a nation. If I look at India, I find the gradual growth of a composite culture of the Indian people.

The origins of this culture may be traced back, on the one hand, to the pre-Aryan period, the civilisation of Mohenjadaro, etc., and the great Dravidian civilisation. On the other hand, it received a powerful impress from the Aryans who came to India from Central Asia. Subsequently, it was influenced by repeated incursions from the north-west and later by the people who came across the seas from the west.

Thus this national culture gradually grew and took shape. It had a remarkable capacity for synthesis and of absorbing new elements. So long as it did so it was dynamic and living. In later years it lost the dynamic quality and became essentially static which led to weakness in all fields. Throughout India's history we see the two rival and contradictory forces at work—those in favour of a synthesis and absorption and those fissiparous tendencies which separate. Today we face the same problem in a different context. There are powerful forces working for unity, not only political but cultural also. There are also forces that disrupt and lay stress on separateness.

The question, therefore, for us today is not an academic one but a vital issue, on the understanding and solution of which depends our future. Normally, it is the business of the intellectuals to give a lead in dealing with such problems, but our intellectuals have failed us. Many of them do not even seem to realise the nature of this problem, others suffer from frustration and a crisis of the spirit, not knowing where to turn.

Marxism and its progeny attracted many of the intellectuals, and there is no doubt that it gave a certain analysis of historical developments which helped us to think and to understand. But even that proved too narrow a creed and, whatever its virtue as an economic approach, it failed to resolve our basic doubts. Life is something more than economic growth, though it is well to realise that economic growth is a basic foundation to life and progress. History shows us two principles at work, the principle of continuity and the principle of change.

They appear to be opposed to each other and yet, each has something of the other. We notice what we consider sudden changes in the shape of violent revolutions or an earthquake. Yet, every geologist knows that the major changes in the earth's surface are gradual, and earthquakes are trivial in comparison to them. So also, revolutions are merely the outward evidence of a long process of change and subtle erosion. Thus, change itself is a continuous process and even a static continuity must yield to gradual change so long as it is not overcome by complete stagnation and death.

There are periods in history when the process and tempo of change are more in evidence. At other times, the appearance is much more static. The static period in the life of a nation is a period of progressive deterioration and weakness, leading to the decay of the creative arts and tendencies and often to political subjection.

Probably, the most powerful cultural element in India came from the union of the Aryan with the older element in India, chiefly the Dravidian. Out of this arose a mighty culture, chiefly represented by our great classical language, Sanskrit. That language, though it had its origin together with old Pahlavi in a common parent in Central Asia, became the national language of India. Both the north and the south contributed to its growth.

Indeed, in later days, the south played a very important part. Sanskrit became the symbol not only of our people's thought and religion, but the embodiment of the cultural unity of India. Ever since the Buddha's time, it has not been the spoken language of the people and yet it continued to exercise this powerful influence all over India. Other great influences came in, which led to new avenues of thought and expression.

Caste, in its innumerable forms, is a typical product of India. Untouchability, the objections to interdining, intermarriage, etc., are unknown in any other country. The result was a certain narrowness in our outlook. Indians even to the present day, find it difficult to mix with others. Not only that, but each caste tends to remain separate even when they go to other countries. Most of us in India take all this for granted and do not realise how it astonishes and even shocks the people of other countries.

Thus, in India, we developed at one and the same time the broadest tolerance and catholicity of thought and opinion as well as the narrowest social forms of behaviour. This split personality has pursued us and we struggle against it even today. We overlook and excuse our own failing and narrowness of customs and habit by references to the great thoughts we have inherited from our ancestors. But there is an essential conflict between the two, and so long as we do not resolve it, we shall continue to have this split personality.

In a more or less static period these opposed elements did not come into conflict with each other much. But as the tempo of political and economic change has grown faster these conflicts also have come more in evidence. In the atomic age, at the threshold of which we stand, we are compelled by over overwhelming circumstances to put an end to this inner conflict. To fail to do so is to fail as a nation and lose even the virtues that we have possessed.

We have to face, therefore, this crisis of the spirit in India, even as we have to face great political and economic problems. The industrial revolution is coming rapidly to India and changing us in many ways. It is an inevitable consequence of political and economic change that there should be social changes also if we are to remain as integrated human beings and an integrated nation. We cannot have political change and industrial progress and imagine that we can continue unchanged in the social sphere. The stresses and strains will be too great and if we do not resolve them, we shall crack up.

It is extraordinary how our professions run far ahead of our practice. We talk of peace and nonviolence and function in a different way. We talk of tolerance and construe it to mean our way of thinking only and are intolerant of other ways. We proclaim our ideal, that of a philosophic detachment even in the midst of action, that of a "*sthitaprajna*", but we act on a far lower plane, and a growing indiscipline degrades us as individuals and as a community.

When the Westerners came here across the seas, the closed land of India was again thrown open in a particular direction. The modern industrial civilisation gradually crept in a passive way. New thoughts and ideas invaded us and our intellectuals developed the habit of thinking like British intellectuals.

Now this faith in western thought is itself being shaken and so we have neither the old nor the new, and we drift not knowing whether we are going. The younger generation has no standards left, nothing to direct their thinking or control their action.

This is a dangerous situation and if not checked and improved, is likely to lead to grave consequences. It may be that we are passing through an age of transition, political, economic and social, and these are the inevitable consequences of such a period. But in the atomic age no country is likely to be given many chances to correct itself, and failure may well mean disaster.

CHAPTER - III

SOCIAL LIFE

INTRODUCTORY

The period intervening between the downfall of the Imperial Mauryas and the rise of the Gupta Emperors marks a crisis in India's social history. The impetus which Aśoka's imperial propaganda had given to Buddhism was continued in the centuries immediately before and after Christ by other royal patrons and by the zeal of pious missionaries. Hence followed both the firm establishment of the faith within India and its expansion into the regions of East and South-East Asia. Buddhism thus, became definitely a world religion, while Jainism under similar influences was transformed into an all-India cult. In the course of these great movements within the fold of Indian society, the situation was somewhat complicated by the influx of large hordes of foreigners with altogether alien social and cultural standards. The first reactions to these changes are seen in the gloomy prophecies of universal decay and dissolution that are met with in contemporary Brahmanical works. And yet in this age of seeming social collapse were sown the seeds of a great revival. Brahmanism, to begin with, so far from being engulfed by the onrushing waves of the rival faiths, girded itself for a fresh struggle and an eventual triumph. While its body of social and religious laws was systematised in the great Smṛitis of Manu and Yājñavalkya, its extensive circle of myths, legends and fables, and its entire code of individual and social ethics, were incorporated into the epic story of the *Mahābhārata* so as to give that work in its present form an authority rivalling that of the Veda. Brahmanism, again, found in some of the ruling houses of Northern India and the Deccan zealous patrons who upheld its social and religious practices, while in the South it won for itself an honoured place in contemporary society. Thus it prepared itself for its crowning triumph in the age of the Imperial Guptas. At the same time, therefore, that the reform movements of Buddhism and Jainism during this age reached their culmination, the Brahmanical counter-reformation strengthened itself to meet its two rivals with success. Simultaneously the problem created by the settlement of foreigners *en masse* was solved by the rapidity and completeness with which they were assimilated into the Indian social system. There was yet another development which, like those just mentioned, stamps this age with the seal of creativity. Though the rise of towns on an extensive scale may be traced back long before this period, a new social type, *viz.* the city-bred man of fashion, portrayed in the *Kāmasūtra* of *Vātsyāyana*, seems only now to have come on the scene.

SOCIAL DIVISIONS AND SUB-DIVISIONS

A. Brāhmaṇas

The division of society into four *varṇas* with their distinctive duties, occupations and status, and the rules relating to their intermarriage and so forth, is the bed-rock of the Brahmanical social fabric. By virtue of their origin the Brāhmaṇas, it was held, take the first place in the order of castes. It is on this and similar grounds that Manu (i 96, x 3) and Yājñavalkya (i 198-9) assert the doctrine of the pre-eminence of the Brāhmaṇas not only over all other *varṇas* but over all created beings. Along with this went as amplification of the rules governing the sacraments and the domestic and other sacrifices that were incumbent upon the Brāhmaṇas. As before, while the duties (*dharma*) of Vedic study, of sacrificing for himself and of making gifts, are shared by the Brāhmaṇa with the two other upper castes, to the Brāhmaṇa alone fall the distinctive occupations (*vṛitti*) of teaching, sacrificing for others, and accepting gifts (*M.* x 75-6; *Y.* i 118). In Manu (x 77-8, 95-6) not only are the other castes expressly forbidden to adopt any of these occupations, but a man of low caste accepting through greed the occupation of a higher one is punished with confiscation of property and imprisonment. The constant and assiduous study of the Veda is the Brāhmaṇa's highest duty according to Manu (iv 147-9), while Yājñavalkya (i 198) stresses the Brāhmaṇa's God-given duties of preserving the Veda, satisfying the gods and the manes, and protecting *dharma*. As to his occupations, teaching the Veda (without stipulating a fee) is the peculiar privilege of the Brāhmaṇa which the other two castes did not share (*M.* i 103; x 1). A Brāhmaṇa in distress may learn the Veda from a non-Brāhmaṇa, but the perpetual student must not reside with such a teacher or even with a Brāhmaṇa who cannot expound the Veda (*ibid.* ii 241-2). A Brāhmaṇa without the means of subsistence may in the last resort accept gifts from any person's hand, but the acceptance of gifts from a low man is worse than teaching or sacrificing for him; a Brāhmaṇa had better maintain himself by gleaning grain or preferably picking up single grains from the fields (*M.* x 102-12). It is indeed the king's duty to support a Brāhmaṇa and especially a Śrotriya who has no means of livelihood, but the Brāhmaṇa who solicits gifts from an unrighteous or low-born king, or from kings in general, or, again, from certain disreputable classes, makes himself liable to severe spiritual penalties (*M.* iv 84-91; *Y.* i 140-l). A Brāhmaṇa, though entitled to accept gifts, should not cultivate that habit too much for danger of losing the divine light in himself (*M.* iv 186). A Brāhmaṇa, accepting gifts from a Śūdra to perform a sacrifice for him deserves the strongest censure (*M.* xi 42-3; *Y.* i 127). In general a Brāhmaṇa is to follow those occupations that cause the least pain to others; be may live by gleaning corn, taking what is given unasked, by begging, agriculture or trade, but never by service, 'a dog's occupation'; he may accumulate as much grain as will fill a granary or a grain-jar, or suffice for three days, or for one day, or he may live by picking up ears of corn from the fields, each succeeding practice among these being a superior alternative to the preceding (*M.* iv 1-9; *Y.* i 128). Though this is the strict law prescribing a Brāhmaṇa's occupation, both Manu (x 80-94) and Yājñavalkya (iii 35) feel constrained to allow Brāhmaṇas when reduced to distress to live by the occupations of the lower castes. This concession is subject, as in the older law, to numerous exceptions touching various objectionable trades and professions. Moreover, having recovered from his distress the Brāhmaṇa must purify himself by performing a penance, and surrendering the wealth thus acquired, and so forth (*M.* xi 193-4; and *Y* iii 35, 289). Man (viii 348-9), again, amplifying the older law, expressly permits Brāhmaṇas as well as Kshatriyas and Vaiśyas to take up arms in self-defence, or in defence of women and Brāhmaṇas, or to prevent the violation of their own duties and to ward off destruction from the three upper classes. Even killing in such circumstances, Manu emphatically declares, is no sin.

It follows from this severe code of discipline that deviations from the ordained standard brought deep discredit and disgrace upon the defaulting Brāhmaṇa. In Manu (iii 150-82) and Yājñavalkya (i 222-4), as in the older Smṛitis, we have long lists of persons not eligible for invitation to *śrāddhas*. Among these are included one not studying the Veda, one teaching for a stipulated fee, and one teaching Śūdra pupils. Not in frequently such degraded Brāhmaṇas are equated with Śūdras (*M.* ii 168; viii 102). When a Brāhmaṇa who neither performs austerities nor studies the Veda accepts gifts, he drags both himself and the donor down into hell (*M.* iv 190; *Y.* i 202). And yet we find already at work a tendency to exalt the Brāhmaṇa irrespective of his qualifications, and even in disregard of his unfitness. In strikingly emphatic language we are told (*Mbh.* xiii 151, 21-3; *M.* ix 317-9) that a Brāhmaṇa, whether learned or not, is a great deity like fire, whether consecrated or not; that like fire which is not contaminated even in a cremation-ground, a Brāhmaṇa employed in the meanest occupations must be honoured as a great deity. After this it is no surprise to learn (*M.* iii 149; *Mbh.* xiii 90, 2) that the merits of the invited Brāhmaṇa need not be closely scrutinised at rites in honour of the gods, though such scrutiny is necessary for rites in honour of the manes. The only exceptions which Manu allows in the former case are a number of notoriously bad characters (iii 150).

It remains to notice the immunities and privileges belonging to the Brāhmaṇas in the old Smṛiti law which are repeated in our present texts. Among the persons entitled to the right of way, the *snātaka* (a Brāhmaṇa who has performed his ceremonial bath after completing his education) has precedence even over the king (*M.* ii 138-9; *Y.* i. 117). A Brāhmaṇa offender is not to be sentenced to death on any account, but he is liable to banishment without confiscation of property, to shaving of the head, to branding or to fines (*M.* viii 123, 378-81, 383-5; *Y.* ii 270). As a rule the

Brāhmaṇa's punishments are less severe than those of the other classes. On the other hand offences against Brāhmaṇas are punished with more severity than those committed against the other classes. As in the older law Brāhmaṇa-murder heads the list of mortal sins (*mahāpātakas*) to be expiated by particularly severe penances (*M.* ix 237; xi 55, 102; *Y.* iii 227, 257), and it is visited with other fearful punishments in the next life (*M.* xi 49; xii 55; *Y.* iii 20). According to Manu (iv 162; xi 90), no injury may be done to a Brāhmaṇa, and intentional slaying of a Brāhmaṇa is an inexpiable sin. But elsewhere (viii 350) Manu himself permits the slaying even of a learned Brāhmaṇa in self-defence. The Brāhmaṇa offender's property is exempt from confiscation while the theft of a Brāhmaṇa's gold ranks among the mortal sins (*M.* viii 380; xi 55; *Y.* iii 227). The heirless property of a Brāhmaṇa is distributed among his fellow-Brāhmaṇas, while that of other castes is escheated to the king (*M.* ix 188-9). The seizure of a Brāhmaṇa's property, as of a god's, is visited with severe penalties in the next life (*M.* xi 26). Not only are learned Brāhmaṇas exempt from taxes (*M.* vii 133), but the king is bound to support them after proper examination of their family, learning and character (*M.* vii 135; *Y.* iii 44). A learned Brāhmaṇa is to act where necessary as the king's substitute for the trial of cases (*M.* viii 9; *Y.* ii 3).

This description of the Brāhmaṇa's status according to the Smṛitis may now be checked by the evidence of other contemporary sources. In the enumeration of castes in the *Milindapañha* (5, 122, 331), as in the older Pāli canonical texts, the Kshatriyas invariably precede the Brāhmaṇas. The superior status of the Kshatriya is pointedly brought out in the Pāli *Nidānakathā* (i 49) and the Sanskrit *Lalitavistara* (i 20): here we are told in the story of Buddha's early life that while the Brāhmaṇa and the Kshatriya are the two highest classes, the Kshatriyas are now admitted to hold the topmost rank. This tendency to glorify the Kshatriya may have been due partly to the desire of the authors to exalt the order to which the founder of their faith belonged, and partly to the strength of the ancient tradition. In any case the *purohita* in the *Milindapañha* (164), as in the Jātakas, is found to combine with his proper office of domestic priest the function of a teacher of the king in early youth. In the story of Nāgasena's early life (*Miln*. 9-10) we find that having been born in a Brāhmaṇa household and reached his seventh year Nāgasena was told by his father that the study of the sciences (*scil*. the Vedas) was compulsory in his family; he was thereupon taken to a Brāhmaṇa teacher (āchārya) who received a substantial fee for teaching him the three Vedas. From this we see that Brāhmaṇa boys went at a tender age, as required by the Canon, to live in residence with a teacher for learning the Vedas, and that it was customary to pay the teacher his fee in advance notwithstanding the denunciation of this practice in the Smṛitis.

In the story of the Buddha referred to above, the circle of Brāhmaṇaslore is said to comprise the three Vedas with their auxiliaries (as known to stock lists in the Jātakas), and knowledge of 'the signs of great men'. More diversified is the curriculum of studies of the Brāhmaṇa mentioned in the *Milindapañha* (178) enumerating the duties of a prince, a Brāhmaṇa youth, a Vaiśya and a Śūdra. It comprises not only the Vedic group (Rigveda, Yajurveda, Sāmaveda, Atharvaveda, Itihāsa, Purāṇa, lexicography, ritual, phonetics and grammar), but also astronomy, astrology and natural philosophy (*lokāyatika*), as well as the interpretation of dreams, omens and portents, of solar and lunar eclipses, of the behaviour of stars and planets, of thunder and the fall of meteors, of earthquakes and conflagrations, and of omens to be drawn from the sight of dogs and deer, the cries of birds, and so on. It is evident that a vast store of sciences and pseudo-sciences had by this time been added to the Vedas in the compass of a Brāhmaṇa's studies. Probably the non-Vedic lore was studied for their livelihood by worldly Brāhmaṇas such as those described so vividly in the Jātakas. Of the type of the true Brāhmaṇa known likewise to the Jātakas, we have a striking reminiscence in a *Milindapañha* passage (225-6) explaining the description of the Buddha as 'an open-handed Brāhmaṇa'. The Brāhmaṇa, we are told, is one who has passed beyond hesitation, perplexity, and doubt, who has escaped from every sort of becoming and is entirely free from evil, who cultivates excellent conditions of heart, who follows the traditional regulations relating to study and teaching, making and receiving gifts, self-control and performance of duties, who enjoys the supreme bliss of ecstatic meditation, and who knows the course of births and all forms of existence. Here we have evidently a picture of the Brāhmaṇa at his best according to the standards of the contemporary smṛitis. As to the Brāhmaṇa's regular occupations, we have historical instances of Brāhmaṇas, notwithstanding the strict Smṛiti injunctions to the contrary, engaged in royal service, and even rising to be founders of ruling houses. Brāhmaṇas are also known to have not only performed sacrifices for themselves, but also officiated as priests at sacrifices celebrated by royalty. Brāhmaṇas, again, are mentioned not only as making gifts, but also as accepting gifts in cash and kind from kings and princes who delighted to honour them.[1]

B. Kshatriyas

In Manu and Yājñavalkya as in the older Smṛitis, the Kshatriyas, while sharing with the Brāhmaṇas and the Vaiśyas the duties of Vedic study, sacrificing for themselves, and making gifts, are assigned the sole occupation of ruling and fighting : only in times of distress is a Kshatriya allowed to live by the occupation of a Vaiśya (*M.* i 89; x 77-89, 95, 117; *Y.* i 119; iii 42). This is confirmed in part and partly corrected and supplemented by references in other works. The list of duties and occupations laid down for the Kshatriyas in the Smṛitis is reflected in the *Mahābhārata* (xii 60, 13 f. etc.). But as Hopkins[2] justly remarks, the essence of the king's duty according to the oft-repeated axiom and motto of the caste in the Great Epic is fighting : for him to die of disease in a house is declared to be a sin, while death in battle is most commended. Repeated references in the *Mahābhārata* again lead Hopkins[3] to conclude that there were three fundamental rules forming the Kshatriya's code of conduct towards his fellows: the first was the 'guest-law', every guest being regarded as inviolable; the second was the law of not forgetting kindness, and the third and last was the sacredness of a 'refugee', *i.e.* a person who threw himself (even in battle) upon one's mercy. The education of the Kshatriya as described in the Epic is somewhat different from that prescribed in the Smṛitis. As Hopkins[4] observes, the descriptions of the early lives of the heroes in the *Rāmāyaṇa* and the *Mahābhārata* prove that the Kshatriyas were trained principally in the art of fighting (*dhanurveda*), and that they passed out of boyhood in their sixteenth year.

The same discrepancy with the Smṛiti law is found in the description of a prince's duties in the *Milindapañha* (178). Here we read that a prince is to learn the arts of managing horses, elephants, and chariots, as well as those of writing and accounts, and of waging war. In this severely practical training, it will be observed, there is no mention of Vedic study such as is attributed in the same context to the Brāhmaṇa youth. Two other slight references in the same work illustrate the current view of the Kshatriya's status. From a simile (190) we learn that the 'Khattiya-secret formula' was current, as in the Jātaka tales, among this order alone. Another and a more striking simile (357-8) shows that a man of low caste presuming to consecrate himself after the Kshatriya fashion was punished with mutilation and torture for usurping a position of authority to which low castes were not entitled. It seems, therefore, that the Kshatriyas were held as in the early Buddhist times, to be an exclusive caste, and that the privilege of ruling was regarded as the monopoly of a member of this order receiving the proper consecration. Other evidence seems to show that the Kshatriyas performed various sacrifices as enjoined by the Smṛiti law. The contemporary inscriptions have preserved the memory not only of kings, but also of private individuals (apparently of the Kshatriya caste) who performed Vedic sacrifices accompanied with the gift of magnificent fees to the officiating priests.[5]

C. Gṛihapatis Etc.

Repeating the old Smṛiti rule Manu (i 90; viii 410, 418; ix 326-33; x 79-80) and Yājñavalkya (i 119) enjoin upon the Vaiśyas, the third in the order of castes, the three-fold duty of Vedic study, performing sacrifices and making gifts, while fixing for them the occupations of agriculture, cattle-rearing, money-lending, and trade. The same three-fold list of duties is laid down for the Vaiśya in the *Mahābhārata* (xii 60, 21 f.) which, however, declares his special occupation to be cattle-rearing. As in the contemporary Smṛiti law, the Vaiśya is entitled to take up arms for self-defence, for the defence of cows and Brāhmaṇas, and for preventing the mixture of castes (*ibid.* 165. 33). In other passages, however (*ibid.* i 126, 13-14, 164; 20; iii 4, 15 etc.), Hopkins[6] detects a tendency to equate the Vaiśya's status with that of the Śūdra. When we turn to the *Milindapañha* (178), we find it assigning, in the fashion of the Smṛitis, the duties of agriculture and trade to the *Vessa* (Skt. *Vaiśya*). In their actual pictures of social life, however, the records of this period make no mention of the Vaiśyas as a separate caste. We are introduced instead to a class well known to the early Buddhist literature, *viz. gṛihapatis* (Pāli *gahapati*, Jaina Prākṛit *gāhāvai*). Of the ten stories of pious Jaina laymen in the *Uvāsagadasāo*, as many as nine deal with the lives of *gṛihapatis* described in the stock phrase as men possessed of vast stores of hoarded wealth and money lent out at interest, enjoying great estates and herds of cattle, who are consulted on all sorts of business by kings, princes and merchants. The tenth story deals with the life of a potter who is described by contrast as owning only one-fourth of the possessions of the *gṛihapati*. The *gṛihapati*, therefore, we may surmise, formed the rich capitalist class consisting of big land owners, money-lenders and ranchers, and they enjoyed high social prestige and were distinguished from the humbler class of artisans. Some light is also thrown upon the status of the *gṛihapatis* by references in the votive inscriptions of the centuries immediately before and after Christ. The *gṛihapatis* are here referred to as following the avocations of a merchant, farmer, caravan-leader or treasurer. In a few instances the donors introduce themselves as relations (son, grandson, mother, wife, daughter, or daughter-in-law) of individual *gṛihapatis*. Apparently, therefore, the *gṛihapatis* followed miscellaneous occupations and formed a special class or rank with high distinctions, but not a rigid caste. Along with the *gṛihapatis* the votive inscriptions commemorate a number of *kuṭuṁbikas* who likewise appear in the Jātakas in the rôle of men of property at the head of a household. Lastly and most important, the votive inscriptions and other records of this period speak of the *seṭṭhi* who is likewise a familiar figure in the early Buddhist literature. In the story of Nāgasena's early life, the *Milindapañha* (17) tells the tale of a *seṭṭhi* of Pāṭaliputra who journeyed at the head of his caravan from North-Western India to his own city. In the votive inscriptions of this period while there are instances of *seṭthis* who themselves make the donations, other donors introduce themselves as their relatives. In a few instances a *seṭṭhi* is referred to simply by his native village or town and without his personal name. Clearly then the *seṭṭhi* was, as in the Jātakas, a rich and influential merchant-prince occupying a special position of honour among members of his profession. A few inscriptions mentioning *seṭṭhis* who were also *gṛihapatis* or sons of *gṛihapatis* suggest that, as in the Jātakas, the *seṭṭhi* was the most important and aristocratic representative of this class.[7]

D. Śūdra Castes, Mixed Castes and Aboriginal Tribes

The disabilities imposed by the old Smṛiti Law upon the fourth and lowest caste, the Śūdras, are emphasised by our present authorities. According to Manu (i 91; x 123-5) and Yājñavalkya (i 120) the Śūdra because of his low origin has only one duty and one occupation, *viz.* to serve the upper classes and especially the Brāhmaṇas who in their turn are bound to feed, clothe and maintain him. Only in times of distress is a Śūdra allowed to live by practising various arts and crafts or by serving a Kshatriya or a rich Vaiśya (*M.* x 99-100, 121), or alternatively by engaging in trades and crafts of various kinds (*Y.* i 120). According to Manu (viii 413-14; 416-17) the Brāhmaṇa can compel a Śūdra, whether purchased or not, to do servile work, and can without hesitation appropriate his possessions. For a Śūdra, so runs the argument, is not released from his inherent servitude even after emancipation, and he has no property of his own. Of the same nature is the clause in Manu (viii 418) enjoining the king to compel the Śūdra to perform his work. That these extreme clauses belonged to times long past is proved by the internal evidence of the works themselves. A verse common to Manu (ix 157) and the *Mahābhārata* (xiii 47, 56), and therefore of respectable antiquity, recognises the Śūdra's right of bequeathing his property in equal shares among his sons. Another clause (*M.* ix 179; *Y.* ii 133) refers to the same right when it allows the Śūdra's son by his female slave to take a share at the Śūdra's discretion. Again, the very clauses (*M.* xi 42-3; *Y.* i 127) declaring a Śūdra's gift to be unlawful for Brāhmaṇas imply the Śūdra's right of giving away his property. The rules (*M.* viii 142; *Y.* ii 38) relating to the legal rates of interest payable by Śūdras presuppose the Śūdra's capacity to follow an independent vocation. In other respects the Śūdra enjoys, as in the Dharmasūtras, limited social, religious and political rights. Thus while the Śūdra's food is unfit to be eaten, specific exceptions are made to this rule (*M.* iv 211, 218, 253; *Y.* i 160, 166). According to Manu (iv. 80 repeating *Vas.* xviii 14) the Śūdra is unfit for sacraments and should not be given advice or religious instruction or made to perform vows. Nevertheless Manu's rule (ii 32) recommending a name connected with service for a Śūdra implies the Śūdra's right to perform the *nāmakaraṇa* ceremony. Elsewhere (x 126-7) Manu says that the Śūdra, though not entitled to the (whole) *dharma*, can fulfil (some portions of) it, and that he who imitates the practice of virtuous men without reciting the sacred texts is praiseworthy. More explicitly Yājñavalkya (i 121) allows the Śūdra the right to perform the *śrāddha* and the vows as well as the five daily sacrifices with repetition of *namaḥ* only. The privilege of Vedic study and the performance of Vedic sacrifices is jealously guarded against the Śūdra (*M.* iv 80, 99; *Y.* i. 148). When, however, we read (*M.* iii 156, 178) that one who is a teacher or a pupil of a Śūdra or sacrifices for him is excluded from *śrāddhas,* we can infer that such practices were not altogether unknown. Finally, the discrimination made against the Śūdra in the branches of civil and criminal law as well as the law of penances, at least implies that he was not without his rights.

In the *Mahābhārata* the status of the Śūdra is much the same as in the Smṛitis. The Śūdra's divinely ordained duty, we are told, is the service of the other three classes especially of the Brāhmaṇas; the latter have to feed and clothe him, to support him in old age and disease, may, even offer funeral cakes for him if he dies sonless (*Mbh.* xii 60, 27-35; xiii 59, 32-3). The Śūdra, however, if without this occupation, can live by trade, animal-rearing, and industry (*ibid.* xii 293, 1 f.; 294, 12 f.). As in Manu, the Śūdra is without property, he cannot commit acts causing loss of caste, and he is not entitled to sacraments, vows, and prayers; but he can perform the smaller sacrifices (*pākayajñas*) and other sacrifices without Vedic texts and, though not entitled to perform the *dharma* laid down in the Vedas, is not forbidden to practise other *dharma* (*ibid.* xii 60. 37-46; 296. 26-7; 327. 49). Only in one extreme text (*ibid.* xiii 59, 33) do we have a hint of the Śūdras being denied the right of touching a Brāhmaṇa or appearing in his presence.

We may now consider the status of the so-called mixed castes derived in the Smṛiti theory from proper (*anuloma*) or improper (*pratiloma*) unions between men and women of the four basic *varṇas*. To the number of these derivative castes enumerated by the older authors, Manu (x. 6-56) and Yājñavalkya (i. 90-5) add a few more, which are all supposed to have been formed from unions of *anuloma* and *pratiloma* castes with the four original *varṇas* or with one another. Inasmuch as Manu assigns them their respective occupations, we may suppose that they were living professional castes or sub-castes formed in the natural course of social development. As for the social status of these castes, Manu (x. 6, 13, 28, 41) says that *anuloma* castes are slightly inferior to their fathers, but are entitled to all the rights belonging to the three upper classes. According to the *Mahābhārata*, however (xiii 48. 4), a Brāmaṇa's son by a Brāhmaṇa or a Kshatriya wife has the same status as the father, while a Brāhmaṇa's son born of a Vaiśya or a Śūdra wife has a lower status determined by the mother's caste.

According to all accounts the *pratiloma* castes have the status of Śūdras. But a specially low rank is assigned to the Chaṇḍālas who are known even in Vedic times as a despised caste. As the lowest of mortals, the Chaṇḍālas are often bracketed together with dogs and crows (*M.* iii 92, 239; x 26). They are excluded from all rights (*Y.* i 93). Their touch is impure (*M.* v 85). They are to take their food from broken dishes, and vessels used by them are to be thrown away (*M.* x 51, 52, 54). They have to wear distinctive dress, ornaments and other outward marks : they are to live outside villages and towns in studiously mean surroundings; their occupations are those concerned with the execution of criminals, the disposal of unclaimed bodies and so forth (*M.* x 51-2; 55-6).

Let us next turn to references in other contemporary works to check the testimony of the Smṛitis. From an important extract in Patañjali's *Mahābhāshya* (on *Pāṇ.* ii 4, 10) we learn that the Śūdras, instead of forming a single caste, really consisted, even so early, of various professional and ethnic groups occupying different social grades. Among the Śūdras, we are told, the lowest place belongs to the Chaṇḍālas and Mṛitapas who, while living in Āryāvarta and within Aryan settlements, are excluded from sacrificial performances, and from eating food on the same plate with an Aryan. Higher in the scale are the carpenters, washermen, blacksmiths and weavers. For while excluded from performance of sacrifices, they can take food from an Aryan's dish without polluting it permanently. Above them are those who, while living outside Āryāvarta but within Aryan settlements, are entitled to perform sacrifices and to eat from an Aryan's plate without making it permanently unclean. In this list are included, besides the Śakas and the Yavanas to be noticed presently, several groups (Kishkindhas, Gandhikas, Śauryas and Krauñchas) who cannot be identified at present. In connections with the foregoing classification it is interesting to observe that blacksmiths, washermen, and carpenters, who could take food from an Aryan's dish according to Patañjali, are included by Manu (iv 210-20) and Yājñavalkya (i 161-5) among those whose food is unfit to be eaten. In contrast with this detailed and apparently realistic account of the status of the Śūdra group of castes, we have a general and evidently formal statement after the Smṛiti fashion in the *Milindapañha* (178); here we read that the Śūdra like the Vaiśya is to live by agriculture and trade. As to the 'mixed castes', lists of their names and occupations are given in the *Mahābhārata* (xiii 48), the Chaṇḍālas and the Pukkasas being described in much the same terms as in the Smṛitis. Similarly the *Lalitavistara* (i 20) mentions the Chaṇḍālas and the Pukkasas along with bamboo-workers and chariot-makers as typical examples of low castes. Of the Śvapākas (allied to the Chaṇḍālas) we are told in the *Uttarādhyayana Sūtra* (xiii 18-19) that they are the lowest of castes, who are loathed by all people and doomed to live in their own hamlets. In the historical inscriptions of this period reference is made to a large number of humble professions, but we have no means of knowing their status.[8]

In the Brahmanical law of this period an attempt is made for the first time to give a recognised status to a number of aboriginal tribes within the orthodox social system. The Pauṇḍrakas, the Choḍas, the Draviḍas, the Kāmbojas and the Kirātas (*M.* x 44), or the Kāmbojas, the Draviḍas, the Kaliṅgas, the Pulindas and the Uśīnaras (*Mbh.* xiii 33, 22-3), or the Mekalas, the Draviḍas, the Lāṭas, the Pauṇḍras, the Daradas and the Kirātas (*ibid.* 35, 17-18), we are told, were originally

Kshatriyas, but they sank to the level of Śūdras by failing to perform the sacred rites and to consult the Brāhmaṇas. This remarkable theory of aboriginal status is laid down in the *Mahābhārata* in the context of a grand eulogy on the greatness of the Brāhmaṇas; but at any rate it shows that the tribes concerned were held to be Śūdras of a fairly high grade. The relatively high status of these tribes is indicated more clearly in the Great Epic (xii 65, 13-22). Here the question is asked how the Andhras, Madrakas, the Pauṇḍras, the Kaliṅgas, and the Kāmbojas, among others, are to perform their duties. In reply it is declared that they should pay respectful attention to parents, teachers, preceptors, kings, and those living in hermitages : they should practise the virtues of non-injury (*ahiṁsā*), truthfulness, purity and forbearance : they should dig wells and construct places for the supply of drinking water : they should perform (and this is most significant) the minor sacrifices (*pākayajñas*) : they should make rich gifts to priests at sacrifices.

In so far as the Dravidian peoples of the far South are concerned their social divisions are revealed to us in the valuable works of the Śaṅgam Age. Among these peoples while the immigrant Brāhmaṇas had an honoured place in society, the classes in order of descending importance were the sages (*aṟivar*), landowners (*veḷḷāḷar*), herdsmen, hunters, artisans and soldiers and, lastly, fishermen and scavengers.[9]

THE MONASTIC ORDERS

The organisation of the orthodox orders of the forest-dwelling hermits (*vānaprastha* or *vaikhānasa*) and ascetics (*yati* or *parivrājaka*) with special rules of life relating to their food, dress, and manner of living, is as old as the Dharmasūtras. These rules are repeated and amplified by Manu (vi 1-85) and Yājñavalkya (iii 45-65). Mention must be made also of members of the Buddhist and Jaina monastic orders of whose fruitful activities we have ample evidence in the history of contemporary literature and missionary enterprise. Testimony to the pious zeal of Buddhist and Jaina monks and nuns in humbler walks of life is borne by the votive inscriptions, and yet the literary records point to the spread of corruption and immorality among these classes. The *Arthaśāstra* of Kauṭilya mentions the employment as spies of pseudo-ascetics, hermits, and mendicant women belonging to Brahmanical as well as non-Brahmanical orders as a well-established institution. What is worse, in pre-Vātsyāyana works on Erotics, Buddhist and Jaina nuns as well as Brahmanical female ascetics are found to be employed in the unworthy rôle of go-betweens among lovers. The low esteem in which female ascetics in general were held in contemporary society may be illustrated by two examples. While adulterous conversation with a married woman made the offender liable to a heavy fine, the penalty for secret conversation with a female ascetic is only nominal according to Manu (viii 361-3) and Yājñavalkya (iii 285, 293). Again Vātsyāyana warns the *nāgaraka's* wife (iv 1, 9) not to associate with female ascetics belonging to Brahmanical, Buddhist, and Jaina orders. Of the sectarian ill-feeling of Brāhmaṇas towards the heretical faiths we have a few examples. Among those for whom no funeral libations are to be offered, Manu (v 89-90) includes monks belonging to heretical orders as well as women joining a heretical sect. Elsewhere (ix 225) he goes so far as to ask for the immediate banishment from the town of the adherents of heretical sects.[10]

RISE AND FALL IN CASTE STATUS

It is desirable in this connection to notice the doctrine of rise and fall in caste status (*jātyutkarsha* and *jātyapakarsha*) advocated by Manu and Yājñavalkya after Gautama. 'According to Manu (x 64) when a Brahmaṇa marries a Śūdra women, the daughter born is *pāraśava* and if this *pāraśava* daughter marries a Brāmaṇa and the daughter of this latter union marries a Brāhmaṇa and this continues for seven generations, then the seventh generation will be a Brāhmaṇa..... Conversely if a Brāhmaṇa marries a Śūdra woman and a son is born, he is a *pāraśava* and if that son marries a Śūdra woman, and their son again marries a Śūdra woman, and this goes on for seven generations, the seventh generation becomes a mere Śūdra.' 'Manu (x 65) extends the same rules to the offspring of the marriage of a Kshatriya with a Vaiśya woman and of a Vaiśya with a Śūdra woman.' 'Yājñavalkya (i 96) speaks of two kinds of *jātyutkarsha* and *jātyapakarsha, viz.* one due to marriage and another due to the avocation followed.' If these rules were observed in practice, they would have done much to soften the rigour of caste distinctions. Such was actually the case according to D.R. Bhandarkar who thinks[11] that the Smṛiti rules above mentioned actually recorded regional customs. But good grounds have recently been given for the view that the doctrine of Manu and Yājñavalkya was in fact only an hypothesis and an ideal.[12]

THE STATUS OF SLAVES

Slavery in India is as old as the Vedas. The Buddhist canonical texts mention various classes of slaves, *viz.* slaves by birth, by purchase, by capture in war and by self-choice. In Kauṭilya (iii 13) we have for the first time a body of laws governing their status. Manu (viii 415) distinguishes seven kinds of slaves, *viz.* one captured in war, one accepting slavery for food, one born in the master's household, one purchased, one given, one acquired by inheritance from ancestors, and one enslaved by way of punishment. This list is confirmed and supplemented by other contemporary literary references. Manu himself, while laying down the primeval law of warriors, says (vii 96) that one who singly gains a woman in battle becomes her owner. The custom of the temporary enslavement of a defeated foe is well known to the *Mahābhārata*.[13] Selling one's own self or wife or child is condemned as a sin of the second degree (*upapātaka*) in Manu (xi 60, 62) and Yājñavalkya (iii 236, 240, 242). In the *Milindapañha* (279), however, the sale as well as the pledge of a son by a father involved in debt or without his livelihood figures as an acknowledged custom. The sale of wives and children is mentioned in the *Mahābhārata* (viii 45, 40) as a reprehensible custom prevalent among the Aṅgas. The gift of slaves is referred to in the same epic (ii 52, 11; 57, 8), while the *Milindapañha* (278) includes women in a list of ten condemned gifts. In the notorious story of the servitude of the Pāṇḍava brothers along with Draupadī as the price of defeat at dice, we have an example of slavery for a wager. Enslavement as a punishment is illustrated by Yājñavalkya (ii 186) who condemns an apostate from asceticism to be the king's slave for life. The enslavement of an adulterous wife caught *flagrante delicto* by her husband as an alternative to other forms of punishment is mentioned in the *Milindapañha* (158) as a prevailing practice. It would appear that slaves in these times were articles of sale, gift, mortgage, and inheritance, their ranks being swelled by capture in war, the sale of minors by their guardians, the voluntary surrender of freedom, and also by punishment for indebtedness, apostasy and adultery. As to the general attitude towards slaves, their humane treatment is enjoined in the sacred texts (*M.* iv 184-5, *Mbh.* xii 242, 20-1). Manu (viii 299-300), however, allows the same limited power of correction over the slave as over the wife and the son to the head of the household. As regards personal rights, Yājñavalkya (ii 183) lays down that slavery (*dāsya*) shall be in the descending order of castes (*varṇas*) and not in the ascending order. With this may be contrasted the far more liberal law of Kauṭilya forbidding an Aryan in any circumstances to be reduced to slavery. As for the slave's rights of property, a dictum common to Manu (viii 416) and the *Mahābhārata* (i 82, 28; v 33, 68), and evidently of high antiquity, categorically denies the slave's right to acquire wealth for himself, though a slight exception is made in favour of a son begotten by a Śūdra on a female slave. Such a son takes a share of his father's property at the latter's choice (*M.* ix 179. *Y.* ii 136) after the father's death; he takes a half share if there are brothers and the whole share if there are no brothers or daughter's sons (*Y.* ii 137). The Smṛitis, however, are silent about the right of slaves in general to acquire, inherit and bequeath property such as is allowed by Kauṭilya under certain circumstances. As regards the right of emancipation Yājñavalkya (ii 185) declares the forcible reduction to slavery, like any sale by robbers, to be void. Emancipation, continues the same authority, is the reward for a slave who saves his mater's life, while one who accepts slavery for his keep is released on payment of the expenses of his maintenance, and one enslaved for debt is freed when he repays it. We miss, however, in Manu and Yājñavalkya the equivalents of Kauṭilya's law entitling a self-sold slave and a slave by capture in war to emancipation on payment of a ransom. On the other hand Yājñavalkya, as we have seen, condemns an apostate from asceticism to be the king's slave for life. We learn, however, from an incidental reference in the *Divyāvadāna* (25) that (as in the Kauṭilyan law) a female slave bearing a child to her master was at once freed with her offspring.

FOREIGN SETTLEMENTS

A Yavana or Yona settlement beyond India's north-western frontier and alongside the territories of the Kāmbojas and the Gandhāras was established sufficiently early to be mentioned in Aśoka's Edicts and endured long enough to be remembered repeatedly in the epic and Purāṇic tradition. In the age of the Mauryas, Yavanas and other foreigners visited the imperial capital in such numbers as to require the care of a special committee of the municipal council. A Yavana-rāja rose to the high position of a provincial governor under Aśoka. It was, however, only with the conquests of the Bactrian Greeks that there occurred largescale settlements of the Yavanas in India. The subsequent invasions of the Śakas and their successors partook of the nature of mass migrations of peoples. The foreign settlers brought with them not only a new social order but also what were held to be repulsive standards of conduct. The havoc wrought by these barbarian invasions and settlements in Indian society is brought home, in the first place, by the pointed testimony of the 'Yugapurāṇa' section of the *Gārgīsaṁhitā*, a work which has been plausibly held to belong to the first century B.C. The author's statements, couched in the form of prophecies in true Purāṇic style, are made in the course of an historical account of the invasions of the Bactrian Greeks and the Śakas. At the end of the Kali Age, so runs his brief but lurid description, all distinctions between the non-Aryans and the Aryans, between Brāhmaṇas, Kshatriyas, Vaiśyas and Śūdras, between orthodoxy and heresy, will disappear : Śūdra mendicants will appear in the guise of Brāhmaṇas : Śūdras will usurp the social and religious privileges of the Brāhmaṇas. The fearful carnage caused by the foreign invasions led to the break-up of family life. Because of the wholesale slaughter of men, we are told in the usual prophetic style, ten or twenty women will marry one husband: women will work in the fields and in business and even serve as soldiers. A twelve years' drought accompanied by famine and plague will be the fitting climax of this series of disasters. We have a more comprehensive account, in the context of the list of evils overtaking the world at the end of the Kali Age, in the *Mahābhārata* (iii 188. 30-64, 190. 12-88). The picture is one of wholesale degeneration and decay, of complete reversal of the social order, of non-Aryan and barbarian rule, and of the predominance of heresy, as a prelude to the destruction of the world by Kalki.[14] There occurs probably another hint of the evil consequences of the large foreign settlements in the contemporary accounts of social manners among the peoples that lived longest under alien rule. Thus the *Mahābhārata* (viii 40, 20-40; 44, 6-44; 45, 5-38) contains a long and vigorous indictment of the customs and practices of the people living in the land of the Five Rivers. Reference is made particularly to the general immorality and the laxity concerning food and drink that prevailed among the Madraka and the Vāhīka men and women. The impure practices of women in this region and in Saurāshṭra too regarding matters of sex are mentioned by Vātsyāyana (ii 5, 25).

Nevertheless, it is an undeniable fact that the Yavanas and other foreigners, so far from upsetting the traditional social order and destroying its accepted canons of morality and conduct, were themselves completely and swiftly absorbed within the indigenous social system. Quite unmistakably, captive India captured her captor. For the Greeks the process of indianisation started as early as the second quarter of the second century B.C. when Demetrius, contrary to the practice of all other Hellenistic kings, introduced a bilingual coinage (in Greek, and in Indian Prākṛit speech with the Kharoshṭhī script). The series of Greek votive inscriptions in Prākṛit, which date from about the beginning of the first century B.C. and are likewise without a parallel in the Hellenistic world, signalised a considerable acceleration of the indianising tendency. What lends significance to these inscriptions is that they belong as much to the regions of the North-West which lay longest within the Greek zone as to those of the interior. With the use of the Indian language and script went the adoption of Indian religions. The object of the inscriptions is frequently to record dedications of Buddhist relics and the like by pious Greek donors. In one instance we find that the donor, Heliodorus, who was the Greek ambassador at the court of Vidiśā, recorded his erection of a Garuḍa column in honour of Vāsudeva, 'the god of gods', and devoutly styled himself a *bhāgavata*. It is also probable that he was versed in the *Mahābhārata*, for an ethical text quoted in the inscription closely corresponds to a couple of verses in the Great Epic. Some of the Indo-Greek kings appear to have figured hellenised forms of Indian divinities on their coins. At a later period a number of Yavana donors with Indian names, whose nationality however is still a disputed point, dedicated caves (or their constituent portions) in Western India for the use of Buddhist monks. When Kanishka dropped the Greek monograms on his coins towards the latter part of the first century A.D. this Greeks generally.[15]

Where the Greeks with their notorious contempt for barbarians had led the way, it was easy enough for the less sophisticated Śakas and other foreigners to follow. The Greeks had been content to adopt the Indian forms of their names. The Śakas, Ābhīras, and others, however, almost from the first took purely Indian names (in a few cases with Kshatriya terminals and in one remarkable instance with the *gotra*-name of the mother). On their coins the Śaka, Pahlava, and Kushāṇa kings adopted from the first the system of bilingual legends (in Greek and in Indian Prākṛit) brought into vogue by their Greek forerunners. Going a step further the Śaka *kshatrapas* of Gujarat and Malwa after the time of Chashṭana converted the Greek inscriptions on their coins into an ornamental border, while substituting a Sanskritised Prākṛit in Brāhmī script for the old pure Prākṛit in Kharoshṭhī letters.[16] Interesting reminiscences of the period of transition when the foreign settlers had partially adopted varieties of Aryan speech are preserved in Manu (x 45) and *Sūtrakṛitāṅga* (i 22, 15-16). With the adoption of the Indian Prākṛit by the Śakas went their official use of a calendar which has been justly characterised by Konow as Indo-Macedonian. Again, the devices and symbols of divinities on the coins of Śaka and Kushāna rulers suggest that while some of them were only patrons of Indian religions, others openly accepted them as their faith. We have more definite evidence of the conversion of the foreign settlers to Indian religions in their inscriptions. For we find them frequently recording their benefactions for the Buddhist faith with formulas associating their relatives (and sometimes even the reigning king or his representative) with the pious act. The Śaka Ushavadāta distributed his charities and acts of piety among the Brāhmaṇa laity as well as the Buddhist monks according to the canonical rules.[17]

While the Yavanas, Śakas and other foreigners were thus being thoroughly indianised, the orthodox authors of social and religious laws were taking steps to meet them half-way. Already in the time of Patañjali, as we learn from the extract (on *Pāṇ*. ii 4, 10) above quoted, the Śakas and Yavanas who were still living outside Āryāvarta were recognised as Śūdras of the higher grade with the right to perform sacrifices and the use of the Aryan's dish. In Manu (x 44) and the *Mahābhārata* (xiii 33, 21; *ibid*. 35, 18) the Śakas and Yavanas are included in a list of Kshatriya peoples who had gradually sunk to the level of Śūdras. Going beyond this point the *Milindapañha* (329) refers to the Kshatriya lineage of king Milinda (Menander) and his Kshatriya antecedents. In the second and third centuries A.D. princesses belonging to the Kshatrapa ruling house of Western India were accepted in marriage by orthodox kings of the Śātavāhana and Ikshvāku dynasties.[18] The Ābhīras, according to Patañjali (on *Pāṇ*. i 2, 72), were a caste separate from the Śūdras. But in the *Mahābhārata* (xiv 29, 15-16) they are included among peoples who were originally Kshatriyas but had sunk to the level of Śūdras. Above all in the Epic (xii 65, 13-22 cited above) Śakas, Yavanas, Tushāras and Pahlavas along with various aboriginal tribes are declared to be eligible for the performance of Vedic religious acts and certain minor sacrifices (*pākayajñas*).

WOMAN'S POSITION IN SOCIETY

A. General Remarks

The Smṛitis of this period repeat the anti-feminist doctrines and principles of the older law. But these are subject in practice, as before, to important exceptions. Thus the ancient doctrine of perpetual dependence of a woman (her father, husband, and son protecting her in childhood, youth, and old age respectively) is repeated and amplified by Manu (ix 2-3) and is paraphrased by Yājñavalkya (i 85-6). Emphasising this principle, they declare (*M.* iv 213; *Y.* i 163) the food of a woman without male relatives (*avīrā*) to be unfit for eating. Nevertheless, as in the earlier law, marriage by mutual choice (*gāndharva*) is not only recognised but approved in a qualified degree both by Manu and Yājñavalkya. Again, a girl who is without guardians or whose guardians have neglected to give her in marriage is allowed as by the older authorities to select her own husband (*M.* ix 91). According to an old dictum quoted by Manu (viii 416 and *Mbh.* v 33, 64) the wife, like the slave and the son, has no right of property. And yet according to Manu (viii 28-9) the property of wives, faithful widows, as well as barren and diseased women, is to be specially protected by the king, and its misappropriation by their relatives is to be punished like theft. Brothers are bound to give a share of their inheritance to their unmarried sister (ix, 118). Above all the mother, according to Manu (ix 217) and Yājñavalkya (ii 135), and for the first time, the widow in the latter's opinion, have the right to inherit a man's property in the absence of his sons. Women again are entitled to own and bequeath their special property or *strīdhana* (*M.* ix 194-8; *Y.* ii 146-8). Concerning religious status, the disabilities imposed upon women by the older law are repeated in our present texts. In Manu (ii 67) a woman's ineligibility for Vedic study and the worship of the sacred fire is masked by the declaration that after her marriage her service to her husband and her performance of household duties are their substitutes. Not by performance of sacrifices nor by offerings to the manes, nor by religious fasts, says the *Mahābhārata* (iii 204) more clearly, but by serving her husband, does a woman attain heaven. In particular we are told (*M.* ii 6; *Y.* i 13) that women's sacraments are to be performed without recitation of sacred texts, Yājñavalkya making an exception in favour of the marriage ceremony. A married or unmarried girl is categorically forbidden to make offerings of oblations to the sacred fires (*M.* xi 36-7; *Mbh.* xii 165, 21-2). As to general treatment of women, both Manu (iii 55-62) and Yājñavalkya (i 82) enjoin in the strongest terms that women should be honoured by their male relatives. As in the older law women have the right of precedence along the road in the same way as the king and the *snātaka* (*M.* ii 138; *Y.* i 117). Newly married and pregnant women are fed even before guests while the householder and his wife take their meals last (*M.* iii 114-16; *Y.* i 105). In the penal law of Manu and Yājñavalkya, as in the older Smṛitis, women are liable to capital punishment for a number of serious crimes such as adultery (*M.* viii 371), breaking reservoirs, killing the husband, preceptor, or child, poisoning or arson (*Y.* ii 281-2). But elsewhere (xi 177-8) Manu himself prescribes simply confinement by the husband and the compulsory performance of appropriate penances even for the very corrupt wife and for one who has repeated the offense with a man of equal caste. According to Yājñavalkya (i 70, 72-3) a woman guilty of adultery should be disgraced (till the performance of the penance, according to the commentator) and in cases of a very provocative nature, abandoned. Manu (ix 230), it may be noted, prescribes a light mode of corporal punishment for woman as for infants, the aged, the poor, and the sick. The penance for killing a wife is the same as for Brāmaṇa-murder (*M.* xi 88), but for killing an adulterous woman it is, as before, only nominal (*M.* xi 139). While such is the law relating to women in general, special consideration is reserved for female relatives. The respectful treatment of paternal and maternal aunts' the elder sister and the mother is enjoined by Manu (ii 131-3). The mother, the wife ('one's own body'), the daughter ('the object of the highest tenderness') and other female relations are persons whose faults should be borne without resentment (*M.* iv 179-80; 184-5; *Y. i 157-8*). Again and again the mother, the father and the teacher are mentioned as entitled to the highest reverence, the place of honour being frequently, though not uniformly, reserved for the mother (*M.* ii 145-9, 225-37; iv 162; *Y.* i 35; *Mbh.* iii 312, 60; xiii 105, 15; xii 109, 17-8). Defaming mother or wife is punishable with an appreciable fine (*M.* viii 275) and casting them off except for loss of caste is visited with a still heavier fine (*M.* viii 389; *Y.* ii 237). The legal penalties are supplemented by religious and social punishments. Casting off the mother is included among the sins of the second degree (*M.* xi 60) and it excludes the offender from *ś*rāddhas (*M.* iii 157.).

We may supplement this evidence relating to a woman's general status form other data. The honourable treatment of women enjoined by Manu is inculcated almost in the same terms in the *Mahābhārata* (xiii 46, 2-12). With this is combined in the same context the familiar doctrine of the perpetual tutelage of women and of the wife's sole duty of serving her husband. The epics repeat (*Rām.* ii 78, 21; *Mbh.* i 155, 2; 158, 31; 217, 4; 219, 7; ii 41, 13) the ancient chivalrous doctrine (not accepted in the Smṛiti law), to the effect that women are immune from capital punishment. An adulterous wife, says the *Mahābhārata* (xii 159, 58) is to be confined, to be reduced to scanty food and clothing, and made to perform penances. The mother, as in the Smṛiti law, is the object of the highest veneration : she is equivalent to ten fathers and is more venerable than the earth (*Mbh.* i 196, 16; iii 312, 60; xiii 105, 15). The daughter, however, is a source of woe (*ibid.* i 159, 11-2; v 96, 15-7). In fine, the stories of Draupadi, Damayantī, Sāvitrī, and others in the *Mahābhārata* and of

Sītā in the *Rāmāyaṇa* have preserved for us pictures of heroic women who are inspired by a high ideal of duty and often by supreme wisdom and goodness. It remains to mention that in the historical records of this period we often find not only queens and princesses but also women in ordinary life making donations of various kinds evidently out of their own property for pious purposes.[19] Nāganikā and Balaśrī were two queens of the Śātavāhana line who ruled as regents on behalf of their minor sons.

B. The Status of the Wife

Regarding the position of the wife in the Smṛiti law of this period, some facts have already been mentioned, but the subject requires a fuller treatment. Referring to older texts Manu (ix 45) lays down the doctrine of the complete identity of husband and wife, and duduces therefrom (ix 46) the corollary of the in dissoluble union of both. Accordingly, to forsake the wife except when she has fallen from caste is held to be a penal offence (*M.* viii 389; *Y.* ii 237). A faithful wife, says Manu (ix 95), is the gift of the gods, and must be constantly cherished by the husband who seeks to please them. According to Yājñavalkya (i 76) a man forsaking his gentle and devoted wife who has given him sons must surrender one-third of his property to her, and if he is without property, he must maintain her. A diseased or a vicious wife or one who bears no son (the last being held to be indispensable for repaying a man's debt to his father) may be abandoned or superseded; but a superseded wife must be maintained (*M.* ix 80-2; *Y.* i 72-4).

As in the older law, the husband has powers of correction over his wife for a number of faults: these extend to beating strictly regulated by law, non-association and depriving her of ornamenıs, confinement, and imposition of penance (*M.* viii 299-300; ix 77-8; xi 177-8), or a temporary disgrace and loss of authority (*Y.* i 70). According to a dictum of Manu (v 152) the wife by virtue of betrothal by her guardian becomes subject to the dominion of her husband, But the sale of the wife is held to be a sin of the second degree, and the gift of the wife is altogether forbidden (*M.* x 162; *Y.* ii 125). The husband's strict duty alike for his own sake and his family's is to guard his wife (*M.* ix 6-7; *Y.* i 81), though it is recognised

(*M.* ix 12) that only those women who keep guard over themselves are well guarded. In particular a wife drinking spirituous liquor at festivals, or goes to shows or assemblies though forbidden, is liable to a fine (*M.* ix 84). As a means of guarding the wife the husband should employ her on household duties (*M.* ix 11). The wife shares in her husband's religious acts, this privilege being reserved for the wife of equal caste where there are others (*M.* ix 86, 87; *Y.* i 88). The wife, however, is forbidden (no doubt in accordance with the ancient doctrine of a woman's perpetual dependence) to perform sacrifices, fasts or vows independently of her husband (*M.* v. 155). The law of husband and wife, according to Manu (ix 101-2), consists in mutual fidelity till death. In the Brahmanical sacred works of this period, however, the duty of absolute obedience and devotion to the husband is strictly enjoined, as never before, upon the wife. The husband is the wife's supreme deity: by serving him she wins heaven, though she may not honour the gods; unlike her other relations and friends, the husband is the wife's sole refuge in this and the next world; unlike her male relatives, the husband gives her immeasurable happiness (*Rām.* ii 24, 20; 26-7; 27-6;39, 30; 117, 24 *Mbh.* xiii 146, 34 *f*; xii 144, 6-7; v 151; 153-4; *Y.* i 77). Hyperbolical descriptions of the spiritual powers of the faithful wife (*pativratā*) occur not only in the *Mahābhārata* (iii 63, 32-9; ix 63, 62 etc.), but also in Tamil works like the *Kuṛal* and the *Śilappadikāram*. When the husband is gone abroad, his wife is required to live a life of studied restraint (*M.* ix 75; *Y.* i 84; *Mbh.* xiii 123, 17). The stories of Sītā in the *Rāmāyaṇa*, of Gāndhārī, Draupadī, Sāvitrī, and Damayantī in the *Mahābhārata*, of Kaṇṇagi in the *Śilappadikāram* enshrine imperishable examples of a wife's deathless devotion to her husband.

We now pass on to the description of the life of the wife of a citybred man of fashion by Vātsyāyana (*Kāmasūtra* iv 1, 1-55; 2, 1-38). This may rightly be regarded as a commentary, drawn on doubt from life, on the Smṛiti code of a wife's duties. The picture exhibits those qualities of devotion and self-restraint combined with sound household management which have remained the possession of Hindu wives to the present day. Where a woman is the sole wife, says the author, she is to devote herself to her husband as to a deity. She is personally to minister to his comforts when he eats his meals of enters the house. She shares in her husband's vows and fasts, brooking no refusal. She attends festivities, social gatherings, sacrifices, and religious processions, with his permission. That the husband may find no fault with her she avoids the company of disreputable women, she shows him no signs of displeasure, and she does not loiter about on the door-step or in solitary places for a long time. She remonstrates with her husband in secret against his improvident or improper expenditure. She serves her father-in-law and mother-in-law and honours their commands. She receives her husband's friends according to their deserts. When the husband goes abroad, she leads a life of self-denial and self-restraint. Besides attending to her husband and his relations and friends, she has complete charge of the household. She engages servants in their work and rewards them on festive occasions. She keeps the house absolutely clean. She looks after the worship of the gods at the household shrine, and makes the religious offering of food thrice a day. In the garden attached to the house she plants various vegetables, herbs, and trees. She frames an annual budget of the family income and regulates her expenses accordingly. She keeps the daily accounts and makes up the total at the end of the day. During her husband's absence she exerts herself so that his affairs may not suffer, and she increases the income and diminishes the expenditure to the best of her power. Where the woman has a co-wife, she looks upon the latter as a younger sister or as a mother according as she is younger or older.

C. The Widow's Status

The status of the widow in the Smṛiti law of this period is a reflex of its strong emphasis upon the wife's supreme duty of serving her husband. It is true that Manu (ix 175, 184) and Yājñavalkya (ii 130, 132) recognise, as of old, the son of the remarried woman among those who are entitled to inherit the father's property in the absence of more respectable classes of sons. Again Manu (ix 176), following the older precedent, permits a virgin widow to perform a fresh sacrament of marriage. Nevertheless we are expressly told (*M.* v 162; ix 65) that remarriage of widows is not in accordance with the prescribed rule. The widow is recommended instead (*M.* v. 156-61; *Y.* i 75) to live a life of strict chastity. On the other hand the Smṛiti law is as yet completely silent about the burning of widows on the funeral pyres of their husbands. Yājñavalkya (ii 135-6), moreover, introduces us for the first time to a very important right of the widow, *viz.* that of inheriting the husband's property in the absence of sons. When we turn to the other literary works of this period, we find that the dreadful rite of *satī* is already supported by a Mahābhārata text (i 74, 46). It is referred to, Hopkins[20] thinks, in a number of other passages (*Rām.* v 26, 24-5; vi 15, 27; *Mbh.* xvi 5, 4; xii 148, 9). We have again a few examples (*Mbh.* i 95, 65; xvi 7, 18) of Kshatriya queens and even one example (*Rām.* vii 17, 14) of a Brāhmaṇī voluntarily submitting to this rite. But the evidence shows, as has been rightly argued,[21] that the practice as yet was rare and confined to royal families. On the whole the widow's lot in this as in the earlier and later periods was hard; her helplessness and misery are vividly brought out in the *Mahābhārata* (i 158, 12; xii 148, 2). Not without reason does the widow head a list of persons who are despised and contemned in this world. (*Milindapañha* 288).

In the far South, as far as the scanty evidence enables us to judge, the widow's lot was essentially similar. From the works of the Śaṅgam Age we learn that ordinarily widows were expected to lead a life of self-denial and that the custom of *satī* was already known and extolled as a high ideal.[22]

D. The Status of the Demi-monde

It remains to notice the social status of some classes of women not included in the above categories. Female ascetics of the Brahmanical order, and Buddhist and Jaina nuns were evidently numerous in these times. We have already discussed their status in the light of contemporary records. On the other hand, the class of female temple-attendants (*devadāsī*), so very common in the following centuries, are as yet of minor importance : only one record[23] refers to a *devadāsī* during this period. Harlots are condemned in strong terms by Manu (ix 259-62). Even the accomplished courtesan (*gaṇikā*), who held a recognised position in city life during early Buddhist times, is included (*M.* iv 209, 219 and *Y.* i 161) among those whose food is unfit to be eaten. But the realistic account in

Vātsyāyana's *Kāmasūtra* shows that the *gaṇikā* still occupied an honoured place in society. A fallen woman of good books and proper conduct who has mastered the arts (*kalā*), says that author (i 3, 20-1), acquires the title of a *gaṇikā;* as such she is honoured by kings, praised by the discerning, sought after by pupils, and accepted by pleasure-seekers. A Mathurā inscription[24] has preserved the memory of a pious Jaina *gaṇikā*. The vivid description of the life of the courtesan in the Tamil works of the Śaṅgam Age amplifies the much shorter notice in Vātsyāyana's work.[25]

E. Seclusion of Women

The custom of the seclusion of royal women was well established during this period. Queens and princesses, we are told in picturesque language, could not see the sun or creatures flying in the sky, and could not be touched by the wind: for them to be seen in public was their greatest misfortune (*Rām*. ii 33, 8; *Mbh*. ii 69, 6; ix 71 etc.). That queens attended sittings of the royal court only when concealed from the public gaze is shown by an incidental reference in the Jaina *Kalpasūtra*. Here we read (iv 62-3) that when the Kshatriya Siddhārtha summoned his ministers and courtiers for the interpretation of the queen's dream, he took his seat on a throne in the hall of audience, but the queen was seated behind a curtain. From a passage in *Lalitavistara* (157) we learn that it was customary for a newly married girl to wear a veil in the presence of her father-in-law, mother-in-law and other elders.

MARRIAGE RULES AND PRACTICES:

A. In the Smṛitis

The Smṛiti rules of this period relating to marriage appear to have been in the same fluid state as before. Following the older authorities Manu (iii 13) and Yājñavalkya (i 57) permit the marriage of a Brāhmaṇa, a Kshatriya, and a Vaiśya with four, three and two wives respectively in the proper (*anuloma*) order; but marriage of the three upper classes, and especially of the Brāhmaṇas, with Śūdra girls is condemned in the strongest terms (*M.* iii 14-19; *Y.* i 56). Nevertheless, both Manu (iii 43-4) and Yājñavalkya (i 62) lay down what rites are to be performed by a Brāhmaṇa, a Kshatriya, a Vaiśya and a

Śūdra girl when marrying a Brāhmaṇa. Again, the respective shares of a Brāhmaṇa's property obtainable by his sons born of wives of the four castes are defined by Manu (ix 149-54) and Yājñavalkya (ii 128), although Manu in the same context (ix 155, 160) disqualifies the son of a Brāhmaṇa, a Kshatriya, and a Vaiśya by a Śūdra wife for any share of the inheritance. It would seem, therefore, that marriages of Brāhmaṇas, not to speak of Kshatriyas and Vaiśyas, with Śūdra girls, though denounced by the Smṛitis, continued to be performed. The rules relating to prohibited degrees of marriage follow the older lines. Manu (iii 5) excludes those who are blood-relations (*sapiṇḍa*) on the mother's side and of the same *gotra* on the father's. Yājñavalkya (i 53) narrows down the restriction to *sapiṇḍa* relations up to the seventh degree on the father's side and the fifth degree on that of the mother. In connection with a custom noted as peculiar to the South by such an early authority as Baudhāyana (*Dharmasūtra* i 1, 2-3), it is worth remarking that Manu (xi 172-3) denounces marriage with the daughter of a paternal or maternal aunt or with the daughter of a maternal uncle. The eight forms of marriage known to the older Smṛitis, are repeated by Manu (iii 27-34) and Yājñavalkya (i 58-61). The list consists of *brāhma, ārsha, prājāpatya* and *daiva* (each involving the gift of a maiden by her father or other guardian), *gāndharva* (marriage by mutual choice), *āsura* (marriage by purchase), *rākshasa* (marriage by capture) and *paiśācha* (marriage by stealth). The views of Manu and Yājñavalkya as to the admissibility of these various forms are as flexible as those of the older authorities. Manu (iii 36-42) and Yājñavalkya (i 39-41) agree in praising the first four forms and condemning the last four. In the same context, however, Manu mentions (iii 23-6) other views declaring *prājāpatya, gāndharva* and *rākshasa* to be lawful, and *paiśācha* and *āsura* alone to be unlawful, and he also recommends different forms for different castes.[26] With regard to marriage by purchase in particular, Manu (iii 51-3) and the *Mahābhārata* (xiii 45, 18-19) repeat the old law which forbids the father to accept a fee, however small, for his daughter, and condemns even *ārsha* marriage as involving such acceptance. We may suppose that, notwithstanding the disapproval of the lawgivers, marriages by mutual choice, by purchase, by capture, and even by stealth, were performed, as before, by the different castes.

It will appear from the above that the gift of a girl (*kanyādāna*) by her parent or other guardian is the form of marriage generally approved in the Smṛitis. In fact, it is the right and the duty of the father (or of other guardians in a fixed order of succession) to bestow the girl in marriage (*M.* ix 88; *Y.* i 63). As to the age of marriage, a young man of the first three classes could marry under the Smṛiti law only after the completion of his studies (*i.e.* at least after twelve years from his investiture with the sacred thread). If he chose, he might remain a perpetual student in residence with his teacher. The girl, on the other hand, in accordance with the strong Smṛiti tradition, was to be married at an early age. As Manu says (ix 88), a girl should be given in marriage even before attaining the proper age, if a very desirable bridegroom of equal caste is available. Going much further than his, Yājñavalkya, like some of his predecessors, says (i 64) that the guardian incurs the guilt of periodically killing an embryo as long as the girl remains unmarried. In the result the relative ages of bridegroom and bride as approved by Manu (ix 94) are remarkably disproportionate, being thirty years to twelve or twenty-four years to eight.

When the guardian fails to give a girl in marriage or she is without a guardian, she is entitled as in the old Smṛiti law to select a suitable husband (*M.* ix 90-1; *Y.* i 64; *Mbh.* xiii 44 16). Manu and the *Mahābhārata* repeat the clause of Vasishṭha (xvii 67-8) and Baudhāyana (iv 1, 14) that she should wait for three years after attaining puberty. This rule, like the one relating to *gāndharva* marriages already mentioned, proves that late marriages of girls were still approved by the Smṛiti authorities in special circumstances, notwithstanding their strong advocacy of early marriages.

On the subject of the remarriage of women, as of marriage itself, the Smṛiti rules are still in a fluid state. The remarriage of widows, as we have seen, is expressly declared by Manu (v 162, ix 65) to be unauthorised by the sacred law. He (viii 226) emphatically declares that only marriage with a virgin is contemplated by the nuptial texts, a non-virgin being excluded from religious ceremonies. Manu (ix 47) and Yājñavalkya (i 65) also declare that a maiden is given once only in marriage. Nevertheless, both (*M.* ix 158f.; *Y.* ii 130 f.) recognise, as of old, the title of the son of a remarried woman (*Paunarbhava*) to inherit his father's property in the absence of respectable classes of sons. The definition of the *paunarbhava* in Manu (ix 175) shows that his mother might be a woman abandoned by her first husband or a widow contracting a second marriage at her free will. Yājñavalkya's definition (ii 130) proves that she might or might not have been a virgin at the time of the second marriage. What is more, a virgin widow and a woman returning to her first husband after living with another man, are entitled to perform a fresh sacrament of marriage (*M.* ix 176). From Yājñavalkya's definition of *punarbhū* (i 67) it appears that whether she was a virgin or not, the sacrament of marriage was again performed on her. A woman whose husband has gone abroad, says Manu (ix 76), is to wait for three, six, or eight years according to the object of his journey. In the parallel texts of Kauṭilya and Nārada she is expressly allowed thereafter to select another husband.

B. In Other Sources

Let us now turn to other evidence touching the rules and practices of marriage in vogue during this period. The Smṛiti rules above-mentioned relating to inter-caste marriages, prohibited degrees of marriage, the eight forms of marriage, the guardian's duty of giving away the girl, and the girl's right of self-choice in its default, are repeated in the *Mahābhārata* (i 73, 12 f.; 102, 12 f.; xiii 44-7), and it is unnecessary to quote them here. It may, however, be noticed that the Epic (xiii 44, 14), slightly varying Manu's rule on this point, gives the relative ages of bridegroom and bride as thirty years to ten or twenty-one to seven. The evil of disproportionate ages of marriage is brought vividly before our eyes in the twice-repeated simile (*ibid.* ii 64, 14; iii 5, 15) of a young girl disliking her sixty-year old husband. Again, the injunction making marriage compulsory for girls is set forth in the Epic (ix 52) in the story of an ascetic's daughter. When after devoting her whole life to ascetic practices, she sought salvation in death, she was told by a sage that she could not be saved since she had not been sanctified by the marriage sacrament. In the epics, marriages in Kshatriya families are performed by purchase, capture, or self-choice, followed in each case by the performance of the appropriate religious ceremony. At the ceremony of self-choice, the bride sometimes selected the victor at a great tournament, having (as the story of Draupadī's marriage shows) the right to refuse a low-born man. Similarly in *Lalitavistara* (136-57) the Bodhisattva as the son of king Śuddhodana wins his bride by exhibiting his superior skill in all arts in competition with other Śākya youths at a great tournament.[27] We have more faithful pictures of contemporary marriage practices in other works of this period. A simile in the *Milindapañha* (47-8) introduces us to the hypothetical case of a man selecting his bride of a tender age by paying the fee, and of another man taking her away in marriage after she is grown up on payment of the same fee, thus giving rise to a dispute triable by the king. It follows that marriage by purchase of girls both before and after puberty was known at this time. In the stories of the *Avadānaśataka* reference is made to procuring a bride from an equal family by a *śreshṭhī* (1, 36), a Brāhmaṇa (19), a Śākya noble (14), a *gṛihapati* (67), and a caravan-leader (60, 83). And yet we are told how the grown-up daughter of a *śreshṭhī* was sought after in marriage by princes as well as sons of ministers and of *śreshṭhīs* (2, 37), while a Śākya noble's daughter was desired in marriage only by princes and minister's sons (16), and a princess by neighbouring kings alone (32). This proves that, as in the Smṛiti law, while marriages within equal castes were usual, those of men of higher castes with women of lower ones were also known.[28] The *Avadānaśataka*, moreover, contains valuable evidence of the independence which girls of the upper classes still possessed in the matter of wedlock. The stories frequently tell us how, when the girls were grown-up and sought after by young men of different ranks, their fathers were plunged in anxiety for fear of displeasing the disappointed suitors. To relieve them of this anxiety, the girls arranged a self-choice ceremony (*svayaṁvara*) at which they dramatically announced their resolve to become nuns (2, 32), or else they entered the Buddhist Order outright with the parent's permission (16), or finally made it a condition with the bridegroom to embrace the monastic life jointly at the proper time (37). In one story (45 f.) we read how two kings engaged to marry their son and daughter born on the same days as a means of ending their hostilities, how when the two were grown-up and the prince sent presents to his future wife she told her father of her resolve to enter the Buddhist Order, how when the king did not need her request and the bridegroom arrived for the marriage, she obtained the pardon of all assembled on the occasion by exhibiting miraculous powers and thereafter became a Buddhist nun. It remains to mention that in the stories above-named, while the princess was able to arrange at once for her *svayaṁvara*, this became possible for the śreshṭhī's daughter only when her father had obtained the permission of the king. *Svayaṁvara* evidently, as in the *Mahābhārata* story of Draupadī's marriage, was held to be the peculiar privilege of Kshatriya girls.

The most complete account of marriage rules and practices prevailing in contemporary society is preserved in the *Kāmasūtra* of Vātsyāyana. Firstly, as regards inter-caste marriages the author tells us (iii 1, 1) that both the secular and spiritual objects of marriage are best secured by union with a virgin of equal caste performed according to canonical rites. Elsewhere (i 5, 1) he observes that the contrary practice of making love to women of higher castes or to other men's wives is forbidden. Making love, the author continues, to women of a caste lower than one's own but still sufficiently pure not to have their dishes cast away after meals, as well as with harlots and *punarbhūs* is neither approved nor condemned, as its object is simply pleasure. Love may even be offered without violation of *dharma* to a woman of higher caste who is a notorious wanton. It will be observed that while marriages within the castes are held alone to be lawful and desirable, and *pratiloma* marriages are condemned outright, even *anuloma* marriages are tolerated but not approved. In contrast with this increased rigidity of caste restrictions in the matter of marriage is the author's avowed sanction of irregular unions with loose women even of higher castes.

In Vātsyāyana, as in the Smṛiti law, marriage is arranged as a rule by the parents or other guardians of the parties. To Vātsyāyana, however, we owe the first detailed and evidently realistic account (iii 1, 4-21) of the way in which the marriage arrangements were made on both sides. For the selection (*varaṇa*) of the bride, the parents and other kinsmen of the bridegroom are to bestir themselves. 'Those charged with *varaṇa* should exaggerate the defects, present and prospective, of other suitors, and should expatiate on the qualifications of their candidate (*nāyaka*) both personal and hereditary. Besides, they should enlarge upon such advantages possessed by him at the time or likely to accrue to him later, as would commend themselves to the girl's mother.' The parents and other relatives of the girl are advised to dress her smartly at the time of giving her away and to allow her to be shown to advantage on festive and similar occasions. 'When the men come to propose marriage, the parents of the girl should receive them hospitably and on some pretext or other show the girl in all her ornaments. They should come to no decision as to giving away the girl before they have consulted the oracles.' 'The *varaṇa* is to fructify in one of the four approved forms of marriage, *viz. brāhma*, *prājāpatya*, *ārsha* and *daiva* or according to the forms in vogue in one's own country.'

When a young man is unable for several reasons to prefer his suit in the ways above mentioned, continues Vātsyāyana (iii 3, 1-44) he should himself woo the girl on whom his heart has been set from childhood. In the Southern Country (Dakshiṇāpatha) a young man separated from his mother in childhood and living in the family of his maternal uncle may try to win the daughter of that uncle, a clear reference to an ancient South Indian custom. Or else he may pay his court to another girl from her childhood, since courting a girl from childhood in righteous ways is praiseworthy. He should begin his advances by collecting flowers, making garlands and joining in suitable sports. He should, besides, propitiate her with presents. He should seek the good offices of her trusted friends (and specially the daughter of her nurse), for these are very likely to promote his suit. When the outward signs of love appear in her, he should try to win her over gradually and completely by various tricks and devices. In fine we are told that the mere child should be wooed by sharing in her games, the young girl by exhibiting knowledge of the arts (*kalā*), and an older woman through her trusted friends.

Like the young man forced to press his suit in person, a girl may be compelled by circumstances to pay court to a prospective husband (iii 4, 36-59). When a girl though possessing excellent qualities is born in a humble family, or though well-born is poor and so is not sought after by equals, or when she has lost her parents and is dependent on her kinsmen, she may try to arrange for her own marriage. This is evidently reminiscent of the Smṛiti rule mentioned above. But the detailed account which follows is peculiar to Vātsyāyana. A girl so situated, says the author, may fix her attention on a young man of ability, good qualities, and handsome appearance, whose affection she has shared from childhood. Or again, when she finds a young man so much smitten with love for her as to be ready to marry her even against his parents' wishes, she may try to win him over by acts of service and frequent meetings with him. But she should never, though smitten with love, make the first overtures, for thereby she would ruin her fortune (*saubhāgyam jahāti*).

As Vātsyāyana gives us the first known accounts of courtship as a preliminary to marriage, so also we owe to him (iii 5, 1-30) some concrete descriptions of different forms of marriage which are mentioned with or without approval in the Smṛitis. In the *gāndharva* marriage, the lovers are to meet by appointment at a secret time and place. Then 'the sacred fire should be brought from the house of a Śrotriya, *kuśa* grass should be spread before it upon the earth, oblations offered to the fire in accordance with the prescriptions of the sacred law, and then they should go round the fire; and after this is completed, the parents should be informed.' For a marriage performed before the fire, as the preceptors concur, can never be annulled. After the marriage is consummated, the relatives should be informed by and by, and they should be persuaded to give away the girl formally to her lover for fear of social obloquy and punishment by the king. The two other forms of marriage corresponding to *paiśācha* and *rākshasa* as being unrighteous, do not require to be confirmed by religious rites. In these cases after the girl has been raped when asleep or when unconscious under the influence of an intoxicating drug (*paiśācha* marriage), or else when she has been abducted after the slaughter or intimidation of her guards (*rākshasa* marriage), her relations are informed and induced to consent to the formal marriage. Vātsyāyana ends by declaring that the *gāndharva* is the most respected of the forms of marriage, since it is attended with happiness, unaccompanied with troubles and negotiations, and is the fruit of mutual preference.

Vātsyāyana's rules as to the age of marriage agree in part with those of the Smṛitis. According to him a man should observe celibacy till the completion of his education (i 2, 6), and one who has finished his education should enter upon the life of a householder (i 4, 1). With regard to the age of the girl, Vātsyāyana, while describing the ceremony of selection of the bride, says that a girl who has just reached puberty should be rejected (iii 1, 12). Nevertheless his rules of marriage and courtship given above are sufficiently comprehensive to apply to girls before and even long after puberty. This confirms the conclusion, hinted at in the Smṛitis, that both early and late marriages of girls were known and practised during this period. It remains to add that Vātsyāyana (iii 1, 2) recommends the bridegroom to marry a girl younger than himself by three years or more.

The description (iv 2, 39 f.) of the remarried woman (*punarbhū*) in Vātsyāyana's work gives us a fuller picture of this type than the meagre references in the Smṛitis. The *punarbhū*, we are told, is a widow who being unable to control her passions unites herself for the second time with a man of good qualities and addicted to pleasure. The *punarbhū's* whole course of conduct is quite unlike that of the married wife who has, as we have seen, to live a life of restraint and seclusion, to manage her household economically, to share in her husband's religious acts, and to be indissolubly bound with him. 'When the *punarbhū* seeks her lover's house, she assumes the rôle of a mistress, patronises his wives, is generous to his servants and treats his friends with familiarity; she chides the lover herself if he gives any cause for quarrel. She shows greater knowledge of the arts than his wedded wives, and seeks to please the lover with the sixty-four *kāmakalās*. She takes part in sports and festivities, drinking parties, garden picnics and other games and amusements. She might leave her lover, but if she did so of her own accord she had to restore to him all presents given by him; if she is driven out, she does not give back anything.'[29]

NIYOGA

On the subject of *niyoga* (the appointment of sonless widow by her guardians to have one or at most two sons by her brother-in-law or other near relative), the Smṛiti law of this period reflects the contradictions of the older authorities. Directions for *niyoga* are given under the usual stringent restrictions by Manu (ix 59-63) and Yājñavalkya (i 68-9). Again, the son born according to the custom of *nigoya* is allowed (*M.*

ix 167, 184; *Y.* i 68-9; ii 128, 131) to inherit, as before, his father's property in the absence of better classes of sons. Nevertheless we find Manu in the above context (ix 57-8; 64-8) condemning *niyoga* itself in the strongest terms. Evidently Manu, while condoning *niyoga* as a practice approved by some earlier authorities, was himself opposed to it. The Great Epic while narrating the stories of the birth of Dhṛitarāshṭra and his brother (i 103-15) and of the five Pāṇḍava heroes (*ibid.* 120-4) refers to or quotes the Smṛiti rule of *niyoga* above mentioned. But the practice actually recommended and in part followed in the stories illustrates an altogether different custom, *viz.* that of appointment a Brāhmaṇa to raise sons on sonless Kshatriya widows. As Winternitz has well remarked,[30] the Smṛiti rule has its parallel in the widespread custom of levirate, while the Mahābhārata rule, like similar rights claimed by priests, chiefs, or landlords, had its origin in the law of might.

TOWN LIFE

The rise of rich and flourishing cities goes back in India to a time long anterior to the Christian era, and called into being a new social type called the *nāgaraka* (the city-bred man of fashion) as early as Pāṇini's time (iv 2, 128). In Vātsyāyana's *Kāmasūtra* (i 4, 1 f.) the *nāgaraka's* way of life is described for the first time with considerable fullness and held up as a model for others to follow. The picture is one of indulgence in a refined epicureanism by an accomplished young man with ample wealth and leisure. When a man has finished his education, says the author, and entered the life of a householder, he has to be take himself to a large or small town or the abode of many good men and adopt the life of a *nāgaraka*. He first builds a house and furnishes it with elegance and taste. The house consists of two parts, an outer section reserved for his amorous enjoyment, and an inner meant for the residence of his wife. The garden round the house has a swing shaded by trees and raised seats strewn with flowers. The outer house is fitted with a pair of couches provided with soft pillows and white sheets. At the head of the couch is a stand for a divine image and a raised seat containing the requisites of the *nagaraka's* morning toilette (unguents, garlands, small pots of beeswax and scents, the peel of citron, and betel-leaves). On a bracket on the wall are deposited his lute, picture-board, and box of paint-brushes, besides a book and a garland of the yellow amaranth. On the floor, not far from his couch, is spread a carpet with pillows and boards for chess and dice. Outside the room are the cages of his sporting birds and in a secluded place is found the spot where he recreates himself with the lathe, the chisel and so forth.

The daily life of the *nāgaraka* is described as follows: Rising in the morning and attending to his physical needs, he arranges his toilette. He uses unguents moderately, perfumes his clothes with the smoke of burnt incense, and wears a garland. He applies collyrium to his eyelids and lacdye to his lips. He finishes with a glance in the mirror, and then chews perfumed betel-leaves. After despatching his business, he takes his daily bath, having his limbs massaged every second day, and cleansed with soap-lather every third day. He shaves his face every fourth day. He takes two meals a day, one in the forenoon and the other in the afternoon (or according to an old authority, in the evening). After his midday meal he amuses himself in various ways such as listening to the talk of parrots, watching the fights of quails, cocks and rams, engaging in exhibitions of artistic skill, and conversing with his companions, or else he enjoys a siesta. In the afternoon he goes out fully dressed to attend social gatherings (*goshṭhī*), and in the evening the enjoys music. Then while his room is being cleaned and charged with the smell of sweet incense, he awaits the arrival of his mistresses. In the alternative he sends female messengers to being them, or goes out himself to seek them.

Besides his daily round of pleasures, the *nāgaraka* has his periodical entertainments. Such are the *samāja* and the *ghaṭa* (assemblies connected with worship of deities), the *goshṭhī* (social gathering), the *āpānaka* (drinking party), the *udyānayātrā* (garden party) and the *samasyā-krīḍā* (public games). The *samāja* takes place on an appointed day every fortnight or every month when the actors and others employed by the *nāgaraka* gather together for performances at a temple of the goddess Sarasvatī, the presiding deity of learning and the arts. On such occasions other actors coming from outside also exhibit their skill and receive their rewards. On special occasions actors of both classes co-operate with one another and the *gaṇa* (guild or club) to which the *nāgaraka* belongs entertains the guests. The *ghaṭas* of different kinds were held in a similar fashion in honour of various deities according to the local custom. The *goshṭhī* takes place when the *nāgaraka* and his associates of the same age, wealth, learning, and character, meet together for pleasant talk at the house of a courtesan, or in a public hall, or at the residence of one of their number. There they engage in the discussion of poetical compositions, and talk about the arts; they conclude by presenting one another with fine dresses. At the *goshṭhī*, says the author, one should not speak too much in Sanskrit or in the vernacular. One should, he continues, avoid *goshṭhī* which are hated by the people, or are harmful to them, or are given over to license. *Goshṭhīs* which are meant only to amuse and divert the people should be patronised. The *nāgarakas* also met at one another's houses to hold drinking parties where the courtezans would give them liquor of various kinds which they themselves afterwards drank. Similar scenes took place at the garden parties and in bathing parties during summer. On these occasions the *nāgarakas* wore rich ornaments and went out in the forenoon mounted on horses in the company of courtezans and attendants, and having spent the day in various diversions, returned home in the evening bringing with them some token of the entertainment. Lastly, the *nāgarakas* joined with the common folk in the various festivals celebrated in different parts of the country and on such occasions they attempted to attract the greatest notice.

A characteristic feature of town life during this period were *goshṭhīs* of fashionable citizens organised not only for intellectual diversion but also for more objectionable purposes. A story in the *Avadānaśataka* (ii 52 f.) narrates how members of the *goshṭhī* in the town of Śrāvastī assembling on a festive day made an agreement to bring their wives with them to a meeting in a garden, non-attendance involving the penalty of a heavy fine. In this case, it will be noticed, the *goshṭhī* partakes of the nature of a garden party, and it is attended not only by the members but also by their wives, and the attendance is enforced by a voluntary fine for default.

Another aspect of the *goshṭhīs* of this period is exhibited by the historical inscriptions. Among the names inscribed on the three relic caskets of the Bhaṭṭiprolu *stūpa* (*c.* 150 B.C.) are those of a *goshṭhī* with its members, the monk (*śramaṇa*) of a *goshṭhī*, and the *goshṭhī* of a certain Arahadina. Referring these *goshṭhīs* to the neighbouring town, we find that unlike the *goshṭhīs* described above, they were purely sectarian associations and that one of them apparently had a monk permanently in its employ. We find also that while one *goshṭhī* was sufficiently aristocratic to be known by the name of its leader, another chose to be remembered by the list of its members. So also among the names of donors commemorated by inscriptions of the *stūpas* at Sāñchī are those of the Barulamisa-goshṭhī from Vidiśā and the Buddha-goshṭhī from Dharmavardhana. The former probably was a *goshṭhī* of the aristocratic type just mentioned, while the latter had its sectarian character stamped on its very name.[31]

FOOD AND DRINK

A. In the Smṛitis

Already in the period of the Vedic Saṁhitās and the Brāhmaṇas we find a tendency to regard certain kinds of meat and even vegetables as unfit for eating.[32] The Dharmasūtras give us for the first time systematic lists of lawful and forbidden food in respect of the flesh of birds and beasts as well as fish and vegetables. Along with this the Dharmasūtras permit or even enjoin the partaking of meat on a number of prescribed occasions. The eating of meat even by Brāhmaṇas on ordinary occasions is condoned by them in other passages.[33] These rules are reproduced and amplified in the Smṛiti law of our period. Thu the lists of lawful and forbidden food given by Manu (v 5-25) and Yājñavalkya (i 169-78) agree on the whole with those presented by the Dharmasūtras. According to Manu (v 41 repeating *Vas.* iv 6) the occasions when animals might be killed are limited to sacrifices, the honey-mixture ceremony, and the rites for the gods and manes. To this Manu (v 27) and Yājñavalkya (i 179) add that the use of meat is permitted when one's life is in danger, when the Brāhmaṇas so desire, and when the meat has been sanctified (*prokshita*). As for the occasions justifying the slaughter of animals Manu (v 35 like *Vas.* xi 34) makes it compulsory for the priest engaged in a sacred rite to partake of meat. Like the older authorities, again, Manu (iii 267-70) and Yājñavalkya (i 257-9) hold different kinds of meat to be acceptable to the manes in an ascending order of preference. In the honey-mixture ceremony (*madhuparka*), the offering of a cow to a student just after the completion of his studies in enjoined by Manu (iii 3), and that of a big bull or goat to a learned Brāhmaṇa is prescribed by Yājñavalkya (i 109). The rules relating to forbidden meat are enforced by stringent penances imposed upon the person partaking of it (*M.* v 20; xi 157; *Y.* i 176). With this denunciation of the unlawful killing of animals is joined a eulogy of complete abstention from meat-eating (*M.* v 31, 33, 34, 38, 43-5, 47-55 and *Y.* i 180-1). It would seem, however, that the practice of meat-eating not only when enjoined by the law but on other occasions also prevailed extensively. This is virtually admitted by Manu (v 56) who concludes his account of the rules touching lawful and forbidden food, with the observation: 'eating meat and drinking wine are natural to human beings, and there is no sin in these acts, but abstention is attended with high rewards.'

In so far as eating the meat of cattle is concerned, we find that even in the period of the Vedic Samhitās and the Brāhmaṇas there was a distinct tendency to sanctify the cow and make her immune from slaughter, although it was usual to slay bulls and cows at sacrifices. From the time of the Gṛihyasūtras, drinking the five products of a cow (*pañcha-gavya*) has been prescribed as a means of purification from various sins. Coming to our period, we find that in Manu (v 18), as in the earlier law, animals with teeth in the upper jaw, with the sole exception of camels, are declared fit to be eaten. This implies (as pointed out by the commentators Medhātithi and Rāghavānanda) that the flesh of cattle was recognised as lawful food. Again, it is true that the slaughter of cows is still reckoned (*M.* xi 60 and *Y.* iii 234), as in Gautama (xxi 11 etc.), among the sins of the second degree (*upapātakas*), and not as yet among the mortal sins (*mahāpātakas*). Nevertheless the penances for killing a cow are particularly severe. They involve for instance a very restricted diet with constant attendance on cows and so forth for three months (*M.* xi 109-17), or continence for one month as well as living on 'the five products of the cow', constant attendance on cows, residence in cow-pens etc. (*Y.* iii 264-5). Again, it is very significant that giving up one's life for the sake of cows or otherwise preserving them is now mentioned for the first time (*M.* xi 80 and *Y.* iii 244-5) as an alternative penance for the murder of a Brāhmaṇa.[34]

Like the offering of meat at sacrifices, the ritual use of intoxicating *soma* juice and to a much less extent the use of liquor (*surā*) are known to the Vedic period. But already in one of the Upanishads we find the drinking of *surā* branded as a grave sin. In the Dharmasūtras, drinking *surā* ranks second in the list of mortal sins coming just after Brāhmaṇa-murder, while the penances of expiation range from death by drinking hot liquor to the performance of severe fasts and a fresh initiation. Even to drinking water from a wine vessel requires a slight penance.[35] These rules are repeated in Manu (xi 91-3; 147-9) and Yājñavalkya (iii 253- 5). For omitting to perform the penance. Manu adds (ix 236-40), the offender is to be punished by the king with branding on the forehead and must be completely cast off by his relatives. The strongest condemnation is reserved for a Brāhmaṇa drinking *surā* (*M.* xi 95-8). Again, in Manu (vii 50-2) drunkenness heads the list in the group of the king's traditional vices. A drunkard wife is liable to immediate supersession, according to Manu (ix 80), and Yājñavalkya (i 73). In particular it is said that a Brāhmaṇa wife drinking wine is reborn in the next life in lower existences forfeiting the world of her husband (*Y.* iii 256 repeating *Vas.* xxi 11).

Yet we notice in these works a tendency to condone the vice of drinking—doubtless, as elsewhere, under pressure of circumstances. Manu (xi 94-8), while strongly condemning the drinking of *surā* in any of its three forms by Brāhmaṇas, implies that the varieties obtained from molasses and from *madhūka* flowers were allowable to Kshatriyas and Vaiśyas. Again, the severity of Manu's denunciation quoted above (xi 91-3) is mitigated by the statement that a man unintentionally drinking the *vāruṇī* varieties of liquor (*M.* xi 147), or *surā* generally (*Y.* iii 255) is purified by a fresh initiation. To this Manu adds that even intentional drinking is exempted from penances involving death. A similar tendency may be traced in Manu (ix 84), where a fine only is imposed upon a wife who drinks liquor at festive shows.

B. In other Sources

In the didactic portions of the Epics the eating of meat and the drinking of liquor are condemned as strongly as in the Smṛitis. The *Mahābhārata* (xiii 114-5) preserves a long discourse in praise of abstention from meat-eating, subject to the exceptional occasions where it is permitted in the Smṛitis. Abstention is particularly recommended during the four months of the rainy season and more specially in the month of Kārtika. According to the Great Epic (xii 35, 20, amplifying the rules of Manu and Yājñavalkya quoted above), he who drinks liquor unintentionally or when his life is in danger is purified by a fresh initiation. Elsewhere, however, (xii 159, 32) we are told that drinking wine is a sin expiable only with death. The strongest censure is reserved, as usual, for Brāhmaṇa drunkards. Once (i 76, 67-8) the sage Śukra is said to have established a rule that a Brāhmaṇa drinking wine should thence forth be held to be guilty of Brāhmaṇa-murder. But in the narratives of the two epics even Brāhmaṇas and Kshatriyas, not to speak of other classes, freely indulge in meat-eating. Wine-drinking is also mentioned there as the habitual practice of Kshatriyas. In the *Mahābhārata* (iii 207-8) we have a remarkable series of arguments justifying the slaughter of animals not only for sacrifice also for other occasions.[36]

When we turn to the Buddhist and Jaina monastic rules, we find the same tendency to modify the fundamental principle of *ahiṁsā* in the light of the widespread practice of meat-eating. Abstention from taking life and from drinking liquor, as is well known, is included among the vows that are binding alike upon Buddhist and Jaina monks and laymen. In the actual rules of the Buddhist Order, however, a monk is permitted to partake of meat, provided it is pure in three respects, *viz.* unseen, unheard, and unsuspected. Again it is laid down that a monk partaking of meat except when he is sick is guilty of a grave sin. According to the Jaina *Āchārāṅga Sūtra* (ii 1, 10, 5 f.) a monk or a nun on a begging tour should not accept from laymen meat or fish with many bones.

We find frequent references in other literature to wine-bibbing and meat-eating as prevalent practices. The *Milindapañha* (278) includes the gift of liquor in a list of ten condemned gifts. But in Vātsyāyana's *Kāmasūtra* (ii 10, 1-22) we read that the *nāgaraka* when being entertained by his mistress is to regale her with liquor as well as varieties of roasted and dried meat and other delicacies. *Nāgarakas,* again, are described in the same work, as we have seen, a indulging in various kinds of spirituous liquor at their drinking parties, garden picnics, and water sports. In the *Divyāvadāna* (136-7) we are told how a big bull was led away for slaughter outside Vaiśālī city by a butcher, and a great crowd followed him hoping to share in the meat. The custom of killing animals for food at wedding feasts is referred to in the story of prince Arishṭanemi's renunciation in the *Uttarādhyayana Sūtra* (xxii 14-7), and that of fattening a ram for slaughter at a guest's entertainment is mentioned in a simile in the same work (vii 1-4). In the story of a pious Jaina layman, the *Uvāsagadasāo* tells us (i 39) that, while limiting himself to a number of stringent restrictions under the householder's vows, he made an exception in favour of a particular kind of liquor. This limitation, with the same exception, is repeated (viii 235) in the tale of another equally pious Jaina layman. The principal wife of the latter, however, because of her habitual indulgence in meat and drink of all kinds, is said to have ended her life miserably under her husband's curse (*ibid.* 240 f.).

A scientific classification of birds and beasts with an analysis of the characteristic qualities of the flesh of each kind is found in a famous medical work of this period, *viz.* the *Charaka-saṁhitā* (Sūtrasthāna xxvii 11-29, 37 f.). The list includes some animals like camels whose flesh is condemned as forbidden food in the Smṛitis.

TOILETTE AND PERSONAL HYGIENE

Rules relating to the daily purification of the body, brushing the teeth and bathing are laid down for householders (*gṛihasthas*) and intending householders (*snātakas*) in the Dharmasūtras. These rules are reproduced with some additions in Manu (iv) and Yājñavalkya (i 97-166). A verse common to Manu (iv 152) and the *Mahābhārata* (xiii 104, 23) neatly sums up the morning routine of the *snātaka*. This consists in answering the calls of nature, toilette, bathing, brushing the teeth, applying collyrium to the eyes, and worshipping the gods. The *snātaka* is required to be clean in his dress and appearance. To quote manu (iv 34-6) and Yājñavalkya (i 131, 133), the *snātaka* should not wear old and dirty clothes but should be dressed in white garments and should keep his hair, nails, and beard clipped; he should also wear two gold ear-rings. According to Manu (ii 209) the student in residence with his teacher is to render him such service as shampooing his limbs and attending on him while bathing. Similar services (anointing the limbs with oil, rubbing or shampooing them with powder and so forth) may be performed for Jaina mendicants by laymen.[37] In the well-known medical work called the *Suśrutasaṁhitā*,[38] a complete course of personal hygiene is laid down with full directions for its practice. This includes the application of the tooth-brush, eye and mouth-washes and collyrium, chewing betel-leaves with the proper spices, anointing the head and the limbs with oil, combing the hair, physical exercise, rubbing and friction, bathing, scented pastes, wearing gems, flowers and clean clothes, washing and anointing the feet, shaving, paring the nails and shampooing.

From the texts, legal and medical, quoted above we turn to those more clearly reflecting contemporary fashions of life. In Vātsyāyana's description of the daily life of a *nāgaraka*, the morning toilette, as we have seen, plays a very important part. What elaborate fashions of hairdressing were known among laymen is indicated by a text in the *Milindapañha* (11). From this we learn that laymen used to adorn their hair and beard, smear them with oil, wash them, apply garlands, scents, myrobalans and dyes to them, making use also of ribbons and combs. Women used to paint their bodies yellow with different substances.[39] They also adorned their bodies with ornamental designs (*viśeshakas*).[40] Dressing in white garments, using sandal, garlands, perfumes, and unguents and so forth, were the distinctive features of the layman's toilette.[41] Even children were anointed with perfumes and used to be rubbed, bathed, and shampooed by their parents.[42] Flowers and perfumes as well as betel-leaves were frequently exchanged between lovers.[43] Perfuming the limbs of a mendicant and fumigating them with incense were permitted to Jaina laymen.[44] The scenting of clothes was a common fashion.[45] Laymen having bought clothes used to wash, dye, brush, rub, clean and perfume them.[46] A perfume compounded of several substances (saffron, aloe, 'Turkish' and 'Yavana' scents among others) was known.[47]

We may next refer to a few texts illustrating the toilette appliances known in this period. The *Rāmāyaṇa* (iv 91, 51 f.) narrative of the entertainment of prince Bharata's host by the sage Bharadvāja at his hermitage, is full of miraculous elements, but the amenities provided by the sage for his guests include a reliable list of toilette articles known to the common folk. It enumerates tooth-sticks, sandal and other pastes, mirrors, combs, brushes and collyrium-boxes. In *Uvāsagadasāo* (i 22-42) we have the story of a pious Jaina *gṛihapati* who, while voluntarily submitting to a whole set of householder's vows restricting him in various ways, expressly reserved for his use a number of toilette articles. Among these are included fragrant red-tinted cloth, a green tooth-stick of sweet taste, the milky pulp of the *āmalaka* fruit (perhaps for cleansing the hair), a specially expensive variety of unguents, powder of scented wheat flour, perfume made of aloes, saffron, sandal, and other substances, the white lotus and a garland of jasmine flowers, incense made of aloes and other substances, and betel with five spices. This inventory may be fairly taken to include articles ordinarily used by members of the rich capitalist class. Lastly the *Sūtrakṛitāṅga* (i 4, 2) in a comic sketch of the woes of a monk seduced from his vows by a woman, acquaints us with the toilette outfit of women in ordinary life. We learn that they used tooth-brushes, combs, ribbons to bind their hair, mirrors, myrobalans, collyrium-boxes with pins attached, sticks to paint marks on their foreheads, oil for the face, lip-salves, powders made of sandal, and other substances.

At the date of the early Buddhist literature a number of professions had arisen to cater for the public taste in toilette. Such professional attendants are mentioned in works of this period when describing city life. A list in Vātsyāyana (vi 1, 9) mentions garland-makers, perfumers, dyers and cleaners of clothes and barbers. In Madhyadeśa gardeners hawked lotuses in the streets (*Avadānaśataka*, I 124). Garland-makers made variegated bouquets from all sorts of flowers, according to the *Milindapañha* (347). In the *Mahābhārata* (iv 9, 19-20) we have the story of Draupadī in disguise seeking employment with the queen of Virāṭa as her attendant. She knew, we are told, the arts of dressing the hair, preparing unguents, and making garlands of wondrous designs; here we have a list of the qualifications expected from a queen's maid in real life. Among the amenities provided for Bharata's host in the Rāmāyaṇa story quoted earlier (ii 9) female bathing-attendants are enumerated. Even the luxury of a shaving saloon is mentioned in a few Jaina canonical texts.[48]

The rich development of toilette-fashions during this period was marked by the elevation of some of them to the rank of technical arts (*Kalās*). In Vātsyāyana's list of sixty-four supplementary arts found in the *Kāmasūtra* are included the preparation of cut-designs from leaves, the weaving of garlands, and the manufacture of perfumes. Among the seventy-two arts (Kalās) known to the Jaina canonical texts are those concerned with the arrangement of dress, the fabrication of unguents, the preparation of powders, the cutting of ornamental leaf-designs, and the beautification of young ladies' complexions. The manufacture of scents and the preparation of leaf-designs are included among the *kalās in* Lalitavistara (156).[49]

The evidence of archaeology confirms and supplements that of the literary texts quoted above. Among the professions commemorated in the contemporary votive inscriptions, that of the perfumers is the one most often mentioned. Again, the excavations of contemporary ancient sites (especially at Taxila) have yielded toilette appliances of various kinds. In the figure sculptures of this period we have more unequivocal testimony to the variety of toilette fashions known at this time. The types of coiffure both of men and women depicted in these sculptures are too varied for detailed notice here. On the bodies of women sculptured in the railing around the Bhārhut *stūpa* are found designs of the sun, the moon, the stars and so forth. Among the sculptures of the Mathurā and the Amarāvatī school, figures of women are found wearing flowers or garlands or else in the act of arranging their toilette.[50]

NOTES AND REFERENCES

1. For descriptions of pure and worldly Brāhmaṇas in Jātakas, see Fick, *The Social Organisation in North-East India*, Eng. tr. pp. 193-250. Examples of Brāhmaṇna high officials etc.: *senāpati* Pushyamitra, founder of the Śuṅga dynasty, *amātya* Vasudeva, founder of the Kaṇva dynasty Brāhmaṇa treasurer of *mahākshatrapa* Śoḍāsa (Lüders, *List*, no. 82), Refs. to Brāhmaṇas making gifts : *ibid*. nos. 82, 1035, 1050. Brāhmaṇas performing Vedic sacrifices: Pushyamitra Śuṇga, Lüders, *List*, nos. 149a *ASIAR*. 1910-11, p. 41; Brāhmaṇas receiving gifts : Lüders, *List* nos. 134, 1099, 1131, 1133, 1135, 1328; *EI*. xxi p. 60. Vedic sacrifices performed and heavy fees paid to officiating priests: Lüders, *List*, no. 1112, *EI*. xx pp. 19, 21, 62; xxiii p. 52 XXIV pp. 250, 253.
2. *JAOS*. XIII pp., 186-7.

3. *Ibid.* p. 104
4. *Ibid.* pp. 109-10
5. Probable refs. to Kshatriyas performing Vedic sacrifices: *El.* XX pp. 19, 31, 62; XXIII p. 52; XXIV pp. 250, 253.
6. Op. cit., pp. 90-4.
7. Stock description of *gāhāvai: Uvāsaga.* i 4-5; ii 92; iii 127; iv 145; v 155; vi 163; viii 232; ix 268; x 273. Description of a potter: *ibid.* vii 182. Refs. to *gahapati* in votive inscrs.: Lüders, *List,* nos. 193, 201, 202, 449, 450 etc. (at Sāñchī); no. 725 (at Bhārhut); no. 1120 (at Nānāghāt); nos. 1170, 1157 (at Junnar); nos. 1206, 1209, 1211, 1220 etc. (at Amarāvatī). Ref. to *kuṭumbika, ibid.* nos. 976, 1121, 1127. For the status of *gahapati* and *Kuṭumbika,* in the Jātakas, see Fick, *op. cit.* pp. 253-7. Fick's description (*ibid.* p. 256) of *gahapatis* as a special class and rank and not a cast is borne out by the votive inscrs. which however do not support his somewhat narrow identification of them (*ibid.* p. 253) with the lower landowning nobility and the rich middle-class families in bit cities. Refs. to *śreshṭhis* and their relatives as donors in votive inscrs.: Lüders, *List.* nos. 24, 41 (at Mathurā); nos. 184, 206, 246, 248, 255, 283, 339, 348 etc. (at Sāñchi); no. 1087 (at Kārle). Refs. to village *śreshṭhi* : *ibid.* nos. 422, 423. Refs. to *śreshṭhi* as *gahapati* or as *gahapati's* son : *ibid.* nos. 1056, 1073, 1075. *Seṭṭhis* are habitually referred to as *gahapaṭis in Avad ānaśataka.* On the status of *seṭṭhis* in the Jātakas, see Fick, *op. cit.* pp. 257-66.
8. Such are the professions of the gardener, perfumer, labourer, blacksmith, brazier, ironmonger, goldsmith, dyer, polisher, carpenter and so forth. See Lüders, *List,* Index of Misc. Terms.
9. K. A. Nilakanta Sastri, *The Colas,* I pp. 106, 113.
10. For reference to Buddhist and Jaina monks and nuns in votive inscrs., see Lüders, *List,* Index on Misc. Terms, *s.v. muni, tāpasa, tapasvin, bhikshu, bhikshuṇi, śramaṇa, śramaṇikā, bhadanta, bhadantī,* etc. Hermit and ascetic (with shaven head or matted hair) as chiefs of stationary spies: *KA.* i 11. Female mendicants of Brāhmaṇa, shaven-headed and Sūdra classes as itinerant spies: *ibid.* i 12. Residences of Buddhist and Jaina nuns and Brahmanical female ascetics as convenient rendezvous for unchaste wives and their paramours: Goṇikāputra quoted in *Kāmasūtra* v. 4, 42. Mendicant women included among female messengers of love : ibid, v. 4, 62.
11. I *A.* 1911, p. 11.
12. The above quotations are from Kane. *History of Dharmaśāstra,* II Part i. pp. 63-4. The method of rise and fall in caste status was an hypothesis and an ideal (*ibid.* p. 65).

13. In *Mbh.* iii 272, 11; iv 33, 50; we are told that according to the law of warfare a foe defeated in battle can save his life by publicly proclaiming himself the victor's slave, but after a year he is acknowledged as the victor's son and set free.
14. Yavanas, Kāṁbojas, Gandhāras mentioned together (RE. V. XIII; *Rām.* iv 43, 12 etc.). Yavanas are the only people without Brāhmaṇas and Śramaṇas (R.E. XIII). Yavanas, Kāṁbojas etc. are fierce barbarians (*Mbh.* vi 9. 65). Yavanas, Kāṁbojas, Gandhāras etc. reckoned among sinful peoples having the nature of *śvapākas* and vultures (*Mbh.* xii 207, 43-5). Ābhīras are sinful and greedy *dasyus* (*Mbh.* xvi 7, 47-9). Text and tr. of relevant extract from the Yugapurāṇa in *JBORS.* 1928, pp. 402, 408, 410, 413-14. Revised text, *ibid.* 1930, p. 18 f. On the date of the Yugapurāṇa, see *ibid.* 1928, p. 399; 1930, p. 45.
15. The unique significance of Indo-Greek bilingual coins and of votive inscrs. Written in Prākṛit is explained by Tarn, *Greeks,* pp. 387, 388-90. On the other hand the account in *Miln.* of Menander's conversion to Buddhism is unconvincing (Tarn, *op. cit.,* pp. 262-4, 267-8). The same remarks apply to the statement (D.R. Bhandarkar, *ASIAR.* 1914-15, p. 78) that a clay-sealing discovered at Besnagar refers to a Greek called Demetrius who was the *yajamāna* at a Brāhmaṇa sacrifice. For refs. to Greek votive inscrs. in prākṛit and Kharoshṭhi, see *CII.* II (i) pp. 4, 8, 65-6, 114 etc. On Besnagar pillar inscr. in Brāhmī, see *ASIAR.* 1908-9, p. 126. For representations of Indra on coins fo Eucratides and Antialcidas and of Lakshmī on those of Agathocles and Pantaleon, see J.N. Banerjea, *The Development of Hindu Iconography,* pp. 123, 163. Inscr. of Yavana donors at Kārle Nāsik and Junnar in Lüders, *List,* nos. 1093, 1096, 1140, 1156, 1182, on end of Greek language etc. see Tarn, *op. cit.*
16. For Indian forms of Greek names, cf. *CII.* II (i) pp. 6, 98; *ASIAR.* 1908-9, p. 126 etc. Names of Yavana donors in West Indian cave inscr. are purely Indian, but their nationality is still disputed. Examples of Sakas etc. with Indian names: (a) Vīryakamitra and Vijayamitra (*EI.* XXIV p. 7), Vijayamitra, his son Indravarman and his nephew Aśpavarman (coins); (b) Jayadāman, Rudradāman etc. of the Kshatrapa dynasty of Western India (Inscr.l and coins); (c) Vudhika, son of Vishṇudata (Lüders, *List,* nos. 1148, 1149); (d) Vishṇudatā, the Śakanikā, daughter of the Śaka Agnivarman and mother of Viśvavarma, temp. King Māḍharīputra Iśvarasena, the Abhīra, son of Śivadatta the Abhira (*ibid.* no. 1137). On the other hand Ushavadāta, usually taken to correspond to Skt. Rishabhadatta, has probably an Iranian name-ending (Lüders

in *SBAW.* 1913, p. 414) or perhaps was a purely Iranian name (Konow in *IHQ.* XIV p. 139). For Kshatriya name-ending *varman* see *Pār. Gṛi. Sū.* i 17; *Baudh. Gṛ. Sū.* i 11, 9 etc. On coin-legends of the Kshatrapas of Western India, see Rapson, *BMCAWK.* P. 1xxxvii f.

17. For epithet Indo-Macedonian applied to Śaka, calendar, see Konow, *CII.* II (i) p. xc. In the Kharoshṭhī records dated both according to the old Śaka era and the era of Kanishka the month-names are mostly Indian, but occasionally Macedonian, while the days are mentioned without the Indian division into *pakshas:* on the other hand, the records in the Śaka era used by the Western Kshatrapas refer not only to the year, month and date, but also to the *pakshas* (Konow, *op. cit.* pp. 1xxxviii-xc). On the devices and symbols of Indian deities on Śaka and Kushān coins, see Banerjea, *op. cit.* p. 122 f. The evidence seems to suggest that while the Śaka and Parthian rulers divided their devotion between Greek gods and hellenized forms of Indian deities (Indra, Lakshmī and probably Buddha), Kadphises II was by faith a Śaiva, and Vāsudeva predominantly so. On the other hand Kanishka and Huvishka were eclectic in their religious inclinations which were centered mainly on Zoroastrian and Indian deities. The epithets *dhramika* etc. borne by Maues and his successors need not necessarily imply, as D.R. Bhandarkar (*IA.* 1911) p. 13; thinks, their conversion to Buddhism. For refs. to dedications of Buddhist relics etc. by Śakas in Northern India cf. *CII* II (i) nos. 28, 48, 137, 145, 150, 151, 170; in Western India, cf. Lüders, *List*, nos. 1137, 1148, 1149; in Eastern India cf. *EI.* xx p. 37. For Jaina benefactions by Iranians with Greek names see Lüders 'The Era of the Matraraja and the Maharaja Rajatiraja' in *D.R. Bhandarkar Vol.* pp. 281-9

18. These are the queen of Vāsishṭhīputra Śātakarṇi of the Kārddamaka royal family and daughter of *mahākshatrapa* Rudradāman (Lüders, *List,* no. 994); and Rudrabhaṭṭārikā, chief queen of Vīrapurushadatta and daughter of the Śaka king of Ujjayinī (*EI.* xx p. 4).

19. The votive inscrs. commemorata donations not only by Buddhist and Jaina female lay-worshippers but also by a housewife and the wives of a cloth-dyer, a merchant, a caravan-leader and the like (refs. in Lüders. *List*, Index of Misc. terms *s.v.*)

20. *JAOS.* XIII p. 173 n.

21. Hopkins, loc. cit; Kane, *Hist. of Dharma.* II (i) pp. 626-7.

22. K.A.N. Sastri. *The Colas,* i pp. 112-13.

23. Lüders, *List,* no. 921.

24. Lüders, *List*, no. 102.
25. Seven years training received by a courtesan girl from her fifth year under expert dancing-masters, music-teachers (skilled in playing tabor, flute and lute respectively) and a composer of songs; her performance after the training before the king and his whole court, and her receipt of the king's prize of 1008 gold coins: (*Śilapp.* tr. pp. 97-104. Mansions of courtesans in Madura: *ibid.* p. 205. Training of courtesans in royal dances, popular dances, singing, lute-playing, flute-playing etc. : *Maṇi.* ii, quoted, K.A.N. Sastri, *The Colas,* I. p. 93.)
26. Approved forms of marriage for different castes, acc. to Manu loc. cit., are as follows: (a) First four forms as well as *āsura* and *gāndharva* for Brāhmaṇas; (b) *āsura, gāndharva, rākshasa* and *paiśācha,* or else *gāndharva, rākshasa* or a mixture of both, or finally rākshasa alone for Kshatriyas; (c) *āsura, gāndharva* and *paiśācha,* or else *āsura* alone for Vaiśyas and Sūdras.
27. Examples of Kshatriya marriages by capture etc. in the epics are as follows:— (a) Daughters of the king of Kāśī carried off by Bhīshma for marriage with his stepbrother: *Mbh.* i 102; (b) Subhadrā carried off by Arjuna in accordance with the precept of Kṛishṇa that in the case of Kshatriyas when the chances of self-choice are uncertain, carrying off by force is also commended: *ibid.* i 219-21; (c) Mādrī purchased from her father for marriage with Pāṇḍu in acc. with family custom of the Madra ruling house: *ibid.* i 113; (d) self-choice of Draupadī, Damayantī Sāvitrī: *ibid.* i 185; iii 57, 292-4; and of Sitā: *Rām.* i 66-73. *Mbh.* i 102, 12 condemns a father's disposal of daughter for a fee, but elsewhere (i 113, 9; 193, 23 etc.) this is mentioned as a recognised custom. That the remarriage of Kshatriya princesses was not thought to be impossible is shown by the trick of Damayantī in announcing her second *svayaṁvara* to find out the whereabouts of her absent husband : *ibid.* iii 70, 24-6. On the whole subject see Hopkins, *JAOS.* xiii pp. 167-9, 356-8. In the *Lalita-vistara* story when Śuddhodana sent a proposal for marriage between the Bodhisattva and Gopā to her father Daṇḍapāṇi, the latter at first withheld his assent, for his family custom required the prospective bridegroom to be an expert in the arts, and the Bodhisattva had not yet shown his skill. Then a great tournament was held at which Gopā was announced to be the victor's prize. It was only when the Bodhisattva had exhibited his superiority to other Śākya youths in all arts that Daṇḍapāṇi gave the girl to him.

28. So also in *Divy.* the bride is said to be procured from an equal family by a Brāhmaṇa (P. 483) and by *gṛihapatis* (pp. 1, 24, 87, 167, 262). Again in *Divy.* (pp. 167-8), a *gṛihapati's* exceptionally handsome daughter is sought for in marriage by princes as well as sons of ministers, *gṛihapatis, śreshṭhis* and caravan-leaders.
29. In the above paragraphs the quotations are from H.C. Chakladar, *Social Life*, pp. 128, 131, 138, 182.
30. *JRAS.* 1897, pp. 731-2.
31. The translation of *goshṭhī* in the inscrs. as 'trustees in charge of temple of charitable endowment, ' (Bühler in *EI.* II followed by Atindrarnath Bose, *Social and Rural Economy of Northern India, c.* 600 B.C. to A.D. 200, I p. 53) or as a 'committee' (Lüders in *List*, loc. cit., followed by N.G. Majumdar in *Monuments of Śāñchī* I, votive inscrs. of *stūpās* I, 2, 3 etc. nos. 96-8, 178, 793); cannot be maintained in view of the refs. in *Kāmasūtra* and *Avadānaśataka* above cited.
32. Cf. TS. ii 5, 1, 1; *AB.* ii 1, 8; *ŚB.* i 2, 3, 9.
33. On the rules about eating vegetables and the flesh of birds, beasts and fishes in the Dharmasūtras see Kane, *op. cit.* II part 2 pp. 777, 781-3.
34. On the sanctity of the cow in the Vedic Samhitās and Brāhmaṇas, see Kane, *op. cit.*, pp. 772-3. On *pañchagavyas*, see *ibid.* pp.773-4. The significance of the alternative penance for Brāhmaṇa-murder in *M.* and *Y.* quoted above is missed by D.R. Bhandarkar, *Some Aspects of Ancient Indian Culture*, pp. 77-8.
35. On the drinking of *soma* and *surā* and the tendency to restrict the latter in the Vedic period, see Kane, *op. cit.*, pp. 792-4.
36. Brāhmaṇas entertained with the flesh of boars and deer and other delicacies by Yudhishṭhira (*Mbh.* ii 4, 1-2). Deer killed by the Pāṇḍavas and their flesh first offered to Brāhmaṇas and then eaten by themselves (*ibid.* iii 50, 4). King Jayadratha and his attendants entertained by Draupadī with the flesh of deer etc. (*ibid.* iii 266, 13-14). Kṛishṇa and Arjuna intoxicated by drinking liquor (*ibid.* v. 57-35), Deer and boar killed for food by Rāma and Lakshmaṇa wandering in the forest (*Rām.* ii 52, 102). Meat of goats, sheep, boars, deer etc. and liquor of different varieties provided for prince Bharata's host by the sage Bharadvāja (*ibid.* ii 91, 51f). Wine and meat abjured by Rāma out of grief for Sītā (*ibid.* v. 36, 41).
37. *Achāra. Sū.* ii 13, 1 f.
38. Chikitsāsthāna xxiv 1-65.
39. *Buddhacharita* iv 46; *Gāthā-sapta śatī* i 22, 58, 80.
40. *Saundarananda* iv 13-6.

41. *Miln.* pp. 243, 338, 248.
42. *Miln.* p. 241.
43. Vātsyāyana v 1, 10; 21, 35; vi 1, 20; 3, 4 etc.
44. *Āchārā Sū.* ii 13, 8.
45. Bhāsa's *Chārudatta* i 26 f.; *Saundarananda* iv 26.
46. *Āchāra, Sū* ii 5, 1, 3.
47. *Miln.* p. 267.
48. Barbers, bathing-attendants, florists, dealers in perfumes among residents of a city; *Miln.* p. 331. Bathing-attendants, toilette-attendants, perfumers, florists, hairdressers among the inhabitants of Ayodhyā; *Rām.* ii 83, 12-28. For *alainkāriyasaha (shaving saloon) see Abhidhānarājendra;* s.v. For refs. to perfumers in votive inscrs. see Lüders, *List*, Index of Misc. Terms s. v. *gāndhika*.
49. On the list of 64 *angavidyās*, see Vātsyāyana, i 3, 16. For the list of 72 *kalās* in Jaina *Samavāyānga Sūtra*, see Abhidhānarājendra, s.v. *kalā*.
50. Examples of toilette appliances from ancient sites:—(a) incense burners, flesh rubbers, perfume sprinklers, copper mirror, ivory handle (for mirror) at Sirkap Taxila: *ASIAR*. 1914-15, pp. 16, 22; 1915-16, pp. 17, 20, 29, 52; decorated ivory comb, ordinary ivory and bone combs at Taxila: *ibid.* 1926-7, p. 119; 1928-9, p. 51; (b) antimony rods at Dharmarājika *stūpa*, Taxila: *ibid.* 1915-16, p. 10; at Sirkap, Taxila: *ibid.* 1914-15, pp. 17, 23; at Besnagar : *ibid.* 1913-14, p. 218; (c) flesh rubbers of pottery antimony rods of bronze, bronze mirror, conchshell, cosmetic holders in form of fish, miniature bronze bottles (as unguent holders?) at Rairh: K.N. Puri, *Excavations*, pp. 42-3. For exhaustive accounts of styles of coiffure, see Moti Chandra, *JISOA*. VIII pp. 89-90. For figures of women with flowers or in act of arranging toilette, see C. Sivaramamurti, *Amarāvatī* Sculptures, pl. vi fig. 9, pl. viii figs. 21, 23, pl. ix figs. 2, 10, 11, 13, 17 etc.

CHAPTER - IV

SOUTH INDIA

EARLY HISTORICAL PERIOD

The extreme south of India from the Tirupati hill (Vēngaḍam) to Cape Comorin (Kumari), bounded by the sea on the east and west, was known as Tamilagam, the Tamil realm. By the fourth century B.C. it had become subject to strong Aryan or Northern influences, though the pre-Aryan (Tamil) culture and language continued to flourish here in much greater strength than in the rest of India. Our knowledge of the history of the country before the Christian era is, however, rather vague and indirect. A scholium of Kātyāyana on Pāṇini (iv 1, 168) which derives the word Pāṇḍya from Pāṇḍu, thus relating the royal family of the extreme south with the Pāṇḍavas of the Great Epic, and the references to the Pāṇḍya country in Megasthenes and Kauṭilya are among the earliest data now accessible to us. Megasthenes knew that Ceylon was an island separated from the mainland of India and that it was more productive than India of gold and large pearls; a good part of the island was forest inhabited by wild beasts including a large breed of elephants. He gives a quaint account of the Pāṇḍyan kingdom making little difference beween fact and fable. He says that Heracles had a daughter Pandaia to whom he assigned the southernmost portion of India including 365 villages, whose people brought by turns their daily tribute to the royal palace, 'so that the queen might always have the assistance of those men whose turn it was to pay the tribute in coercing those who for the tme being were defaulters in their payments.'[1] What is described as tribute here seems to have been the supply of the daily provisions needed for the royal household; the *Śilappadikarām*, written nearly a thousand years after the date of Megasthenes, contains a reference to the shepherds in the suburbs of Madurai supplying ghee every day to the palace by turns.[2] Kautilya's references to the fine cloth from Madurai and the trade routes to the South have been noticed already (p. 73).

Late inscriptions and legends recall events long past, and mention the rule of the Nandas in the Deccan, and the migration of Chandragupta Maurya with the Jaina Patriarch Bhadrabāhu to Śravaṇa Beḷgoḷa in Mysore. But perhaps the oldest and most tangible evidence that there was contact between North and South leading to a certain uniformity of culture throughout India is to be found in the 'punch-marked' coins of copper and silver, rectangular to start with, but later round also, 'which long served as the common currency of most of the states of ancient India, and were wonderfully uniform in weight and general style from the Himalayas to Cape Comorin.' Cunningham was disposed to date the most ancient coins of the class as early as 1000 B.C. though others think the estimate 'much in excess of the truth'. In the South they were used 'from the most remote times down to about A.D. 300'.[3]

The second and thirteenth Rock Edicts of Aśoka mention the southern kingdoms and Ceylon; the list in the second Edict, which is longer, comprises by name the Choḍas, Pāṇḍyas, Satiyaputa and Keralaputra, besides Tāṁbraparṇī. These countries lay outside the empire of Aśoka, but they were so friendly to the emperor that he could arrange for the medical treatment of men and animals in all these lands, and for the importation and planting of useful medicinal herbs and roots wherever they were needed. The *dūtas* (emissaries) of Aśoka also visited these countries for preaching *Dhamma* there. The bare mention of such facts is enough to warrant the inference that there existed in these parts a settled life with an ordered polity and a fairly high level of civilization. The Tamils believed in fact that the three monarchies of the Cheras, Cholas, and Pāṇḍyas were of immemorial antiquity, 'dating from the time of creation' as a mediaeval commentator quaintly puts it.[4] A late Pallava charter counts Aśokavarmā among the earliest rulers of Kāñchī, and this may well be a relic of Mauryan rule in the South.

Of the three Tamil monarchies the Pāṇḍya country occupied the extreme south and included the modern districts of Tirunelvēli, Madurai, and Ramnad, besides South Travancore, often called Nāñjilnād, plough-land. Its capital was Madurai, the city on the Vaigai river, and Koṟkai on the east coast at the mouth of the Tāmbraparṇī river was its main seaport, though we hear of another port further north by name Sāliyūr; there must have been some port or ports on the west coast as well round about modern Trivandrum. The Chola country comprised the lower Kāvērī valley, the coastal plain between two rivers both bearing the name Veḷḷār, the north Veḷḷār entering the sea near Porto Novo, and the smaller southern stream passing through Pudukkōṭṭai territory. The Chola kingdom thus roughly corresponded to modern Tanjore and Trichinopoly districts; its inland capital was Uṟaiyūr, and Puhār or Kāvēripaṭṭanam (the Khaberis of Ptolemy) at the mouth of the Kāvērī was its main port. The Chera or Kerala kingdom was the western coastal strip above the northern limit of the Pāṇḍyan kingdom. It had a number of good ports, Toṇḍi and Muśiri being the best known. The capital of the Chera kingdom was called Vañji, and its location has been the subject of an inconclusive debate, some identifying it with some place on the Periyār river or at its mouth, others locating it inland in Karūr or Karuvūr, the centre of the westernmost taluq of the Trichinopoly district. The mention of Karu-ur in a Brāhmī record of the third century B.C. from the neighbourhood, and of Karuvūr *alias* Vañjimānagaram in a much later inscription,[5] may be taken to support the inland location of the Chera capital. Ptolemy's reference to Korura as the Chera capital and the discovery of Roman coins near Karūr lend further support to this view. If it is correct, the Chera country was not confined to the western coastal strip but had a notable inward extension by way of the Palghat gap. The identity and location of Satiyaputa are uncertain. The best view now seems to be that first put forward by K.G. Sesha Aiyer (*Cera Kings*, page 18) and confirmed by Burrow on what appear to be sound philological grounds (*BSOAS*. xii, 1948, pp. 136-7, 146-7). Satiya corresponds, not to skt. *Satya*, but later Tamil *Atiya;* and *puta* becomes *magan* later *mān* in Tamil, so that Satiyaputa was the Tamil chieftain Adigamān (of Tagaḍūr)—who was quite prominent in the

Śaṅgam period and may have risen into importance earlier. This is a much more satisfactory identification than that of Satiyaputa with Kośar which was accepted by some scholars till recently. Old Tamil was the only language that prevailed in the whole area, possibly[6] with dialectical variations, which, slight at first, developed in the course of centuries into the separate languages of Malayālam and Kannaḍa. The Gulf of Mannar was famous for its pearl fisheries which were shared by the Pāṇḍyas, Cholas, and the rulers of Ceylon.

Among the earliest monuments of the Tamil country to which we may assign a date with some confidence are the Brāhmī inscriptions found in natural caverns in hills, which have many features in common with the hundreds of similar records found in Ceylon. The script of these inscriptions resembles closely that of the brief inscriptions from Bhaṭṭiprolu, and may well be assigned to the third and second century B.C. These inscriptions from caverns have not been fully elucidated, but they are clearly either brief donative records, or only give the names of persons who made the caverns fit for habitation, or of the monks who occupied them thereafter. Kalugumalai (Tamil for Gṛidhrakūṭa) is the name of one of the hills containing these caverns. The name Pañcha Pāṇḍavamalai often applied to them 'strongly reminds us of the Pāṇḍava-pabbata at whose foot the Buddha after his renunciation took his first meal which he had obtained by begging.' One of the caves bears the name '*uṇḍānkal*', 'the rock of the man who took the meal'. The caverns of South India resemble one another and the similar monuments of Ceylon which are assuredly Buddhistic. For these reasons it has been suggested that these caves 'were the abodes of Buddhist monks to the exclusion of the other sects'.[7] It is, however, premature to formulate such a definitive conclusion. Some of these caverns are called Śamaṇar-kuḍagu, cave of the Jainas; new caverns are still being discovered from time to tme throughout South India, *e.g.* the natural cavern at Mālakoṇḍa in Nellore district. And tradition is strong that Jainism came to South India at the same time as Buddhism, if not earlier.

Though the script of the inscriptions in Brāhmī of the southern variety, their language is seen to be Tamil still in its formative stages. The script was alphabetic and already included signs for the peculiarly Dravidian sounds like ṟ, ḷ, ḻ, and ṉ. Vocalized consonants were represented by two symbols, that for the consonant being followed by the complete vowel sign, *yu* being written as *ya u*. There is no doubt that these peculiarities were the result of a pretty long process of trial and error that had by no means come to a stop in the second century B.C., a fact often overlooked by some ardent Tamilists who would carry back the date of the literature of the Śaṅgam to the third century B.C. or even earlier. Tentative studies of these records have provided a glimpse into their contents. Polālaiyan, a *kuṭumpikan* (*i.e.* peasant or householder) from Iḻa (Ceylon) figures as a donor; and a woman, some members of the Karaṇi caste, and merchants (*Vāṇikan*) also figure in the same capacity. The ascetics pursuing their life divine in solitude were thus already enjoying the support of all classes of laymen.

Much has been written about a Maurya invasion of South India, and the Podyil hill adjoining the Tirunelveli and Madurai district to the west has been fixed as the farthest limit of this invasion which is supposed to have occurred in the period between Chandragupta's treaty with Seleucus and the thirteenth year Aśoka.[8] This theory rests on references to Mauryas in the Śaṅgam poems which have been interpreted by others as a reference to a branch of the Konkaṇi Mauryas.[9] The view last mentioned would place the Śaṅgam poems in the sixth or seventh century A.D. which is far too late for any of them. The references to the Mauryas occur in five poems, three by Māmūlanār, and one each by two other poets. The relative chronology of the poets is not clear, but the whole body of Śaṅgam literature clearly belongs to the first three centuries of the Christian era. Therefore the mention of Nandas and Mauryas in these peoms can only be a reference to events long past, but somehow preserved in the popular memory. There is good reason to doubt whether the two poets other than Māmūlanār were actually referring to the Mauryas of history or to some aspects of an obscure mythology. That they both refer to the same fact or myh is evident. The expressions used are identical, though one of them, Kaḷḷil Āttiraiyanār,[10] gives more details than the other, Paraṅgoṟṟanār.[11] The more detailed account mentions the Mōriyar, their victorious lance, their skyscraping umbrella, and their chariots bearing banners. It then states that their strong bright-rayed wheel cut across a mountain at the end of the earth and rolled past it, and past the broad disc of the sun fixed near the pass so made. The commentator amplifies the sense by additions of his own; he states that the Mōriyar ruled the whole world, and that the mountain severed by their discuss was the silver mountain which separated the earth from another world, and that the Mōriyar were the Chakravāla emperors or Vidyādharas and Nāgas, an interpretation which would suit the alternative reading 'Ōriyar' much better than 'Mōriyar' (Mauryas). Stress need not, however, be laid on the alternative reading 'ōriyar', for the cutting of the hill and the rolling of the wheel are features that recur in the unmistakable references of Māmūlanār to the Mauryas. But these other poets, if indeed they were thinking of the Mauryas, had but the vaguest notions about them and their achievements, and were ready to class them with the superhuman beings whose deeds, according to the Purāṇas, fill the annals of the universe for many ages after the dawn of creation.

Māmūlanār exhibits better historical knowledge, and his statements are much more precise, though he too retains the quasi-legendary feature which is all that is known to the other poets concerning the Mauryas. He mentions the Nandas and the enormous treasure which they accumulated. 'What is it,' asks a lovelorn lady, 'that has attracted my lover better than my charms ?'; and among the alternatives postulated by her occurs this:[12] 'Is it the treasure accumulated in prosperous Pāṭaliputra and hidden in the waters of the Ganges by the Nandas of great renown, victorious in war ?' Here we find much that is known of the Nundas from other sources, and one fact that is new—the manner in which they kept the treasure hidden under the waters of the Ganges, which reminds one of a similar practice attributed to the Mahārājas of Zabag by Arab travellers of the eighth century A.D. Māmūlanār's mention of the Mauryas is accompanied by equally clear and precise indications of historical events. There are two passages for consideration, both from the *Ahanānūṟu*. One[13] starts by saying that the lover would not stay behind even if he got the wealth of the Nanda for doing so—a second reference to this topic by the poet; it then proceeds to say that the Kōśar of the victorious banner started operations against their foes and gained several victories; but as Mōhūr did not submit to them, the Mōriyas who had a large army led an expedition in which their chariots rolled across a cutting made in the mountain for that purpose. The Mauryas were so friendly to the Kōśar as to aid them in war. This active intervention in the politics of the Tamil country brings to our view a phase of Mauryan imperialism that has so far escaped notice. The last reference in Māmūlanār[14] adds some more details. It says that when the Mōriyar turned to the south, the warlike Vaḍugar preceded them in the van, and the mountain which was cut to make a way for the chariots is on this occasion described as the large snow mountan reaching up to the skies, obviously the Himalayas. This last detail betrays that Māmūlanār also is by no means free of legendary notions about the Mauryas; only he managed to convey some facts besides the legend. Vaḍugar is a rather vague term in Tamil literature; it means literally northerners, and was genrally applied to the Kannaḍa-Telugu peoples of Southern and Eastern Deccan together. They were included in the Mauryan empire, and they may have been called upon to take the lead in any movement further south. One last reference to the Nandas in the *Kuṛundogai*[15] is simple and clear; it refers to the abundance of gold in Pāṭaliputra and to the elephants bathing in the Son river near the city. These Tamil texts, three to five centuries later than the age of the Mauryas, thus indicate that the Tamil states were within the sphere of Mauryan influence, a fact already attested by the Aśoka inscriptions, and that at least on one occasion the Mauryas went to the assistance of the Kōśar to enable them to subdue the rebellious chiefain of Mōhūr; the Vaḍugar took a hand in this expedition.

II. THE AGE OF THE SANGAM

Introduction

The serious study of the earliest strata of Tamil literature known as the Śaṅgam literature was inaugrated towards the close of the last century by the publication of texts from the hand of scholars like Damodaram Pillai and Swaminantha

Aiyer. P. Sundaram Pillai began the critical use of these classics for purposes of historical reconstruction with his articles on *Neḍunalvāḍai* and *Maduraikkāñji* in the *Madras Christian College Magazine*. But he did not attempt any systematic chronology, and the first scholar to take this in hand was Kanakasabhai Pillai. In his *Tamils 1800 years ago* (Madras, 1904) he accepted the *Śilappadikāram* as a Śaṅgam classic and made it the sheet-anchor of his chronological scheme, though he consulted in manuscript many poems that were still unpublished. But it has since become clear that the *Śilappadikāram* in its present form and the stories and legends of Karikāla Chola recorded in it cannot claim such high antiquity; even a cursory study of the word-forms and grammatical endings and the complex system of prosody known to this work would be enough to show that it could not be assigned to a time much earlier than the sixth century A.D.; and this conclusion is reinforced by some other features such as borrowings traceable to other works and verbal citations from them, besides the social and political traits of a relatively late age which may be discerned in the text. The relation of Iḷaṅgō, the reputed author of the *Śilappadikāram*, to Śeṅguṭṭuvan, the Chera king, who is said to have been his elder brother, is not heard of in the *Padiṟṟuppattu* which makes no mention of the brother of the monarch. Neither the poet Iḷaṅgō nor his work finds a place among the authors and works of the Śaṅgam listed in the commentary to the *Iṟaiyanār Ahapporuḷ*—our main source for the traditions relating to the Śaṅgam; though that commentary cites the *Śilappadikāram* and knows of Nakkīrar, but not of *Maṇimēkalai* which is said to have been composed at the same time as the *Śilappadikāram*. It should be added that the commentary is sometimes ascribed to Nakkīrar himself. M. Srinivasa Aiyangar in his essays on the *Tamil Academies* and the *Ten Tens*[16] reviewed the legends of the *Iṟaiyanār Ahapporuḷ* and the work of Kanakasabhai in so far as it concerned the Cheras. Pandit M. Raghava Aiyangar's work on *Śēran Śeṅguṭṭuvan* (1915) and the discussion it gave rise to mark the next important stage in the study of the subject. Raghava Aiyangar argued for a date in the fifth century A.D. for the Śaṅgam; but his arguments were subjected to devastating criticism by K.S. Srinivasa Pillai in his contributions to the *Śen Tamiḻ* and in his *History of Tamil Literature*,[17] and

Raghava Aiyangar withdrew the chronological argument from his book in its second edition (1929).

The most comprehensive of all the efforts so far made to determine the chronology of the Śaṅgam period from a study of the internal evidence available is that of K.N. Sivaraja Pillai in his *Chronology of the Tamils* (1932). But this work starts with wide a *priori* assumptions, accepts only selected works like the *Puṟanāṉūṟu*, *Ahanāṉūṟu*, *Naṟṟiṇai* and *Kuṟundogai* as of primary value, and discards the evidence of the *Padiṟṟupattu* and *Pattuppāṭṭu* when it conflicts with that of the four favoured collections (p. 41); moreover the author interprets many texts in a forced way to suit his theories, and, in an extremity, rejects particular lines and passages as interpolations, claiming in some matters to know more of the authentic tradition than the redactors of the collections as we have them now. His work is therefore not as conclusive or convincing as it might otherwise have been.

The most recent discussion of the subject is that of K.G. Sesha Aiyer in his *Cēra Kings of the Śaṅgam Period* (1937). His primary concern is with the Chera monarchs, and naturally he bases his work on the *Padiṟṟuppattu*, though he takes account of other poems mentioning the monarchs. He also briefly reviews the controversies about the age of the Śaṅgam and himself advocates a date in the second century A.D.

Sources and Chronology

The comprehensive study of the political history of the Śaṅgam period cannot be undertaken without a full and unbiased sifting of the data in all the authentic poems that have been preserved. The *Śilappadikāram* and *Maṇimēkalai* must be left on one side for reasons already indicated; but the synchronism suggested by the first work between Śeṅguṭṭuvan and Gajabāhu of Ceylon may be accepted as historical, because it fits in very well with the other lines of evidence derived from the general probabilities of history in North and South India, besides Greek and Latin authors on the one side, and the Śaṅgam poems and archaeology on the other; and without it there is no means of importing any exactitude into the chronological system derived from a study of the internal evidence.

Let us begin by trying to determine the number of generations of monarchs and authors that are reflected in these poems, accepting as genuine the traditions, recorded in the colophons and *padigams* (epilogues) to them.[18] The *Padiṟṟuppattu, Ainguṟunūṟu* and *Pattuppāṭṭu* are compact groups with a manageable number of kings and poets; and the *padigams* in the *Padiṟṟuppattu* give the genealogical relations in the Chera line that go far to simplify our task. The *Naṟṟiṇai* and *Kuṟundogai* may for the most part be left alone, because the number of poets involved is numerous and many of them are obscure; the theme of these poems moreover is love, and they contain little of political interest; but political references wherever found in them will be taken into account and accommodated in the scheme as they should be. *Paripāḍal*, a collection devoted to love and religion and belonging to the class *iśaittamiḻ* (Tamil set to music), will be treated in the same manner. *Kalittogai* raises a problem of its own; it is not settled if Nallanduvanār was the author of the whole collection or its compiler. In any event, it too is a collection of love poems with few facts of history coming in anywhere. There is indeed a reference to the flooding of the South Pāṇḍya country by the sea for which the Pāṇḍya ruler compensated himself by overthrowing the Chera and the Chola.[19] but who can decide if this is legend or history? The *Śilappadikāram* too has a similar tale, and there the compensatory conquest reaches the Himalayas. Lastly, the collections known as the *Ahanānūṟu* and *Puṟanānūṟu* are important and will come for a good deal of discussion, particularly the latter, for the sake of the numerous events of political history which they contain.

We shall begin by setting forth the genealogical data for the Cheras from the *padigams* to the *Padiṟṟuppattu (Ten Tens)*, the only collection which yields such data in any considerable measure. While all writers have recognised the existence of two branches of the Chera royal line, they are not agreed about the details of the arrangement, and some, particularly Kanakasabhai, have combined in their tables data from the *Ten Tens* and *Śilappadikāram*. It would be tedious to state in detail the reasons for our differences with these writers, it is enough to give the genealogy as it is made out from the *padigams*, stating authyority for each link, and drawing attention to difficulties and weak spots where the celebrated

in the remaining eight groups of poems are indicated by the numbers in Roman numerals placed after their names in the table. The particular *padigam* of which each link in the table rests is set forth in separate footnotes under the two tables.

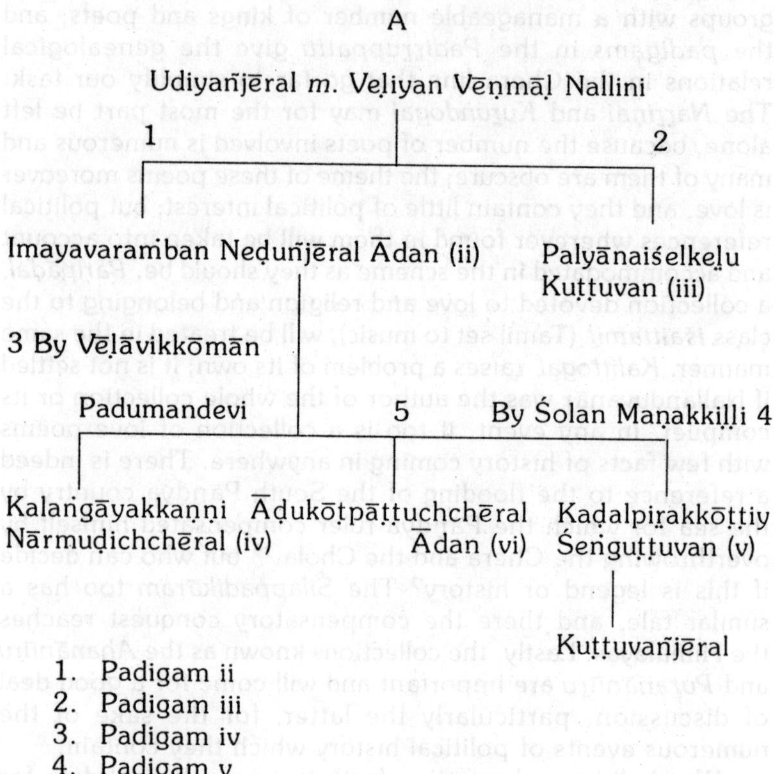

1. Padigam ii
2. Padigam iii
3. Padigam iv
4. Padigam v
5. Padigam vi

The name of the Chola princess who was the second queen of Imayavaramban Neḍuñjēral is given as Naṟchōṇai by Aḍiyārkkunallār in his commentary on the Padigam to the *Śilappadikāram* which mentions for the first time Iḷangō, the brother of Śenguṭṭuvan and the reputed author of the *Śilappadikāram*. These facts are of course less authentic than the rest. Note also that we have assumed the identity of Imayavaramban Neḍuñjēral Ādan with Kuḍakkō Neḍuñjēral Ādan (vi) and Śēral Ādan (iv).

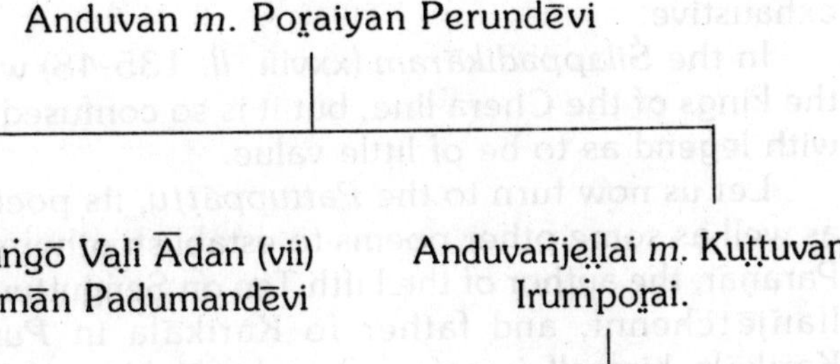

6. Padigam vii
7. Padigam viii
8. Padigam ix

Padigam ix on which Kuḍakkō's position rests calls for some notice. It reads : *Kuṭṭuvan Irumpoṟaikku Maiyūr kiḻān vēṇmāḷ Anduvañjeḷḷai inṟa magan Iḷañjēral Irumpoṟai i.e.* Iḷañjēral Irumpoṟai, the son born of Anduvañjeḷḷai, the daughter (*vēṇmāḷ*) of the lord of Maiyūr. The name Anduvañjeḷḷai naturally means Śeḷḷai, the daughter of Anduvan; Anduvan is a name which occurs in this form in *padigam* vii also. He was also the lord of Maiyūr.

Can we connect the two lines chronologically ? A hint is given by the occurrence of a common name, that of Vēḷāvikkōmān Padumandēvi in both the tables. *Dēvi*, like *vēṇmāḷ*, may be understood to express the relation of daughter, though possibly these different designations indicate some difference in the status of the ladies concerned. The occurrence of this common name, Padumandēvi, in the two lists can best be explained by our supposing that it refers to two sisters married to two Chera princes, and if this view is correct, we get the important result that Imayavaramban Neḍuñjēral and Śelvakkaḍuṅgō Vāḻi Ādan who married the sisters must have belonged to one and the same generation. It would follow further that our tables A and B include three generations of two contemporary branches of the Chera royal family. There were doubtless other Chera princes *e.g.* Kuṭṭuvan Irumpoṟai, the husband of Śeḷḷai; and our present list is by no means exhaustive.

In the *Śilappadikāram* (xxviii. *ll.* 135-48) we find a list of the kings of the Chera line, but it is so confused and mixed up with legend as to be of little value.

Let us now turn to the *Pattuppāṭṭu*, its poets and heroes, as well as some other poems to establish other synchronisms. Paraṇar, the author of the Fifth Ten on Śeṅguṭṭuvan, celebrates Iḷañjēṭchenni, and father fo Karikāla in *Puṟam* 4, while Karikāla himself is referred to by Nakkīrar in terms which imply that his reign ended some time earlier (*Aham* 141). We may assume (1) that Kapilar, author of the VIIth decad, was a younger contemporary of Paraṇar, because the Padumandēvi who married Vāḻi Ādan was a younger sister of Neḍuñjēral Ādan's queen, and (2) that the second generation of table B was more or less comtemporary with the third of table A, so that the two together will give us not three but four generations of rulers. However that may be, we seem to get an extension of time by way of Uruvappahrer Iḷañjēṭchenni and his son Karikāla, and one further generation appears to be added in an unmistakable manner; but these results are tentative.

Now Karikāla is celebrated in *Porunarāṟṟuppaḍai* by Muḍattāmakkaṇṇiyār and in *Paṭṭinappālai* by Kaḍiyalūr Uruttiraṅgaṇṇanār (Rudrāksha) who also celebrated Toṇḍaimān Iḷandiraiyan in the *Perumbāṇāṟṟuppadai*. Here then is a bunch of contemporaries of the generation of Karikāla, and some hint of the relative age of three out of the ten poems in the *Pattuppāṭṭu*. Kapilar's *Kuṟiñjippāṭṭu*, another poem in the same collection, must also belong to about the same time.

We get the next link from a reference of Nakkīrar to Kapilar and Pāri in *Aham* 78; Nakkīrar sang the *Neḍunalvāḍai* on Talaiyālaṅgānattuchcheruvenṟa Neḍuñjeḻiyan, on whom there is another poem in the *Pattupāṭṭu*—the *Maduraikkāñji* of Māṅguḍi Marudan. Here is the next bunch of poets and kings of the generation after Karikāla. To this we may add as a prefix Nannan, son of Nannan, celebrated in the *Malaipaḍukaḍām* of Peruṅgauśikan (great Kauśika), because Māṅguḍi Marudan mentions this Nannan, the son of another Nannan, and in a manner that invites comparison with some lines of the *Malaipaḍukaḍām*.[20]

The *Mullaippāṭṭu* has no hero; but its name resembles that of *Kuṟiñjippāṭṭu* and it mentions *mlechchhas* and *yavanas* like the *Neḍunalvāḍai;* its poet Nappūdanār may be assigned therefore to the same period, more or less, as Nakkīrar.

Lastly, the *Śiṟupān-āṟṟuppaḍai* is a poem on Nalliyakkōḍan by Nattattanār; it refers to all the seven *vaḷḷas*—chieftains noted for charity, as dead and gone, and obviously belongs to the closing period of the Śaṅgam age. There remains the *Tirumurugāṟṟuppaḍai*, a quasi-religious poem, which passes under the name of Nakkīrar and has found entry into the anthology called *Pattuppāṭṭu* (Ten Idylls). The contents of this poem are vastly different from those of the others in the collection, and by a careful study of its diction and language, Vaiyapuri[21] has demonstrated that it cannot be of the same age as the other pieces we assign to the Śaṅgam, but must be the product of much later time. We have therefore to postulate a Nakkīrar II.

The foregoing consideration lead us to the following grouping of the poems of the *Pattuppāṭṭu* with reference to their relative age :

Group I (1) Porunar—āṟṟuppaḍai—Muḍattāmakkaṇṇiyār on Karikāla.
(2) Paṭṭinappālai—Kaḍiyalūr Uruttiraṅgaṇṇanār on Karikāla.
(3) Perumbāṇ-āṟṟuppaḍai—Do. on Toṇḍaimān Iḷandiraiyan.
(4) Kuṟiñjippāṭṭu—Kapilar to the Ārya king Pirahatta (Prahasta).

Group II (1) Malaipaḍukaḍām—Peruṅgauśikan on Nanna's son Nannan.
(2) Maduraikkāñji—Māṅguḍi Marudan on Talaiyālaṅgānattuchcheruvenṟa Neḍuñjeḷiyan.
(3) Neḍunaivādai—Nakkīrar I on do.
(4) Mullaippāṭṭu—Nappūdanār (no hero).

Group III Śiṟupāṇ-āṟṟuppaḍai—Nattattanār on Nalliyakkōḍan. And the much later Tirumurugāṟṟuppaḍai—Nakkīrar II.

This arrangement receives confirmation from a verse (*Puṟam* 53) in which Śēy of the Elephant-look, a Chera prince, is said to have regretted that Kapilan was no longer there to celebrate his victories in a suitable manner; and this Chera was a contemporary of Neḍunjeḷiyan of Talaiyālaṅgānam as we see from another poem (*Puṟam* 17) addressed to Śēy after he had escaped from the Pāṇḍya's prison and occupied the Chera throne by force; thus our assignment of the Kuṟiñjippāṭṭu to the first and earlier group which preceded that of the Maduraikkāñji fully borne out by these references.

The *Aiṅguṟunūṟu* (The Five Short Hundreds) was compiled by Yānaikkaṭchēy Māndarañjēral Irumpoṟai and comprises poems by five poets, *viz.* Ōrambōgi, Ammūvanār, Kapilar, Ōdalāndai, and Pēyanār. The compiler, Śey of the Elephant-look, is seen from *Puṟam* 17, 20 and 22 to have been a contemporary and enemy of Neḍuñjeḷiyan, victor of Talaiyālaṅgānam. The inclusion of a hundred short pieces of Kapilar in an almost contemporary anthology by a prince of the Chera royal line is noteworthy for at least two reasons; the practice of literature and literary criticism transcended the boundaries and passions of politics and united the whole Tamil country in a common bond; secondly, criticism was briskly at work, collecting, assessing and clarifying and grouping poems as they were composed from time to time—proper work for an Academy. This anthology while it does not add much to the stock of information except the names of four poets, goes some way to confirm the relative chronology reached from a study of the other collections especially as regards Kapilar and Neḍuñjeḷiyan.

Next we may consider the names of other kings and chieftains mentioned by the poets so far named; this would enable us to check and revise our tentative conclusions in the light of the new data and thus strengthen the links in the internal chronology of the age. Only important and outstanding names will be considered, and no attempt made at an exhaustive enumeration of all, as that would be both tedious and futile.

The authors of the Second and Third Tens in the *Padiṟṟuppattu* refer to no important contemporaries other than their heroes. Kāppiyāṟṟukkāppiyanār, the author of the Fourth Ten, mentions Nannan as the foe vanquished by his hero Kaḷaṅgāykkaṇṇi Nārmuḍichchēral (*Padiṟṟ*. 40); we have seen that there were two Nannans, father and son, and that the son is mentioned by Māṅguḍi Marudan, the contemporary of Neḍuñjeḷiyan of Talaiyālaṅgānam; Nārmuḍichchēral belonged definitely to an earlier generation and we may assume that the Nannan whom he vanquished was the father.

Paraṇar, the author of the Fifth Ten on Śeṅguṭṭuvan, mentions a number of rulers, great and small, and we must consider their relative positions with some care. Most important among these in Karikāla Chola whose victories at Vāhaippaṟandalai (*Aham* 125) and Veṇṇi (*ibid.* 246) are known to Paraṇar, and who is mentioned once again in another poem along with Marandai, a town belonging to Kuṭṭuvan (*ibid.* 376). We have noted before that Paraṇar belauded Karikāla's father also. Karikāla should be treated therefore not as altogether of the generation succeeding that of Śeṅguṭṭuvan, but as his younger contemporary. The tradition preserved in the *Śilappadikāram* that Śeṅguṭṭuvan and Karikāla were contemporaries is thus confirmed by the evidence of these early poems. Paraṇar also sang of another Chola prince Verpahṟaḍakkaip-Peruviṟaṟkiḻḻi who fought against a Chera Kuḍakkō Neḍuñjēral Ādan (*Puṟam* 63) in the battle of Pōr; both the princes laid down their lives on the field. The latter may be identical with the father of Śeṅguṭṭuvan as already noted. The incident is the subject of two poems by Kaḻāttalaiyār (*Puṟam* 62, 368). Aḻiśi of Ārkkāḍu on the banks of the Kāvērī, father of Śendan, is another prince mentioned by Paraṇar, but not as a contemporary (*Kuṟundogai* 258); at the latest he may have been of the same age as Karikāla's father; perhaps he belonged to an earlier time. Perumbūṭpoṟaiyan (*Kurun.* 89) was another Chera of whom Paraṇar sang as in the past; also Māndaram Poṟaiyan Kaḍuṅgō (*Aham* 142) who may have been contemporary. Māvaṇ Tittan of Uṟandai (Uṟaiyūr) (*Aham* 6, 122 and *Puṟam* 352) and his daughter Aiyai (*Aham* 6) are mentioned by Paraṇar in a manner that leaves no room for any doubt about their contemporaneity. Not so his references to Śeḻiyan, Paśumpūṭpāṇḍiyan and Evvi, all of whom appear definitely to have belonged to earlier generations. Śeḻiyan is said to have once upon a time put to flight the two great monarchs (Chera and Chola) in a battle at Kūḍalpaṟandalai in the neighbourhood of Madurai (*Aham* 116); the identity of the Pāṇḍyan victor in this battle can be ascertained, if at all, only with more definite evidence from other sources. Again Paśumpūṭpāṇḍiyan is stated to have commanded the services of Adigan in a battle against the Koṅgar at Vāhaippaṟandalai (*Aham* 162), but apparently he himself fell in this battle together with Adigan's elephant on which he was riding (*Kurun.* 393); the incident is also mentioned as a past event by the later poet Nakkīrar who says that the Koṅgar were driven off the field by Paśumpūṭpāṇḍiyan who took many lands (*Aham* 253) in consequence of his victory (also *Naṟṟiṇai* 358).

Paraṇar makes two references to Evvi, the chieftain of Nīḍūr; Evvi ordered extensive feeling (*peruñjōṟu*) at Uṟattūr in Arimaṇavāyil (*Aham* 266), and the death of Evvi caused distress to minstrels by the loss of a very liberal patron of their class (*Kuṟun.* 19). But the name Evvi is famous in the literature of the age and occurs in many other poems; Māṅguḍi Kiḻār (Māṅguḍi Marudan) relates that the great Vēḷ Evvi lost the divisions of Miḻalai and Muttūṟu to the Pāṇḍya Neḍuñjeḻiyan, victor of Talaiyālaṅgānam (*Puṟam* 24); Kapilar says that Iruṅgōvēḷ belonged to the ancient line of Evvi (*ibid.* 202); Veḷḷerukkilaiyār laments the death of Evvi in two short poems in the *Puṟam* (233-4), and Nakkīrar and Māmūlanār mention Evvi in the past in *Aham* 126 and 115 respectively, the latter making a pointed reference to his death in battle. Was Evvi a dynastic name like Āy and Adigan, and borne by all the chieftains of Nīḍūr ? If that was so, the references to Evvi will cease to have much importance for the construction of our chronological scheme. It seems more probable, however, that Evvi was a personal name, and that there were two Evvis, grandfather and grandson, the former being a contemporary of Paraṇar, the latter of Neḍuñjeḻiyan. Iruṅgōvēḷ, the contemporary of Kapilar and Karikāla, belonged to the same line as the two Evvis.

Paraṇar has references, none of them necessarily contemporaneous to Ōri, one of the *vaḷḷals* (patrons), and to his Kollimalai and forest (*kānam*) (*Aham* 208, *Kuṟun.* 199, *Naṟṟiṇai* 6 and 265). That Ōri was killed by Kāri and his Kollimalai transferred to the Cheras thereby is mentioned by Kallāḍanār (*Aham* 209). Paraṇar's reference to the flight of Kaṭṭi from the darbar (*nāḷavai*) of Tittan Veḷiyan at Uṟandai (*Aham* 226) obviously recalls a past occurrence; but there must have been more Kaṭṭis than one, for a Kaṇgan Kaṭṭi is mentioned as having fallen in battle with the Chola commander Paḻaiyan before the battle of Kaḻumalam (*Aham* 44 by

Kuḍavāyiṟ Kīrattanār); and Parṇar himself names this Chola commander in two poems (*Aham* 186 and 326). Māmūlanār speaks of the region beyond the good country of Kaṭṭi with the strong spear—*valvēṟ Kaṭṭi nannāṭṭumbar* (*Kuṟun.* 11), where a different language begins to be spoken. Naḻḻi, another *vaḻḻal*, was certainly the contemporary of Paraṇar (*Aham* 152) for both Kākkaipāḍiniyār Nachcheḻḻaiyār and Kapilar also sing of him. Paraṇar refers to Nannan in a number of poems; he was a chieftain of Pāḻi and of Pāram (*Aham* 142, 152); a friend of his is Āy Eyinan, said to have fallen in the battle of Pāḻi fighting his foe Miñili (*Aham* 208, 396). This Nannan, so often referred to by Paraṇar, must be taken to be the father of Nannan, the hero of *Malaipaḍukaḍām*. Paraṇar knows also of another Nannan who attained ill fame as a woman-killer for having sentenced to death a woman whose only fault was that she ate a fruit that came to her floating down the stream in which she was bathing (*Kuṟun.* 292); he refused to commute the death sentence even though he was offered eighty-one tusker elephants and a gold image of the woman as recompense. Whether this incident is fact or legend, it belongs to the time of a still earlier Nannan; how much earlier we have no means of deciding. Yet another Nannan is mentioned by Paraṇar (*Aham* 258) as a celebrity of the past; in his town of Pāḻi, the ancient *Vēḻir* (*tonmudir vēḻir*) had kept much gold; he is called Nannan Udiyan, and certainly belonged to a time earlier than that of Nannan, the father of Nannan of Malaipaḍukaḍām; possibly even to the age of Udiyan of Peruñjōṟu fame. The Nannans were a line of *Vēḻs*. Pēhan, another *vaḻḻal*, and his liberal gifts from the subject of three poems by Paraṇar (*Aham* 262, *Puṟam* 141 and 142); when some difference arose between Pēhan and his wife, they were reconciled by the intercession of poets, Paraṇar being among them (*Puṟam* 144, 145) as also Kapilar (*ibid.* 143), Ariśil Kiḻār (*ibid.* 146), and Perunguṇṟūr Kiḻār (*ibid.* 147). Perunguṇṟūr Kiḻār was younger than Kapilar, the junior contemporary of Paraṇar. Yet another *vaḻḻal*, named Tērvaṇmalaiyan (also Kāri) was known to Paraṇar (*Naṟṟiṇai* 100), and this chieftain was celebrated also by Kapilar who has many references to him, by Kallāḍanār, and by Ammūvanār, one of the poets of *Ainguṟunūṟu*. Lastly, there was Paḻaiyan of Mōhūr, a chieftain of the Pāṇḍya country, who was defeated in battle by Kuṭṭuvan (*Padiṟṟu.* 44) who went to the aid of his friend Aruhai; there were also other *vēḷir* fighting on the side of Paḻaiyan on that occasion (*ibid.* 49 and *padigam* v).

Paraṇar also names Agudai more than once (*Aham* 76, 208 erc.) and the same chieftain seems to be mentioned as the lord of Kūḍal by Kapilar (*Puṟam* 347); we have already noticed other connecting links between the generations of Paraṇar and Kapilar which were close to each other. Kapilar refers to Iruṅgōvēḷ *alias* Pulikaḍimāl (*Puṟam* 201 and 202) to whom he offers Pāri's daughters in marriage; as we have seen, he belonged to the line of Evvi. Iruṅgōvēḷ seems to have been a common name or title, as Nachchinārkkiniyar explains (*Paṭṭinappālai, l.* 282). Among the *vaḷḷas*, Kapilar had Pāri for his patron and naturally speaks of him very often in his poems; Ōri of Kollimalai (*Kuṟun.* 100) was killed by Kāri (*Naṟṟiṇai* 320). Kapilar also records the legends of the rise of the Agnikula kings from a sacrificial fire-pit of the northern sage Vasishṭha in connection with Pulikaḍimāl (*Puṟam* 201).

Ariśil Kiḻar, the author of the Eighth Ten, mentions Adigamān of Tagaḍūr, the enemy of his Chera patron Peruñjēral Irumpoṟai (*padigam* viii) and Eḻini, a commander who fell in the sack of Tagaḍūr (*Puṟam* 230).

Peruṅguṉṟūr Kiḻār has two poems on Kuḍakkō Iḷañjēral Irumpoṟai (*Puṟam* 210 and 211) besides the Ninth Ten; he gives him the title *Nilandaru-tiruvin-neḍiyōn*, an expression which is applied to the Pāṇḍya in the *Maduraikkāñji*,—and this should warn us of the need for caution in using these titles as marks of identity. A Māndaran is mentioned by the poet in *Padiṟṟupattu* 90 in a way which implies that he was a remote ancestor of the Cheras, anterior to Anduvan—*viṟal Māndaran viṟal maruga*. The Kiḻār addressed a poem to Uruvapahṟēr Iḷañjeṭchenni, the father of Karikāla (*Puṟam* 266)—a fact which goes far to confirm our scheme of synchronisms. There is mention also of an Iḷam Paḻaiyan Māṟan as the enemy of Kuḍakkō (*padigam* ix); his relation to Paḻaiyan Māṟan of *Maduraikkāñji* is a problem. The number of towns received by Kapilar as presents from his patron is referred to as a past event in *Padiṟṟuppattu* 85.

Turning now to the poets of *Pattuppāṭṭu*, Māṅguḍi Marudan and Nakkīrar I are the most prolific in their references to other contemporaries besides their heroes. Māṅguḍi Marudan refers to Paḻaiyan Māṟan and his capital Mōhūr

(*Maduraik. ll.* 508 and 772); Nakkīrar mentions (*Aham* 346) as a past event the combat of this chieftain with Kiḻḻi Vaḻavan on the outskirts of Kūḍal (Madurai); Māmūlanār (*Aham* 251) has a reference to Mōhūr which seems to recall a state of affairs long anterior to the times of Māṅguḍi Marudan and belonging to the Mauryan epoch as already noted (p. 502). The Kōśar and the chieftain of Mōhūr were clearly friendly in the days of Māṅguḍi Marudan who says that the *sabhā* of Mōhūr was adorned by the Kōśar (*Maduraik. ll.* 508-9). We have noted already that the relation between Paḻaiyan Māṟan and the enemy of Kuḍakkō is not apparent; the latter is called Iḷam (Junior) Paḻaiyan Māṟan. Was Paḻaiyan Māṟan then a hereditary dynastic title, there being two persons bearing the title at any time—the ruling chieftain and the heirapparent ? this assumption seems best to satisfy all the data at hand. If, as seems likely, Māṅguḍi Kiḻār was only another name for Māṅguḍi Marudan, we must assume that Eḻini Ādan of Vāṭṭāṟu, celebrated in a poem (*Puṟam* 396), was a contemporary of his. In the *Maduraikkāñji* (*ll.* 203-4) the poet makes a mysterious reference to the vast wealth with which Vāṇan filled the mountains of the southern region; the annotator glosses Vāṇan with *Vāṇan ennum śūran*, thus suggesting a legendary origin to the idea; at any rate the Vāṇan of this passage has nothing to do with the minor chieftain of the same name who is associated with Śiṟukudi in the Pāṇḍya country by Nakkīrar (*Naṟṟiṇai* 340) and two other poets—Madurai Kāmakkaṇi Nappālattanār (*Aham* 204) and the anonymous author of *Aham* 117.

The most notable reference in Nakkīrar's poems is the list of the enemies whom Neḍuñjeḻiyan faced and defeated at Talaiyālaṅgānam (*Aham* 36); they were Śēral, Śembiyan (Chola), Titiyan, Eḻini, Erumaiyūran, Iruṅgōvēṇmān, and Porunan, seven in all. His reference to Karikāla's (*Aham* 141) settlement of wandering tribes is in the past, as may be expected. In another poem (*Aham* 346) Nakkīrar mentions the joy of Kōdaimārban at the defeat of Paḻaiyan Māṟan near Madurai at the hands of Kiḻḻi Vaḻavan who captured a great number of horses and elephants on that occasion; by itself this need not be a contemporary reference. Nor can we be sure if this Kiḻḻi Vaḻavan was the same as the homonymous Chola prince who is said to have died at Kuḷamuṟṟam and concerning whom a number of songs by several poets are found in the *Puṟanāṉūṟu*. But Nakkīrar has another reference to Kōdai, strong in his elephants and chariots, and ruler of Karuvūr (*Aham* 93); he is perhaps the same ruler whom Māṅgudi Marudan mentions in *Maduraikkāñji* (*l.* 524), and who is said to be the protector of Vañji (*Aham* 263) by the poet Kaṇṇambāḷanār of Karuvūr; he is celebrated in two songs by Poygaiyār (*Puṟam* 48, 49), and possibly also in a song by Erichchalūr Māḍalan Maduraikkumaran (*Puṟam* 54), though this is somewhat doubtful as the colophon describes the prince as Śēramān Kuṭṭuvan Kōdai. Considering the number and nature of these references it is not unlikely that the combat between Kiḻḻi Vaḷavan and Paḻaiyan Māṟan which turned out to the satisfaction of Kōdai was an event of the time of Nakkīrar and Māṅguḍi Marudan. Nakkīrar's reference to Kuṭṭuvan and Toṇḍi (*Aham* 290) has no chronological significance, nor has his mention of Vānavaramban (*Aham* 389). Pāri and Kapilar are also referred to as belonging to the past (*Aham* 78). The Pāṇḍya prince Nanmāṟan who died in Ilavandigaippaḷḷi is praised in high terms by Nakkīrar (*Puṟam* 56) and was obviously his contemporary; the poet Madurai Marudan Iḷanāganār who obviously his contemporary; the poet Madurai Marudan Iḷanāganār who also celebrates this prince (*ibid.* 55) must have been contemporary too.

Iḍaikkaḻanāṭṭu Nallūr Nattattanār, author of *Śiṟupaṇāṟṟup-paḍai* on Nalliyakkōḍan, clearly declares himself to be among the last of the Śaṅgam poets when he mentions Kuṭṭuvan of Imayam fame, the seven *vaḷḷals,* and the story of Auvai getting a myrobalan fruit from Adigamān Añji (*l.* 101), all events of past history.

Before proceeding further, we may consider briefly the relative positions of two major poets, Kallāḍanār and Māmūla-nār. Kallāḍanār was a contemporary of Talaiyālaṅgānattu Neḍuñjeḻiyan for he addḍanād poems to him (*Puṟam* 23, 371 and *Aham* 25); he also refers to Ambar Kiḻān Aruvandai (*Puṟam* 385) as a contemporary besides the minor chieftain Poṟaiyāṟṟu Kiḻavōn (*Puṟam* 391). He mentions as a past event a fight between Kaḷaṅgāyakkaṇṇi Nārmuḍichchēral and Nannan,—possibly the father (*Aham* 199). The author of *Kallāḍam* must be regarded as another and much later writer of the same name. Māmūlanār must have been among the last poets of the Saṅgam age, coming almost at the close of it; he knows all the major events and persons of the entire period and his numerous poems contain valuable references to occurrences in the Tamil country and even in the rest of India, from the age of the Nandas and Mauryas to the very end of the Śaṅgam period. Yet there occurs not a single reference in all thse poems that gives a direct clue to his exact age.

We have so far discussed the data bearing on the relative chronology of the events and the number of generations of rulers and poets reflected in the anthologies of the Śaṅgam; we have seen that the extant poems appear to contain the transactions of four or at the most five generations; a period extending over a century or a little more. We may now consider the means of determining where to place this period in the Christian era. The only concrete evidence that aids us here is the synchronism between Śeṅguṭṭuvan and Gajabāhu of Ceylon attested by the *Śilappadikāram*; and this evidence has been treated with suspicion by several scholars. They argue that the chronology of early Ceylonese history is far from settled and can hardly be expected to throw light on South Indian history; and that, the *Śilappadikāram* being a relatively late work, its testimony can have no value for the history of a time preceding it by several centuries. There is force in these objections; but there are not wanting strong considerations on the other side. Though late in its present form and mingled with much that is palpably legendary, the *Mahāvaṁsa,* as Geiger has demonstrated, is based on a genuine tradition and may well be accepted as history except for its opening chapters. Its chronology has been subjected to acute and exhaustive discussion by the same scholar, and we might well do worse than accept his date for Gajabāhu I as A.D. 173-195, the only Gajabāhu known in Ceylonese history before the twelfth century A.D. As for the *Śilappadikāram,* in its extant from it certainly belongs to an age much later than that of the Śaṅgam, but there is reason to hold that this work too preserves the elements of a correct tradition for its historical setting. Its testimony to the contemporaneity of Śeṅguṭṭuvan and Karikāla is borne out by the earlier poems of their own time. It is true that its evidence to the fact of Gajabāhu's being the contemporary of both these rulers lacks corroboration from any other source; but there is nothing improbable in the synchronism, and we shall see that the general historical trend strongly favours its acceptance. The Pattini (Kaṇṇagi) cult found a congenial home in Ceylon, and Gajabāhu may have been its founder. We get of course no hint of this possibility in the *Dīpavaṁsa* or the *Mahāvaṁsa*—both being works written from an exclusively Buddhist point of view.[22] The Gajabāhu synchronism thus rests on a slender foundation and involves an assumption regarding Gajabāhu's religious persuasion which finds no support in the only chronicle of his reign accessible to us. Or it may be that the Kaṇṇagi cult was a late institution and in the classic account of its origin, the *Śilappadikāram*, the real names of contemporaneous kings were correctly employed.

Normally we should feel justified in refusing to base any firm conclusions regarding the general history of South India on such insecure evidence; but the position improves considerably when we turn to the general probabilities. That Ceylon and South India had much to do with each other in those remote days becomes apparent in many ways. They are first mentioned together in the inscriptions of the great Mauryan emperor Aśoka who maintained an active and friendly intercourse wth these two countries throughout his long reign in the third century B.C. According to the *Mahāvaṁsa* the island of Ceylon began to fall under powerful Chola influences very early in its history. The relations between the Damiḷas (Tamils) and the natives of Ceylon form one of the main strands in its narrative, and the distinction between the Pāṇḍya and Chola divisions of the Tamil country is well recognized in it. Towards the middle of the second century B.C., a Damiḷa of noble descent, Eḷāra by name, came to Ceylon from the Chola country, overpowered Asela for fortyfour years, administering even justice towards friends and foe.[23] Many stories are told to illustrate the justice of his rule, and among them is the tale of how the king sentenced his only son to death for his having unwittingly killed a young calf by driving the wheel of his chariot over its neck—a typical Chola legend. Though not a Buddhist, the king was on friendly terms with the *bhikkus*. Duṭṭhagāmaṇi led the native opposition against him and put him to death in a battle fought at the gates of Anurādhapura. Also worth noticing are the names of some Tamil chieftains mentioned in the *Mahāvaṃsa e.g.* Paṇaya Māraka, Paḷaya Māraka which seem to be obvious variants of names known to us from the *Puṟanāṉūṟu* and *Pattuppāṭṭu;* and these chieftains are placed by the chronicle in the latter half of the first century B.C. There is also a poet from Ceylon among the Śaṅgam authors Iḻattu Pūdan Dēvaṉār. If we remember that the *Mahāvaṁsa* was composed in the fifth century A.D. with the aid of earlier chronicles, we shall see that the somewhat confused account of the Tamil invasions of the island in this early period are not bottomless fabrications, but preserve the faded memory of real events, and the dates assigned to these events cease to be altogether valueless for Tamil chronology. The similarity of Brāhmī inscriptions found in natural caverns in Ceylon and the Madurai and Tirunelvēli districts, all of which may be dated between the second century B.C. and the first century A.D. must also be allowed some significance.

Another line of evidence strongly confirms the chronology indicated by these facts. There is perfect agreement between the Śaṅgam anthologies, the notices of South India in the works of European writers of the early centuries of the Christian era, such as the *Periplus* and Ptolemy's *Geography*, and the numerous finds of Roman coins of the early empire in several places in South India.[24] The *Periplus of the Erythrean Sea* is the interesting handbook of an Alexandrian merchant 'which was written in the time of Domitian (A.D. 81-96) and by the evidence furnished by Pliny the Elder'.[25] Ptolemy wrote half a century later and his work marks a decided advance in the regularity and volume of trade between the Roman Empire and India. Ptolemy's account shows that the Roman trade with the East which began sometime in the reign of Augustus had by the first quarter of the second century A.D. reached beyond India to Indo-China and Sumatra. The recent discovery of a 'Roman factory' of the first century A.D. in the proxmity of Pondicherry deserves particular mention.[26] Relatively few Roman merchants visited the lands of the Far East themselves; Southern India obviously acted as the intermediary in the trade between China and the West. The direct trade between Rome and Southern India did not long survive the second century A.D.; it declined and died out in the period of military anarchy which distracted the Roman Empire of the third century.

Practically no Roman coins of the third century have been found in India, and business relations were not resumed till order and a stable gold currency had been re-established in the Byzantine period, and then mostly through intermediaries.

The first and second centuries A.D. formed the period when Roman trade with India was brisk and the Tamil countries had many opportunities of contact with the *Yavanas* (Graeco-Romans) and their wares of which precious wines formed no small part. Muśiri and Toṇḍi on the west coast of South India, Koṟkai and Kāvēripaṭṭanam on the east were among the chief ports of the Tamil land where these foreigners crowded, and sometimes they found their way into the interior in various capacities—as palace guards, doorkeepers and so on. All this is vouched for by references in the Tamil poems of the period, and it is difficult to assign these poems to any other age. And the merit of the Gajabāhu synchronism lies in its fitting in so exactly with the data gathered from the classical authors, the Tamil poems, and the coin-finds.

Attempts to settle the age of the Śaṅgam with the aid of astronomical data found in a few of the poems have led to no conclusive or satisfactory results. *Paripāḍal* No. 11 is the most crucial piece. L.D. Swamikkannu Pillai discusses it at length[27] and the other in A.D. 634, the first as satisfying the data of the poem as interpreted by its annotator Parimēlaḻagar and the second as closer to the text. In the course of the discussion he makes a statement which is most valuable from our point of view; it is that the *Paripāḍal* 'horoscope' which describes the planetary positions at the time of the flood in the Vaigai river, is just what it might be expected to be if the Tamils derived their knowledge of astronomy direct from Babylon.[28] So that the astronomical lore exhibited in the eleventh *Paripāḍal* and in such poems as *Puṟam* 229 on the death of Yānaikkaṭchēy Māndarañjēral Irumpoṟai, cannot by any means be held incompatible with our holding the early centuries of the Christian era to be the age of the Śaṅgam. We shall do well to grasp the general position quite firmly as it seems to be the one certainty that emerges from the intricate and many-sided discussions of the astronomy of the poems by different writers.

As for the dates suggested above, Swamikkannu considered A.D. 634 more satisfactory than A.D. 17 both astronomically and historically. We may accept his statement without question on the astronomical aspect; moreover A.D. 17 does appear too early a date for the poem in the light of the general scheme of chronology relative and absolute, advocated here. On the other hand A.D. 634 is equally clearly too late. The date brings us well into the period of the Pallavas of the Siṁhavishṇu line and the age of Nāyanārs and Āḻvārs; and no student of the history of the Tamil language and literature can fail to note that the *Paripāḍal* must have preceded the hymns of Sambandar by about a couple of centuries, if not more.

Accepting thus the Gajabāhu synchronism as valid evidence, we may assign Śeṅguṭṭuvan to *c.* A.D. 180 and work backwards and forwards allowing roughly twenty-five years to a generation. The result so far as it concerns the outstanding figures among kings and chieftains is as follows, the dates suggested being approximations :

	Māndaran
130. Udiyañjēral	140. Anduvan
155. Im. Neḍuñjēral Ādan	165. Selvakkaḍuṅgō Vāli Ādan
Palyānai Śelkeḻukuṭṭuvan	Kuṭṭuvan Irumpoṟai
	165. Uruvapahṟēr Iḷañjēṭchenni
180. Śeṅguṭṭuvan	(Māndaram Poṟaiyan Kaḍuṅgō)
Āḍukōṭpāṭṭuch-chēral Ādan	190. Karikāla
Kaḷaṅgāykkaṇṇi Nārmuḍi	190. Tagaḍūr eṟinda Peruñjēral
	Irumpoṟai.
	Kuḍakkō Iḷañjēral Irumpoṟai
Gajabāhu 173-195 (Ez-III p. 9)	
215. Śéy of Elephant-look;	
Kôdaimārpan	210. Nannan (son)
215. Talaiyālaṅgānattu Neḍuñ-	215. Toṇḍaimān Iḷandiraiyan
jeḻiyan	235. Nalliyakkōḍan

It is thus seen that the poems we have so far considered, and they form a good part and perhaps the most significant part of the Śaṅgam anthologies, reflect the history of the period ranging from A.D. 130 to about 230. We have indeed some casual references to earlier events and persons, but for the most part we lack the means of assigning any precise dates to them. One thing is certain. We have before us only a segment of the Tamil history of the early centuries A.D.; the beginnings are lost and the anthologies seem to start rather late. And the end is also equally abrupt. The transition to the conditions of the next great epoch, that of the Pallavas and the Pāṇḍyas, is also hidden from view, and we have very little direct evidence on the period of three centuries intervening (*c.* A.D. 250-550).

History : The Cheras

Udiyañjēral: C. A.D. 130. His queen was Nallini, the daughter of Viḷiyan, and he had two sons by her—Imayavaramban Neḍuñjēral Ādan and Palyānaiśelkeḻu Kuṭṭuvan.[29] Veḷiyan must not be confused with his namesake who came much later and was the son of Tittan of Uṟaiyūr, the contemporary of Paraṇar (*Aham* 152, 226).[30] There is every reason to think that Udiyañjēral was the hero of the missing first decad of the *Ten Tens*. The titles Vānavaramban and Peruñjōṟṟu Udiyan are applied to him by the poet Muriñjiyūr Muḍināgarāyar in *Puṟam* 2. The first title was borne by other kings also who came later in the line; it means 'skybounded'. Another poet, a Chera prince Mākkōdai, who died at Kōṭṭambalam[31] speaks of Udiyan's celebrated kitchen (*aṭṭil*) at Kuḻumūr (*Aham* 168) and thus confirms his title to fame as a great distributor of food. Māmūlanār also mentions the age of Udiyañjēral, who had a great regard for his ancestors and indulged in extensive feeding—*mudiyaṟ pēṇiya Udiyañjēral peruñjōṟu koḍutta ñānṟai* (*Aham* 233).[32] The author of *Puṟam* 2 roundly asserts that Udiyañjēral got his title of a great dispenser of viands by feeding both the armies engaged in the great battle of the Mahābhārata war. Literally understood, this statement would make the poet and the king contemporaries of the heroes of the Mahābhārata; and this is obviously impossible. Some writers explain it as a memorial feeding on the anniversary of the war,[33] but there is really no warrant for the supposition. Perhaps the best way is to look upon it as a legend attributting this rôle of playing the host to the armies of the Great War to some remote ancestor of the Cheras and here employed by a well-known poetic convention in praise of Udiyañjēral. The same honour is claimed by the Pāṇḍyas and Cholas as well, and it is a feature common to royal familes all the world over to claim some connection, direct or remote, with well-known heroes famed in war and song. The inclusion of the poet of *Puṟam* 2 among the authors of the first Śaṅgam in the *Iṟaiyanār Ahapporuḷ Urai* is the natural consequence of a literal understanding of the poem! The relatively late poet Māmūlanār has a vague reference to Udiyañjēral expanding the Chera country—*nāḍu kaṇ agaṟṟiya* (*Aham* 65); but as no details are forthcoming from contemporary authors, this can be only treated as conventional praise.

Imayavaramban Neḍuñjēral Ādan c. A.D. 155, son of Udiyañjēral, is said to have ruled for fifty-eight years. He married two queens and had, as already noted, three sons by them. His achievements form the subject of the Second Ten by Kumaṭṭūr Kaṇṇanār, who is said to have obtained from the monarch in reward for his composition 500 villages of Umbaṟkāḍu as *brahmadāya* and a share in the revenues of the southern country (*tennāḍu*) for thirty-eight years! Letters have seldom been so lucrative an occupation, and the staggering statements that occur in the epilogues (*padigam*) to the decads must be accepted with much reserve. In the body of the ten poems, the one concrete achievement ascribed to the king is the overthrow of the Kaḍambu tree which was situated on an island (*iru munnīrtturutti, ll.* 1-2 of 20) and was the palladium of some hostile power; the king crossed the sea, defeated the enemy, uprooted his guardian tree and made a war-drum out of its trunk (*vv.* 11, 12, 17, 20). The enemy with the Kaḍambu emblem has been regarded as a class of pirates by one modern writer[34] and identified with Nannan by another.[35] The first view rests on the references to piracy on the Kanara coast occuring in classical authors, and the second lacks all basis. Whether the kaḍamba dynasty who ruled some centuries later in Vanavāsi and other places had any connexion with this enemy of Śēral Ādan is not clear. Whoever he was, the overthrow of this enemy and the destruction of his guardian tree was a great achievement of the Chera monarch, and he won much praise by it.

Another achievement of the monarch finds a place only in the epilogue; on one occasion he captured several Yavanas, bound their hands behind them and poared oil on their heads, and did not release them until he received a heavy ransom in the form of diamonds and other precious stones and many utensils of fine workmanship. These Yavanas were doubtless Graeco-Roman merchants and sailors; how they offended the Chera monarch is not explained but they were well punished for their contumacy. This was evidently no more than an episode of transient importance.

The king's title Imayavaramban (who had the Himalayas as boundary) is explained by the round assertion that he conquered the whole of India from the Himalayas to Cape Comorin (*v.* 11, *ll.* 23-5) and carved his emblem of the bow on the face of the great mountain after subjugating the kings of the North (epilogue). In the same way his ancestors are said to have ruled the entire world (*v.* 12, *ll.* 19-20). These statements can only be treated as fond poetic exaggerations, possibly founded on successful military raids or even quasi-religious, quasi-military pilgrimages. Less incredible are the verses which describe the effects of his good rule and the ruin of the countries which pitted themselves against him (13), the wars he waged for many years spent in camps parted from the company of his queen (15, 16), and his liberality to poets and others who sought his patronage (18, 20). In war, the king rode on an elephant adorned with garlands and lace ornament (11, *ll.* 17-20). He wore a garland of the seven crowns of enemy kings whom he had conquered and subjugated (14, *l.* 11. and 16, *l.* 17). This feature, however, tends to become conventional at least for the later monarchs of the *Ten Tens*.

In two poems (*Aham 127, 347*) Māmūlanār mentions the war against the Kaḍambu and the carving of the bow on the Himalayas by Śēral Ādan as past events; he also states that his capital Marandai (*Aham 127*) was thronged with enemy kings who, vanquished in war, had come to the city bearing tribute.

We have already noted the identity of his monarch with Kuḍakkō Neḍuñjēral Ādan; there are two poems, one each by Kaḻāttalaiyār (*Puṟam* 62) and Paraṇar (*ibid.* 63), in which the poets lament the death on the battle-field of Pōr of this monarch together with his Chola opponent Veṟpahṟaḍakkaip-Peruviṟaṟ Kiḻḻi; the queens of both the fallen monarchs are said to have performed *satī* with their husbands. We have no information of the cause of the conflict.[36]

Palyānaiśelkeḻu Kuṭṭuvan, younger brother of Imayavaramban, ruled for twenty-five years. The decad concerning him was composed by Pālaik Kautamanār, a Brahmin poet, who, as the reward for his literary effort, desired the king to help him and his wife to attain heaven; the king is said to have consulted learned Brahmins and resolved to help the poet to perform ten Vedic sacrifices at the end of which the poet and his wife became invisible, evidently attaining the object of their desire. The intrusion of the miraculous and supernatural into ostensible historical narratives is common in all early literature, and we can only set down the data as we find them, leaving the reader to interpret them as he may. The name of the poet, his reward, the duration of the king's reign and some other facts not known to the text of the poems in the decads are given only in the *padigam* in every case.

In the text of the decad, the specific achievements attributed to the king are the conquest of Koṅgu (22, *l* 15) and the capture of the fortress of Agappā (*ibid. l.* 26) and more generally the expansion of the Chera power and the ruin of enemy countries. He is also called the lord of the Pūḻiyar of the Śeruppu mountain (21. *l.* 23), lord of Aiyirai mountain (*ibid. l.* 29), and the armour of armed soldiers (*ibid. l.* 24). He is styled once the Kuṭṭuvan of many great elephants (29. *l.* 14) and he is also said to have sumptuously fed his entire army on the eve of his battles by beat of drum (*peruñjōṟu*).

In the epilogue the king is said to have established his rule in Umbaṟkāḍu; but as this country was already under Chera rule, we must suppose that some rising in the land was suppressed, and Chera rule firmly re-established in it. Next, the destruction of the Agappā fort is mentioned, and this is followed by the distribution of conquered territory among the senior kinsmen of the monarch. He is said to have caused the water of the western and eastern oceans to be brought at the same time for his *abhisheka* by a system of relays of elephants detached for the purpose—an indication of the extent and splendour of his royal power. He worshipped the goddess of Victory on the Ayirai mountain; finally, led by his learned Brahmin *purohiṭ* Neḍumpāradāyanār (Bhāradvāja) he relinquished the monarchy, to enter the forest and turn ascetic.

The *Śilappadikāram* has a reference to the king's enabling Kautamanār to perform the sacrifices and reach heaven (*Śil.* xxiii *ll.* 62-6).

Kaḷangāykkaṇṇi Nārmuḍichchēral: c. A.D. 175. One of the two sons of Imayavaramban by his senior queen, the daughter of Vēḷāvikkōmān Paduman. He ruled for twenty-five years, and was the hero of the fourth decad sung by

Kāppiyāṟṟuk-Kāppiyanār who was rewarded by a gift in gold of four million *kāṇam* and a share of the kingdom.

In the text of the decad (38, *l.* 4) the king is accorded his full title as given above; the title means that his crown was made of palmyra fibre and the festoon upon it was made of *kaḷangāy*, a small dark berry; why he had to wear these insignia is nowhere explained; we have only the annotator's surmise that somehow the proper crown and festoon were not on hand at the time of his coronation—which explains nothing.[37] We learn from the next poem in the decad (39) that the crown was really not made entirely of fibre, but had a golden frame and festoons of precious pearls calculated to mitigate the shortcomings of the fibre crown. There must have been some real reason for the king choosing such an extraordinary tiara, but we have no means of getting at it now. The king is also called Vānavaramban (38, *l.* 12).

Nārmuḍi was a brave warrior, and he waged wars with success against Neḍumiḍal (32, *l.* 10) who according to the commentator bore the personal name of Añji; if this is correct, he must be distinguished from the more famous Adigamān Neḍumān Añji, the opponent of a later Chera monarch. Neḍumiḍal's country is said to have been occupied by the Chera conqueror (32, *l.* 14). The other achievement of Nārmuḍi was his victory against Nannan I and the destruction of his guardian tree of *vāhai* (40, *ll.* 14-16). Kallāḍanār refers to this event as a past occurrence in a poem (*Aham* 199) which says that the king recovered some lost territory after a battle with Nannan, and he locates the scene of battle at Vāhaipperunduṟai—a name that might have had something to do with the guardian tree of Nannan. The *padigam* to the decad describes Nannan's city at Kaḍambin-peruvāyil and states that Nannan was decapitated by the victor who also uprooted his tree. An expedition into Pūḻi-nāḍu is placed at the head of these operations against Nannan, and it seems probable that this was the name of the territory intervening between the Chera country proper and Nannan's land which was probably the Tulu country. The title of lord of Pūḻiyar was borne by Palyānai Kuṭṭuvan.

Nārmuḍi is said generally to have waged many wars, worn the garland of seven crowns (40, *l.* 13), and attended personally to all matters of administration, and thus rendered it impossible for his enemies to get the better of him (34). He lived for others rather than for himself (38, 39).

This decad (iv) is an *andādi*, the closing words of one poem occurring also at the beginning of the next. It contains details regarding Vishṇu worship, mentions the *tulasi* (basil) garland of Vishṇu and the practice of fasting in the temple to obtain the grace of the deity, and alludes to the story of the burning of Tripura (32).[38]

Śeṅguṭṭuvan: c. A.D. 180. The hero of the fifth decad by Paraṇar, one of the most celebrated and longest-lived of the poets of the Śaṅgam age. Śeṅguṭṭavan is said to have rewarded Paraṅar with the gift of the entire income (*vāri*) from Umbaṟkāḍu and of his son Kuṭṭuvan Śēral. What the gift of the son means is hard to say.

Śeṅguṭṭuvan was the son of Imayavaramban Neḍuñjēral Ādan by his junior queen, a Chola princess whose name seem to figure as Maṇakkiḻḻi in the *padigam* to our decad, while Aḍiyārkkunallār, the commentator of the *Śilappadikāram*, calls her Naṟchōṇai and states that she had a second son after Śeṇguṭṭuvan. Infact the life and achievements of Śeṇguṭṭuvan have generally been viewed in the light of the late and legendary data of the *Śilappadikāram*, and it takes a mental effort to view them in their proper perspective. We shall do well to follow the story step by step.

It is remarkable that there is no other contemporary poem on this monarch except one by Paraṇar himself (*Puṟam* 369) nor even clear allusions to him and his work in the later poems gathered in the anthologies accessible to us. In the decad of Paraṇar the only definite martial achievement attributed to Śeṅguṭṭuvan is a war with the chieftain of Mōhūr, the fierce foe of Aruhai, a firend of Śeṅguṭṭuvan in a distant country; from this war the Chera monarch emerged victorious, destroying the guardian *margosa* tree of the Mōhūr princeling from the stem of which a war-drum was made (44, *ll.* 11-16); in this conflict Mōhūr commanded the support of other kings and *vēḷir* (49, *ll.* 4-7) but without avail; and many warriors lost their lives in the fierce battle (*ibid. ll.* 8-16). Mōhūr must clearly be the seat of the Paḻaiyans in the Pāṇḍyan kingdom, famous in many other contexts. Of Aruhai we have no further information. Paraṇar also says that Śeṅguṭṭuvan exerted himself greatly on the sea (41, *l.* 27; 42, *ll.* 21-3), but it is not certain if this was a separate historical event of the nature of a sea-fight, or has reference only to a quasi-legendary achievement attributed to him elsewhere in the decad (45, *ll.* 18-23; 46, *ll.* 11-13), *viz.* to have secured the retreat of the ocean by throwing a spear against it from which the monarch got the title *kaḍal piṟakkōṭṭiya,* 'who drove back the sea'. The commentator explains even this as meaning that Śeṅguṭṭuvan destroyed the efficacy of the sea as a protection for his enemies who relied upon it. If this is correct, Śeṅguṭṭuvan must be credited with a naval victory, his own, or his ancestors' *e.g.* the war against Kaḍambu. For the rest we learn little more from Paraṇar except that Śeṅguṭṭuvan was a skillful horseman, presented a vast number of horses to troupes of actors, rode a war-elephant, conquered many kings between the Himalayas and Cape Comorin (43), wore the garland of seven crowns (45,*l.*6), was adept in the siegh of fortresses (46), supplied unlimited toddy in his darber (ibid.), and loved war better then women (50).

The epilogue to the decad adds a number of new particulars, the most important of them relating to the establishment of the Pattini cult. It says that to get the stone on which the image of the divine Pattini was to be made, Śeṅguṭṭuvan crossed forests, killed an Aryan chieftain, bathed the stone in the Ganges, and captured numberless cows of good breed with their calvas. This brief sketch of the monarch's action regarding Pattini is in striking contrast with the very elaborate story in the *Silappadikārum,* of which more presently. The next event mentioned in the *padigam* is his camping by the forest of Iḍumbli for an attack on Viyalūr in which many tiger-like warriors fell; we learn from a poem of Māmūlanār (*Aham* 97) that Viyalūr belonged to Nannan, so that this section of the *padigam* is a reference to the war against that chieftain, of which we have no further particulars; possibly it was a case of rebellion suppressed by the suzerain. Seṅguṭṭuvan is said then to have reached Akkarai, overthrown the fortress of Koḍukūr, cut into pieces the hard trunk of the darkboughed *margosa* tree guarded by Paḻaiyan, and had the logs drawn in a cart by elephants yoked with ropes made of the hair shorn from the heads of Paḻaiyan's womenfolk. The location of Koḍukūr has been sought in the south Mysore country[39] and its destruction treated as part of Śeṅguṭṭuvan's war against the Kongar mentioned in the *Silappadikāram* but nowhere else. This may be so, though the evidence cited is late and inconclusive. The refinement of barbarity in the treatment of the womenfolk of Paḻaiyan is, one hopes, no more then an exaggeration born of the acceptance of the false conventions by the poets of the age. The last event mentioned in the epilogue is a battle at Vāyil in a war of Chola succession in which nine Chola chaimants to the throne are said to have lost their lives; this encounter is located at Nērivāyil, a village to the south of Uṟaiyūr, by the commentator of the *Silappadikāram*.[40] This work states in detail that the ruling Chola monarch Kiḻḻi was related to Śeṅguṭṭuvan as *maittuna* (wife's brother?), that he had trouble from nine princes of the blood royal, who would not accept subordinate positions and began to fill the country with their quarrels and were likely to ruin it; this intolerable situation was brought to an end by Śeṅguṭṭuvan's intervention which restored the unity of Kiḻḻi's rule after destruction of his nine rivals at Nērivāyil.

Not in connection with this battle only, but in many other respects the *Śilappandikāram* embellishes the life story of Śeṅguṭṭuvan; the one Aryan chief conquered by him in his northen expedition becomes a thousand kings, and the expedition itself takes place not once but twice, once to bathe his mother in the Ganges and again to win the stone for the Pittini image. Regarding the maternal bath in the Ganges, the commentator himself entertains doubts and says that it is a story,[41] possibly because acording to *Puṟam* 62, the king's mother committed *satī* on the pyre of her husband when he fell in combat with a Chola.The *Śilappadikāram* says further that Śeṅguṭṭuvan engaged in constant war for at least fifty years, but no fresh details are forthcoming. The work purports to be that of a younger brother of the monarch.

The estimate of *Śeṅguṭṭuvan* will vary according as we base it on contemporary poems only or on the *Śilappadikāram* also. The general tendency has been to follow the second course and to make a very great hero of him. In reality he was just like any other monarch of the age. He may have taken a leading part in the institution of the Pattini cult, unless indeed that cult was a later institution which was ascribed to Śeṅguṭṭuvan by the *Śilappadikāram*, the saga of the cult. How far again the incidents in the story of Kōvalan and Kaṇṇagi are to be treated as historical is another vexed question on which no confident opinion can be expressed. The Pāṇḍyan contemporary of Śenguṭṭuvan was Neḍuñjeḻiyan known as Āriyappaḍai-Kaḍanda, who conquered the Arya forces.[42] He is the author of one poem (*Puṟam* 183).

The antiquity and popularity of the Kaṇṇagi story is well attested by other evidence. A song in the *Naṟṟiṇai* (216) by Marudan Iḷanāganār of Madurai contains a casual and all the more valuable reference, to Kaṇṇagi tearing off one of her breasts from grief for her husband and her appearance under a *vēṅgai* tree where the gods came to her in response to her wish; both these elements are found woven into the story of the *Śilappadikāram* as we have it now. Again a verse cited in the commentary of the *Yāpparuṅgalavirutti*[43] is obviously part of the lament of Kaṇṇagi after the murder of her husband; the verse is cited as an instance of metrical irregularity to be treated as *ārsha;* here we have proof of the existence of other works, now lost, on the Kaṇṇagi saga.

Paraṇar had many notable contemporaries among the monarchs and poets of the age—Karikāla's father and Karikāla himself among the Cholas; Naḷḷi, Evvi, Ori, Kāri, Nannan I, Pēhan, and Paḻaiyan, among chieftains; and all the authors of the sixth to the ninth decads of the *Ten Tens* among the poets. Facts like these must be firmly kept in view when determining the duration of the age depicted in the Śaṅgam literature.

Āḍukoṭpāṭṭuch-chēral Ādan: c. A.D. 180, half-brother of Śaṅguṭṭuvan, and brother of Nārmuḍi, is said to have held sway for thirty-eight years. He is the hero of the sixth decad by the poetess Kākkaipāḍiniyār Nachcheḷḷaiyār whom he rewarded with gold, weighing 9 *kā* for making jewels and 100,000 *kāṇam* in cash, besides entertaining her in his court permanently thereafter.

The poetess acquired her title from having introduced a crow as a leading feature in a song in the *Kuṟundogai* (210) in which Naḷḷi and Toṇḍi are also mentioned—the song being to the effect that even the fine rice of Toṇḍi mixed with the ghee yielded by the cows of Nāḷḷi's shepherds would not be adequate recompense (*bali,* offering) for the crow that by its cawing announced the return of the lover to his love! Naḷḷi is mentioned also by Kapilar, the author of the next decad, in a poem in *Aham* (238) where Naḻḻi's mountain and his liberality are selected for particular praise.

In the body of the sixth decad there is little history; Ādan's good rule is praised in general terms, as also his heroism in war and his liberality. He is said to have indulged in mixed dances (*tuṇaṅgai*) and roused the jealousy of his queen (52). He had the title Vānavaramban (58, *l.* 12, also *Aham* 389 Nakkīrar) and Naṟavu on the sea-shore was one of the towns belonging to him (60, *l.* 12).

In the epilogue the king's title is accounted for by the statement that he compelled his enemies who had carried off into the Daṇḍāraṇya a flock of *varuḍai* (mountain sheep) belonging to the Cheras to return them safe to Toṇḍi. He is said further to have given a village in Kuḍanāḍu with cows to Brahmins and thereby caused his name Vānavaramban to shine forth. This seems to imply that we have to understand the title as a metaphor suggesting the conquest of heaven by pious deeds, an idea known to the Gupta coin-legends. Lastly, the king defeated the Maḻavar in battle and routed monarchs and ruled his subjects as parents guard their children with a loving mind.

This monarch may well have been the famous Karikāla's Chera opponent, who received a wound in his back in the battle of Veṇṇi and expiated the disgrace by starving to death on the battle-field sword in hand—as we learn from three poems (*Puṟam* 65, 66 and *Aham* 55).[44] One of them, by Māmūlanār (*Aham* 55), states, that many eminent men gave up their lives when they heard of the Chera monarch's demise and the reason for it.

From the next decad, the seventh, the collection proceeds to treat of monarchs of another branch of Cheras, and before taking up their study, we may stop of consider the nature of the Chera monarchy implicit in the data yielded by the epilogues. In them the five monarchs of the line of Udiyañjeral whose reigns we have so far studied are said altogether to have reigned for over two centuries (58+25+25+55+38= 201); and we shall see further that the monarchs of the seventh, eighth and ninth decads respectively are assigned periods of 25, 17 and 16 years, giving a total of another 58 years. Surely we cannot consider these periods as successively running one after another; we must necessarily postulate a very considerable degree of overlapping. How exactly the rule of the kingdom was shared among the different princes of the blood royal, and the rules of precedence, if any, that prevailed among them, we have no means of ascertaining now. The Chera kingdom must have been a sort of family estate in which all the adult males of the line had a share and interest—what Kauṭilya has called *kulasaṅgha*, a family-group. Kauṭilya attributed great merit to this type of state organisation, saying that a *Kulasaṅgha* was invincible—*kulasaṅgho hi durjayaḥ.*[45] A similar clan-rule might have prevailed in the Chola and Pāṇḍya kingdoms as well; in the case of the Cholas such an assumption would be the best means of explaining of occasion for Śeṅguṭṭuvan to intervene in a war of succession in which nine Chola princes laid down their lives; it would also furnish a natural explanation for the occurrence of so many names of kings—all necessarily to be accommodated within a space of three, four or at most five generations for the reasons already stated. Our knowledge of the genealogy of the royal families being so limited, the dates we assign to different persons and incidents can only be rough approximations. The kings of the last three decads of the *Ten Tens* as well as their ancestors must be taken to have ruled contemporaneously with the kings of the house of Udiyañjēral. Let us now see what the poems have to tell us about these monarchs.

Anduvan: c. A.D. 140, was the father of Śelvakkaḍuṅgō Vāḻi Ādan; his wife was the daughter of a certain Orutandai. Her name figures only as Poṟaiyan Perundēvi, the great queen of Poṟaiyan (Chera). Anduvan is said to have had a stout heart and taken his enemies captive; he was also celebrated for his wide and accurate scholarship (*padigam* vii). He was the lord of Maiyūr (*pad.* ix). Doubtless also he was the monarch addressed by the poet Eṇichchēri Muḍamōśiyār of Uṟaiyūr (*Puṟam* 13); the occasion was furnished by a Chola prince Muḍittalaikkō Perunaṟkiḷḷi who was carried into the precincts of Karuvūr by the uncontrollable must elephant on which he was riding; the poet explains the situation to Anduvan in order to assure him that it was no act of hostility on the part of the Chola thus to ride into the Chera capital, and prays for the safety of the Chola prince. We get no other information about Anduvan.

The poet of Uṟaiyūr just mentioned is celebrated as a Brahmin Protégé[46] of the chieftain Āy; many of his poems celebrating his patron are found in the *Puṟam* besides poems of other poets on the same chieftain. Āy was thus clearly a contemporary of Anduvan, and we may stop to consider the information to be gathered about him from the poems before we proceed to the decad dealing with Anduvan's son, Śelvakkaḍuṅgō Vāḻi Ādan. Further, as Kapilar, the author of that decad, declares at the outset (61) that he went to the Chera monarch after the demise of his former patron Pāri, we may also discuss the incidents of Pāri's life and his relations with Kapilar at this stage.

Āy, a *vēḷ* chieftain, is mentioned in two poems by Paraṇar; in one (*Aham* 152) his name occurs with the names of other chieftains—Nannan, Naḷḷi. Piṇḍan, and Tittan Veḷiyan, and he is said to have owned numerous elephants and presented them liberally to his favourites; in the other (*ibid.* 198) mention is made of Āy's good country in the south. In fact Āy appears to have held sway in the mountainous marches of the southernmost section of the Western Ghats which divided the Pāṇḍya and Chola countries on the east from the Kerala on the west. The region abounds in elephants even at the present day and it is no surprise to find these noble animals figuring so largely in the poetry that celebrates. Āy and his country. In fact Mōśi Kīran, a somewhat later poet who was contemporary with Peruñjēral Irumpoṟai who won Tagaḍūr (*Puṟam* 50), says clearly that the Podiyil mountain belonged to Āy (*Kuṟn.* 84). Another poet Kārikkaṇṇanār of Kāvirippūmpaṭṭinam, compares the rain clouds gathering in the sky to the crowd on elephants that Āy Aṇḍiran ever kept ready for presentation to the bards and minstrels who visited him (*Naṟṟiṇai* 237). There is a reference to Āy's forest (*kānam*) in the only poem (*Aham* 69) of Paraṅgoṟṟanār, son of Umaṭṭūr Kiḻār; and another poet also, Tuṟaiyūr Ōḍai Kiḻār, is only known by the single poem which he addresses to Āy soliciting a present (*Puṟam* 136). A quasi-legendary reference to Āy occurs in the rather late poem, *Śirupāṇāṟṟuppaḍai* (*ll.* 96-9), in which he is said to have presented to God Śiva a very fine cloth given to him by a Nāga (*nīla-nāgan*).

It is to Muḍamōśiyār that we owe many songs of great literary finish and intense personal feeling celebrating the virtues and eminence of Āy. In one poem (*Puṟam* 127) he describes the luxurious palace of Āy depleted of all its wealth after the visit of *pāṇars* (minstrels); in another (*ibid.* 128) he says that the mountain Podiyil was accessible only to dancing-girls (*pāḍinis*) coming to look for Āy's patronge; but not to enemy kings, however strong their forces. Several poems attest the ingenious strivings of the poet to convey to us the richness of Āy's country in elephants and Āy's great liberality in parting with them as presents to his guests—thus, the stars must fill the entire sky to equal the number of elephants given away by Āy Aṇḍiran (*ibid.* 129); such elephants were more numerous than the spears employed on the field where the Kongar were driven to the western sea by Āy—almost the only martial achievement of Āy to be mentioned—and the poet questions Āy if in his country one she-elephant brought forth ten calves at a time (*ibid.* 130); again did the mountains sing the praises of Āy and win presents from him, that they should harbour so many elephants (*ibid.* 131)? Āy's *kaṇṇi* (the festoon on his crown), was of *vaḻai* (*ochrocarpus congifolius*) (ibid.). In one poem the poet laments that at one time he thought of others before Āy, and maintains that Āy in the south belances the Himalayas in the north of India (*ibid.* 132), thus recalling the cycle of legends centring round Agastya and his residence in the Podiyil mountain. Another poem (*ibid.* 133) is an exhortation to a dancing-girl (*viṟali*) to resort to Āy in all haste if she wanted to meet the embodiment of fame. Āy was no trader in *dharma*, seeking the reward of comfort in the other world for the good he did here, but only sought to be an example to others (*ibid.* 134). The poet says in another poem (*ibid.* 135) that he went with the dancing-girl with her lute behind him just to meet Āy, not to apply for any presents, but adds slyly: 'May Āy ever be in a position to dispense with the things coveted by his visitors.' Two other poems conclude the theme of Āy's liberality, one by contrasting the sun unfavourably with him (*ibid.* 374) and the other by lauding his appreciation of literature (*ibid.* 375). Finally the poet mentions the death of Āy and the welcome he received in the abode of the gods in heaven, saying that the drum in Indra's palace reverberated at the arrival of Āy (*Puṟam* 241). The death of Āy Aṇḍiran is mentioned also by Kuṭṭuvan Kīranār who is known only by a single poem (*Puṟam* 240) which records the event, recalls the presents of elephants, horses, and chariots that Āy gave to poets in his lifetime and mentions the fact that the wives of Āy immolated themselves on his funeral pyre, performing *satī*. Āy appears to have been a dynastic name, while Aṇḍiran may be the Sanskrit word meaning hero. Ptolemy knew of Āy and his mountain country.

Pāri was another *vēḷ* chieftain, the friend and patron of Kapilar who found his way to the Chera court only after Pāri's death. Of the origin of the *vēḷs* there is a legend recorded by Kapilar himself (*Puṟam* 201) according to which they belonged to a line of kings who appeared from the sacred fire-pit of a northern sage and ruled in Tuvarai for forty-nine generations. Tuvarai may stand for either Dvārakā or Dvārasamudra. It is perhaps better identified with the latter, because in the same poem Kapila describes Iruṅgō-vēḷ as *puli-kaḍi-māl*, the great man who drove off the tiger, an attribute that anticipates by centuries the Kannaḍa legend regarding the origin of the dynastic name Hoysala.

Many minor chieftains of the Tamil country in this period claimed to be of *vēḷ* origin, and Pāri is one of the best known among them. His principality lay in the Pāṇḍya country round about the hillock known as Koḍuṅguṉṟam or Pirāṉmalai, where there is a temple of Pāriśvara commenmorating perhaps the ancient connection of Pāri with the shrine.[47] The fame of Pāri's liberality finds an echo in later ages in Sundaramūrti's lament: 'there is no one ready to give, even if an illiberal patron is addressed by the name of Pāri.'

Kapilar was not a mere bard who sought to win the favour of Pāri by celebrating him in song, but his lifelong friend and adviser. He stood by the chieftain through thick and thin, and devised ways of prolonging resistance when Pāri's hill was completely surrounded by 'the three crowned kings' of the Tamil country; after Pāri's death, Kapilar took charge of his two unmarried daughters and did his best, apparently without success, to get them suitably married.

The story of Pāri and his daughters and Kapilar grew into a popular saga, embellished from time to time by the addition of fresh details; all these later accretions have found their lodgement in the compilation of literary legends known as *Tamiḻ Nāvalar Charitai*, hardly two centuries old. Leaving these late legends alone, we shall confine ourselves to the data from the Śaṅgam anthologies.

In a song in the *Naṟṟiṇai* (253) Kapilar describers the strongly guarded hill of Pāri. A number of his poems on Pāri figure in the *Puṟam* collection. One of them (105) is a *viṟaliyāṟṟuppaḍai* in the conventional style exhorting a *viṟali* (danching-girl) to go to Pāri and seek his patronage; Pāri's gentleness and liberality to visitors, she is told, are more refreshing than the cool waters of the springs for which his hill was famous. The next poem (106) says that Pāri's liberality was so universal that even bad poets returned from him not empty-handed. In another short poem (107) Kapilar says that poets praise only Pāri, and seem to forget that the rain has also a part in ensuring the well-being of the world. The fertile land of Pāri with its sandal-wooded hillsides was really the property of those who praised him in song (108). The riches of Pāri's hill in forest produce is described in detail by the poet in a song (109) which concludes on the note that access to them is easier to minstrels and dancers, than to kings who seek to enter by force. The next song (110) begins with a brief repetition of the same idea, and dissuades kings from resorting to Pāri even as minstrels, declaring that all the three hundred villages of his fiṇe country have been distributed as presents and there remains only the poet Kapilar, Pāri, and the hill. Kings will find it hard, repeats Kapilar in another song (111), to take Pāri's hill by the force of their lance, but a *viṟali* may win it if she approaches with a song to the accompaniment of a lute.

Then comes a short poem of five lines attributed to Pāri's daughters; it is a direct and simple statement, full of pathos, of the change in their fortunes due to their father's death. 'In those days, we enjoyed the moonlight happily with father, and the foe could not take our hill; now this day, in this bright moonlight, kings with victorious resounding wardrums have won the hill, and we have lost our father.' The annotator explains in his gloss that the first half of the verse refers to the period when the three kings were besieging Pāri's hill for a long time without success, and that the reference to their victorious war-drums is ironical, as they killed Pāri not in open fight, but by treachery. Considering how often Kapilar asserts the impossibility of reducing the hill by force, the commentator's statement may well be accepted as the record of a correct tradition. According to one of the early legends that grew round this celebrated siege, Kapilar trained a large number of birds to fly out from Pāri's fortress into the open country behind the besieging troops and bring in enough corn to feed the city and the army for several days and months; thus he helped to stave off an early surrender. Kapilar himself has nothing to say on this; but poets who came very soon after him make pointed references to it. Auvaiyār has (*Aham* 303) a poem which speaks of Pāri's gifts to poets of elephants and jewels besides the story of the sparrows flying out in the morning to fetch grain in the evening for provisioning the beleagured fortress; Nakkīrar (*Aham* 78) mentions the same incident and names Kapilar as the inventor of the ruse which prolonged the siege for years; and roundly asserts that Pāri triumphed in the end, which is not borne out by the earlier series of poems. We may mention here to other poets who speak on Pāri and his munificence as belonging to the past—Miḷaikkaṇḍan (*Kurun*. 196) and Nannāganār (*Puṟam* 176).

To return to Kapilar's poems. They continue the story after Pāri's death and give hints of some things that Kapilar did thereafter. Two songs (*Puṟam* 113. 114) are touching farewells to Pāri's hill and country pronounced on the eve of Kapilar's departure from that land with Pāri's daughters to find in search husbands for them; they recall the planty and splendour of the past and contrast them with the penury to which the poet and his protégés had sunk after Pāri's death. Another poem (*ibid*. 115) is also reminiscent of the feast and song of Pāri's lifetime, while others (*ibid*. 116, 117 and 119) draw a poignant contrast between the condition of Pāri's hill and its city in his life and after his death, one poem (*ibid*. 118) laying particular stress on the neglect of irrigation, and another (*ibid*. 120) on that of agriculture.

Three poems bear on Kapilar's attempts to marry off Pāri's daughters. One of them (*Puṟam* 200) is addressed to Vichchikkōn, a minor chieftain; it praises Vichchikkōn and his valour, describes the noble descent of Pāri's daughters, and ends with a request that the chieftain should accept them as his brides. Incidentally the poem alludes to Pāri's gift of a chariot to a creeper of the *mullai* flower, an act which sounds absurd in modern ears, but was held up by many old Tamil poets as the leading instance of Pāri's liberality. The suit to Vichchikkōn was apparently unsuccessful, for the next two poems (*ibid*. 201 & 202) record that Kapilar took the girls to another chieftain Iruṅgōvēḷ with the same result. The first opens with the statements that the girls were the daughters of the famous Pāri who had been Kapilar's great friend and that consequently he, a Brahmin poet, looked upon them as his own daughters; it then adverts to the legends of the origin of the *vē!s* already noticed, and exhorts Iruṅgōvēḷ to accept the girls as brides. The other poem is the utterance of the poet of his distress at his second failure, he prophesiesthe destruction of Araiyam, the capital of Iruṅgōvēḷ, but attributes it to the curse of the poet Kaḻāttalaiyār whom one of the chieftain's ancestors had insulted; and apologies for having spoken to him at all about Pāri's daughters!

The colophon to one of Kapilar's poems in the *Puṟam* (236) records that the poet failed in all his efforts to marry off the girls, and that he left them finally in the charge of Brahmins and starved himself to death. The poem itself is only poignant expression of the poet's grief at the death of Pāri and of his desire that they should be united again as friends in another birth. But the tradition recorded in a late Chola inscription[48] at Kiḻūr (Tirukoyilur tq., S. Arcot) is very different; it mentions only one daughter of Pāri and states that Kapilar had given her in marriage to the Malaiyan before he entered the fire to attain heaven, a fact commemorated by a stone set up on the spot. We have no means of deciding between the rival stories. There are, however, four songs in the *Puṟam* (121-4) in which Kapilar celebrates Malaiyamān Tirumuḍikkāri of Muḷḷūr, the excellence and defensibility of his country, the desire of each of the crowned kings of the Tamil land to have him as his friend, and his liberal patronage of poets and minstrels. This renders probable the story of the marriage of Pāri's daughter recorded in the Kiḻūr inscription, though our literary sources seem to know nothing of it. Kapilar has other poems on Kāri in the other anthologies. He mentions the sandal-wood of Kāri's mountain and the Muḷḷūrkkānam of Kāri in two poems in the *Kuṟundogai* (198 & 312); he also refers to Kāri's victorious combat against Ōri of Kollimalai in which Ōri lost his life, and his mountain was thereupon transferred to the Cheras by Kāri (*Naṟṟiṇai* 320); this incident, as already noted, is mentioned in some detail (*Aham* 209) by the somewhat later poet Kallāḍanār, the contemporary of Pāṇḍya Neduñ-jeḻiyan of Talaiyālaṅgānam. Another poem of Kapilar (*Naṟṟiṇai* 291) mentions (Kāri) the king of Muḷḷūr, riding on horseback to lift the cattle from his enemies' herds. Kāri's heroism is mentioned by Kapilar in another poem (*Naṟṟiṇai* 77).

Kāri is also celebrated in songs by a poetess Māṟōkkattu Nappaśalaiyār. In one song (*Puṟam* 126) she states that Kapilar has praised Kāri so well that there is no room for others to essay the task; yet she made the effort to overcome her poverty. In another (*ibid.* 174) she makes a further reference to Kapilar' praise of Kāri, to the death of Kāri himself who went to the other world to enjoy the results of his good deeds here, and then celebrates his successor Malaiyamān Tirukkaṇṇan, who was the younger brother of Kāri (*l.* 18 *nummun*) and a commander (*ēnādi*) of the Chola monarch.

The poetess has yet another song (*ibid.* 226) in which she wittily says that Death must have gone to a certain Chola prince as a beggar to have got away with the life of that prince, for it could have been taken in no other way. The name of the Chola is Kiḻḻi Vaḷavan who died in Kuḷamuṟṟam and we have to find him a place near this generation. A song of Kōvūr Kiḻār (*Puṟam* 46) addressed to this Chola prince is said to have resulted in his commuting the sentence of death passed on the youthful sons of Malaiyamān (Kāri) in the *sabha* of Uṟaiyūr; the reason for the sentence is not mentioned; but the young men were about to be thrown to an elephant, when the poet interceded with the song in which he recalled the charity of Śibi, a mythical ancestor of the Cholas, to the dove, and pointed out that the line of Malaiyamān had patronised learning and was entitled to mercy; the sentence was not executed and Malaiyamān's sons were saved. Another Chola prince who was of the same generation was Rājasūyam-vēṭṭa Perunaṟkiḻḻi who was aided by Kāri, called Tērvaṇmalaiyan (*Puṟam* 125) in a war against Māndarañjēral Irumpoṟai; the poet Vaḍamavaṇṇakkan Pēri Śāttanār says that by his act Kāri earned the praise of both sides in the war, the victor being grateful for help received, and the vanquished attributing his defeat more to kāri's aid than to the strength of his Chola opponent.

Lastly Kapilar is said to have composed the *Kuṟiñjippāṭṭu*, one of the *Ten Idylls* (*Pattuppāṭṭu*) in order to convey an idea of Tamil culture (ideals of marriage) to the Ārya king Piraḥattan (Prahasta?) of whom we know nothing else. The fame of Kapilar's poetry and his relative chronological position are made clear by a poem of Porundil Iḷangīranār (*Puṟam* 53) in which he says that Kapilar ought to have been alive to do justice to the great qualities of Māndarañjēral Irumpoṟai.

NOTES AND REFERENCES

1. McCrindle, *Meg. & Arr. pp. 62-3; 158-9*
2. *xvii*, l. 7
3. Smith, *CCIM*. I p. 135
4. Parimēl-Aḷagar on *Kuṟal*, 955
5. *ARE*. 1927-8, ii. 1.
6. For other views see (p. 26) *ante* and Barua, *Aśoka and his inscriptions*, pp. 111-2, Also *Age of the Nandas and Mauryas*, ed. K.A.N. Saṣtri, (1952) pp. 250 ff.
7. *PAIOC*. (III 1924) p. 278
8. *The Beginnings of South India History*, ch. ii
9. *CHI*. I p. 596
10. *Puṟam* 175
11. *Aham* 69
12. *Aham* 265
13. *Ibid*. 251
14. *Ibid*. 281
15. No. 75 by Paḍumarattu Mōśikiranār
16. *Tamil Studies*, ix and x (1914)
17. *Tamil Varalāṟu* (Kumbakonam, 1st ed. 1922, 2nd ed. 1924)
18. See essay i on *Puṟanāṉuṟu* in *Studies in Cola History and Administration by* K.A.N. Sastri for a discussion of the authenticity of the colophons. The *padigams of Padiṟṟupattu* are of course late, but may well be taken to embody a correct tradition. See p. 4-5 intro. to Swaminatha Iyer's edition (1920).
19. *Kali*. 104, *ll*., 1-4. cf. *Śilap*. xi. *ll*. 18-22
20. *Maduraik*. *ll*. 618-9 and *Malai*. *ll*. 70-2
21. *Tirumurugāṟṟuppaḍai* ed. S. Vaiyapuri Pillai, 1943, Madurai. For a further discussion of the chronology of the *Pattuppāṭṭu* see ch. xxi *post*.
22. D.V. xxii *vv*. 14, 28; *MV*. xxxv vv.
23. *MV*. chh. xxi-xxv.
24. For details and references see *Colas* 1
25. Rostovtzeff, *Social and Economic History of the Roman Empire*, p. 91
26. *Ancient India*, no. 2 (July 1946), pp. 17-124, esp. 22-4
27. *Ind. Eph*. I. (i)
28. *Ibid*. pp. 100-1
29. ii and *padigam* iii.
30. *Contra:* K.G. Sesha Aiyar's *Cera Kings*, p. 10 evidently based on com. to *Puaṟm* 80.
31. His only other poem (*Puṟam* 254) is a short and poignant lament on the loss of his wife.

32. See also *Śil.* xxiii, *l.* 55 and *Kalingattupparaṇi* v. 181 and notes in Gopala Aiyar's edition.
33. Sesha Aiyar, *op. cit.*, p. 7.
34. S.K. Aiyangar, *The Beginning of S. Indian History,* pp. 231-2.
35. Sesha Aiyar, *op. cit.*, p. 11.
36. The word *māṇḍana* occurs in *l.* 27 of v. 19 in the sense of 'died', 'ceased to exist'. In the Śangam works this word is usually employed in another and better sense, *viz.* attained celebrity. Here is a textual problem; but an easy solution for it is to suggest that the word is a mistake for *māyndana* which will suit the context and the metre very well.
37. M. Raghava Aiyangar improves on this and says (*Śeran Śenguṭṭuvan,* p. 13) that enemies had carried them off, a statement for which there is no support.
38. It also contains the verbal form *adirpaṭṭu-muḻangi* (39, *l.* 6) which sounds rather unusual for the age of the poem.
39. M. Raghava Aiyangar, *op. cit.*, p. 29 citing *IA* XVIII p. 367.
40. *Śil.* XXV, *ll.* 115-9; XXVII, *ll.* 118-23; M. Raghava Aiyangar, *op. cit.* pp. 32-3.
41. *Śil.* XXV. *ll.* 160-1.
42. *Śil.* Madurai, Kaṭṭurai.
43. Ed. Bhavanandam (1916), p. 351.
44. Sesha Aiyar, *op. cit.*, pp. 29-32.
45. *KA.* I 17.
46. *Tol.* Marapu 74 *urai.*
47. M. Raghava Aiyangar, *Vēḷir Varalāṟu*, pp. 63-4.
48. *SII.* VII 863, *l.* 2.

CHAPTER - V

ORIGINS OF THE INDIAN VILLAGE SYSTEM

Indian Migration: There has been a great deal of migration in ancient times, and the institution of the village community has travelled, like other things, far and wide. It is believed by some that it was by way of the Euphrates valley that the Indian village communities made their way into Europe, for their village system is exactly reproduced in that of Palestine, where at the present day the lands are every year distributed among the cultivators exactly in the way that is usual in India. It was there that they apparently first found out how to develop the local grasses into wheat and barley, good substitutes for their Indian grass developed into rice, or *ragi*. Thus it is probable that, while the domestic animals came to Europe from West Central Asia, the older staple crafts may have come from South-East Asia, from Asia Minor, or Northern Palestine. Hewitt believes that the constitution of the Dravidian village community made its way to the Persian Gulf through coasting voyages, and ultimately reached South-Eastern Europe. According to him, the Spartan from of government reproduces Dravidian customs, and gives, along with other evidences, an historical clue to the origin of the race. The five *ephors* are the five members of the Indian village council, called the *panchayat*, or council of five (*panch*), while the two kings are the Dravidian supreme king, judge, and law-giver, and his chief subordinate and almost coequal, the *senapati*, lord (*pati*) of the army (*sena*), the commander-in-chief. Thus the village hall of the Indian Dravidians which is found in every Dravidian village in India, and in those of Burma, Siam, and Annam, was also to be found later among the Southern Suevi or

Swabians in Europe, either as a common dancing or meeting place, or as a building similar to that of the German village, owned by the community as a place for public meetings and for the entertainment of strangers. It is among them that we alsofind, according to the descriptions of Caesar and Tacitus, that magistrates and princes in assembly divide the land annually in proportion, as in the Indian village community, while the village tenants of the lord, who have no separate and private fields with proper boundaries, each occupies his own house and pays a tribute of corn, cattle and flax. The system of Indian rural economy and village settlement thus ultimately found its way into Western Europe with changes brought about by successive migrations and invasions, and there it had a different and chequered career. These are matters which cannot be finally decided before sufficient evidences in the following directions are brought eogether : the anthropometric affinities of racial types, the affinities in language, myth, and social customs, as well as the testimony of stone, iron, and wood implements in the diverse regions marked by homogeneity in physical and social types and species.

But some of the Indian evidence is sufficiently clear and definite. The *panchayats*, or the village councils, and the village or ward policemen, as well as the allotments of lands for village headmen, accountants and employees, are the most vital of the Munda-Dravidian survivals, still found wherever the social composition shows a large aboriginal admixture. The *panchayats* and the communal villages have not been obscured, whether by the Mitakshara and Dayabhaga codes of property, or by the Muhammadan superimposition of overlords, biefs, and feudal tenures, or again by the British superimposition of the rights of individual property. In Bengal the unions of villages in a circle, *mandala*, and *panchagrama*, or five villages, the officers now called the *mandalika* and the *panchagramika*, the divisions of villages and urban congregations into *parhas* and pattis, and the larger devisions now called parganas, have their original affinities to manda institutions.

Caste Government: In the gradual process of absorption of the Munda-Drvidians by the Hindu social organization, We find survivals of their polity in the *panchayats* of almost all the non-Brahman castes. In matters of social administration, each caste is an autonomous unit, having its headman and peon, and often its vice-headman. Appeals against the decision of the village headman, whose jurisdiction extends over each endogamous subdivision of the cdaste or tribe in each village, are referred to a higher tribunal, consisting usually of a council of these headman, presided over by the tribal or caste chief, or head. This tribunal exercises its authority over a number of villages, the number varying with the strengh and distribution of the communities concerned. In South India the territorial jurisdiction of such a tribunal is variously known as a *nadu* or *pati*, both of which denote old tribal divisions of the Dravidians. In most castes the decisions of the second court are subject to a third, or even to a fourth tribunal, the constitution of which varies with almost every caste. In some castes several *nadus* are grouped together under the jurisdiction of an officer called *pattakkaram*, *periyanattan*, *peria doraoi*, *padda ejaman*, *raja*, *gadi-nattan*, etc. Sometimes the decisions of pattakars are referred to a board of *pattakars* and sometimes, when Brahmanical influence is stronger, to a *guru*. Such are the vestigial remains of the old Munda-Dravidian tribal organization, seen in its purer form even today in Chota Nagpur, Malabar, Cochin and Coorg, with its divisions or tribal territory into a number of villages, each under its headman, its groups and unions of villages, called *parhas* or *pattis* or *nadus*, and the hierarchy of tribunals composed of the board of headmen, presider over by a chief or a raja, who still exercises a certain vague supremacy over a group of tribal divisions. Caste administration is of a strictly hierarchical character, like tribal administration, and monarchical or republican forms survive as vestiges of the older tribal types. In each caste tribunal, again, we find the two assessors selected by each party advocating each side of the case before the *panchayat*, as we find in the tribal councils among the Mundas and oraons, for instance, in Chota Nagpur. Among almost all South Indian castes matrimonial disputes are sent, after a preliminary inquiry, by the village headmen to the head of the *nadu*, who decides them with the help of a few village headmen. This is clearly a vestige of the Dravidian custom of the sanction of marriages by the chief.

VILLAGE LAND SETTLEMENT

Question of Origins: Turning to the agratian settlement, we find that in the Munda-Dravidian village organisation *khunt* lots are divided into blocks, one for the chief's descendants, one for the *mahto's*, and one for the tribal priest's. Vestigial remains of this custom are still to be found among many Dravidian tribes and castes in the South who still set apart the fines levied by the *panchayat* under three heads : for the *sarkar*, for the members of the *panchayat*, and for the priest. In Sandur State, Bellary, the first third is still paid into the State coffers, whence it is handed over to deserving charities. Among the Pallans of South India, a fine of Rs. 1¼ is thus apportioned : 10 annas goes to the *aramanai*, *i.e.*, place or government; 5 annas towards feasting the villages; the *ilangali* and *odumpillai* receive 1½ annas each, the barbar and dhobi 1 anna each. The village sweeper or scavenger, *kulawadi, tothi*, or *kotwar*, as he is variously called, is the guardian of the village boundaries, and his opinion was often taken as authoritative in all cases of disputes about land in many parts of India. This position he perhaps occupied as a representative of the pre-Aryan tribes, the oldest residents of the country, and his appointment also may have been based partly on the idea that it was proper to employ one of them as the guardian of the village lands, just as the priest of the village gods of the earth and fields was usually taken from these tribes. The reason for their appointment seems to be that the Hindus still look on themselves to some extent as strangers and interlopers in relation to the gods of the earth and of the village, and consider it necessary to approach these through the medium of one or other member of the non-Aryan communities, who were former owners of the soil. The words *bhumka* and *bhuniya* for the village priest both mean the lord of the soil or belonging to the soil. But with regard to the common ownership of the pasture-lands, water-courses, and the village temples in the Indo-Aryan village community, it would be difficult to say whether Munda or Dravidian institutions found ready to hand were copied, whether they were natural outgrowths of early Aryan tribal conditions or whether they were inevitable under the conditions of Indian economic geography and physiography. We find in Manu that grazing grounds are the common property of the village; the people encroaching upon them are liable to penalties, and Yajnavalkya lays down substantially the same rule. This was so even as early as the Vedic age, when it was called *khila* or *khilya*, as surrounding the plough-land. The village land appears also to include adjoining forest tracts, over which the entire village has a common right. Besides these, there were the water-course, the village temple, and the village gods, which were the communal properties of the entire village. And even with regard to the arable land occupied or cultivated by the villagers which was considered to be the separate property of the joint families we find a trace of the communal right of the village in the rule that such lands could not be alienated without the consent of the entire village (*Mitakshara*, chap. I, sect. I). In such cases the question of origins is not easy to solve. A nearly certain test of Munda-Dravidian affinities may be found in the regional prevalence of the worship of local spirits, and the sacredness ascribed to the earth, fields, and trees. This anthropoligical test should be applied for discrimination between Dravidian or Aryan political forms and institutions. Again, the data furnished by Comparative Ethnology help us a great deal in finding out the gradation of social values in Aryan origin and development, and in isolating, accordingly, the distinctive features of the Aryan polity.

Aryan and Dravidian features in the Village System: Thus difficult though it may be to sift the Aryan observances and rural practices, we may yet enumerate briefly the characteristics which bear upon the evolution of the Aryan village community.

(1) The Aryan settlement corresponds to the Munda-Dravidian division of tribes and villages into exogamous clans; but, unlike the latter, these are not totemistic, but eponymous. Common descent from a saint replaces connection of totem, even as the holding of land in common supersedes tribal bonds under the control of the chieftain.

(2) Unlike the organisation of Munda-Dravidian settlement, which exhibits tribal government and a more or less centralised control under the divisional chieftain as well as elected or hereditary clan-chiefs, subsequently utilised as wardens of the outlying regions and connected by feudal ties, the Aryan

settlement partakes of the nature of a group of self-governing village communities bound together by common descent, and paying a share of the Crop (collected at harvest-time on the village threshing-floor) to the local *raja*. The Hindu raja's portions are usually allotted by counting groups of eighty-two, forty-two, or twenty-four villages, a practice which survives in various parts of Northern India. Local clan chiefs with appropriate allotments of territory pay no revenue to the *raja*, but help him in time of war. This system of chiefs in subordination to the king differs from the Western type of monistic feudalism in that they are held together by slenderest bonds, the fiefs being sometimes actually movable and unconnected with ownership of land. The king makes no claim to be owner of the soil; the chiefs exercise a co-ordinate and quasi independent jurisdiction; and both the king and his chiefs are bound together by clan-relationship. This has been the general feature in the purely Aryan settlements, as in Mewar, Oudh, and Orissa. The more evolved form of the Hindu State, or the mere local lordship of the *thakurs* or *rawats, rajas* or *ranas, talukdars* or *zamindars*, adventurous Kshatriyas or scions of noble houses in almost all parts of India, shows this peculiar type of pluralistic feudalism with its landlord estates and village communities on the Aryan clan basis.

(3) The Aryan tribal settlement brings to the fore ethnic distinction by creating two classes of villagers, the original conquerors or settlers or their descendants, and strangers or new settlers, upon whom a fee is levied. Cultivators other than the proprietary body are their tenants, though the manner in which this liability is distributed is different in different parts of the country. This distinction between a privileged and a non-privileged class is now most marked in the Punjab, the United Provinces and Oudh and in the Rajput and Kunbi settlements in Western India. Such a distinction is always associated with conquest or usurption by superior agricultural, clans, castes, and families, or with grants of lands made by rulers, and

is not to be found in settlements and expansions by a gradual peaceful process where there were no superimposed rights, at least as a general rule. Thus develops a distinction between what Bandan-Powell calls a landlord and a *ryotwari* village community.

(4) Though tribal divisions or the territory are equally marked, the Munda-Dravidian system of the allotments of land set apart for the services of the chief of the district, and the elaborately organised system of remuneration of village officers (*servi*), bondsmen, and hired labourers, are absent. Village and district officers, originally appointive, and eventually hereditary, looked after the collection of the king's share in the crop and attested any sale of village lands in the Aryan scheme.

(5) The Aryan clans superimpose upon the agrarian distribution an elaborate kinship and casteorganization according to which rights and duties in the village communities are determined. Lands are subdivided among the various shareholders, at first in large family subdivisions, and these again in smaller shares on inheritance according to Hindu law. The proprietary body at the outset probably held their lands jointly in one or more of the forms in which joint tenure is possible, but subsequently lands were subdivided into definite family shares. The *samudayam* (Sanskrit), implying collective proprietary rights, was universal throughout the Brahman settlement in the Tamil country, and still prevails in many villages in every part of it; the periodical division of the cultivated lands of the village is not entirely forgotten in Tinnevelly, while in Tanjore, Madura, Dindigul, etc., the villager still claims to participate in the common lands, tanks, irrigation channels, threshing-floors, burial-grounds, cattle-stands, etc., or to use them according to the share or parts of a share he holds in the proprietary body.

(6) The local spirits or boundary godlings, clan deities of the forest where the village clearing was made, are gradually superseded by household and village gods as well as ancestral deities, though these latter are

equally important in the Munda socio-religious system. The periodical sacrifices in the village temple, which replace the older communal feasts, serve to knit together the village community, and a close intercourse with strange and impure aboriginal races is avoided, though they are utilised as watch and ward, drummers, sweepers, etc., in the village festivals.

(7) The Aryan village community follows the open-field system each of the equitable subdivisions of the arable allotment being often given an appropriate name from the Epics. It recognises the joint ownership among the proprietary body of the common land, which is available for partition, or for lease on behalf of the community, or is used for grazing, etc. It euqalises rights as regards meadow, waste, or forest. But it recognises much more generously than the Dravidians, the sacred and inalienable rights of families and individual households, independent alike of communal laws and communal economy.

(8) As contrasted with the Dravidian promiscuity, the Indo Aryan family stands forth before the world as free and self-supporting. Gardens or orchards are attached to individual houses, though the common forest which is such a marked feature in the Dravidian village community, is also to be seen.

(9) Finally, the Aryans superimpose an elaborate village-planning, stamped with ethnic distinction in the segregation of caste wards, and with the symbolism of the Puranas in the location of the presiding deities of the village and in the arrangement of village streets, courts, quadrangles, and temples.

CHAPTER - VI

THE IDEAL SOCIAL ORDER

Writing in medieval India on the ideal Muslim social order, as on other aspects of the Islamic revelation, was confined to those educated in Muslim religious sciences. Therefore its approach is academic and doctrinaire. This is no crisis-literature; it does not offer practical answers to contemporary social problems, but rather repeats ideas which entered Hindustan from the outside Muslim world. Any correspondence between the ideal categories of Muslim "social" thought and the actualities of the Indian scene is attributable more to the general similarity of the economic order and class structure of Asian society in the pre-industrial age, whether in Hindustan, Persia, or Iraq, than to actual observation of society in India.

The ideal Muslim social order is essentially a religious order. Society is not a venue for individual self-realization, a contrivance for the satisfaction of human wants; the only kind of human happiness which it should make possible is the happiness which comes from obedience to God. Since obedience to God meant obedience to a revealed Holy Law; the Sharīa, Muslim social ideals envisage a conservative order in which repetition and submission are reckoned more worthy than innovation and enterprise. The good society was the old society—that which existed during the lifetime of the Prophet. The modern American hopes and intends change to be for the better; the medieval Muslim believed it to be for the worse.

As has been seen, for the Muslim, earthly society should be so ordered as to make possible the godly life and the welfare of the students of the godly life, the ulamā and the mystics. Harmony is the keyword; man should be in harmony with God, nature, and his fellows. If he is not in harmony with his fellows, his attention will be diverted from God, for then he will be intent upon self-preservation. But harmony depends upon being in his proper place and a man's proper place is that for which his nature fits him. The ultimate whole within which each individual finds his place is not economic, although economic activity is essential to the welfare of that whole. The ultimate whole is Islamic—the Muslim community defending itself successful against attack from outside, devoting itself to the practice of the True Faith, and providing itself with a livelihood sufficient both to bear the cost of its own defense and to keep its members alive and active in the service of God.

In India (following pre-Muslim Iranian tradition) society is seen as four main classes—men of the pen, men of the sword, men of business, and men of the soil. The first are guardians of religion and learning, the second are the guardians of those guardians, and the third and fourth are the sustainers of the first two classes. Attempts by any member of any class to change from his class can only, it is believed, result in chaos and disorder. Muslim social ideas are essentially hierarchical and organic. But how was each to be sure of his proper class and function? Indo-Muslim thinkers, adapting Greek and Persian ideas, answered that God had decided the problem at the creation. Social harmony between classes of men endowed with different aptitudes is willed by God.

The ideal social classification advocated by Indo-Muslim theorists of the Ulamā class did correspond in large measure to the social stratification, viewed from a Muslim point of observation, in that area of Hindustan under Muslim rule—except that the people of the sword took precedence in practice over the people of the pen and often ignored them. But it was nevertheless very much the theory of a pen-man's utopia which ignored actual social differences in Muslim India—the distinction between Turk and non-Turk in the first century of Muslim rule, between immigrant Muslim and Indian-born Muslim, between hereditary Muslim and converted Muslim, Delhi Muslim and Bengali Muslim, between descendants of Afghan tribes and non-Afghans, between those with light skins and those with dark, between slaves and free men. However, in its picture of a static society in which men performed those duties for which heredity and inherited education had designated them—of soldiers who would not conceive of becoming agriculturists or traders, and of traders who would not think of becoming ulamā or soldiers—the idea was not very far from the actual: a society of small cultivators and traders supporting, with its labour and taxes, a military and learned aristocarcy.

The institution of slavery was important in politcs, administration, and in household economy in medieval India under Muslim rule; it does not figure as an important theme in Indo-Muslim writing on the ideal social order. Turiksh rulers like Qutub ud-dīn Aibak (1206-1210, Iltutmish (1211-1236), and Balban (1266-1287),began their careers as slaves, and slaves from within the sultans' households were often appointed to high administrative and military offices, but no organized system of slave training, promotion and rule, similar to the Janissary system under the Ottoman Turks, existed in medieval India.[1]

Similarly, the status of women in Muslim law and thought did not change with the conquest of Hindustan by Muslims, although, in practice, Hindu customary law was influential among certain groups of Muslim converts from Hinduism.[2]

For statements on the social and political discrimination which, ideally, should be enforced against non-Muslims, reference should be made to Chapter XVII.

THE FOUR-CLASS DIVISION OF SOCIETY

The first reading has been taken from a Persian work on ethics written outside India in the second half of the fifteen century. The work is *Jalālī's Ethics* (*Akhlāq-i-Jalālī),* by Muhammed ibn Asad Jalāl ud-dīn al-Dawwānī (1427-1501). It was popular in Mughal India.

[From Thompson, *Practical Philsophy of the Muhammadan People*, pp. 388-90]

In order to preserve this political equipoise, there is a correspondence to be maintained between the various classes. Like as the equipoise of bodily temperament is effected by intermixture and correspondence of four elements, the equipoise of the political temperament is to be sought for in the correspondence of four classes.

1. *Men of the pen*, such as lawyers, divines, judges, bookmen, statisticins, geometricians, astronomers,

physicians, poets. In these and their and exertions in the use of their delightful pens, the subsistance of the faith and of the world itself is vested and bound up. They occupy the place in politics that water does among the elements. Indeed, to persons of ready understanding, the similarity of knowledge and water is as clear as water itself, and as evident as the sun that makes it so.

2. *Man of the sword*, such as soldires, fighting zelosts, guards of forts and passes etc.; without whose exercise of the impetuous and vindictive sword, no arrangement of the age's interests could be effected; without the havoc of whose tempest-like energies, the materials of corruption, in the shape of rebillious and disaffected persons, could never be dissolved and dissipated. These then occupy the place of fire, their resemblance to it is too plain to require demonstration; no rational person need call in the aid of fire to discover it.

3. *Man of business*, such as merchants, capitalists, and craftsmen, by whom the means of emolument and all other interests are adjusted; and through whom the remotest extrèmes enjoy the advantage and safeguard of each other's most peculiar commodities. The resemblance of these to air—the auxiliary of growth and increase in vegetables—the reviver of spirit in animal life—the medium by the undulation and movement of which all sorts of rare and precious things traverse the hearing to arrive at the hedquarters of human nature—is exceedingly manifest.

4 *Husbandmen*, such as seedsmen, bailiffs, and agriculturists—the superintendents of vegetation and preparers of provender; without whose exertions the continuance of the human kind must be cut short. These are, in fact, the only producers of what had no previous existence; the other classes adding nothing whatever to subsisting products, but only transferring what subsists already from person to person, from place to place, and from form to form. How close these come to the soil and surface of the earth—the point which all the heavenly circles refer—the scope to which all the luminaries of the purer world direct

their rays—the stage on which wonders are displayed—the limit to which mysteries are confined—must be universally apparent.

In like manner then as in the composite organizations the passing of any element beyond its proper measure occasions the loss of equipoise, and is followed by dissolution and ruin, in political coalition, no less, the prevalence of any one class over the other three overturns the adjustment and dissolves the junction. Next attention is to be directed to the condition of the individuals composing them, and the place of every one determined according to his right.

The four-class classfication is found in India in Abū'l Fazl by whom the learned are relegated to the third position.

[From Abū'l Fazl, *Ā'in-i, Akbarī, iv - v*]

The people of the world may be divided into four classes:

1. *Warriors,* who in the political body have the nature of fire. Their flames, directed by undestanding, consume the straw and rubbish of rebellion and strife, but kindle also the lamp of rest in this world of disturbances.
2. *Artificers and merchants,* who hold the place of air. From their labors and travels, God's gifts become universal, and the breeze of contentment nourishes the rose-tree of life.
3. *The learned,* such as the philosopher, the physician, the arithmetician, the geometrician, the astronomer, who resemble water. From their pan and their wisdom, a river rises in the drought of the world, and the garden of the creation receives from their irrigating powers, a peculiar freshness.
4. *Husbandmen and laborers,* who may be compared to earth. By their excertions, the staple of life is brought to perfection, and strength and happiness flow from their work.

It is therefore obligatory for a king to put each of these in its proper place, and by uniting personal ability with due respect for others, to cause the world to flourish.

Social Precedence

The essentially religious color of the medieval Muslim ideal social order is brought out in the following passage, which purports to be an order by the Caliph Ma'mūn establishing social precedence. The passage is from the *Rulings on Temporal Government's*, by Ziā ud-dīn Barnī.

[From Barnī, Fatāwa-yi-Jahāndāri, folios 128a - 129b passim]

It is commanded that the inhabitants of the capital, Baghdad, and the entire population of the Muslim world should hold in the greatest honer and respect all man of the Hāshimite family who are related to the prophet by ties of blood, especially the Abbāsids to whose line the caliphate of the Muslim community has been confirmed, and, in particular the saiyids whose discent from and relationship to the prophet is certain. In all circumstances they should strive to reverence to the honor them and not allow them to be insulted and humiliated. They should consider the rendering of honor and respect to them to be among their religious duties and a way of doing homage to the prophet himself. People should consider the causing of any harm or injury to them as equal to infidelity and unbelief.

In accordance with God's commands a share of the fifth of the spoils of war which accrues to the public treasury, after having been converted to cash, should be delivered to them at their homes for their maintenance. They are to have precedence in seating over all my [the Caliph Ma'mūn's] helpers, supporters, courtiers, and high officers and dignitaries of the realm. In other assemblies and meetings, religious scholars, shaikhs, wazirs, maliks [princes], and the well-known and distinguished people of Baghdad are to sit below them. All classes of the Baghdad population are to pay them due regard and to deem the salvation of Muslims of the classes attainable through paying the relations of the prophet honor and respect.

As regards the Sunni religious scholars and the Sufis of Baghdad, it is commanded that they should be respected in the capital; to do them honor is to be considered a part of piety. It should be throught that the mandates of the Ture Faith are adorned by there words and deeds and the elevation of the banners of Islam is a result of a honor paid to them.

[And Ma'mūn ordered that] in accordance with the instructions of the Chief Qādī and with the records kept by the Shaikh ul-Islām, they should cause religious scholars and Sufis to be given what would be sufficient and salutary for them, and enable them to live in the best of circumstances and to avoid that neediness which makes both knowledge and the learned contemptible.

For the warriors and champions of the faith, he commanded sufficient salaries, allowances and assistance to be given them cash from the public treasury of the Muslims, in accordance with the instructions of the muster master at Baghdad and the ranks and graders named and fixed by the muster master's department. Respect and honor are be paid to holy warriors both in the Caliph's palace and in all Baghdad for they are the protectors of the territory of Islam and of its inhabitants. They fight in the way of God and overthrow the enemies of God and of His prophet.

DIVINE ORIGIN OF THE "DIVISION OF LABOR"

Ideally a man's status in the godly society is related of his innate virtues or vices for which God as creator is responsible. A man's occupation denotes his moral degree in God's sight. The superior social rank of the learned and the literary, implied in the first reading, should be noted.

[From Barnī, *Fatāwa-yi-Jahāndārī*, folios 216b-217b]

All men in creation are equal and in outward form and appearance are also equal. Every distinction of goodness and wickedness which has appeared among mankind has so appeared as a result of their qualities and of their commission of acts. Virtue and vice have been shared out from all eternity and were made the associate of their spirits. The manifestation of human deeds and acts is a created thing. Whenever God obliges good actions and wicked actions, and good and evil. He gives warning of it so that those good and bad deeds, that good and that evil, may be openly manifested, and when, in the very first generation of Adam, the sons of Adam appeared and multiplied, and the world began to be populated, and in their social intercourse the need for everything befell mankind, the Eternal Craftsman imparted to mens' minds the crafts essential to their social intercourse. So in one he implanted writing and penmanship, to another horsemanship, to one the craft of weaving, to another farriery, and to yet another carpentry. All these crafts, honorable and base, from penmanship and horsemanship to cupping and tanning, were implanted in their minds and breasts by virtue of those virtues and vices which, in the very depths of their natures, have become the companions of their spirits. To the hearts of the possessors of the virtues, by reason of their innate virtue, have fallen the noble crafts, and in those under the dominion of vice, by reason of their innate vice, have been implanted the ignoble occupations. Those thus inspired have chosen those very crafts which have been grafted upon their minds and have practiced them, and from them have come those crafts and skills and occupations with which they were inspired; for them the bringing of those crafts into existence was made feasible.

These crafts, noble and ignoble, have become the hidden companions of the sons of the first sons of Adam. In accordance with their quickness of intelligence and perspicacity, their descendants have added to the crafts of their ancestors some fine and desirable features, so that every art, craft, and profession, of whose products mankind has need, has reached perfection.

As virtues were implanted in those who have chosen the nobler occupations, from them alone come forth goodness, kindness, generosity, valor, good deeds, good works, truthfulness, keeping of promises, avoidance of slander, loyalty, purity of vision, justice, equity, recognition of one's duty, gratitude for favours received, and fear of God. These people are said to be noble, freeborn, virtuous, religious, of high lineage, and of pure birth. They alone are worthy of offices and posts in the realm and under the government of the ruler who, in his high position as the supreme governor, is singled out as the leader and the chief of mankind. Thus the government of the ruler and his activities are given strength and put in an orderly condition.

But whenever vices have been inserted into the minds of those who chose the baser arts and the mean occupations, only immodesty, falsehood, miserliness, perfidy, sins, wrongs, lies, evil-speaking, ingratitude, stupidity, injustice, oppression, blindness to one's duty, cant, impudence, bloodthirstiness, rascality, conceit and godlessness appear. They are called lowborn, bazaar people, base mean, worthless, "plebeian," shameless, and of impure birth. Every act which is mingled wityh meanness and founded on ignominy comes very well from them. The promotion of the low and the lowborn brings no advantage in this world, for it is impudent to act against the wisdom of creation.

RULERS TO PRESERVE THE SOCIAL ORDER WILLED BY GOD

[From Barnī, *Fatāwa-yi-Jahāndārī,* folios 58a-58b, 130a]

It is a [religious] duty and necessary for kings whose principal aims are the protection of religion and stability in affairs of government to follow the practices of God Most High in their bestowal of place. Whomsoever God has chosen and honored with excellence, greatness, and ability, in proportion to his merit so should he be singled out and honored by kings. .....He whom God has created with vile qualities and made contemptible in his sin, rascality, and ignorance, who as a sport of the Devil has been brought into existence as a slave of this world and a helpless victim of his lower self, should be treated and lived with according to the way he was created, so that the wisdom of the creation of the Creator may illumine the hearts of all. But if the ruler, out of a natural inclination or base desire, self-will, or lack of wisdom honors such a scoundrel, then the ruler holds God in contempt and treats Him with scorn. For the ruler has honored, in opposition to the wisdom of creation, one whom God has dishonored and treats him as one distinguished and honorable, making him happy out of the bounty of his power and greatness. Such a ruler is not worthy of the caliphate and deputyship of God. To use the name of king for him becomes a crime for he has made the imcomparable bounty of God into an instrument of sin. Opposition to the wisdom of creation hurts him in this world and finally he will be punished in the next world.

. . . . .

Teachers of every kind are to be strictly enjoined not to thrust precious stones down the throats of dogs or to put collars of gold round the necks of pigs and bears—that is, to the mean, the ignoble, the worthless; to shopkeepers and the lowborn they are to teach nothing more than the mandates about prayer, fasting, alms-giving, and the pilgrimage to Mecca, along with some chapters of the Qur'ān and some doctrines of the Faith, without which their religion cannot be correct and valid prayers are not possible. They are to be instructed in nothing more lest it bring honor to their mean souls. They are not to be taught reading and writing, for plenty of disorders arise owing to the skill of the lowborn in knowledge. The disorders into which all the affairs of religion and government are thrown is due to the acts and words of the lowborn, whom they have made skillful. For by means of their skill they become governors, revenue-collectors, accountants, officers, and rulers. If the teachers are disobedient and it is discovered at the time of investigation that they have imparted knowledge or taught letters or writing to the lowborn, inevitably punishment for their disobedience will be meted out of them. [folio 130a]

The next two readings from the Mughal period express a similar point of view to Barnī's. The first work, Muhammad Bāqir Khān's *Admonitions on Government*, was written in 1612-13; the second, though entitled *Institutes of Timūr*, was written abut 1637 by Abū Tālib al-Husainī.

[From Muhammad Bāqir Khān *Mau'iza-yi-Jāhāngīrī*, folio 29-31 *passim*]

Rulers should not permit unworthy people with evil natures to be put on an equality with people with a pure lineage and wisdom and they should consider the maintenance of rank among the fundamental customs and usages of rulership. For, if the differences between classes disappear and the lowest class boast of living on an equality with the "median" class, and the "median" boast of living on an equality with the upper, rulers will lose prestige and complete undermining of the bases of the kingdom will appear. For this reason rulers of former days used not to allow base people of rascally origin and who had been taught writing to understand problems of fulfilling promises and rules of order because, when this habit is perpetuated and they emerge from their professions to take their place among the servants of the government, verily, injury will spread and the life of all classes become disordered.... Consider worthy of education him who has an intrinsically fine nature and avoid educating rascals with an intrinsically bad nature, for every stone does not become a jewel nor all blood fragrant musk. In him who has a vile person, a base nature, and an inner nastiness, there will not be seen either sincerity, capacity for government, or regard for religion—and when the quality of sincerity and of piety, which is the root of intellect, has been removed, every fault which it is possible to have can be expected from him.

[From Abū Tālib al-Husainī, *Tūzuk-i-Tīmūrī*, pp. 158-60]

Fourthly, by advice and institute, I regulated the affairs of my household and by advice and institute I firmly established my authority so that the amirs [nobles] and ministers, soldiers and subjects, could not transgress the just bounds of their ranks and degrees, and each one was the keeper of his own station. [p. 160]

. . . . .

Be it known to Abū Mansūr Tīmūr [on whom be the blessing of Almighty God!] that the organization of the business of this world is paterned on the organization of the business of the next, in which there are public functionaries and officials, deputies and chamberlains, each in his own station performing his own work. They do not overstep their bounds and they await the commands of God. Therefore you must take precautions that your wazirs, soldiers, officials, servants, and officials, each being within the confines of their own stations, await your commands. Keep every class and group within their proper limits so that your dominion may be properly established and ordered. But if you do not keep everything and everybody in their proper place, then chaos and sedition will make their way into your state. Therefore you should watch that everything and everybody remain in their rank and degree. [p. 158]

NOTES AND REFERENCES

1. For an extensive discussion of the status of slaves under Muslim law, see the article, " 'Abd" in the *Encyclopaedia of Islam* (new edition, 1954). No changes in legal doctrine on slavery appear to have occurred in medieval Muslim India; readings from lawbooks used in India have not been given.
2. See the article, " 'Āda" in the *Encyclopaedia of Islam* (1954).

CHAPTER - VII

THE RELIGION AND SOCIAL ORGANIZATION OF THE SIKHS

Sikhism is the religion of some six and a quarter million Indians. The homeland of the Sikhs is the Sutlej valley, the region around Amritsar, Jullundur, and Ludhiana, in the Punjab. Smaller numbers of Sikhs, in service or commerce, are to be found in many other parts of India, especially since the exodus from West Pakistan at the time of partition. The Sikhs are not racially distinct from other Punjabis, from whose main stocks they are drawn.

Sikhism began as one of the many religious movements called forth in northern India by the confrontation of Hinduism and Islam. What has survived of the teaching of its founder, Nānak, is not so vigorous as that of his predecessor Kabīr, nor so original as that of the later Dābu, both of whom founded small sects which survive to this day. But Sikhism revealed a power of growth, religious and political, not possessed by the Kabīr or Dābū-panthīs, so that whereas they are today minor sects, the Sikh community is still politically important. Sikhism has a double interest then, as an example, first, of syncretist religious thought in Nānak's teaching, and second, of the clothing of a spiritual idea in corporate institutions.

The Punjab, when Nānak was born (A.D. 1469), had been for four centuries under Muslim rule and influence. More particularly, from the thirteenth century onward the Sufi orders had been active, firth the Chishti and Suhrawadi, and then the Qadiri and Naqshbandi orders. The teaching and shrines of the Sufi saints alike were venerated—by Hindus as well as by Muslims. The Punjab was also influenced profoundly by the Bhakti movement, that outburst of devotional religion which swept across India, a vigorous Hindu reaction to the shock of persecution and the monotheistic teaching of the Muslim invaders.

Between the two movements, Sufi and Bhakti, for both of which doctrine was unimportant and the personal, emotional relation of the individual to God vital, there was much in common. The three successive exponents in northern India of this new religious approach were a Muslim, Kabīr (1440-1518), a Hindu, Nānak (1469-1538), and a Muslim, Dādu (1544-1603). All three used a common Bhakti vocabulary to preach a message which, under different emphasis, remained at root the same. Indeed the Sikh and Dādūpanthī scriptures incorporate much of Kabīr's teaching and verse. Both Hindus and Muslims were attracted by their preaching, and the popular accounts of Kabīr and Nānak picture Muslims and Hindus claiming the bodies of the dead teachers as theirs to bury and to cherish.

So far did the *rapprochement* go that the orthodox on either side took alarm. At the very moment when, under Aurangzib, orthodox Muslims were acting to restrain the Sufis, orthodox Hindus were denouncing the Sikh gurus for betraying Hinduism. As Dādu cried: "Fierce and terrible have they become, whey they saw I was of neither faction."[1]

NĀNAK AND HIS TEACHING

The founder of Sikhism, Nānak, was a Hindu and a kshatriya. His native village, largely Hindu, had a Muslim zamīndār (landholder), however, and it is said that a Muslim neighbour provided for Nānak's further education after he had finished the schooling given by the village pandit.[2] Nānak married a Hindu girl, who bore him two sons, and possibly a daughter also. Through his brother-in-law's influence he secured a job as storekeeper in the service of Daulat Khān Lodi, the great Afghan governor of the province.

Nānak's early life thus illustrates the interdependence of Muslims and Hindus in the Punjab. The accouts of his life also speak of his early interest in the teachings of wandering ascetics; Muhsin-i-Fānī[3] suggests that Nānak, a Hindu, finally decided to adopt the wandering religious life at the prompting of a Muslim darwish. Leaving the service of Daulat Khān Lodi in early middle age, he abandoned his wife and family, and, accompanied by a Muslim musician, Mardāna, began a period of wandering which traditionally took him all over India, to Ceylon, and even to Mecca and Medina. At intervals he revisited the Punjab where he spent the last ten or fifteen years of his life at Kartarpur, a newly founded "Sikh" village. There he lived with his family as a householder,[4] preaching in the villages and teaching the disciples gathered round him, until his death in 1538.

Nānak was not a systematic theologian, and his thought, drawn from many sources, is not always coherent. But his personal working faith proclaims insistently the majesty and unity of God, the comparative insignificance of prophets or avatārs, the fleeting vanity of worldly life, and the need to approach God in fear and love. God creates, God disposes, but God is gracious. All can approach Him, therefore, in a spirit of service and devotion, without which all formal ritual is worthless.

God, and the worship of God, rather than man's salvation, is at the centre of Nānak's preaching. His Being is beyond men's capacity to know, relate, or understand, shrouded in mystery, "The Unseen, Infinite, Inaccessible, Inapprehensible God."[5] But if there is something here of the Hindu attitude (or the Mu'tazilite), defining God by negatives until God becomes a mere philosophical abstraction, normally Nānak stresses the reality of God, whose power and glory are displayed in His creation. "There is but one God whose name is true, the Creator"[6] Here the influence of Islam is evident and strong. And it is seen again in the vision of God sustaining and disposing by His will. This transcendence and omnipotence are carried indeed to the logical conclusion of orthodox Islam, to predestination and a fatalistic acceptance of God's decree.

But the background of Nānak's thought is Hindu—the metaphors and basic concepts of Hinduism come naturally to him. So, though in his writings as a whole, the vision of God the Creator is dominant, there are also passages about the immanence of God—"He Himself is the Relisher; He Himself is the relish; He Himself is the Enjoyer"[7]—which strike a quite different note. In the same way he accepts the Hindu doctrines of māyā and rebirth, though forcing them into a form which is scarcely reconcilable with Hindu philosophy. Thus the almost autonomous system of karma to which that philosophy consigns men is in Nānak made subject to the will of God.

The round of transmigration becomes a punishment, a hell, to which God may condemn men, but from which, whatever his burden of evil action, God in His grace may save man. "Even if he be drowning in sin, God will still take care of him."[8]

What then is the relationship of men and God? It has already been suggested that for the Muslim "the reason for man's existence on earth, the purpose of his daily life, was submission to and worship of the One God, the Omnipotent." Nānak, when he is thinking of God as omnipotent, likewise urges absolute and joyful submission. He stresses man's weakness, his own consciousness of failure or sin, and his consequent wholeome fear of the Lord.

But he also thinks of God as a loving God—a bestower of unmerited grace:

As a herdsman guardeth and keepeth watch over his cattle,
So God day and night cherisheth and guardeth man and keepeth him in happiness.
O Thou compassionate to the poor, I seek Thy protection; look on me with favour.[9]

In this mood Nānak throws himself upon God's mercy, calling upon Him also to pity all suffering humans.

But Nānak does not conceive of man as merely passive. Man may be misled by māyā—but here māyā is not that pure illusion of Vedantic monism which keeps man from the realization that God alone exists, but something much nearer the Puritans' view of a snare and a delusion. If man chooses the world, the flesh, and the devil, he is to some degree responsible; Nānak contritely recognizes that he has sinned, if only by omission, "I have done no good act."[10] He outlines how responsible men should act in this world so as to "abide pure amid the impurities of the world."[11]

There is no constant belief, however, in human free will, and even where man chooses the good life, he is still utterly dependent upon God's grace. He cannot earn, still less compel the gift of salvation. "God cannot be overcome by other ceremonial acts."[12] Nevertheless, worship and devotion are given as the means of approaching God. He is in fact bounteous, the great giver, but even if He were not, wholehearted devotion would be man's only way.

Man can avoid entanglement in māyā by surrender and devotion to God.

By obeying Him wisdom and understanding enter the mind.
By hearing the Name [God revealed] sorrow and sin are no more.[13]

But God does not reveal Himself directly, nor can man learn to love the Creator unaided. A mediator is needed between the transcended Lord and man. The mediator is the gurn.

With Nānak, who had no human guru of his own, the world is used less of human guides then for God Himself, For the Holi spirit. But his teaching accorded well with the ancient Hindu doctrine of the teacher being all in all for the pupil, with the emphasis on the realationship of pīr and murīd among Sufis, even perhaps with the Shīa doctrine of the Imām. The doctrine of the guru was one destined to grow in importance in Sikhism.

Finally, what of the negative, the puritan, aspect of Nānak's teaching? There is an attack upon whatever sunders man from the One True Name-pride in book learning, pride in fasts and penances, pride in ritual purity or the five prayers daily made. There is an attack upon whatever is set up as a substītute for God, whether it be prophet or avatār. There is an attack upon whatever distracts-wealth, leisure, even family ties. And there is the most relentless attack upon idol worship.

Kabīr had been a trenchant iconoclast: "The beads are of wood the gods of stone, the Jumnā of water Rāma and Krishna are dead. The four Vedas are fictitious stories."[14] Nānak's monotheism is not quite so unqualified. Sometimes he echoes Kabīr, pointing out the inconsistencies in the four Vedas,[15] the false lesson taught in the *Rāmāyana* and *Mahābhārata*.[16] He several times makes the point contained in the lines.

At God's gate there dwelt thousands of Muhammads, thousands of Brahmas, of Vishnus, and of Shivs.
There is one Lord over all spiritual Lords, the Creator, whose name is ture.[17]

But the prophet, or the Hindu Gods, through created, have a reality, and honest worship of them has some value. It is heard to be a good Muslim or Hindu, hard to give alms, fast, or say one's prayers meaningfully, but to be or do so is good. Caste, which he treats as irrelevant, is seen as a source of spiritual pride. In all of these what Nānak deplores is the confusion of outward from for inner purpose. "Thou shalt not go to heaven by lip service, it is by the practice of truth thou shalt be delivered."[18]

NĀNAK

The teachings of Nānak, which have come down in the *Ādi Granth*, are in the form of hymns and of sayings, often short and pithy, which are made more memorable by being in vegorous verse. His verses, like those of all the gurus, are often repetitions, for they represent his perching to many different audiences, and to unlettered villagers at that.

Sikhs hold that the essence of Nānak's teaching is found in the Japji, or morning prayer. From it, the opening invocation, three of the thirty-eight verses, and the conclusion are given below. Here we find Nānak's conception of God, the transcendent Creator, the Disposer of all things; and also his view of man, predestined, sinful, brought to judgment.

[From M.A. Macauliffe, *The Sikh Religion*, I, 195-98, 204, 217]

There is but one God, whose name is true, the Creator, devoid for fear and enmity, immortal, unborn, self-existent; God great and bountiful. Repeat His Name.

The True One was the beginning, the True One was in the primal age,
The True One is now also, O Nānak; the Ture One also shall be.
By His order bodies are produced; His order cannot be described.
By His order souls are infused into them; by His order greatness is obtained.
By His order man are high or low; by His order they obtain preordained pain or pleasure.
By His order some obtain their reward; by His order others must ever wander in transmigration.
All are subject to His order; none his exempt from it.
He who understandeth God's order, O Nānak, is never guilty of egoism. [pp,195-96]

True is the Lord, true is His name; it is uttered with endless love.
People pray and beg, "Give us, give us"; the Giver giveth His gifts;
Than what can we offer Him whereby His court may be seen?
What words shall we utter with our lips, on hearing which He may love us?
At the ambrosial hour of morning meditate on the true Name and God's greatness.
The Kind One will give us a robe of honor, and by His favour we shall reach the gate of salvation.
Nānak, we shall thus know that God is altogether true.
[pp.197-98]

. . .

Numberless are the fools appealingly blind;
Numberless are the thieves and devourers of others' property;
Numberless are those who establish their sovereignty by force;
Numberless the cut-throats and murderers;
Numberless the liars who roam about lying;
Numberless the filthy who enjoy filthy gain;
Numberless the slandered who carry loads of calumny on their heads;
Nanak thus describethe the degraded.
So lowly am I, I cannot even once be a sacrifice unto Thee.
Whatever pleaseth Thee is good.
O Formless One,Thou art ever secure. [p.204]

. . .

Merits and demerits shall be read out in the presence of the Judge.
According to men's acts, some shall be near, and others distant from God.
They who have pondered on the Name and departed after the completion of their toil,
Shall have their countenances made bright, O Nānak; how many shall be emancipated in company with them!
[p.217]

The Guru and the Ungodly
[From Macauliffe, *The Sikh Religion*, I, 228, 272-83, 326-31]

As a fish out of water, so is the infidel—dying of thirst.
If thy breath be drawn in vain, O Man, thou shalt die without God.
O Man, repeat God's name and praises;
But how shalt thou obtain this pleasure without the guru ? It is the guru who uniteth man with God.
Meeting the society of holy men is as a pilgrimage for the holy. [pp. 330-31]

. . .

Man is led astray by the reading of words; ritualists are very proud.
What availeth it to bathe at a place of pilgrimage, if the filth of pride be in the heart ?
Who but the guru can explain that the King and Emperor dwelleth in the heart ?
All men err; it is only the great Creator who erreth not.
He who admonisheth his heart under the guru's instruction shall love the Lord.
Nānak, he whom the incomparable Word hath caused to meet God, shall not forget the True One. [pp.272-73]

. . .

The Hindus have forgotten God, and are going the wrong way.
They worship according to the instruction of Nārad.
They are blind and dumb, the blindest of the blind.
The ignorant fools take stones and worship them.
O Hindus, how shall the stone which itself sinketh carry you across ? [p. 326]

. . .

What power hath caste ? It is the reality that is tested.
Poison may be held in the hand, but man dieth if he eat it.
The sovereignty of the True One is known in every age.
He who obeyeth God's order shall become a noble in His court. [p. 283]

They who have meditated on God as the truest of the true, have done real worship and are contented;
They have refrained from evil, done good deeds, and practiced honesty;
They have lived on a little corn and water, and burst the entanglements of the world.
Thou art the great Bestower; ever Thou givest gifts which increase a quarterfold.
They who have magnified the great God have found Him.

[p. 228]

THE DEVELOPMENT OF SIKHISM AS A DISTINCT RELIGION

Tolerance, a belief that there are many roads to God, is a feature of Hinduism. The Bhakti and Sufi movements both subordinated doctrine to the establishment of a direct communion with God. Akbar attempted an eclectic approach; Dārā Shikōh argued that nothing separated Muslim and Hindu but terminological differences. Kabīr of Dādu called God indifferently Allāh, Rāma, Karīm. For his part Nānak probably sought neither to fuse Islam and Hinduism, nor to found a new religion of his own. He did allow that the Muslim or Hindu who lived up to the best in his creed achieved something—but of incomparably less value than the worship of the True Name. God was within—the externals of Islam or Hinduism could not lead man to Him. On the other hand, as far as the records go, he did little or nothing to organize those whose spirit he had quickened, to prescribe for them a distinctive way of life, or a distinctive form or ritual of worship.

Yet Nānak's personal influence did not die away; Sikhism emerge as a distinct religion. Nānak's personal rejection of the ascetic life, and of his son Sri Chand because he had formed a quietist sect, may have been one factor, along with his stress on living the good life in this world, which contributed to a distinctive Sikh way of life. His unusual decision to appoint a successor, whom he regarded as the guru for his followers, certainly was another, for it made possible the emergence of the Sikhs as a separate body.

The guguships of Nānak's first four successors—Angad (1539-1552), Amar Dās (1552-1574), Rām Dās (1574-1581), and Arjun (1581-1606)—passed in peaceful development. Akbar admired their saintly lives and there was no quarrel with Islam or the State. But each added something to the separate identity of Sikhism.

Angad elaborated a distinctive script, Gurmukhi, based on that of the Punjab moneylenders, in which to write down Nānak's life and teaching. He also made the institution of the *langar*, or free kitchen, more important. Under Amar Dās the self-conscious organisation of Sikhism went further. It may have been in his day that "the active and domestic Sikhs" were set apart from the ascetic Udasis who followed Sri Chand.[19] By thus barring the ascetic, Sikhism acquired a distinctive social character. Amar Dās, by even greater stress upon the *langar*, possibly weakened caste feeling among those who shared the common meal. He certainly provided a common purpose for the Sikhs who contributed to support of the *langar*, as he did when the great step-well (*bawali*) was built at Goindwal, the first Sikh place of pilgrimage. His appointment of three days in the year on which Sikhs should foregather, his provision of specifically Sikh funeral and marriage ceremonies, his discuragement of sati and indulgence in wine all served further to separate the sikhs from their fellow Punjabis, Hindu or Muslim. Moreover there were so many recruits, from both communities, as to require the setting up of some twenty-two *manjas* or circles, each under a pious Sikh, where the Sikhs assembled for worship and whence missionaries were sent out. (This congregational worship is perhaps another Islamic contribution.)

Rām Dās completed the most famous shrince of Sikhism, the *amritsār*, tank of nectar, from which the town takes its name, and began the Golden Temple in its midst. He took the significant step of sending out agents (*masands*) to collect funds for this. His successor, Guru Arjun, was still more active in organizing the circle (*manjas*) and the collection of the tithe levied on the faithful through this agents. Amritsar in his day became a centre for all Sikhs. His greatest contribution, however, was the compilation of the *Ādi Granth* (first book), the official collection of the hymns and saying of Nānak and his successors, together with a very large selection from Kabīr and other Bhaktas and Sufis whose message was consonant with that of Nānak. Sikhism now had its Book, which was to receive the reverence among Sikhs given by Muslims to the Qur'ān. By Arjun's day Sikhism had a distinctive language, scripture, ritual, communal life, and centre. He himself emphasized this fact :

I have broken with the Hindu and the Muslim,
I will not worship with the Hindu, nor like the Muslim go to
Mecca.
I shall serve Him and no other.[20]

This claim, however, conceals the fact the Sikhism was turning more strongly against Islam than Hinduism. Angad and Amar Dās had been zealous Hindus before their conversion, and the writings of Amar Dās, Rām Dās, and Arjun are very Hindu in tone. There were some Muslim but many more Hindu converts. Moreover since the Sikhs were now emerging as an organized community under gurus with great temporal power, there was more likelihood of friction and conflict developing between them and their Muslim rulers. In 1606 Arjun was involved in the unsuccessul rebellion of Prince Khusrau against his father, the Emperor Jahāngīr. Punished with a fine, Arjun refused to pay and was executed. Though Jahāngīr, once secure on his throne, was almost as tolerant in religious matters as his father, Akbar, nevertheless in the eyes of the Sikhs Arjun became a martyr and the Muslims their enemies.

Hargobind (1606-1645) succeeded Arjun at the age of eleven, and obeying his last injunction, assembled a military force about him. There were several clashes with Mughal troops during his guruship, notably in 1628, 1631, and 1634, and conflicts also with the rājas of the Himālayan foohills. The guru had become a military as well as spiritual leader. Later the ninth guru, Teg Bahādur (1664-1675)—who had served with the Mughals in Assam—was called to Aurangzib's court and offered the choice of conversion to Islam or death. He chose martyrdom.

It was his son, Gobind Sing (1675-1708), who completed the final transformation of the Sikhs into a militant community.[21] His father, he said, had died "to protect the frontal marks and the sacred threads of the Hindus."[22] Now he would uproot tyranny from the land. Gobind Singh's life is a record of continuous warfare, largely unsuccessful against the Mughals, more successful against the hill rājas. But if he failed as a soldier, he succeeded as a Sikh. In 1699 he inaugurated the khālsa, the sworn brotherhood of fightings Sikhs. At baptism into the khālsa, Sikhs were given five signs marking them off from Hindu or Muslim—notably the uncut hair and beard—and received the name of Singh. Their joint drinking from one bowl of baptismal nectar cut at caste withing Sikism. Association with Hindu or Muslim was declared sinful. Paradise was promised to those who died in the Sikh cause.

In the fighting with the Mughals Gobind Singh lost all his sons. He provided in two ways for the succession to the guruship, first, by making his obeisance and offering to the *Granth Sahib* (he had added a considerable body of his own writing to the *Ādi Granth*), with the instruction, "Obey the *Granth Sāhib*. It is the visible body of the guru";[23] and second, by making the khālsa likewise an emodiment of the guru : "Wherever there are five Sikhs assembled who abide by the guru's teaching know that I am in the midst of them. Henceforth the guru shall be the khalsa and the khālsa the guru."[24]

In the institutions of the Gobind Singh may be seen the coming together of three distinctive strands in Sikhism, the idea of the guru, of the *Granth Sāhib*, and of the Brotherhood of the Sikhs. Nānak had said, "Through the guru, man obtaineth real life,"[25] and the same stress is laid upon the guruship's importance by the succeeding gurus. This was no more than Kabīr had done, however. What gave the guruship such importance was the practice of the guru choosing his successor, to whom he made an offering and obeisance. That choice was made, in the case of he Angad and Amar Dās, from among the disciples, on the grounds that these two excelled all others in the completeness of their surrender to the guru's will. Rām Dās, the fourth guru, was the son-in-law of Amar Dās, but even so it was stressed that he excelled in submission and humility. Here was emphasized for all Sikhs, the merit of absolute obedience to the guru. There was also developed the theory that the gurus were in fact one spirit, passing from one body to another. Since from Rām Dās the guruship passed by hereditary succession, it was easy for the Sikh to think of the guru as somehow divine. The gurus, notably Gobind Singh, denounced any such idea as sacriligious, but it persisted. Indeed when boys of five or nine (Har Kishan and Gobind Singh) were recognized as spiritual leaders, it is clear that the idea of incarnation had superseded that of the human teacher.

Something of the same process is seen in the Sikh attitude to the *Granth Sāhib*. To the concept of a book were added the overtones associated with Nānak's mystical use of the words *The Name*, or *The Word*, until the book itself became sacred and an object of worship.

The third basic concept was that of the Sikh brotherhood (compare this with the brotherhood of Islam). The union of Sikhs in cooperative efforts—sometimes opposed by Muslims or Hindus—gave a practical sense of corporate life. To this was added a sense of being elect. Rām Dās cursed those who left the community, and promised the faithful sure salvation. "God himself is the protector of the True Guru, and will save all who follow him."[26] The true Sikh was not merely saved himself, he could save others.[27] The fellowship of these saints was likewise given a peculiar sanctity, until Gobind Singh could equate any five of the khālsa gathered together with the guru himself. These ideas, and the practical organization acieved under the gurus, served to preserve Sikhism and the Sikh community in the very difficult years after the death of the last of the gurus.

ANGAD

The Succession to the Guruship

Little from Angad has survived, but these lines from the Coronation Ode by the minstrel Balwand reflect the growing *mystique* of guruship and the importance of obedience as the prime qualification for it. Here "Lahina" refers to Angad (1539-1552).

[From Macauliffe, *The Sikh Religion*, II, 25, 26]

Guru Nānak proclaimed the accession of Lahina as the reward of service.
He had the same light, the same ways; the king merely changed his own body. [p. 25]

The divine umbrella waved over him; he obtained possession of the throne in the place of Guru Nānak....
Lahina obeyed what the guru had ordered him, and earned the reward of his acts. [p. 26]

AMAR DĀS

The third guru, Amar Dās (1552-1574), was a powerful preacher, who to Nānak's teaching added even greater stress upon the guru—the *human* guru—together with a sharper disdain of Brāhmans and those who reject Sikhism.

[From Macauliffe, *The Sikh Religion*, II, 166-67, 221, 238]

They who turn their faces from the true guru, shall find no house or home.
They shall wander from door to door like divorced women of bad character and evil reputation.
Nānak,[27] they who are pardoned through the guru's instruction shall be blended with God. [p. 221]

Let none be proud of his caste.
He who knoweth God is a Brāhman.
O stupid fool, be not proud of thy caste;
From such pride many sins result.
Everybody saith there are four castes,
But they all proceed from God's seed.
The world is all made out of one clay,
But the Potter fashioned it into vessels of many sorts.
The body is formed from the union of five elements;
Let anyone consider if he hath less or more in his composition.
Saith Nānak, the soul is fettered by its acts.
Without meeting the true guru salvation is not obtained.
[p. 238]

If the perverse be admonished, will they ever heed the admonition ?
If the perverse meet the good, these will not associate with them; they are doomed to transmigration.
There are two ways—one the love of God, the other of mammon; the way man treadeth dependeth on God's will.
The believer chasteneth his heart and applieth to it the touchstone of the Word.

It is with his heart he quarreleth, with his heart he struggleth, he is engaged with his heart.
Whoever loveth he true word shall receive what his heart desireth.
He shall ever eat the ambrosia of the Name, and act according to the guru's instruction.
They who quarrel with others, instead of quarreling with their own hearts, waste their lives.
The perverse are ruined by obstinacy and by the practice of falsehood and deception.
He who by the guru's instruction subdueth his heart, shall fix his affection on God.
Nānak, the believer practiceth truth; the perverse suffer transmigration, [pp. 166-67]

RĀM DĀS

Rām Dās (1574-1581), the fourth guru, gave further form to Sikh religion by his teaching and direction of the Sikh community.
[From Macauliffe, *The Sikh Religion*, II, 264]

Let him who calleth himself a Sikh of the true guru, rise early and meditate on God;
Let him exert himself in the early morning, bathe in the tank of nectar,
Repeat God's name under the guru's instruction, and all his sins and transgressions shall be erased.
Let him at sunrise sing the guru's hymns and whether sitting or standing meditate on God's name.
The disciple who at every breath meditateth on God, will please the guru's heart.
The guru communicateth instruction to that disciple of his to whom my lord is merciful.
The slave Nānak prayeth for the dust of the feet of that guru's disciple who himself repeateth God's name and causeth others to do so.

ARJUN

Guru Arjun (1581-1606) wrote a great deal and, unlike the second, third, and fourth gurus, addressed Hindus and Muslims alike.

[From Macauliffe, *The Sikh Religion*, III, 13, 28-29, 64, 311, 422]

I practice not fasting, nor observe the [month of] Ramazan;
I serve Him who will preserve me at the last hour.
The one Lord of the earth is my God,
Who judgeth both Hindus and Muslims.
I go not on a pilgrimage to Mecca, nor worship at Hindu places of pilgrimage.
I serve the one God and no other.
I neither worship as the Hindus, nor pray as the Muslims.
I take the Formless God into my heart, and there make obeisance unto Him.
I am neither a Hindu nor a Muslim.
The soul and the body belong to God whether He be called Allāh or Rām.
Kabīr hath delivered this lecture.
When I meet a true guru or pīr, I recognize my own Master.
[p. 422]

Without the society of the saints, man ever wavering, suffereth great misery :
By love of the one Supreme God the profit of God's essence is earned. [p. 311]

. . . .

To the word and the Name are now added as instruments of salvation bathing in the Amritsar tank, and the *Ādi Granth* compiled by the guru.

By bating in the tank of Rām Dās
All the sins that man commiteth shall be done away,
And he shall become pure by his ablutions.
The perfect Guru hath given us this boon.
When we meditate on the Guru's instructions,
God bestoweth all comfort and happiness,
And causeth the whole cargo to cross over safely,
In the association of the saints uncleanness departeth,
And the supreme Being abideth with us.
Nānak by meditating on the Name
Hath found God the primal Being. [p. 13]

. . . .

Three things have been put into the vessel [the *Ādi Granth*]—
truth, patience, and meditation
The ambrosial name of God, the support of all, hath also been
put therein.
He who eateth and enjoyeth it shall be saved.
This provision should never be abandoned; ever clasp it to
your hearts.
By embracing God's feet we cross the ocean of darkness;
Nānak, everything is an extension of God. [p. 64]

. . . .

O my soul, grasp the shelter of the Supreme and Omnipotent
God.
Repeat the name of God who supporteth the regions of the
earth and the universe.
O saint of God, abandon thine intellectual pride, understand
the will of God, and thou shalt be happy.
Accept the act of God as good : in weal and woe meditate on
Him.
The Creator saveth in a moment millions of fallen ones, and
in this there is no delay.
The Lord is the destroyer of the pain and sorrow of the poor;
He rewardeth whom He pleaseth;
He is mother and father, cherisher of life and soul, and a sea
of comfort for all.
There is no deficiency in the Creator's gifts; He is omnipresent,
and a mine of jewels.
The beggar beggeth Thy name, O Lord; Thou abidest in every
heart.
The slave Nānak hath entered the sanctuary of Him from
whom nobody departeth empty. [pp. 28-29]

GOBIND SINGH

The tenth guru, Gobiṇd Singh (1675-1708), was founder of the khālsa, the sworn brotherhood of fighting Sikhs. His hymns sound a warlike Note.

[From Macauliffe, *The Sikh Religion*, V, 117, 261-62, 286]

May we have the protection of the immortal Being !
May we have the protection of All-steel !
May we have the protection of All-death !
May we have the protection of All-steel ! [pp. 261-62]

. . .

Thou art the Subduer of countries, the Destroyer of the armies of the wicked, in the battle-field Thou greatly adornest the brave.
Thine arm is infrangible, Thy brightness refulgent, Thy radiance and splendor dazzle like the sun.
Thou bestowest happiness on the good, Thou terrifiest the evil, Thou scatterest sinners, I seek Thy protection.
Hail ! hail to the Creator of the world, the Savior of creation, my Cherisher, hail to Thee, O Sword !
[p.286]

Finally, as an example of how far Sikhism had traveled since Guru Nānak's day, here is part of Guru Gobind's instructions on the means of salvation.

Have dealings with every one, but consider yourselves distinct. Your faith and daily duties are distinct from theirs. Bathe every morning before repast. If your bodies endure not cold water then heat it. Ever abstain from tobacco. Remember the one immortal God. Repeat the Rahirās in the evening and the Sohila at bedtime. Receive the baptism and teaching of the guru, and act according to the *Granth Sāhib*. Cling to the boat in which thou hast embarked. Wander not in search of another religion. Repeat the guru's hymns day and night. Marry only into the house of a Sikh. Preserve the wife and thy children from evil company. Covet not money offered for religious purposes. Habitually attend a Sikh temple and eat a little sacred food thereform. [p. 117]

LATER DEVELOPMENTS IN SIKHISM

It is evident that in Gobind Singh's day there were many among the Sikhs who clung to Hindu ways, despite the elaboration of a distinctive pattern for Sikh life by the gurus. The years of Mughal proscription, from the days of Aurangzib's attack upon both Hindus and Sikhs, threw the Sikhs into the arms of the Hindus, to whose civil usages and customs they largely adhered. At the death of Ranjīt, founder of the Sikh kingdom in the Punjab, the Hindu rite of satī was observed. Veneration of the cow, never taught by the gurus, led to rigid prevention of cow slaughter, Malcolm stresses the tremendous strength of caste within Sikhism, ruling absolutely over marriage, but also affecting commensality.

This continued drift away from the teaching of the gurus called forth a series of reform movements. First was that of Dyāl Dās (1783-1855), the *Nirankāris* (the formless), who attacked the worship of idols—even images of the gurus. He also attacked the adoption of Hindu marriage ceremonies and pilgrimage. His son Bhāi Dārā did win back the Sikhs to ceremonial conforming to the scriptures. There was also an antimilitarist element in the movement. The *Nāmdhari* movement of Sāin Sāhib (d. 1862) attacked the introduction of caste distinctions and taboos, satī, and idol worship. Later in the nineteenth century, when Hindu and Christian missionaries were active, the *Singh Sabhā* (or Association) was formed. Its influence was marked in fostering Sikh education, with particular emphasis on the teaching of Gurmukhi and the Scriptures. Missionaries were appointed and the Khālsa Tract Society formed to distribute religious literature.

One unexpected aid to the reformers was provided by the attitude of the British military authorities. Impressed by Sikh fighting capacity and grateful for Sikh aid during the Mutiny, they freely recruited Sikhs into the Indian army. The army insisted, however, on recruiting khālsa Sikhs; an order of the commander-in-chief read, "Every countenance and encouragement is to be given to their comparative freedom from the bigoted prejudices of caste, every means adopted to preserve intact the distinctive characteristics of their race, their peculiar conventions and social customs."

In the twentieth century the most powerful reformist movement was the Akāli, whose greatest achievement was the Sikh Gurdwāras Bill, passed in 1925, which restored to the Sikh community control of the gurdwāras (temples), which had in many cases fallen into the hands of mahants (priests) who were far more Hindu than Sikh but who exercised a hereditary control. With the intensification of the Indian struggle for independence, the Akāli movement took up increasingly the political cause of the community, the latest aspect of which is the demand for a separate Sikh state in East Punjab.[29]

NOTES AND REFERENCES :

1. W.G. Orr, *A Sixteenth-Century Indian Mystic*, p. 63.
2. Ghulām Husayn Khān Tabātabā'i, *Siyar-ul-Mutaak-khirin*, I, 110.
3. Muhsin-i-Fāni, *Dabistān-i-Mazāhib*, II, 247-48.
4. Bhāi Gurdās, *War*, I, 38.
5. M.A. Macauliffe, *The Sikh Religion*, I, 330.
6. *Ibid.*, I, 195.
7. *Ibid.*, I, 265.
8. Macauliffe, *The Sikh Religion*, I, p. 107.
9. *Ibid.*, p. 301.
10. *Ibid.*, p. 178.
11. *Ibid.*, p. 60.
12. *Ibid*, I, 308.
13. *Ibid.*, I, 201.
14. G.H. Westcott, *Kabir and the Kabir Panth*, p. 58.
15. Macauliffe, *The Sikh Religion*, I, 236.
16. *Ibid.*, I, 269.
17. *Ibid*, I, 40-41.
18. Macauliffe, *The Sikh Religion*, I, 39.
19. Sir J. Malcom, *Sketch of the Sikhs*, p. 27. (Nānak, Angad, and Amar Dās were all Married, Family Men.)
20. Cf. Macauliffe, *The Sikh Religion*, III, 422.
21. Not all the Sikhs had Approved of this Conflict with the Mughal Authority, Either in Hargobind's day or in Gobind Singh's.
22. Macauliffe, *The Sikh Religion*, IV, 392.
23. Macauliffe, *The Sikh Religion*, V, 244.
24. *Ibid.*, V. 243-44.
25. *Ibid.*, I, 149.
26. Macauliffe, *The Sikh Religion*, II, 301.
27. "He had saved himself and his family, and he shall save twenty one generations, yea the whole world." *Ibid.*, II, 292.
28. As may be judged from the preceding examples, it was a poetic convention for he poet's name to appear in the last lines. Use of the name of Nānak by later gurus reflects the belief that his spirit spoke through them.
29. For a Full Account of Reform Movements, see Khushwant Singh, *The Sikhs* (London, 1953).

CHAPTER - VIII

PROSPECTS OF AN INTEGRATED APPROACH TO SOCIAL REALITY

I. SCOPE OF THE DISCUSSION:

Ever since Peter Berger and Thomas Luckmann (1971) wrote their famous book *The Social Construction of Reality*, it has become rather difficult to write on 'social reality' with flippant ease. Although the general tendency among social scientists is to commonly use the concept 'social reality' as a term whose meaning is deemed to be known to its users, Berger and Luckmann have made us aware of the deep philosophical and epistemological connotations of the word 'reality' and 'social reality'. The formulation 'social reality' involves intriguing questions in the sociology of knowledge—such as 'what is real'? and how is one to know it? and how best the gap between 'reality' and its conceptual reconstruction in the process of knowing can be narrowed down? Apart from these questions pertaining to 'reality', and 'knowledge' in which a sociologist should be no less interested than his colleagues in social philosophy, the problem of social relativity of 'reality' and the ultimate validity or invalidity of knowledge are equally vexing.

This paper, however, is not an attempt to discuss the meaning of 'social reality' in the framework of the sociology of knowledge. We shall, therefore, by pass the deep philosophical questions without underrating their importance. Here we shall take 'social reality' as given - implying that society is an objective reality, although it may be differently perceived, conceived and interpreted. We assume that it is possible to understand society—its basic structures and dynamics—through procedures of empirical observation and verification as well as through intuitive philosophical reflection. The ways of understanding society are manifold and those who seek to know it may not necessarily agree on the adequacy and utility of a particular mode of understanding. It is with this broad positivist conviction that this paper seeks to examine alternative approaches to the understanding of social reality. Particularly our focus will be on the nature, scope and limitations of the integrated approach. We shall also discuss later the status of theory and the role of social values in the context of our advocacy in favour of an integrated approach to the understanding of social reality.

II. TWO CONCEPTIONS OF SOCIETY:

There are two broad conceptions of society—or of the relationship between man and society. One of these may broadly be called the 'emergent' conception which views society or social order as *sui generis*. Man's interrelationships with his environment, human or otherwise, produce institutions, norms of conduct and all forms of typifications which imply historicity and control. This conception, therefore, treats 'social order' as prior, as something that transcends the individuals who constitute it. The intellectual tradition that subscribes to this emergentist notion of society is often traced to Emile Durkheim's (1964) writings.

The other may be termed as the immanent conception which views 'social order' as basically a human product. It implies that society exists only as a product of human activity. Externalization is a fundamental biological need; and human beings have the necessary biological equipment to realise it. The so-called '*sui generis*' social order is thus reduced to the human individuals who constitute it. Thus, society is conceived as nothing more than summation of its constituents. Both these conceptions are somewhat 'ideal type'polarities that miss the fundamental dialectical nature of relationship between human activity and experience on the one hand and the institutional order that is not only the product of human activity but also an objective reality in its own right. For our purpose then, we may proceed with the following basic premises:

(a) That society as a social reality is a human product;

(b) That it is an objective reality that is independent of its component and one which is amenable to empirical verification and understanding and,

(c) That man is a social product at the same time as society is viewed as a human product (Berger et. al., 1971, pp. 78-79).

The purpose of restating these somewhat hackneyed premises is to highlight the integral nature of man-society relationship, or of the relationship between man, nature and society. The three are only abstractions and conceptualizations drawn from what is an extremely complex, and yet indivisible, set of interconnections. This is not to suggest that the founding fathers of modern social sciences in the late eighteenth and in the nineteenth centuries were grossly unaware of this basically indivisible interrelationship between man, nature and society. Despite the fact that this awareness did often reflect in the writings of social philosophers of the pre-industrial era, attempts to study man, in relation to nature and society got compartmentalized into a host of specialized disciplines. These attempts eventually got institutionalized into independent scientific domains. Even a cursory look at the schemes of classification of 'sciences' in the writings of August Comte, Herbert Spencer down to wilhelm Dilthey and Max Weber would reveal the underlying intellectual justifications for creating separate sciences— with peculiar sets of concepts and methodologies which were meticulously sustained and preserved, though seldom advanced, by their disciples in the present day social sciences.

III. UNITY AND DUALITY OF SCIENCES:

The intention here is not to deny the fundamental duality of sciences—a notion to which we subscribe. At the level of the spirit and ethic of scientific enquiry one could find a basic identity between the 'natural' and 'Humanistic or social' sciences. Philosophical evidence suggests that method in the natural sciences is based on the same kind of cycles of interpretation commonly associated with social sciences (Kuhn, 1970). Empirical observations suggest that natural science investigation is grounded in the same kind of situational logic and marked by the same kind of indexical reasoning which we are used to associate with the symbolic and interactional character of social systems/or social world (Knorr 1977 : 669-96). However, more recently methodological discussions have pointed out the essential inadequacies of the positivistic model for social science methodologies and have highlighted the significant differences in concrete method, analysis and research procedures of social sciences and those of natural sciences (Knorr-Cetina, 1931: 335-36). Therefore, the two realms of sciences had to follow entirely different sets of logic of proof, of verification and bases of generalizations in their development throughout the nineteenth century and thereafter. What is interesting is the fact that the compartmentalization did not stop at the simple binary division between 'natural' and 'social sciences' the process of specialization by disciplines got proliferated not altogether without any purpose or justification. Growth of sociology, psychology, anthropology, comparative religion and politics, economics was mainly in the form of branching off from social philosophy which in its classical formulations had viewed the integral nature of social reality. The development of various specialized social science disciplines was in large measure a response to the nature of transformation wrought about by the industrial capitalism throughout the nineteenth century. Elaborate division of labour based on high degree of specialization characterized the work organization in modern industrial societies.

Advancement in science and technology and their application to productive processes led to atomization and gradual fragmentation of the integral unity of the man-society relationship. Specialization in social sciences, emergence of a number of sub-disciplines, and a somewhat pathological keenness to demarcate boundaries of one science from the other were only manifestations of that fragmentation. The branching off of various specialized social science disciplines and subdisciplines may be viewed as the need of the time and yet it reflects the segmental view of man which this process encouraged. Specialization in modern society thus acts as a double-edged weapon. It ensures high degree of expertise in a sector of learning but at the same time, it creates conditions of self-imposed isolation from other pursuits of learning. The latter typifies the present day social science scene in our academies.

The recent trend, therefore, favours interdisciplinary collaboration and exchange in teaching and research. In India, the University Grants Commission has also laid special emphasis on interdisciplinary activities which will apparently receive fresh impetus in the form of developmental grants in the Sixth Five Year Plan on priority basis. The euphoria apart, the need for integrating efforts of various disciplines—their theory and research can hardly be overemphasized for a proper appraisal of social reality.

IV. INTERDISCIPLINARY EXCHANGE:

The Natural vs. Social Science Experience:

Before examining the scope and potential for an integrated approach in social sciences, it would be quite instructive to acquaint ourselves with the experience of natural sciences. In this area there has been more meaningful interaction among different disciplines over several centuries and their progress has been more orderly and better regulated. This is not to suggest that natural sciences have reached the pinnacle of perfection and have solved all problems and riddles. But, among the natural sciences there is a common trunk, going from mathematics to quantum mechanics, then to physics from there to chemistry, biology and from there even to physiological psychology, we can certainly discover in the main a series of 'decreasing generality' and 'increasing complexity'.

Using these August Comte's classificatory criteria, we can certainly place various natural sciences in a hierarchical order where specialists in one would need collaboration of research workers belonging to the preceding sciences in the order (Piaget, 1973: 9-10).

Thus, we find that a physicist constantly finds mathematics indispensable, and theoretical physics, while lending itself to experimentation, is essentially mathematical in its form as well as in technique and application. Similarly, mathematicians are concerned with physics in that they, by deduction, solve certain problems posed by physics. A chemist cannot go very far without physics and a biologist needs chemistry, physics and mathematics. In all these fields, therefore, interdisciplinary research is becoming imperative for attempting integration of perspectives and for enriching our understanding of the material world. It must, however, be stressed that such integration is facilitated by the nature of things (subject-matter) on the one hand and by a clearly defined hierarchical order of disciplines determined by the principles of decreasing generality and increasing complexity that find wider acceptance in the field of natural sciences. Consequently, a whole range of new sciences such as biophysics,biochemistry, biometry etc. are emerging with their increasing complexity.

In the field of human sciences, interdisciplinary research can result from two separate but interrelated needs. First is the 'need for more information' and the second is the need for common structures or for analytical integration. At the first level an interdisciplinary collaboration poses little or no problems. It involves exchange of information among related disciplines in the hope that it enriches a discipline's own understanding of the phenomena under study. A discipline's boundaries and autonomy in explanatory terms are not eroded by interdisciplinary contacts at the level of information. It may sometimes lead to adoption of common methods by related disciplines which in turn may pave way for a possible integration at the level of analysis or perspectives. The fulfilment of this second need for common structures, or what we have termed as analytical integration, is beset with a number of difficulties. Unlike in the natural sciences, in social sciences there is no linear order of sciences ranged between 'decreasing generality and increasing complexity'. On the contrary, in some of the social sciences there is a marked tendency to reduce explanations of diverse social phenomena to a single perspective peculiar to that science. Sociologists are often accused of reducing everything to sociology and their reductionism is called, in somewhat pejorative terms, as 'sociological imperialism'. Similar tendencies are noticeable, with difference of degrees though, among some economists, political scientists, linguists, psychologists and so on. In our opinion, the challenges posed by reduction particularly in social sciences to some extent explain the growing interdisciplinary trend that is receiving a continual impetus today. Consequently, like in the natural sciences, even in the field of social sciences a whole range of new specialization is growing and we have 'political sociology' and 'economic anthropology' (Godelier, 1977) and the like. These are paying way for an integrated approach in the field of social sciences.

Implicit in our argument is integration of perspectives *i.e.* analytical integration, which is possible by synthesizing theoretical formulations and empirical findings produced across social science disciplines. This is possible by, what Piaget (1973 :

11) has called, 'reciprocal' assimilation by partial reduction of the 'higher', but also by enrichment of the 'lower' by the 'higher'. Going over the bounds of one's own discipline at analytical level implies a synthesis of perspectives, and an assimilation of scientific explanations. Such convergence is warranted more by the nature of social facts or social phenomena that social scientists deal with. For such a convergence, social scientists must begin by comparing their problems first; if there is convergence of certain general problems, then they must see whether the two sets of problems and social realities they deal with have connections with other areas that are dealt with by other disciplines; and finally to solve those problems, they must examine whether it is necessary to take recourse to any seminal ideas which actually rest on common machanisms, or on integrated synthesized analytical scheme.

V. STATUS OF THEORY IN INTEGRATED APPROACH:

Fortunately, logic and structure of certain social theories and perspectives are conducive to such an integration. But neither their explanatory powers have been fully tapped nor are their adaptive and innovative potentialities sufficiently revealed so far. Reference may be made here to the Marxian general theory of history, particularly 'dialectical materialism', Talcott Parson theory of social systems (1970 : 3-23) and action frame of reference, (1977: 43-51, 731-57), and also to more recent advances made in structuralism. This is only by way of illustration and not an exhaustive list of perspectives which we consider as inherently facilitating synthesis. Functionalism and structural-functionalism in Anthropology too had this potential for synthesis. However, in the heydays of functionalism 'structure' was used more as a static concept. Consequently, complex social processes tended to be reduced to simple mechanistio formula mostly derived from anologies and isomorphism with biological systems. Later, and at a higher level of abstraction, in the systemic analytical framework this narrowness was overcome character and 'change' was seen as the result of 'structural differentiation'. These developments paved way for some dialogue between the adherents of the dialectical theoretical tradition and those of the systemic theoretical tradition. Such attempts to synthesize these two or more approaches for theoretic assimilation could be mentioned as one of the striking features of the European intellectual tradition today. Qualitative differences in their emphases still persist. For example, the systems approach continues to focus on functional equilibrium as 'homeostasis' whereas the dialecticians treat it as 'homeorhesis' or dialectical equilibrium as the essence of the process of structural transformation (Ball, 1979 : 785-96). Althusserian attempts to combine structuralist and Marxist perspectives are points in this direction of synthesis and assimilation at the theoretic level (Althusser et. al., 1970 Rex 1974) Alan Tournaine's (1977) recent work may also be cited as an important landmark in this context.

In India, so far such an integration or theoretical synthesis is not in sight. Few social scientists demonstrate even awareness of theory and those who recognise the relevance of theory for any systematic understanding of social phenomena are still fewer. Even where theory is taken seriously, as is the case of sociology in India, to confine to my own discipline alone, the systemic theoretic exercises have been made by Yogendra Singh (1973) (1978), Y.B. Damle (1965 : 32-52; 1967: 250-81) and others, whereas Marxian dialectical analyses have grown somewhat independently (*e.g.*A.R. Desai, 1948; 1969) of the former. Even rudimentary efforts inthe direction of synthesis are lacking in India.

Basically all the theories only represent different alternatives of appraising social reality. But, Ramkrishna Mukherjee notes some striking features of theoretical orientations in sociology. First, that these theoretical alternatives have a deductive-positivist base and that 'there is no objective basis from which to infer their relative powers of explanation and prediction vis-a-vis the contextual reality'. Instead it is left to the subjective judgements of the proponents of the various theoretical alternatives. Therefore, although theories are mutually distinct, they in effect express both 'fact' and 'values'. Secondly, this undoubtedly influences the cause and effect ordering of acts in various theoretical alternatives. The ideological loads and differences among sociologists thus lead them to promote one or another alternative appraisal of social reality — (Mukherjee, 1977 : 123-32) — an appraisal which is based on 'a subjective but critically impartial evaluation that in the ultimate analysis is dictated by meta-academic dictates'(Mukherjee, 1977 : 33-34). As a reaction to this situation, Mukherjee prefers to come out of a vicious-circle of an ideologically loaded deductive positivism and advocates what he calls an inductive - inferential approach to social reality. Two points could be raised on Mukherjee's proposed approach. First, he presumes that inductive sociological exercises will *not* demonstrate oppositional value preferences as deductivepositivist alternatives do. Secondly, what kind of theoretical break-through induction will achieve ? Mukherjee confesses that in the immediate future inductive-inferential approach will not achieve such a break through (*ibid.* : 135). But, the precise contribution such an approach is likely to make either to development of a new theory or integration of existing theories is not precisely spelled out by Mukherjee. In the absence of these, his views practically border on nihilism or an anti-theoretical position or both.

At the level of theory, to what model of theory should protagonists of integrated approach subscribe? Here, monistic and pluralistic theoretical models provide us with two clear alternatives. Seen in the true spirit of integration the monistic theory model looks incompatible with the tasks of synthesis and assimilation which face social scientists today. Such theories are possible only where scientists have succeeded in establishing causal explanations that facilitate predictions and control. The credit for having achieved these is often given to natural sciences but even there skepticism over the tenability of 'causal explanation is growing.' In our opinion the nature as well as objectives of 'social causation' is basically different from causation in natural sciences. The goal of social science inquiry could at best be 'understanding' (implying Max Weber's exegesis-interpretation) or 'trend analysis' and not 'prediction' (Kaplan, 1964:346-56). The nature of scientific explanation, and therefore of theory, in humanistic sciences is 'stochastic' or 'probabilistic'. Various alternative explanations of social phenomena are possible. This leads us to a theoretical pluralist position. However, the tasks involved in integrated approach must not remain confined only to recognizing the plurality of social forces that operate; they must also include evaluation of the relative importance of those social forces. An attempt must necessarily be made to indicate which of the interpretations is more tenable and which social forces prove to be more decisive over a period of time. Social scientists have to tackle problems of analysis at the 'synchronic' and diachronic levels. Real success of integrated approach would like in explaining social reality at both the levels. Moreover, theoretical pluralism implies relativism which means that there need not be *the* theory, or *the* explanation for all time to come. What is relatively a more important and determining force at a particular phase in societal development may not remain so in time and space.

VI. THREE ORIENTATIONS IN INTEGRATED APPROACH:

All those social scientists interested in studying social reality in an integrated and interdisciplinary perspective may have three possible alternative types of orientations, viz., cognitive, affective and conative. Conventionally, cognitive orientation has been considered not only necessary but also desirable as an integral part of any scientific pursuit. The cognitive orientation itself operates at two levels. At one level it manifests in description of the phenomenon which is being observed in terms of the concepts commonly used by diverse social science disciplines. Here, similarities and differences in the conceptual connotations familiar in respective social science fields must be carefully sorted out first. This will ensure multifaceted descriptions that are mutually complementary and reinforcing. At the other level, the cognitive orientation manifests in explanatory exercises. Scientific explanation is an attempt to answer questions 'why' and under what conditions the phenomenon occurs and with what consequences Gore (1976 : 9-10). Most of the social sciences in the Anglo-American intellectual tradition have laid emphasis on both these aspects of the cognitive orientation.

The other two orientations—affective and conative—have so far been considered as inappropriate for 'pure' scientists. The canons of positivism, objectivity and, more particularly, of value-reeness discourages social scientists from adopting affective or even conative orientation towards social realities. These orientations involve emotional or affective involvement of a scientist and his will or desire that would ultimately reflect in social action. The controversy over 'value-free' and 'value-based' social science is age-old and yet an unresolved one.

But, there has been a marked shift in favour of the latter in more recent years (*e.g.* see Mullick : 1979). The role of value judgements in (a) the selection of problems, (b) the determination of the contents of conclusion, (c) the identification of facts and in (d) the interpretation and assessment of evidence is most vital. As Ernest Nagel has put it : 'social scientist selects what is the socially important values; and he attributes' cultural significance 'so that value-orientation is inherent in his choice of material for investigation' (Nagel : 1961 : 1-14). Thus although Max Weber was a vigorous proponent of "value-free social science", his contention nevertheless was that the concept of culture itself is a value-concept and an empirical reality becomes 'culture' to us as we relate it to value-ideas. Thus, we cannot, and must not, discover what is meaningful to us by means of a 'presuppositionless' excursion in empirical data. Orthodox social scientists, however, continue to cling to 'value neutrality' as the essence of science. To them affective orientation is by its very nature non-objective and conative orientation presupposes certain prescriptive, normative concerns or 'end-states' in terms of which existing reality is sought to be evaluated, modified, and changed if necessary. Unfortunately, most of social scientists today choose to accept the role of self-appointed guardians of objectivity and prefer to talk of 'social change' as if it is value free.

Social scientists operating within an integrated frame have then two options. They may choose to refrain from prescriptive and 'end-state directed activities' and thus confine themselves to purely cognitive-type of scientific studies whether descriptive or explanatory or both. Implicit in this position is an assumption that complete objectivity and value-freeness are possible. In such an ideally detached frame of analysis researchers function purely as technocrats and do not wish to, or pretend not to be committing to any set of value preferences. Alternatively, social scientists can opt for a committed science in which research pursuits have social relevance and are anchored in certain end-states—whether directly or indirectly. Social reality would not only be understood but sought to be modified or changed in relation to value preferences. An interdisciplinary research team must be homogeneous in terms of its orientation. A team with some members trying to remain 'aloof and detached' and others with avowed commitment will not be a viable one because its members are likely to engage themselves in activities that pull them apart and can function at cross purposes.

Our own preference is for a social science that is committed and is socially relevant (Dhanagare 1980 : 25-26). This choice is dictated by two considerations. First, that any absolute 'valueneutrality' is not possible except in the form of pure and simple abstraction or mental construct. That 'valuefreeness' borders on 'valluelessness'. Often value-choices tacitly influence scientific endeavours and still claims to 'scientific objectivity' are voiced most vociferously. This is far more dangerously misleading because in that case value-loads operate at the unconscious level under the facade of scientific objectivity. Therefore, the best course for social scientists is to make their value-preferences explicit, whatever they may be, and then try to conform to rigours of scientific objectivity. In fact, 'to be aware of ones own valuepreferences itself is a step towards scientific objectivity (Srinivas, 1970 : 4-5). Secondly, in the methodology of social sciences, that is styled mostly on the model of natural sciences, unfortunately 'value-preference' and 'scientific objectivity' are pitted against each other as mutually incompatible polarities. At least in Weber's writings value freeness of social science did not 'presuppositionless' investigation of social reality (Weber, 1949, 1-47) as it tends to be accepted in the present-day empirical sociology. Within the framework of ones accepted values and desired end-states it should still be possible for a social scientist to maintain the standards of objectivity, avoid distortion and examine and present facts in a manner that is replicable so that inter-subjective verifiability could be possible. Our position is that it is possible to distinguish between 'fact' and 'value' and to identify value-bias whenever it occurs in social inquiry. When we take this position we are aware of the tension inherent between the positivists and the intuitionist camps. This tension is apparent even in Weber's famous notion of 'understanding' or *Verstehen* itself. It raises some far reaching philosophical issues into which we need not go. According to Weber, 'action' covers all behaviour to which a subjective meaning is attached by the agents, and social action covers all action that takes account of the behaviour or others by virtue of the subjective meaning attached to it by the agents. Some interpreters of Weber have taken this sense of *Ver-*

stehen to entail an intuitionist position. But this is not so. Weber is emphatic that even the most self-evident interpretation requires to be validated by reference to concrete empirical evidence. Verification of subjective meaning or interpretation, as in case of all hypotheses is indispensable. To that extent Weber never compromised with the basic tenets of positivism, but nevertheless he always believed that 'some form both of 'internal' comprehension and of 'external' confirmation are necessary to justify any sociological explanation (Runcilman, 1974: 11-13). Likewise, when we argue in favour of a value based understanding of social reality we do believe that the test of empirical demonstration and verification within the methodological canon of objectivity is still inescapable for the committed social science inquiry also.

Let me illustrate how this is possible. If a social scientist is associated with a particular action-oriented agency that is working for the welfare of the weaker sections, he or she would naturally be looking for the sources of the 'weakness' of those sections. In searching these sources he or she may find that the bulk of the weaker-sections are engaged in agriculture labour and that their miseries could be attributed to a large measure to their exploitation by the landowning classes. If, however, in course of his/her enquiries it is discovered that actually over the years landowners had increased agricultural wages, either voluntarily or in response to the dispensations of the Minimum Wage Act etc., then it is not necessary at all to suppress that fact. In fact, this will not do any harm to the researchers value-preferences and desired end-states. A comparative picture of the increase in agricultural wages on the one hand and profits earned by landowners on the other could be constructed by a further probe. Similarly, prices of essential goods could be investigated to highlight 'real wages' and purchasing power. One can still pursue the 'exploitation' thesis without suppressing facts of wage-hikes and benefits accruing to the weaker sections as a result of land-redistribution measures by the state. One must, however, follow a methodology of analysis and interpretation that will yield similar results when others try it with the set of facts presented.

In our view, suppression and distortion of basic facts are most injurious to one's own values and to that extent they weaken the cause or the efforts in the direction of the desired end-states, Within the matrix of value-commitments, a certain objective methodology could be followed without any wavering on ones ultimate value-choices. For social scientists, therefore, 'ends and means'question is of vital importance. Neither is to be subordinated to the other. So far, efforts were aimed at pursuing one at the expense of the other. Our submission is that it is possible to blend these two together. This will also end the ivory towerisolation of which social sciences are often held guilty and will render them as socially relevant and serviceable. One of the reasons why contribution of social scientists to social change in India is dismally poor is that they are preoccupied with spinning 'theories of action' rather than 'for action'. Consequently, a philosophical theory of social reality seldom gets translated into the process of social transformation, for which political demagogues and academicians both spare no platitudes.

NOTES AND REFERENCES

Althusser, L. and E. Balibar, 1970
Reading Capital (Translated by Ben Brewster) New York : Pantheon Books, pp. 13-24.

Ball, Richard A., 1979
'The Dialectical Method : Its Application to Social Theory', *Social Forces*, 57 (3) March 1979, pp. 785-98.

Berger, Peter L. and T. Luckmann, 1971
The Social Construction of Reality - A Treatise in the Sociology of Knowledge, Harmondsworth: Penguin Books.

Damle, Y.B., 1965
'For a Theory of Indian Sociology', in *Sociology in India* (Report of a Seminar, 15-20) December 1964 (), Agra University Institute of Social Sciences.

'..........',1967
'The School and College as a Social System', in M.S. Gore et. al. (eds.) *Papers in Sociology of Education in India*, New Delhi, NCERT, pp. 250-81.

Desai, A.R., 1948
Social Background of Indian Nationalism, Bombay: Oxford University Press.

'........', 1969
'Introduction to Rural Sociology in India', in A.R. Desai (ed.) *Rural Sociology in India*, Bombay : Popular Prakashan, Pp. 1-99.

Dhanagare, D.N., 1980
'Search for Identity' *Seminar* (Special Number on Studying Our Society), No. 254 (October) pp. 23-26.

Durkheim, E., 1964
The Rules of Sociological Method, (8th ed. Translated by S.A. Solovay & J.H. Mueller, and ed. by George E.G. Catlin) London: The Free Press (Paper-back).

Godelier, M., 1976
Perspectives in Marxist Anthropology, Cambridge University Press (Paper-back).

Gore, M.S., 1976
'Inaugural address', in Indian Institute of Advanced Study, Simla; *Social Sciences and Social Realities*, Simla, pp. 9-13.

Kaplan, A., 1964
The Conduct of Inquiry: Methodology for Behavioural Science, San Francisco : Chandler Pub. Co.

Knorr, K., 1977
'Producing and Reproducing Knowledge : Descriptive or Constructive ?' *Social Sciences Information*, Vol.16, pp.669-96.

Knorr-Centina, K.D., 1981
'Social and scientific Method or What Do We Make of the Distinction Between the Natural and the Social Sciences ?' *Philosophy of the Social Sciences*, Vol. 11, pp. 335-59.

Kuhn, T., 1970
The Structure of Scientific Revolution, Chicago.

Mukherjee, R., 1977
Trends in Indian Sociology (Reprinted from *Current Sociology, Vol. 25, No.3*). London : Sage Publications.

Mullick M. (ed.), 1979
Social Enquiry : Goals and Approaches, Delhi : Manohar.

Nagel, E., 1961
Structure of Science — Problems in the Logic of Scientific Explanation, New York : Harward Bruce & World Inc.

Parsons, T., 1970
The Social System, London : Routledge & Kegan Paul (Paperback).

'............', 1974
The Structure of Social Action, Delhi : Amerind Publishing (Indian Edition).

Piaget, Jean, 1973
Main Trends in Inter-Disciplinary Research, (Main Trends in the Social Sciences — Series 5), London; George Allen & Unwin Ltd.

Rex, John (ed.), 1974
Approaches to Sociology : An Introduction to Major Trends in British Sociology, London: Routledge & Kegan Paul.

Runciman, W.G., 1974
Social Science and Political Theory (2nd Edition), Cambridge University Press.

Singh, Y., 1973
Modernization of India Tradition, Delhi: Thomson Press (India) Ltd.

Srinivas, M.N., 1962
Caste in Modern India and Other Essays, Bombay : Asia Publishing House.

'.........', 1970
'Sociology and Sociologists in India Today' (Presidential Address Ninth All India Sociological Conference, Delhi) *Sociological Bulletin*, XIX(1), pp. 1-10.

Touraine, A., 1977
The Self-Production of Society (Translated by D. Coltman), Chicago : University of Chicago Press.

Weber, Max, 1949
The Methodology of the Social Sciences, New York : The Free Press.

—*D.N. DHANAGARE*

CHAPTER - IX

RELIGION AND ITS IMPACT ON INDIAN SOCIETY

A search for right perspective on religion has been one of the major problems confronting India and the world. This paper aims at an examination and understanding of the growth and evolution of Annie Besant's concept of religion and studying its impact on the Indian society during the crucial period in the Indian History in the late ninteenth and the early twentieth century.

I

Due to impact of industrial revolution in the late 19th and early 20th century India in common with many other nations was faced with the problem of adopting and adjusting the ancient heritage to a set of new rapidly altering social condition brought about by the immense technological changes.[1]

The special characteristics of 19th and 20th century social reform movement was that, that much of it originated from secular motives based on rationalistic critiques of society which lead to secular as well as religious movements of social reform.[2]

History is an integral part of social consciousness. Every individual and group inherit history as constructed and disseminated by society. The presence of history and social consciousness enables its appropriation by those who are sensative to its force. Therefore appropriation of history is a common occurence in any society particularly by social and political movements. Indian society is no exception to this. Rewriting and reconstructing the history of a society is a continuing process.[3]

Colonial domination induced some scholars to inquire into the social formation. Efforts made by European and the Indian scholars mainly emphasis on theorising of Eurocentric ideologies.

There is no denying that while western world started realising the drawbacks of their material existance and started examining religious and social aspects of human existance, India started looking seriously towards the western ideas to bring about social change and modernization.[4]

The contemporary social reformers considered the prevailing social evils in the Indian society to be the root cause of the Indian religion.[5] They held the hyponotic control over society of corrupt Brahmins as the cause of India's down fall. Indian society as it existed during the period was considered to be a race degenerated, paralysed in all their energies.[6]

The Hindu civilization based on the ancient Aryan institutions was heading for a doom.[7] It was realised that Christian missionaries had brought much social wisdom to India.[8]

2

Annie Besant was born in victoria England to a secptical London doctor and a very religious Irish mother. She was no doubt physically English emotionally and ideologically Irish, but culturally and spiritually Indian. Young Annie, appears to me, devoted to the christ as Meera was to Lord Krishna.

Passionate love of religion made her wish to die a martyr for truth as Jesus Christ did. Her marriage at the age of twenty to an orthodox christian priest was due mainly to her love of religion.

But when her infant girl fell seriously ill with whooping cough and watching her suffering child in agony and finding no answer to her anguished prayers, she began to question the ways of Providence. Her faith in God was snapped and she became an agnostic like the Buddha.

This led to her leaving the church and to her being expelled from her home, and even to her being deprived of the custody of her too little children. This was the price which she had to pay to assert the integrity of her soul. She wrote.

> "I went out into the darkness alone, not because religion was too good for me, but because it was not good enough; it was too meagre, too commonplace,

> too little exacting, too bound up with earthly interests, too calculating in its accommodations to social conventionalities".

Forsaken and forelone, her love for them everflowed as love for every child, for everyone who was weak and helpless, for even animals, birds, trees and plants. Having lost her faith in a beneficent diety, she sought man's salvation from himself.

Annie Besant saw her three dearest one's die. Two in her tender age when she was just 5 years old her father and her little brother, and now her dearest mother, who was a friend, philosopher and guide to her and with whose apron string she wanted to be tied for ever.

But she was a warrior soul. She studied at the British Musium, wrote articles, lectured and became a close associate of charles Bradlaugh, the formost freethinker of those times. In her search for truth she became closely associated with Fabian socialism led by Bernard Shaw.

Inspite of the way she sought to forget herself in work for others, she always felt a certain spiritual emptiness. She had written extensively on agnosticism and socialism. Now she carried out thorough research on spiritualism, hypnotism and various other fields in order to find solutions to the mystery of life and death in her quest for understanding the nature of Ultimate Reality.

It was in this state of mind when she was asked to review the too bulky volumes of Madame H.P.Balavatsky's 'The Secret Doctrine'.

She later wrote.

'Home I carried my burden and sat me down to read. As I turned over page after page the interest became absorbing; but how familiar it seemed; how my mind leapt forward to presage the conclusion; how natural it was, how coherent, how subtle, and yet how intelligible. I was dazzed, blinded by the light in which disjointed facts were seen as parts of a mighty whole, and my puzzles, riddles, problems, seemed to disappear. The effect was partielly illusory in one sense, in that they all had to be slowly unravelled later, the brain gradually assimilating that which the swift intuition had grasped as a truth. But the light had been seen and in that flash of illumination I knew that the weary search was over and the very Truth was found.'

What brought Annie Besant to India? Why she read profusedly of the Veda, the Upanishads, the Puranas, the Gita and all the religions and phelosophies of India? Why and how did she so meticulously write commentries and translated so clearly on the Indian religions? All this should give us clues to the growth and evolutions of her concept of religion and society.

3

Let us take some illustrations from her Volumious Writings, on our topic.

1. I should define Religion as that inner urge that we find in the human being to realise that life which is the life of God in man, the God within the man, cramped, cabined by his material surroundings, reaching out, as it were, to the God outside him, Universally enveloping him as well as entering him, Called often in Philosophy, God immanent in the first cause, Transcendent in the second case.[10]
2. Modern Life is becoming petty because we are not strong enough to reverence. Modern Life is becoming base, sordid, and vulgar, because men fear that they will sink if they bow their heads to that which is greater then they are themselves.[11]
3. To know Him everywhere is the true wisdom;
   To Love Him everywhere is the true desire;
   To Serve him everywhere is the true action.[12]
4. Brotherhood means holding everything for all, so that others may share in what we have, and rise to where we are today. It means sharing all willingly, not by compulsion of Law, but by the most imperious compulsion of the spirit within, which knows the unity of all.[13]
5. I plead for Social Reconstruction on the basis of the family, and that is that the weaknest shall be most cared for, that the baby shall have the least toil and the most amusement. It was put into a splendid sentence by a French Socialist:

   "From every man according to his ability; to every man according to his needs".

That is the true rule of human society.[14] •

6. A great word was spoken by the Christ.
   "Let him that is the greatest among you be as your servant".

Such preaching of the Law of Brotherhood means social justice.[15]

7. Important as economies may be and are, behind economics lies men and women and unless those men and women are trained into a noble humanity, economic schemes will fail as hopelessly as any political schemes can possibly do.[16]
8. I suggest that the moral training which should make men and women understand that growing knowledge and power is duty, is one of the most vital lessons for these modern days.[17]
9. We must change our estimate of the relative value of things, and substitute intellectual and spiritual wealth for material riches as a standard of social consideration.[18]

4

On Annie Besant, it appears, fell the responsibility of giving right orientation and necessary strength and stability to its degenerating society. On her arrival in India in 1893 Annie Besant made up her mind to rouse self-respect of Indians:—

To a people imprisoned in alien ideals and bewiched by western standards and modes of life, to awake them from dungens of their own musings and imaginations and inferiority complex.

The Adyar headquarters over which she presided was the centre of cultural activity which had led to a wider appreciation of India's ancient culture. It also worked for peace in the broadest sense of world by studying the essential features of the great religions of the world.

Thus she not only made a scientific study of the Indian religions but also paved the way for the world religion. Through her service to India and revival of its culture she worked through out her life to bring about a healthy social change in India.

Annie Besant reply to the glowing tributes at the Queen's Hall, London, on the occasion of her golden jubilee of public work further explains her concept of religion when she said that there was no joy like the joy of sacrifice for a great cause. She believed all men and women were simply carrying out the will of the creator. She made the point from a discussion with his socialist friend:—

> "Herbert, I wonder why on earth we go on doing this," and his answer was: "We can't help it".

And in that there was a great truth, for the God, she added who unfolds within us pushes us onwards even when our eyes are blinded to His Glory. She concluded by saying:-

And - if I may finish with words which I believe to be intensely true, and that are so often left only half said— when Kipling spoke about the East and the West and "never the twain shall meet," he went on to say:—

> "But there is neither East nor West,
> Border, nor Breed nor Birth,
> When two strong men stand face to face.
> Though they come from the ends of the earth."

And that is true, whether they be from Britain or form India. Whether it be from one side of the world or the other, there is only one Life, and we are one in Him, and we shall bring the outer lands together because the Inner Life is ever one.

5

I would like to conclude that inspite of the fact that the great scientific inventions had liberated the mankind from servitude to nature, people seemed to suffer from a type of neurosis from cultural disintegration. Science had relieved individuals of grinding poverty, mitigated the tortures of physical pain, yet they suffered from an inward loniliness. All growth was marked by pain. All transition belonged to the realm of tragedy. The transition that they had to effect, to survive, was a moral and spiritual revolution.

The enemy to fight was not capitalism or communism. It was folly, spiritual blindness, love of power and lust for domination.

NOTES AND REFERENCES

1. Works of Arnold Toynbee, Radha Krishnan and A.L.Basham have been referred for developing basic understanding on the topic.

2. *Ibid.*
3. K.N. Pannikkar, Appropriation of History and Historian's Role, Presidential Address, South Indian History Congress, March 1-3, 1991, Calicut.
4. Raj Kumar, Theosophy and Social Change in India, Sansthan.
5. M.G.Ranade and Iswar Chandra Vidyasagar quoted, *Ibid.*
6. K.T. Telang, *Ibid.*
7. The Indian Social Reformer, 8 March, 1903.
8. Freid B. Fishes, India's Silent Revolution, P.85
9. Section Two of this paper has mainly been developed from Annie Besant's Autobiography and other biographies besides my book on Annie Besant's Rise to Power in Indian Politics 1914-1917, New Delhi, 1989.
10. Annie Besant, The Religion of the New Civilisation.
11. Annie Besant, The Spiritual Life.
12. Annie Besant, Esoteric Christianity.
13. Annie Besant, Evolution of Man's Destiny.
14. Annie Besant, The Problems of Reconstruction.
15. Annie Besant, *Ibid.*
16. Annie Besant, The future of Socialism.
17. Annie Besant, *Ibid.*
18. Annie Besant, Some Problems of Life.
19. The Fourth Section is based upon my study of:
    a) Annie Besant, Four Great Religion, Adyar, 1978 (Reprint)
    b) Annie Besant, The Indian Ideals, Adyar, Madras, 1965.
    c) A Woman World Honoured.
    d) Annie Besant, Hints on the Study of the Bhagavad Gita, Adyar, 1973 (Reprint).
    e) Annie Besant, The Wisdom of the Upanishads, Adyar, 1974 (Reprint).
    f) Annie Besant, Theosophy, Adyar, 1961 (Reprint).

—DR. RAJ KUMAR, ICHR

CHAPTER - X

BESANT ON SOCIAL REFORM

Last December Mrs. Besant appeared in the new role of the Social Reformer. In her lectures on "Ancient Ideals in Modern Life" she discusses some of the most important questions of Hindu Social Reform. The questions are of course delth with in a most moderate spirit and the tone is apologetic throughout. Mrs. Besant feels that she is saying things which her audience never expected from her, and dealing with subjects for the discussion of which an anniversary meeting of the Theosophical Society was the least likely place. But the mere fact that the High Priestess of Theosophy should enter the Reform arena is in itself of very great significance. It is a happy sign of the times and shows that even those who in their zeal for Hinduism have left the most orthodox far behind, and who have been spending any amont of ingenuity in reconciling Hindu superstitions with the "heterodoxies" of modern science and preaching the doctrines of the old faith with all the zeal of new converts, even these good people are realising the necessity and urgency of Reform. The Reformers will of course welcome with open arms this most unexpected aid and we have every reason to hope that Mrs. Besant will be able to influence that large section of the Hindu community which lies outside the Reform plane and which could never have been influenced by the Radical wing.

The series consists of four lectures dealing with (1) the four Ashrams, (2) Temples, Priests and Worships, (3) the Caste system, and (4) Womanhood. Mrs. Besant's plan is to put the ancient ideal before her audience first, then to describe the deterioration which that ideal has undergone, and lastly to point out the means of regeneration. One may or may not agree with all the assertions and arguments of Mrs. Besant, but there can be no doubt about the sincerity of her intentions and the practicability of her Reform Scheme. I have neither the ability, nor can the *Samachar* afford space for an adequate treatment of the many Reform questions raised by Mrs. Besant but I will try to discuss them briefly from the "heterodox" standpoint and to impress on the readers of this Journal as strongly as I can the urgency and feasibility of the Orthodox Reform Scheme.

In the introductory part of her first lecture she tells us that the future world-empire belongs to the Teutonic race with England at its head. The place of India, forming as it does politically an integral part of the British Empire, will be that of the spiritual teacher of mankind but before this can happen India must fit herself to her new environment and move with the spirit of the age. She says,"To set ourselves stubbornly to stand one place and to say: 'Because this in the past was good therefore it must be good for the present and the future, therefore I will not mould myself to the tendencies of the age nor adapt myself to my environment'—that is to be fossilized, that is, to be left behind in the forward march of evolution. On the other hand, to go forward with headlong precipitancy without thought or consideration, without reverence for the past, without understanding the causes it has set up, the tendencies it has bequeathed—that spells ruin, as much as immovability and fossilization spell death." But I doubt very much whether any section of even our extreme reformers now holds the latter view. In all their utterances and writings the responsible leaders of the Reform party describe the past glories of their country with awe and reverence and exhort their hearers and readers to adopt the virtues of their ancestors and discard their vices. The Indian Social Conference is the best representative gathering of the Social Reform movement, and Mr. Ranade was the life and soul, the guide, philosopher and friend, of the Indian Social Conference. In his Madras Address he very clearly defined the position of Reformers in the following words: "We have not to unlearn our entire past, certainly not the past which is the glory and wonder of the human race. We have to retrace our steps from the period of depression, when in panic and weakness a compromise was made with the brute force of ignorance and superstition. If this unholy alliance is set aside, we have the Brahmanism of the first three Yugas unfolding itself in all its power and purity, as it flourished in the best period of our history." So we see that there is no great difference as regards "the virtues of our ancestors "question.

Coming of the main part of the lecture, Mrs. Besant puts before her hearers the ancient ideal of the Student, the Householder, the Vanprastha, and the Sanyasi. The education given the students was very perfect indeed, spiritual, moral, intellectual and physial training forming part of it. The persent Educational System of Europe is based on the same lines and that is no doubt one of the main causes of European progress. The conditions of modern civilization are such that only those nations can advance which give as thorough an education as is possible to their future citizens. But unfortunately for ourselves, the present system prevalent in India is bristling with a thousand faults, which neither the authorities care to remove nor the agitators to point out. We have yet to realise that above everything else—even above political reform—we require a complete reorganization of our Educational System on more progressive lines. The system adopted by the Central Hindu College authorities, will, let us hope, do much, not only by its actual work but also by putting before other institutions, a higher and nobler ideal on education. Unless physical and moral education is imparted on some regular plan, the status of the teacher raised and the educational career made worth his while, the intercourse between the teacher and the taught extended beyond the schoolroom and the collage compound, and the boarding house system—in which boys are taught to live a corporate life-introduced, the sham education by rote replaced by a real training of faculties of observation and thinking, and the examination slavery abolished, we can only hope to go on as we have been going on far the last half-century, our colleges turning out boneless weaklings of very doubtful intellectual merit and our Universities awarding them diplomas.

Another point on which Mrs. Besant rightly lays great stress is the early marriage of boys, and there can no doubt that the great physical degeneracy of the higher classes which is going on before our eyes, must be attributed in a very great measure to this most pernicious custom. The Hindu College has taken the lead in this matter by refusing to admit married boys in the middle section of the school and below it. But the reform will not be thorough until parents come to realize that to marry a boy before he can earn enough to maintain himself and his family is crime. I would even go further and say that the marriage of a boy does not fall within the category of parental duties and must be left to himself. But this remark of mine I am sure will not be relished even by the advanced reformers.

The second Ashram, that of the householder, nowadays forms the last stage of a man's life. No doubt there are Sanyasis in plenty but most of them are so many rogues and cheats. It is refreshing to read Mrs. Besant's denunciation of these pests of Hindu Society. "Robust and lazy, such men swarm over the country by thousands, living on the earning of others, and giving nothing back in benefit to the community; too often profligate, taking advantage of their sacred garb to corrupt and lead astray, sensualists not ascetics, luxurious not self-controlled." As for the last two Ashrams I doubt whether this part of the Hindu system can be practically worked on a large scale in India for a long time to come. Poverty has increased, competition has become keener the great majority even of the higher classes hardly make both ends meet by hard daily toil. Indian families cannot afford to left any of their members remain idle; no, not even for the sake of spiritual contemplation. This aspect of the question will deserve the attention of the revivalists.

The second lecture is one long and bitter complaint against the priestly class and its immoral practices. That a class of priests is necessary for the spiritual needs of a people and therefore must be allowed to stand between a man and his maker is a controversial point. But even if we grant that, we must admit that a priest to be of any use must be learned, pious and pure. Is it so in India? Mrs. Besant speaks with no uncertain voice on this question: "Do we not know that the very names of Mahants and Pandas carry to the ears of many who hear them association of degradation and not so spiritual power, of shame and not of pride? Do we not know that if we stand at a sacred Tirtha, we see there scenes that make us turn away in bitter shame, shocked at the rapacity of those who gather round the pilgrims, and who in the very water that should be sacred to the blessed Gods absolutely strive with each other physically to drag the pilgrims into their own hands, for the sake of money?... Do we not know that too often the family Guru is not looked upon with love and honour, not always because of western education and falling off from religion, but because it is hard to give respect, where there is nothing respectable?... But for those who thus prostitute the holiest of names, who by ignorance and profligacy blaspheme the most sacred of relations, for them there lies in the future the lowest of Narakas, the doom of those who blaspheme the Divine in man, have outraged that which is the holiest and the most pregnant with the salvation of mankind." Mrs Basant proposes two remedies, the education of the priests—for which by the way a Theological Class is to be opened in connection with the Central Hindu College and the raising of the standard of spiritual advancement among the people. This is quite right and if we could get priests trained for their work in an institution like the Central Hindu College many of the present abuses will vanish. Speaking of the community of Kashmiri Pandits in Lucknow I can say that a certain number of youths of our priestly families who have been educated in the Oriental Depertmant of our local college are morally and intellectually far superior to their fathers. This is a significant fact and shows that if our priests were to take the trouble of submitting themselves to the discipline and training of a well-organized religious seminary it will do them immense good. But the question is, will they do so?

But while denouncing the faults of the present priesthood with her usual earnestness and eloquence Mrs. Basant curiously enough says, "If a man has in him a heart that is strong enough, a faith that is heroic enough to look through the unworthy Guru to the great Guru whose power may come down even through the unworthy channel, if a man has courage, devotion, insight enough to disregard the unworthy form, and see in it merely a channel for the power that is divine; then the mantra given by even such a Guru will purify and spiritualize the man who takes it, and he will not suffer because the one who gave it was not worthy to be the giver. Do not break the tie of love, the tie of duty, even when the representative is unworthy. Be patient for a little time. Bear with these unworthy ones for the sake of the ideal they represent, for the sake of the glory of the past, and for the holiness of the name, that is cast as a veil over the unworthiness of the present." Further on she remarks: "The words of a wise teacher of ancient times should be remembered, when he told his disciples not to pull up too hastily the weeds that had grown along with the wheat, lest they should also pull up the young corn; but rather wait until the corn was strong enough to bear the movement round its roots, so that the weeds might be gathered and thrown into the fire which was their proper place, without injuring the corn." Either I have not been able to grasp her real meaning or Mrs. Besant in her intense zeal for religion and all that is connected with religion has not been able to explain herself quite clearly. The office of a priest is the holiest on this Earth, and can we, should we treat with forbearance a man who prostitutes the sanctity of this holy office? Do our Pandas, Mahants and Gurus, ignorant, licentious and brutal as they are, deserve sympathy and generous treatment? Are they fit for being mediators between a pure and noble soul and its God? Has not the time yet come for an open revolt against these wretches who blaspheme by their words and their acts, the great God when they pretend to worship, and whose very touch is pollution? Mrs. Besant asks us to forbear but will not this very forbearance be a sin? Will not the weeds, while we are waiting for the corn to be strong enough to bear the movement round its roots, gather strength and choke the corn itself? I wonder how Mrs. Besant who in her early life fought so bravely against the abuses of Christian priesthood can tolerate this compromise with the powers of darkness and evil.

The Tribunal of Priests which Mrs. Besant wants to set up "to redress flagrant scandals, to interfere with and prevent unworthy priests from continuing to receive emoluments belonging to their office," will be a very good thing indeed, if it were practicable. But I am afraid that at present at least public opinion is too weak and the forces of ignorance and superstition too strong for the effective carrying out of such a scheme. In the first place, it will be difficult to get a sufficient number of men who should be not only pure and noble in their lives but public spirited enough to take such a burden on themselves. We know full well how weak in public spirit are even our best educated and enlightened classes. To expect such an amount of public spirit and patriotic feeling as will be necessary for the establishment and proper working of such a

Tribunal from our priesthood is I am afraid quite vain.

In her third lecture Mrs. Besant deals with that most thorny of our social questions, the caste system. Mrs. Besant regards the four-fold division of caste as a Divine institution but this view of hers cannot be accepted by a heterodox critic. I regard caste as a purely human institution built up by those social forces which are working out the evolution of human society. Human institutions are always changing with the changing needs and environments of human society. New environments give birth to new institutions, new wants bring into existence new instruments for their satisfaction. And the birth of new institutions goes on hand in hand with the decay and death of old ones. "Old order changeth yielding place to new" and in its onward progress human society outgrows the need of many old institutions which served it at a certain period of its evolution but which have now become excrescences and therefore must die. We may prolong the death struggle but we cannot prevent their dissolution. If we regard this view as correct then we must be prepared to accept the dissolution of caste sooner or later. Whether such a time has yet come or not may be a disputed question but the coming of it sooner or later must be a certainty. And when that time comes, then the system will die and be displaced by a broader, nobler and better institution suited to the more advanced age of society.

But this view the orthodox will never accept. Human institutions may change but Divine institutions are unchangeable because they are suited for all time. "Our little systems" are based on human experience, and human wisdom may err and human experience may be faulty. They at best can devise means for the satisfaction of present needs. But Divine wisdom can look forward as well as backward from eternity to eternity and Divine institutions are therefore Eternal, Immutable.

Let us see how Mrs. Besant explains the caste system from her point of view. "The next thing to remember is that this system, as regards the soul, is a great educative system. Reincarnation is always implied in it. The soul passes from one caste to another according to the actions it had performed. It may rise upwards, or it may sink downwards, but the effect of one birth always shows itself in another birth, and the soul is led, stage by stage, along the pathway of evolution. And very plainly is this shown when you look upon the caste system in its pure form. The higher the caste the greater the restrictions, the heavier the duties, the more burdensome the weight of responsibility placed on its shoulders." But someone might object that at present we do not see the purity and nobility of any particular caste corresponding with the evolution of a soul belonging to that caste. The case is rather the reverse. There is no class of people worse off in this respect than the Brahmans. Here is Mrs. Besant's explanation of this phenomenon.

"Gradually, however, a change arose. This system, originally founded and worked by great Rishis, the different castes inhabited by souls of strongly marked and different characteristics, worked well enough in those days. But as less and less developed souls were born into the system, their qualities no longer coincided with the special caste into which they were born. Less and less evolved souls came into Indian bodies, for training and instruction and were no longer able to fulfil the Dharma of the caste in which they were born." But how came the less evolved souls to be born in the higher castes for which they were not fit? Why was the law broken? If the souls of men had degenerated and were not fit for the performance of noble duties and high responsibilities of the higher castes, why were they not put in the lower ones? And why this sudden degeneracy of souls, and what explanation is there for this phenomenon in the spiritual world? Who is responsible for this state of chaos? Be what, however, as it may, Mrs. Besant pronounces with no uncertain voice against sub-castes. And that itself is no small gain.

Foreign travel is a very important plank in the Social Reform platform and people will be glad to find that Mrs. Besant supports the sea-voyage movement and poohpoohs the show of a penance called *Prachitt*. "I have heard a man boast that he travels backwards and forwards constantly and pays Rs. 5, on his return to his priest and performs *Praschitt* and then is received without demur. Such *Praschittas* are blasphemies and dishonour all who take part in them." And her outspoken remarks on the stupidity of the system of outcasting as it prevails among the Hindus today, will not be relished I am afraid even by the most enlightened among the orthodox. "It is largely a matter of intrigue and private interest, a matter of active exertion by some who have personal motives behind the work they are doing; that is a well-known fact, and too often the decision of a caste is swayed by men who by outer formality of religion gain an outer respect, not warranted by purity of life, by learning, by wisdom and nobility of character; you know further, as well as I do, that when you come to deal with outcasting, as now practised, it is not only that the people who practically control the decisions are those who ought not to do it, but also they exercise their authority over those, over whom that authority should not be exercised. You know perfectly well that within the limits of caste a man may fairly outrage every principle of morality and yet no man will think of outcasting him. In life he may practically disregard the caste principles but if he keeps up an outward show, he is not outcasted. The man may go to a hotel, may eat beef, may get drunk, but provided he goes in by the back door and not by the front door, his castemen will shut their eyes to his errors. Whereas if a man travels out of India, however well educated he may be, however pure the life he may lead, however useful he may be to his community, you will find that in some sub-division of a caste, he is outcasted for the mere fact of travelling. How can a system last where such injustice is done?" And so the wretched system is doomed.

WOMEN

In her last lecture Mrs. Besant pleads for the elevation of Hindu women. She draws the picture of the Hindu woman as she was in the old days, pious, learned, and pure, a helpmate of her husband and an ornament of society. She was not shut up behind the *purdah*. She was not stupefied and dulled by the despotism of the husband and the tyranny of the mother-in-law. The ideal of womanhood as depicted in ancient Sanskrit literature is very high indeed and we may be sure that at least in that section of the Hindu society which was influenced by that literature, the place of woman was a place of honour. But times changed, political and religions convulsions shook the Hindu Society to its very depths, everywhere there was chaos and confusion. The old order passed away, Hindus had to fight for centuries for their very existence, everywhere there was struggle and strife, and the shedding of blood like water. In such a society how can we hope for the maintenance of a high ideal of womanhood. This naturally told upon our ideal of womanhood and the disastrous consequences of it any one who runs may read. Mrs. Besant proposes the following remedies: "First, it is clear that the elements of the ordinary vernacular education must be given to them, with a knowledge of Sanskrit and its literature so that they may be able to read of the great ideals of Womanhood, and desire to reproduce these in their own lives. This should be the foundation of a woman's education; a knowledge of the vernacular from the literary standpoint, and a knowledge of mother-tongue Sanskrit in which is stored up the sacred literature of India. It would be wise, though many of you will probably disagree with that, as a novel idea, if you introduced also the knowledge of the English tongue... Then you should add to that education, an education scientific in its character, along the lines which should make the woman more useful as the queen of the home. She should be taught in modern India as she was taught in ancient India, the elements of Hygiene, Physiology and Nutrition, so that she may guide the household wisely and well, so that you may not have to call in a doctor for every trivial ailment and difficulty... It might be well in addition, if you added to that literary, scientific, and religious education, some elements also of artistic training." This is the education which ought to be given to Indian women before we can hope to see them influencing for good the destinies of the race. No race can improve if its women are degraded, and that the condition of our women is degraded no one would deny. The intellectual gulf which separates man from woman in India is very wide, the mental planes in which they move are very different. There is no intellectual sympathy between husband and wife, mother and son. It is hard to ask a youth to honour and obey his mother when he knows that the mother is ignorant and superstitious. It is still harder to ask him to take as his life's companion a woman who is a century behind him in culture and intelligence, who can give him neither help nor sympathy in the realization of that splendid though very vague and undefined dream which has risen before his mind's eye with the dawn of the New Light. Mrs. Besant is fully conscious of this and her words deserve the very best attention of those whose conscience still remains untouched by the wrongs of Indian Womanhood. "There are two ways in which a woman may be treated—one the ancient way, one the modern way; one I venture to say a natural and so a wise way, the other an artificial and so a foolish way; one that makes for construction and the other that makes for gradual destruction. The ancient and wise way was training, educating, raising the woman, putting her more and more on a high level, and then giving her a reasonable and dignified liberty. The modern and foolish way is keeping her ignorant and undeveloped, childish and irrational, and then shutting her within a narrow environment. There are few things more beautiful in life than the way in which the Indian son loves, reverences and obeys his mother. But if that most beautiful of relations is to continue under the modern conditions for boys in India, you will have to meet their needs by educating the women who are their mothers.....

In order that the woman's influence may be preserved; in order that she may not lose her hold over the respect as well as the hearts of her husband and her sons; in order that she may be really one-half of humanity as she ought to be; in order that she may play her part will in the home, may train up her sons as they ought to be trained; in order that she may exercise an elevating power over the children round her knees, may prove a worthy mother to worthy sons, this question must be considered and dealt with by the wise amongst you; else the gulf between western-trained men and uneducated woman will widen despite all love, all tenderness, despite all longing to remain together. For the influences are mighty that are tending to divide and unless those influences are checked, that old great ideal of marriage will disappear and be seen no more."

This is a brief summary of the New Teaching of Mrs. Besant and she places before her orthodox followers the following scheme of Reform.

1. A resolve not to marry their sons before 18, nor to allow the marriage to be consummated before 20; the first marriage (betrothal) of their daughters to be thrown as late as possible from 11 to 14 and the second (consummation) from 14 to 16.
2. To promote the maintenance of caste relations with those who have travelled abroad, provided they conform to Hindus ways of living.
3. To promote intermarriage and interdining between the sub-divisions of the four castes.

4. Not to employ in any ceremony (where choice is possible) an illiterate or immoral Brahman.
5. To educate their daughters and to promote the education of the women of their families.
6. Not to demand any money consideration for the marriage of their children.

Some people will perhaps think that Mrs. Besant does not go far enough, but I think that for all practical purposes Mrs. Besant's scheme is very good indeed. And the best of it is that it is meant for the orthodox people and contains very little which clashes with the theory of the orthodox creed. It will be all the more acceptable for being forth in the garb of "Revival." But rose with any name will smell as sweet and the Reformers need not quarrel with Mrs. Besant for putting forth her suggestions in the form most acceptable to her disciples. But though agreeing with Mrs. Besant on most of the points dealt with, I would like to say a few words about one or two general principles which run throughout the whole of her teaching but which are not quite intelligible to a non-theosophist.

In the first place, I find that when dealing with spiritual theories, she is satisfied with making a series of assertions. She does not seem to think that people may require a little more logical proof before they accept all this even on her authority. For instance she says that Caste system is based on a system of progressive evolution of souls, that the rustle of garments of Devas is heard in Hindu temples, that even an immoral and ignorant priest may be a fit channel for the reception of Divine influence, and she is satisfied. But these assertions might be questioned and there are many honest people who do not believe in the visit of Mahatmas who leave their turbans behind them. Whatever other Theosophist leaders may say we expect something more reasonable and rational from Mrs. Besant. Her lectures are meant not only for the Theosophists but also for the heterodox who believe, rightly or wrongly, in nothing but pure Reason, yet who honestly try to understand her teaching. To say that you must believe before you can understand, and give your faith without adequate rational proof is a stock missionary argument which I am sure Mrs. Besant is too clear-headed and broad-minded, to use. In the second place, it seems as if all this higher teaching is meant only for the Dvijas. What about the bulk of the Hindu people, the Sudras? It is true that Mrs. Besant says something about the elevation of Southern Parias in her third lecture but this is not sufficient. It is a most lamentable fact that vey little attention is paid even by the enlightened Reformers to this all-important question. If the Sudras are to be retained in the Hindu Social system, our present rules must be relaxed. We know what lately happened in the South when the people of a particular caste were refused admittance in Hindu temples, and if such things are to be checked they can only be checked by tact and foresight. The Sudras form the bulk of the Hindu race, and treated as they have always been with contempt by the three higher castes, they have always been the cause of our great political weakness. Dynasties rose and fell, wars were waged, the country was lost and won on a hundred battlefields but the mass of the people stood by careless and indifferent. They have been made the hewers of wood and drawers of water by the tyranny of the Brahman scriptures and the Rajput sword, and what did they care whether the Government was Rajput, Scythian or Afghan. When the Rajput army was once defeated it was all over and the country passed quietly under foreign rule. Perhaps this mistake came to be realized afterwards and many a socio-religious reformer like Kabir and Nanak preached the lesson of salvation by Bhakti and not by caste. The acceptance of this doctrine involved in no small measure the elevation of low castes, and the example of Islamic Brotherhood worked in the same direction, it is a most significant fact that when the Moghal power came to be overthrown in the 17th and 18th centuries it was overthrown not by the high-caste Rajputs of Oudh and Rajputana but by the low caste Jat Sikhs of the Punjab and the Marathas of the Deccan. I know that I have somewhat digressed from the main point but I want to explain to my high-caste fellow Hindus is that the Sudra problem cannot be shirked and will have to be faced sooner or later. A Sudra civil servant will not bow to a Brahman beggar and if we refuse him a place in our society he will seek it somewhere else, because he knows full well that though high-caste Hindus may deride him or look down upon him as long as he remains a Hindu, they will not do so if he becomes a Christian. This desire to rise in the social scale has been the main cause of Sudra conversions, and we cannot solve the problem offhand by saying that a Sudra has got a less evolved soul in his body and therefore he must be content with his lot, however hard and cruel it may be.

And lastly, I beg to point out that the best instrument for the reformation of all social and religious abuses is the education of the people themselves. As above everything else the rise of National Spirit and strong Patriotic Feeling is necessary for our political salvation, so more than any Reform or Revival we require the cultivation of the Scientific Method and Critical Spirit for our intellectual, social and religious salvation. The credulity and the Hindus is remarkable and however beautiful it may look when we admire ourselves for our simplicity and childlike faith, it is doing us any amount of mischief in our every-day life, and makes us the laughing stock of the whole world. Religious impostors abound in India and every Sanyasi who puts on the orange garb can do anything he likes with impunity. You cannot remove these evils by erecting Tribunals of Priests, the people themselves must learn to sift the false from the true, the real from the unreal, and spurn with disdain all that is base, wrong and impure, howsoever strongly it may appeal to their national vanity. The shackles of Authority have been borne too long. It is not for Mrs. Besant who fought in Europe so valiantly and so well in the van of the Army of Free-thought by the side of Charles Bradlaugh, to stifle the spirit of inquiry and doubt in India. Excesses may be committed as they are committed everywhere, and the pendulum may swing a little too much to the other side. But we must not forget that this is a reaction against centuries of ignorance, superstition,and social tyranny, and even a little excess of red-hot Radicalism is better than fossilised Orthodoxy. The Rationalistic spirit has done so much for Europe; there is no reason why it should not do as much for India. The Hindus must learn that even the holiest and greatest things are not above criticism, that Doubt, honest Doubt, is better than half the creeds. Inquiry must be encouraged, people must be taught to think for themselves. It has been said that "Undying Hope is the secret of vision" and perhaps I will be accused of seeing a little too far ahead and taking a too optimistic view of things. But I sincerely believe that if we go on, on the lines laid down by the great Rationalistic thinkers of Europe and accept the great fact of

Human evolution we have no reason to despair. There may be obstacles, there may be even dangers in the way. But our leaders bid us be of good cheer. On the one hand, we hear the eloquent voice of Mrs. Besant cheering us onward and pointing out the way of righteousness, regeneration and truth. On the other hand, we still seem to hear as from afar the tones of that voice which preached so earnestly and so fervently year after year the Gospel of Hope from the platform of the Indian Social Conference. The music of that voice is in our ears, the words of encouragement and hope that have come on its wings have sunk deep in our hearts. The goal may be distant, the way narrow, and the march toilsome, but still we must not lose heart. Surely men like Ram Mohan Roy, Dayanand and Ranade have not toiled in vain. The day will come when East and West will unite, the darkness of ages born of ignorance, sin and superstition which hangs over us like a pall, shutting out from our eyes the Light of Knowledge and Hope will be dispelled by the Dawn of Reason, and the victorious thunderpeal of a triumphant Rationalism will resound through the length and breadth of the Indian continent.

CHAPTER - XI

THE THEOSOPHICAL SOCIETY AND ITS CONTRIBUTION TO TAMIL SOCIETY IN THE 19TH CENTURY*

INTRODUCTION

In this paper, an attempt is made to study the impact made by the Theosophical Society on the 19th Century Tamil Society. The Theosophical Society was a reform body within the Hindu fold. Scholars like R.N. Saksena hold the view that the Theosophical Society was a Hindu revivalist body. Founded in New York in 1875 as an international association,[1] It was shifted to Bombay, India in 1879. R.C. Majumdar is of the opinion that the Theosophical Society was an offshoot of neo-Hinduism (The other branch being the Ramakrishna Mission, 1897) which glorified Hindu religion and society in their current forms.[2] According to him, "Brahmaism was the result of an effort to check Christianity and influence of Western ideas by emphasizing the essential principles of Hinduism. These were regarded as free from the evil accretions of a later date, which formed the chief target of attack by Christian Missionaries and were held out to be opposed to the true spirit of Hinduism. This rationalistic attitude provoked a reaction in Bengal which gathered force in second half of the nineteenth century, and gave rise to what may be called neo-Hinduism.** Its common characteristic was the glorification of Hindu religion and society in their *current forms*, and a spirited defence of these against hostile criticism both by Indian refor-mers and European missionaries."[3] Prof. C.E. Ramachandran holds similar view that the religious bodies like the Brahmo Samaj (1828), the Prarthana Samaj (1867), the Arya Samaj (1875), the Theosophical Society (1879) and the Ramakrishna Mission (1897) were the Hindu reform bodies which endeavoured to cleanse the impurities that had encrusted the Hindus religion with the passage of time. He also feels that these religious organizations could not be called revivalist bodies of Hindu religion as the latter was never dead even at the hey days of Jainism or Buddhism.[4]

EMERGENCE OF SOCIAL REFORM MOVEMENT IN INDIA IN THE 19TH CENTURY

Though scholars differ on the nature of the Theosophical Society, it is agreed on all hands that Hinduism suffered a serious set-back at the hands of Christianity when India came under the direct control of the British rule in the 19th century. India, once the seat of a great civilization, came to be criticised by the Christian Missionaries as the land of myths and superstitions. There was a concerted move on the part of the Missionaries to spread the Gospel of their religion and convert Hindus to their faith. Charles Grant, a British Missionary who later became an influential member in the Court of Directors in the East India Company, criticised Hinduism as "idolatry with all its rabble of impure deities, its monsters of wood and stone, its false principles and corrupt practices, its ridiculous ceremonies and degrading superstitions, its lying legends and fraudulent impositions."[5] William Wilberforce who led the Anti Slavery Movement in England, declared in Parliament that Christianity was sublime, pure and beneficent whereas Hindu religion was licentious and cruel.[6] Alexander Duff, another Missionary described the Indian people as a 'multiple of heathens'. He wrote in his book, '*India and Indian Missions*' that of all the religions, Hinduism was the only religion that had the brunt of perversion.[7] The Missionaries launched a multi-cornered attack on Hinduism through schools, societies, books, pamphlets and press. As one writer has pointed out, Hinduism received a challenge calculated to reduce its vaunted supremacy.[8]

The wholesale condemnation of the Christian Missionaries led to a serious rethinking and a critical evaluation of the past. Social customs, hitherto found valid, came to be criticised as injurious to social health. Educated Hindus in Bengal, with a view to preserving the purity of Hindu religion, criticised and condemned social institutions such as *Sati*, childmarriage and untouchability.

BIRTH OF THE SOCIAL REFORM MOVEMENT

It was against this background that Social Reform Movement emerged in Bengal in the 1820's. Being an intellectual movement, it endeavoured to remove the excrescences that had encrusted the Hindu society over the years. Socio-religious reform bodies like the Brahmo Samaj (1828), the Prarthana Samaj (1867) and the Arya Samaj (1875) were formed. By emphasizing the eternal truths of Hinduism and re-emphasizing the Vedic thought of monotheism, the Brahmo Samaj aimed to check Christianity and Western Influence.[9] The Prarthana Samaj, an offshoot of the Brahmo Samaj, was started in Bombay in 1867 by Atmaram Pandurang (1823-1898). He undertook the spread of worship and social reform. the Arya Samaj, another offshoot of the Brahmo Samaj, founded in Bombay in 1875 by Dayananda Saraswati (1824-1883), aimed at reviving the Hindu religion by reconverting to Hinduism those who got converted to Christianity and Islam.

EMERGENCE OF NEO-HINDUISM

The downright condemnation of Hinduism both by the Indian reformers and the European missionaries stirred up the consciousness of the Bengalis and this gave brith to neo-Hinduism.[10] According to R.C. Majumdar "Its common characteristic was the glorification of Hindu religion and society in their current forms, and a spirited defence of these against hostile criticism both by Indian reformers and European missionaries."[11] R.C.Majumdar includes the Theosophical Society (founded in New York in 1875 and shifted to Bombay, India in 1879) and the Ramakrishna Mission (1897) as belonging to neo-Hinduism. Thus, the Theosophical Society was Hindu reform body as it aimed "to check, to a certain extent, the influence of the Christian as well as materialistic thoughts of the period."[12]

MEANING OF THE WORD 'THEOSOPHY'

The word 'Theosophy' literally means 'knowledge of divine matters'. It meant divine illumination *i.e.*, knowledge of God by direct spiritual intuition. The Encyclopaedia Britannica gives the meaning of the word 'Theosophy' as "... those forms of philosophic and religious thought which claim a special insight into the divine nature and its constitutive movements or processes... it starts with an explication of the divine essence and endeavours to deduce the phenomenal universe from the play of forces within the divine nature itself..."[13] It was an exact translation of the well-known Sanskrit word 'Brahma Vidya.'[14] According to Annie Besant, it mean an all embracing religion and ethics.[15] It is made up of two Greek words, "Theos", meaning God and "sophia", meaning wisdom. Therefore, Theosophy meant knowledge about God. It was first used in the third century A.D. in Alexandria by the Greek philosopher Iamblichus. He is believed to have used the word to mean the inner knowledge of things related to God which were taught in Greek mysteries. It is the synthesis of science, religion and philosophy.[16] To a Theosophist, God and the world are inseparably one. To him, man is the replica of God and in him divinity is inherent. The Theosophists were believed to have been interested in occultism*** and transmitted it is a secret doctrine by a brotherhood of mahatmas spread over the world.

NATURE OF THE THEOSOPHICAL SOCIETY

The Theosophical Society was a non-sectarian body of seekers after Truth whose aim was to promote Universal Brotherhood. "It was a group of people who believed in the unity of all religions and brotherhood of man."[17] It was essentially a movement which started outside India but it was brought to India by its leaders like madame Blavatsky (1832-1892), Colonel Olcott (1832-1907) and W.Q. Judge. They held the ancient Indian culture in high esteem and advocated new ways and means by which it could be brought back to its original glory. Truth forms the basis of the Theosophical Society. 'There is no religion higher than Truth' is its motto. Though Theosophy aimed at reviving *the true spirit of religions*, it was not a religious body as it had no creed or dogmas. Its membership was thrown open to all seekers after Truth. It had among its members Hindus, Parsees, Jews, Jains, Buddhists, Confucianists, Christians and Muhammadans. At Adyar in Madras, one can find in the spacious compound of the Theosophical Society all the temples representing the cardinal faiths of the world. The writer has visited the place.

FOUNDERS OF THE SOCIETY

The Theosophical Society was founded in New York in 1875 by Madame Helena Petrovna (Blavatsky), Col. Henry Steele (Olcott) and W.Q. Judge. Olcott was born on August 2, 1832 at Orange in New Jersey, U.S.A. After undergoing several vicissitudes in life as colonel and miner, he took to spiritualism.

Blavatsky was born in 1831 at Ekateri Noslav in Southern Russia. In 1874 she visited the United States and came into contact with Olcott. In 1876 she met Annie Besant in London. In 1888 she published her first two volumes of her work, '*The Secret Doctrine, the Synthesis of Science, Religion and Philosophy*'. In 1889 she published her book, '*The Key to Theosophy*'. She was believed to have been gifted with the extraordinary powers of extra-sensory perception including clairvoyance.**** She was believed to have got the vision of the future of humanity in terms of universal brotherhood and harmony, based upon the teachings of the Buddha. Her aim was not to make personal gains through her extraordinary powers, but to prove the existence of a universal spirit and promote universal brotherhood.[18] Theosophy's emphasis on universal brotherhood helped the social reformers to promote their cause. Theosophists were required to give up their (castes) and superstitious beliefs. To be a member, one need not have to recognize the existence of any special God or a deity. But at the same time, one need only worship the spirit of nature and try to identify oneself with it.

FOUNDATION OF THE THEOSOPHICAL SOCIETY

a) New York, 1875

It was with the purpose of creating a universal organization for the promotion of Universal Brotherhood, that both Olcott and Blavatsky founded the Theosophical Society in New York on November 17, 1875.

b) Bombay, 1879

Since the founders of the Theosophical Society felt that Hinduism was one of the ancient religions of the world, and that they had the proper climate to propagate Universal Brotherhood, they shifted the Society to Bombay, India, the birth place of Hinduism, in 1879. Both Olcott and Blavatsky demonstrated a series of occult powers which made the Society popular in India among the elites.

c) Adyar, Madras, 1882

Since the Theosophical Society was plagued with financial problems, it was shifted to Adyar, a suburb of Madras, in 1882.[19] In Madras there were more subscribers and so it was hoped that the financial difficulties of the Society could be tided over.

OBJECTIVES OF THE SOCIETY

The original object of the Theosophical Society was to diffuse knowledge of the laws which govern the universe.[20] Subsequently, its aims were expanded as follows:[21]

1. To form a nucleus of the Universal Brotherhood of humanity without distinction of race, creed, sex, caste or colour.
2. To encourage the study of comparative religion, philosophy and science.
3. To investigate the hidden mysteries of nature and the latent physical forces of men and,
4. To recognise the Universality of God as the one Creator Preserver and Regenerator.

ESTABLISHMENT OF THE SOCIETY IN TAMILNADU

After the Theosophical Society was shifted form Bombay to Madras, Olcott and Blavatsky undertook in 1883 an extensive tour of Tamil Nadu, visiting Trichinopoly, Tanjore, Kumbakonam, Mayavaram, Nagapatam, Madura, Srivilliputtur, Tinnevelly, Coimbatore and Cuddalore where they were accorded a warm welcome.[22] Olcott underscored the fact that the only remedy for the country's malady was the dissemination of the knowledge of the Vedas to the people. While visiting Tamil Nadu, Olcott felt that he had ushered in the real revivalist movement.[23] V. Yasoda Devi however points out that in South India, aristocrats, officials and educated middle class people alone became its members and the common people had no attraction for it.[24] Theosophical Lodges were opened in various parts of the Madras Presidency. A list of branches is given below:[25]

	Place	*Name of the Branch*	*Date of Charter*
		Madras District	
1.	Adyar	The Adyar Lodge, T.S.	18[illegible]
2.	Egmore	The Sachidanand Lodge, T.S.	19[illegible]
3.	Madras	The Madras, T.S.	18[illegible]
4.	Mylapore	The Mylapore, T.S.	19[illegible]
5.	Triplicane	Parthasarathy Lodge, T.S.	18[illegible]
		Madurai District	
6.	Dindigul	The Dindigul, T.S.	1884
7.	Kodaikanal	The Kodaikanal, T.S.	1905
8.	Madura	The Madura, T.S.	1883
9.	Periyakulam	The Periyakulam, T.S.	1884
		Tanjore District	
10.	Nannilam	Ramakrishna Lodge, T.S.	1908
11.	Nagapatam	The Sundara Lodge, T.S.	1883
12.	Neyyatankarai	The Ashwathama Lodge, T.S.	1908
13.	Palakurichi	Shri Varadha Lodge, T.S.	1903
14.	Porayure	The Porayure Lodge, T.S.	1915
15.	Shiyali	The Shiyali, T.S.	1910
16.	Tanjore	Shri Beasan Lodge, T.S.	1883
17.	Thalamayur	Shri Nataraj, T.S.	1913
18.	Thirupanivataram	The Maireya Lodge, T.S.	1917
19.	Tirukamapuram	The Maireya Lodge, T.S.	1917
20.	Tirunichiyur	The Santa Lodge, T.S.	1912
21.	Tiruvadi	The Panchanatha Lodge, T.S.	1912
22.	Ukkadi	The Ukkadi, T.S.	1906
23.	Valakari	Sri Ranga Lodge, T.S.	1908
24.	Valivalam	The Mahendra Lodge, T.S.	1908
25.	Valkai	The Ganapathi Lodge, T.S.	1910
26.	Vedaraniam	The Vadavichara Lodge, T.S.	1898
27.	Vilakudi	The Rajagopala Lodge, T.S.	1909
		North Arcot District	
28.	Arni	Shri Krishna Lodge, T.S.	1885
29.	Ranipet	The Ranipet, T.S.	1898
30.	Tiruvannamalai	The Tajas Lodge, T.S.	1909
31.	Vellore	The Vellore, T.S.	1885

Place	*Name of the Branch*	*Date of Charter*
	South Arcot District	
32. Alampundi	Shri Ganesh Lodge, T.S.	1913
33. Bhuvanagiri	Shri Chamundeeswari, T.S.	1913
34. Chidambaram	The Chidambaram, T.S.	1902
35. Cuddalore	The Cuddalore, T.S.	1883
36. Cuddalore	The Maireya, T.S.	1910
37. Eyyalur	Shri Krishna Lodge, T.S.	1913
38. Kallakurichi	The Gomutti Lodge	1911
39. Kattumannarkoil	Shri Rajagopal Lodge, T.S.	1913
40. Manampundi	Bhakta Balsamajam Lodge, T.S.	1913
41. Malakadumpur	The Amritagaliswar Lodge, T.S.	1909
42. Nallikuppam	The Paranava Lodge, T.S.	1909
43. Panruti	Shri Sadguru Lodge, T.S.	1909
44. Reddiyur	The Visalakshi Lodge, T.S.	1910
45. Sorattaperum	Shri Ram Lodge, T.S.	1912
46. Tindivanam	The Tindivanam, T.S.	1900
47. Tirukkoyilur	The Tirukkoyllur, T.S.	1900
48. Villupuram	The Vasudeva Lodge, T.S.	1900
49. Vriddhachalam	The Vriddhachalam, T.S.	1900
	Coimbatore District	
50. Anamalai	The Anamalai Narayana, T.S.	1904
51. Bhavani	The Bhavani, T.S.	1893
52. Chittoor	The Ganesh, T.S.	1914
53. Coimbatore	The Coimbatore, T.S.	1883
54. Erode	The Erode, T.S.	1900
55. Kollegal	The Kollegal, T.S.	1913
56. Tirupur	The Tirupur Lodge, T.S.	1888
57. Pollachi	The Pollachi, T.S.	1900
58. Udumalpet	The Udumalpet, T.S.	1888
59. Vettagaram Pudur	The Vettagaram Pudur, T.S.	1913
	Chingleput District	
60. Chingleput	The Chingleput, T.S.	1863
61. Conjeevaram	The Satyavarata, T.S.	1897
62. Kadambur	Gana Vilas Lodge, T.S.	1913
63. Nugambol	The Nugambol, T.S.	1913

Place	*Name of the Branch*	*Date of Charter*
64. Poonamallee	The Poonamallee, T.S.	1893
65. Puthonamkottai	Shri Krishnamurti, T.S.	1912
66. Saidapet	The Srikrishna Lodge, T.S.	1901
67. Thiruvallur (Chingleput)	The Veera Raghaa Lodge, T.S.	1898
68. Tonnadu		1913
69. Washermanpet		1909
	Tinnevelly District	
70. Ambasamudram	The Ambasamudram, T.S.	1889
71. Srivaikuntam	The Agasthya, T.S.	1897
72. Tinnevelly	The Tinnevelly, T.S.	1881
73. Tuticorin	The Tirumantra Lodge, T.S.	1904
	Trichinopoly District	
74. Attankudi	The Attankudi, T.S.	1914
75. Illupur	Shri Kaliyana Venkata-chalapathi Lodge, T.S.	1909
76. Kulittalai	The Kulittalai Lodge, T.S.	1910
77. Lalgudi	The Shrimathi Lodge, T.S.	1903
78. Namakkal	The Namakkal, T.S.	1887
79. Trichinopoly	The Trichinopoly, T.S.	188[illegible]
	Salem District	
80. Karur	The Karur, T.S.	1900
81. Salem	The Salem, T.S.	1897
	Ramnad District	
82. Paramakudi	The Paramakudi, T.S.	1885
83. Rajapalayam	The Gnanand, T.S.	1915
84. Ramnad	The Ramnad, T.S.	1904
85. Sivaganga	The Sivaganga, T.S.	1897
86. Srivilliputur	The Natchiyar, T.S.	1883

ITS MEMBERS

The Theosophical Society had lawyers and teachers as its members. In the Madras Branch R. Raghunatha Rao was chosen as its President, G. Muthuswamy Chetty and P. Srinivasa Rao, both judges of the High Court of Madras, were chosen as its Vice-Presidents and T. Subba Rao, a lawyer in the High Court, was chosen as its Secretary. It inspired the educated youths. By June 1884, it had eighty branches in South India, with its members and sympathisers running into thousands.

Formation of Sanskrit Schools

Olcott and Blavatsky decided to start enduring institutions for the promotion of Vedic studies. To realise their dream, they started Sanskrit schools at Triplicane, Mylapore and Black Town.[26] The Society's members sent their children to these schools before admitting them into English medium schools. Sanskrit schools were opened by the Society's branches in Madura and Trichinopoly.

The Aryan League of Honour, 1884

In 1884 at the annual conference of the Theosophists at Adyar, a resolution was passed to the effect that an 'Aryan League of Honour' should be established in all centres to promote the cause of Aryan regeneration.[27]

The Adyar Oriental Library, 1886

In 1886, the Adyar Oriental Library was established, Olcott's main aim in starting this Library was to make it accessible not only to Indian scholars but also to scholars from the West to train Sanskrit Pandits.

THE CONTRIBUTION OF THE THEOSOPHICAL SOCIETY TO SOCIAL REFORM

i) Education

Though the Theosophical Society, in the beginning, was mainly concerned with spiritual problems, its leaders slowly became interested in social reform activities also. One of the social problems to which they paid their attention was education. Olcott, with a view to improving the lot of the Pariah children, started schools for them, an account of which is given below.

ii) Hindu Boys' Association, 1874

Olcott took delight in speaking to the Indian students, reiterating the past glories and rich traditions of India. In his lecture on 'India—*Past, Present and Future*' which he delivered at Lahore, he stressed on the inherent beauty of Indian tradition. He infused in them a sense of pride which was a prerequisite for the salvation of the country. With this aim, he formed the Boys' Clubs and Societies in Madras which in 1874 became the Hindu Boys' Association. The Association aimed to weld all Hindu boys together so as to enable them to come to know and practise their religion in a true national spirit. It was an attempt to revive the old Hindu faith and reconcile the traditional with the modern.

iii) Olcott's Contribution to Education for Pariah Children

The outstanding work for which Olcott is remembered is the foundation of 'Pariah Schools' in Madras which were given the name 'Panchama Schools'. He was deeply moved by these unfortunate ones who were called 'the untouchables'.

In his pamphlet on 'The Poor Pariah', Olcott described the lot of the untouchables and appealed for help from the reformers. It was with the aim of promoting the welfare of the Pariah children that Olcott founded five schools in the greater Madras region in the period 1894-1906.[28] The first school was opened on June12, 1894, near the Theosophical Society at Adyar.[29] This was a pioneering undertaking, as hardly anyone was interested in educating or caring for the 'outcastes' at that time.[30] With less than Rs. 250, Olcott built the 'mud-walled palmyra' thatched school house in which fifty-five Pariah children were given instruction.[31] The building was declared open by one S. Ryden. To begin with, the school had twenty-five boys who were given free board and lodge. They were given instruction upto the Fourth Standard. Instructions were given in English, Tamil and Hindustani. He also taught them cooking, mending clothes and managing household.[32]

The second school, named after Blavatsky, was opened in 1898, the third one named after a young Brahmin, Damodar K. Mavalankar in 1899 and the Fourth named after the Tamil poet Thiruvalluvar in 1902.[33] These schools were supervised by Miss. S.E. Palmer of Minnesota, U.S.A.

iv) Number of Students Studied

By 1901 the total number of Pariah children who studied in the Olcott schools was 384 boys and 150 girls.[34] The total number of teachers employed was sixteen.[35]

The following table shows the number of Pariah children getting educated at the Olcott Free School and H.P. Blavatsky Memorial School between 1894 and 1899.[36]

Year	Number of students sent for examination	Number passed	Percentage
1895-96	14	12	86
1896-97	33	25	75
1897-98	34	21	62
1898-99	54	33	61

The percentage of the Pariah children who passed from this school was eighty one per cent which was five per cent more than the entire presidency average.[37]

When Pariah children became grown up to support their families, they were discharged from the school.

The following table shows the number of Pariah children getting educated at the Olcott Free (Pariah) Schools between 1899 and 1902.

OLCOTT FREE (PARIAH) SCHOOLS

	1899-1900			1900-1901		
Standard	No.of students sent for examination	Number passed	%-age of passes	No. of students sent for examination	Number passed	%-age of passes
Infant	37	27	73	29	25	86
First	28	24	85	26	16	61
Second	10	10	100	24	23	95
Third	10	10	100	10	9	90
Fourth	5	5	100	7	7	100
Total	90	76	84	96	80	83

v) Govt.'s Takeover of the Schools

In 1926 due to financial crisis, three schools were transferred as gifts to the Corporation of Madras. The Olcott Memorial School established by Olcott in 1894 and a Primary school at the fishing village of 'Olcott Kuppam' on the beach adjoining the Theosophical Society Estate still continue to be run by a Board of Management under the Chairmanship of the President of the Theosophical Society.[38] It was upgraded into a high school in 1974.

ANNIE BESANT'S CONTRIBUTION TO THE THEOSOPHICAL SOCIETY

Annie Besant (1847-1933), born in Ireland, came to India in 1893. She advocated abolition of caste system. She wanted the common people and also the women of India to get educated. On the death of Olcott in 1907, Annie Besant became the President of the Theosophical Society. To improve the lot of women, she founded the Women's Indian Association at Adyar in 1917. The momentum gained strength when the All India Women's Conference was organised in 1927. To encourage inter-dining and inter-marriages, she along with her friend, N.Subba Rao founded in 1904 the Madars Hindu Association.[39] In her book, *'Wake Up, India: A Plea for Social Reform'*, she rejected the caste system and exhorted the Madras audience to marry virgin widows.[40] In 1919, she founded the Training College of Teachers at Adyar, the Brahma Vidyashrama at Adyar in 1922 and after her death in 1933, the Besant Memorial School at Adyer in 1935 and the International Academy of Arts at Adyar in 1936 were established.

CONCLUSION

From the foregoing discussion, it could be inferred that the Theosophical Society was founded with the noble purpose of promoting Universal Brotherhood and unity of religions. It made Indians proud of their hoary past. It inculcated among its members a spirit of broad-minded appreciation of each other's faith.

In Tamil Nadu, during the period under review, the Theosophical Society endeavoured to mitigate the severities of the caste system. It encouraged widow re-marriage and promoted the welfare of the downtrodden. The Theosophists felt that education alone could remove the social disparity among the people. It was with this end that they established educational institutions for the Pariahs. Yet the Depressed Classes and the untouchables could not be drawn into it as its ideals centred round higher philosophy. It was only in the first quarter of the 20th century when the Non-Brahmin Movement spearheaded by P. Thiyagaraya Chetti and Dr. M.N. Nair, the Self-Respect Movement spearheaded by E.V. Ramasami and the Untouchability Removal Movement spearheaded by M.C. Rajah took up the cause of the downtrodden, a social awareness was created among the common people.

The Theosophists promoted the study of Sanskrit as it was the 'Key to treasures of ancient Indian learning and culture'. To this end, they started Sanskrit schools in the Presidency. They promoted the study of Tamil also. Thus the composite culture that was ushered in the Tamil land in the wake of the Aryanization of the South, got cemented. This was the significant contribution of the Theosophists to Tamil society which is discernible even today.

To promote the welfare of women, Annie Besant started in Madras the Madras Hindu Association (1904), Women's Indian Association (1917-18), Training College of Teachers (1919), and the Brahma Vidyashrama (1922). After her death in 1933, the Besant Memorial School (1934) and the International Academy of Arts (1936) were founded. One cannot ignore the services rendered by Annie Besant to Tamil society and politics. Besant, a lady of Irish origin, started the Home Rule Movement for the Indians to attain their goal of self-rule and this speaks volumes of her involvement in Indian politics too.

All told, the Theosophical Society was not free from its shortcomings. Though it was started to promote unity of religions, it became the advocate of Hinduism and upheld Sanatana Dharma as its cardinal principle. It was further charged with promoting feelings of casteism from which criticism it has yet to recover.

Yet the Theosophical Society was a landmark in the history of that time. At a time when the people of this land had lost all their pride in their heritage, the Theosophical Society fostered in our countrymen a feeling of pride and a sense of values. The purpose once served, the Society receded to the background as is the case with all historic institutions and movements. At a time when man was bedevilled by distinctions of caste and creed, the Theosophical Society contributed its mite to bring men's minds in unison and to perceive nobler values transcending narrow grooves of sectarian thinking. Certainly Tamil Nadu benefited from it.

NOTES AND REFERENCES

* The writer places on record his grateful thanks to Prof. R. Gopalan Shastri for his unflinching help in overseeing this paper. A part of this paper has been published in the book entitled, *Prof. T.K. Venkataraman's 81st Birthday Commemoration Volume* edited by S. Nagarajan, (Madurai, 1981). This is only a partial study.

** The Brahmo Samaj, the Prarthana Samaj, the Arya Samaj together with the new Hindu reform bodies like the Theosophical Society and the Ramakrishna Mission have been given the name Hindu reform bodies.

*** Occultism = a perception of the mysterious which normally remians hidden to the ordinary human eyes.

**** Clairvoyance—The alleged power of seeing things not present to the senses—Chambers's *Twentieth Century Dictionary*, p. 193.

1. R.N. Saksena, *Indian Social Thought*, (Meerut, n.d.), p. 170
2. R.C. Majumdar, *British Paramountcy and Indian Renaissance* (The History and Culture of the Indian People Series), Vol. X, Part II (Bombay, 1981), p. 115.
3. *Ibid.*, p. 115.
4. Interview with Prof. C.E. Ramachandran, Head of the Department of Indian History, University of Madras.
5. Cited by V.K.R.V. Rao, *Swami Vivekananda—The Prophet of Vedantic Socialism* (Builders of India Series), (New Delhi, 1979), p. 2.
6. *Ibid.*, p. 2.
7. *Ibid.*, p. 3.
8. Mukund, R. Jayakar, *Social Reform and Social Service*, Presidential Address delivered at the Bombay Provincial Social Conference at Nasik 1917, (Madras, 1917), p. 4.
9. R.C. Majumdar, *op. cit.*, p. 115.
10. *Ibid.*, p. 115.
11. *Ibid.*, p. 115.
12. Haridas Bhattacharya (ed.), *The Cultural Heritage of India*, Vol. IV (*The Religions*), Reprint, (Kolkata, 1975), p. 655.
13. *Encyclopaedia Britannica*, Vol. I, 1970 Edn. p. 1000.
14. Haridas Bhattacharya (ed.), *op. cit.*, p. 640.
15. Annie Besant, *The Ancient Wisdom*—An outline of Theosophical Teachings, Reprint, (Adyar, 1949), p.1.
16. Stephen Neill, Gerald Anderson and John Goodwin (ed.), *Concise Dictionary of the Christian World Mission*, (London, 1970), p. 596.
17. R.N. Saksena, *op. cit.*, p. 170

18. S.P. Sen (ed.), *Social Contents of Indian Religious Reform Movements*, (Kolkata, 1978), p. 399.
19. Henry Steele Olcott, *Old Diary Leaves: The History of the Theosophical Society*—Second Series, 1878-1883; Reprint, (London, 1974), p. 392.
20. 'The Golden Book of the Theosophical Society' (Pamphlet), p. 23.
21. *Ibid.*
22. *Supplement to the Theosophist*, (Madras, Sept. 1883), Vol. 4, No. 12, No. 48, pp. 1-3.
23. Henry Steele Olcott, *Old Diary Leaves: The History of the Theosophical Society*—Second Series, 1878-1883, Reprint, (Madras, 1974), pp. 454-455.
24. V. Yasoda Devi, 'Social and Religious Reform Movements in Andhra Pradesh in the Nineteenth and Twentieth Centuries' in S.P. Sen (ed.), *Social and Religious Reform Movement in the Nineteenth and Twentieth Centuries*, (Kolkata, 1979), p. 366.
25. Cited by M. Rani, *The Role of Mrs. Annie Besant in Tamilnadu* (Unpublished M. Phil. Thesis, Madurai Kamaraj University), (Madurai, 1981), Appendix-I.
26. R. Suntharalingam, *Politics and Nationalist Awakening in South India*, (Arizona, 1974), p. 303.
27. *Supplement to the Theosophist*, Vol. 6, No.5. (Madras, Feb. 1885), No. 65, p.1.
28. 'Souvenir'—Centenary of the Theosophical Society, (Dec. 20-30) (Adyar, 1975).
29. Henry S. Olcott, 'The Poor Parish' (Pamphlet), (Adyar, 1902), p. 17.
30. 'Souvenir'—'Olcott Memorial Schools', 75th Anniversary.
31. Cited by Dale R.C. Mc Coy, *The Theosophical Movement And National Regeneration in India* (Unpublished Ph. D. Thesis) (University of Madras, 1978), P. 181.
32. Henry S. Olcott, 'The Poor Pariah' (Pamphlet), (Adyar, 1902) p. 17
33. *Ibid.*, pp. 17-18.
34. *Ibid.*, p. 18.
35. *Ibid.*, p. 19.
36. *Ibid.*, p. 21.
37. *Ibid.*, p. 22.
38. 'Souvenir'—*Centenary of the Theosophical Society*, (Dec. 20-30), 1975, (Adyar, 1975).
39. N. Subba Rao Pantulu Garu (ed.), *Hindu Social Progress*, (Madras, 1904), Appendix-B, p. 55.
40. Annie Besant, *Wake Up, India: A Plea for Social Reform*, (Adyar, 1913), p. 68.

—DR. C. PARAMARTHALINGAM

CHAPTER - XII

THEOSOPHY AND SOCIAL CHANGE IN INDIA

Theosophical Society was established in America in 1875 by Madam Blavatsky and Col. H.S. Olcott. The founders of the Society came to India in 1879. This was the period of rapid social changes in India. Christian missionaries had started some work to improve the position of the weaker and depressed sections of Indian society. Annie Besant joined the Theosophist group in India in 1893. Besant made her mission the saying:

> They are slaves who fear to speak for the fallen and weak.[1]

The main objective of Theosophy was brotherhood of man and acquisition of knowledge about the common truth of all the great religions. It advised their followers to remain within the religion to which they belonged and to deepen it, broaden it and spiritualize it.[2]

While the Western world had come full circle. While they had started realising the trials and tribulations of their meterialistic existence. While they had started examining the spiritual aspects of the human éxistence, Indians looked for Western ideals to bring about social change. English manners, English behaviour, and English language became the means of their salvation. English ideals dominated their lives and thought. Immorality, licentiousness, riotous living were the order of the day. Denationalising emasculation was the prevailing characteristic. Young men took delight in wounding the religious susceptibilities of their countrymen and in cutting their way to salvation through ham and beef and wading their way to liberalism through tumblers of beer.[3]

Much of the social change in the 19th and 20th centuries originated from secular motives based on rationalistic critiques of society and led to secular as well as religious movements for social reform. Caste was considered the root of all problems.[4] The reformers held that due to prevailing social evils in Indian society the land of virtue had become the land of depravity. K.T. Telang and M.G. Ranade felt that system had become petrified. Rammdhun Roy and Keshub Chandra Sen attributed the decline to false religion and Dayananda Saraswati held the hypootic control over society of corrupt Brahmins as the cause of India's downfall. Indians were—a race, degenerated, paralysed in all their energies. The *Indian Social Reformer* declared:

> "The Hindu civilisation based on the ancient Aryan institutions is doomed."[5]

N.G. Chandavarkar and K. Natarajan admitted that Christian missionaries had brought much social wisdom in India.[6] Vithal Ramji Shinde founded the Depressed Classes Mission of Indian in 1906, with the help of the Bombay Presidency Social Reform Association under Chandavarkar.[7] This Mission and the Brahmo Samaj were the first examples of non-Christian efforts on an organized basis to improve the outcastes' conditions.[8] By 1913 the Depressed Classes Mission maintained thirty educational institutions throughout Bombay and Madras provinces. Efforts in this direction were also made by the Arya Samaj, the Dev Samaj, Sikh Associations and by some rulers.[9]

These were some of the illustrations of social change in India when Theosophical Society and Annie Besant emerged on the scene in India with Somewhat different ideas.

To begin with the Theosophical Society took an interest in the Untouchables. The Society established schools for them in 1890. Four such schools were in operation by 1902 under the direction of Miss E.E. Palmer of the University of Minnesota. The number of Olcott Pariah Schools, as they were called, was compared by their founder, in 1902, to the approximately four thousand Christian Missionary institutions for pariahs which were then in operation.[10]

Annie Besant's work for women's upliftment in India which later developed in the form of All India Women's Conference is a lasting testimony of her concern for women's upliftment in India. Throughout her life she stood committed to the ture and not politicized elevation of the cause of weaker sections and depressed classes. She wrote that for a Theosophis the most dynamic idea was the universal Brotherhood of Humanity. Only imagine a world people in the majority with men and women who not only believe but have discovered the joys inherent in that principle; would a man woman then care to ask to what race other belongs, to what God he or she bends the knee? The one joyous truth which the stranger brings with him is then: "You are my brothers. I am your brother." How could wars ever arise in such a civilisation? How could poverty exist as contrasted with callous luxury? These human evils the source of the struggle for existence disappear, as the morning mists disappear with the rising of the sun.[11] Hence, for Annie Besant service and upliftment of the weaker sections and depressed classes of the colonial Indian society was the performance of the Dharma and a duty also which she had to discharge for the sins her countrymen as rulers of the country had committed towards the Indian society by their exploitative and wanton acts.

An examination of the references made by scholars on Annie Besant's works and her activities in India show a lack of true grasp of the lady's personality and her ideas. She has been often denounced as a Hindu Revivalist or as a 'Putna' who was playing an imperial game. But tons of literature available at Adyar, Madras, Nehru Memorial Museum and Library and the National Archives of India, New Delhi, alone give us different pictures of her works and antedents, which is born out by many living Indians who directly or indirectly came in contact with her works and activities in India. To understand her ideas clearly let us go back a little and briefly.

Annie Besant was born with a total faith in God. After marriage, sufferings of children and separation from the husband she studied and reflected and turned non-believer and a stark rationalist—a free thinker with Charles Bradlaugh. Then an anti-imperialist, a birth control agitator and a Fabian socialist. She continued experimenting with truth and finally became Theosophist and claimed to have ultimately found her moorings.

Hence her ideas and activities do not need to be analysed on the basis of any Euro-centric methodologies and theoretical formulations. She was a humanitarian and social reformer according to her own light and not under any external pressures and motives as is often made out:

> "Olcott and Leadbeater were joined in 1893 by Annie Besant, who within a few years established herself as the outstanding revivalist of Hinduism in South India....Mrs. Besant held forth on the glories of ancient and modern Hinduism in all its facets. Social reformers stood nearly helplessly by while a great-voiced, cultivated English woman be sought Hindus to avoid the pitfalls of so-called Western advancement and revere their own great culture."[12]

Annie Besant was not the first nor the only advocate of the philosophy of social reform, discussed in the preceding paragraphs. Dayanand Saraswati had already given a call to go back to Vedas and the whole lot of orientalists who had by now drunk deep of the original and translated Indian classics had started examining them more carefully for a happy and healthy social order.

Annie Besant had herself read and written extensively on Upnishads, Gita and other Indian classics and through her varied experiments and experiences was fully convinced that any social change brought about on the basis of mere human rational was not enough, it must also confirm to the perennial truth as revealed in the divine revelations.

Throughout her exhortations for social change in India she propounded and advocated Indian ideals, howsoever she was misunderstood or criticized by those for whom she lived and died at Adyar (Madras) on 20 September 1933. She believed:

> Each truth can only be seen by a man as he develops the power of vision corresponding to it.

NOTES AND REFERENCES

1. Raj Kumar, *Annie Besant's Rise to Power in Indian Poilitics 1914-1917*, New Delhi, 1989.
2. Annie Besant, *A Sketch of Theosophy*, T.P.H. Adyar, Madras, 1951, p. 6.
3. *Hindustan Review*, May 1907, p. 480.
4. M.G. Ranade, *The Miscellaneous Writings of Mr. Justice M.G. Ranade*, Mumbai, 1915, p. 192.

Also Rammohan Roy, *The English Works of Rammohan Roy* (ed Jogendra Chunder Ghose), Allahabad, 1906, pp.929-30.

5. Iswar Chandra Vidyasagar, Marriage of Hindu Widows, Kolkata, 1956, p. 94.
6. K.T. Telang, *Selected Writings and Speeches,* Mumbai, 1916, p. 97.
7. *The Indian Social Reformer,* 8 March 1903, pp. 1, 112.
8. Fred B. Fisher, *India's Silent Revolution,* p. 85.
9. J.N. Farquhar, *Modern Religious Movements in India,* p. 372.
10. *Ibid.,* p. 372.
11. S. Natarajan, *A Century of Social Reform in India,* Mumbai, 1959, p. 156.
12. Henry S. Olcott. *The Poor Pariah,* Madras, 1902, p. 23.
13. Annie Besant, *A Sketch of Theosophy,* Adyar, Madras, 195
14. Charles H. Heimsath, *Indian Nationalism and Hindu Social Reform,* Princeton, 1964.

—DR. RAJ KUMAR, ICHR

CHAPTER - XIII

NATIONALISM AND SOCIAL CHANGE

The emergence of a national movement of epic dimensions in India, and its culmination in the transfer of power from British into Indian hands, constituted one of the most important historical processes of the twentieth century. The repercussions of this movement, which were manifest in the transformation of India from a colonial into an independent polity, extended far beyond its immediate political consequences. Within the physical confines of India, this national movement set afoot processes which sought to redistribute social and economic power in the community, and which continue to characterize politics in the subcontinent after three decades of independence. Outside the country, this national movement initiated a political revolution in the Third World as a result of which other colonial societies in Asia and Africa were able to free themselves of European domination. Both in its internal and in its external reprecussions, therefore, the rise and fulfilment of nationalism in India was a phenomenon of outstading significance, comparable in its sweep, its complexity, and its consequences to the Russian Revolution of 1917, or the emergence of a revitalized China in 1949.

When we consider the significance and scale of the national movement in India it should occasion no surprise that it has inspired a very rich corpus of historical literature. Nor should it be a matter of surprise that this literature reflects conflicting scholarly perceptions of the nature of the national movement in India. A process as complex as the one under consideration is bound to reflect different facets of its reality to different scholars. But over and above the complexity of the national movement, there is the question of the influence which grand theory exercises over historical writing; of the philosophical assumptions, or the political presuppositions, which scholars bring to bear upon the task of examining society and politics in India under the British *imperium*. One touches here upon the vexed question of bias and commitment in history. Since the author subscribes to the view that all historical writing rests upon explicit or implicit assumptions, one can legitimately infer that different scholarly perceptions of nationalism in India are just as much related to the empirical focus of particular studies as they are related to the presuppositions with which a scholar examines this political phenomenon.

Our own particular bias in this essay touches upon the relationship between social structure and political process. It is further assumed that the growth of nationalism can best be studied by relating it to the structure of society in India, and the changes which came about in this structure as a result of British rule. Yet before we embark upon such an exploration, it would be useful to spell out our understanding of nationalism.[1] Such an exercise is necessary because the absense of conceptual clarity often leads to considerable confusion in studies on nationalism in India. It is clear that the species of nationalism which is under cnsideration here first manifested itself in Europe during the late eighteenth and the early nineteenth centuries; and further, that it rested upon the organization of culturally homogeneous polities into autonomous States, which were characterized by popular participation in politics. The ideology of nationalism, to put it formally, leads societies which are culturally and ethnically homogeneous to organize themselves into independent States; and it encourages them to do so in the belief that political autonomy will heighten their material as well as their cultural creativity. Indeed, one cannot overemphasize the fact that in any nationalist movement moral and material motives are inextricably linked, and it is impossible to decide where the one begins and the other ends. When we apply our definition of nationalism to India, we run into some serious problems. It is clear, for instance, that the cultural homogeneity or ethnic cohesion which underpinned the nationalist movements of Europe were conspicuously absent in India. It is also clear that the social structure and political texture of society in India were qualitatively different from the social structure and political texture of those European societies which underwent nationalist upheavals in the nineteenth century. These aspects of society in the subcontinent are emphasized merely in order to prepare the ground for our enquiry into the national movement in India.

I

This essay takes as its point of departure the social system of India as it existed towards the middle of the nineteenth century, at a time when British policies had interacted with pre-colonial institutions to create a fairly will-defined organization of society. We do so in the belief that politics in general, and the politics of nationalism in particular, can best be understood by looking at social structure and social change, and by examining the tensions latent in a society as well as their articulation in ideology.

Our attempt at exploring the social system of India as it stood towards the middle of the nineteenth century can be successful only if our task is reduced to manageable proportions. For this purpose, it would be advisable to break up the social system into two broad divisions, namely, the urban and the rural sectors. If we first examine the structures of these two sectors, and then focus upon the linkages which held them together in a composite system, it may be possible for us to grasp something of the complexity of society in India as a whole.

It would be profitable, in the first instance, to examine the rural sector in India in the second half of the nineteenth century. As is well known to historians of modern India, in the rural districts of Bengal, Bihar, Orissa and eastern Uttar Pradesh the British attempted to create an aristocratic landed society, in the belief that such a Society would, on the one hand, generate a powerful sentiment of loyalty for the British Government and, on the other, provide the basis for economic growth in the rural community. These expectations were based upon the experience of political control and economic growth in Britain in the eighteenth century; they also rested upon the assumption that social and economic institutions which had yielded favourable results in Britain would yield favourable results in India.

While the Permanent Settlement of Bengal rested upon a British model of economic growth, it was applied to a social context characterized by a very complex organization of property rights and tenurial relations in the land.[2] Some of the great territorial magnates 'created' by the British were genuine zamindars, who were merely confirmed in respect of rights which they had enjoyed for generations; some of them were clan and lineage heads, who had formerly acted as revenue collecting intermediaries in respect of the lands controlled by the clan or the lineage as a whole; others were newly enriched civil servants, or men of business, who had accumulated considerable properties during the time of troubles which followed upon the decay of Mughal imperial authority; others, yet again, were tribal chiefs, who suddenly found themselves in full ownership of territories over which they had formerly exercised a vague political authority. Yet whatever be the origin of the territorial magnates created by the British, most of them shared a common quality, or a lack thereof. They were incapable of acting in the capacity of improving landlords, as envisaged by contemporary Western theories of economic growth; instead, they preferred to lease portions of their properties to others, who in turn played the role of rentiers, so that within a short span of time, as many as four or five layers of parasitic intermediaries stood between a great zamindar, who tendered account to the British Government for an estate bequeathed to him in perpetuity, and the humble tenant in the village, who cultivated a few acres to provide the barest of subsistence for himself and his dependants.

It is only recently that historical research has revealed to us the full consequences of the great experiment in social engineering which the British introduced under the Permanent Settlement of Bengal. It has been suggested, for instance, that profits in agriculture were so attractive till the 1850s that urban capital and urban enterprise were drawn irresistibly towards agriculture, thus giving to Bengali society, more particularly to the life styles of the upper classes, that 'feudal' character the cultural residues of which can be discerned even till the present day. Of course, the stranglehold which British commerce, assisted by the policies of the British Government, had established over the region served a similar purpose by driving Bengali capital and Bengali enterprise to the land. Be that as it may, the contemporary picture of the upper and middle classes of Bengal, as classes which abhorred commercial and entrepreneurial activity and preferred to maintain themselves on rents drawn from their lands or through employment in the liberal professions, is largely related to a deliberate act of policy by the British Government. The results of this policy were obvious by the close of the nineteenth century, and they are crucially related to nationalist politics in the region. Within the span of a few generations, the incomes of substantial sections of the Bengali landed gentry had declined to an extent where they were unable to sustain the life styles to which they had become accustomed. The professions, too, were unable to accommodate all those sons of the impoverished gentry who had obtained a liberal education in the hope that they would make their careers as lawyers, doctors, teachers, or journalists. The frustration of this class, a class rich in its intellectual culture and possessing a great measure of expectations, was the great driving force behind nationalist activity in Bengal, and we shall touch upon its activities later in this essay.

The social process which underpinned nationalist politics in Bengal is well known to scholars of modern Indian history. But we know far less of what was happening in the nineteenth century in other parts of the country where policies different from the Permanent Settlement were pursued. In the Presidencies of Madras and Bombay, and in the provinces of north India, the strategy of basing the stability of the British Raj upon a territorial aristocracy was abandoned in favour of a very different strategy. This new strategy is conventionally described as the *raiyatwari* system, and it is to the examination of this system, and to a critique of its social and political consequences, that we shall now turn our attention.[3]

At the very outset, we would like to point out that the objectives with which the British Government launched the *raiyatwari* system have never received much scholarly attention. We know equally little of the social transformation which the *raiyatwari* system brought about in the regions where it was applied. However, it may be possible to extrapolate the findings of a few investigations in southern and western India to the *raiyatwari* areas as a whole. According to conventional wisdom, the *raiyatwari* system was an attempt by the Birtish Government to establish an egalitarian peasant society in the south, the west and the north of the country. But the egalitarian tone of this policy should not blind us to the fact that social mobility and economic growth, albeit within the parameters of a peasant society, were encouraged rather than discouraged in the *raiyatwari* areas. Orderly government and the magic of private property, so the advocates of the *raiyatwari* policy believed, would encourage thrifty and enterprising peasants to reinvest their capital in the land, thus ensuring for themselves expanding horizons of prosperity, and for society as a whole a regime of steady economic growth. Such an economic strategy could be expected to provide a far more stable political base for the British Raj than that conjured into existence by the Permanent Settlement. For, so the advocates of the *raiyatwari* policy argued, their strategy would ensure for the British Government the loyalty of hundreds upon thousands of small peasant-proprietors, whose growing prosperity would tie them in firm bonds of allegiance to the British Government.

The realities of social mobility and economic growth in the provinces subject to the *raiyatwari* system were quite different from the expectations with which the policy had been introduced in vast regions of India. It is probably true that a small proportion of the peasantry—we would not put their strength at higher than ten per cent of the cultivators—was able to reap substantial benefits from the *raiyatwari* system and from the infrastructure of law and government which sustained this system. But the growing prosperity of this class of peasants, whom we shall call the rich peasants, was only one of the consequences flowing from the *raiyatwari* system. A considerable proportion of the remaining ninety per cent of the peasants were unable to cope with the market-oriented rural economy generated by the British Raj, with the result that they became increasingly impoverished and often sank to the status of tenant cultivators or landless labourers.

Since the *raiyatwari* system generated as much upward mobility as it generated downward mobility—it made the rich peasants richer, and the poor peasants poorer—it posed very awkward problems of political control and economic management for the British Government. The disaffection of the peasantry which was sliding down the scale of prosperity erupted quite frequently in agitations which threatened to undermine the fabric of the British Raj in India. In 1857, for instance, in large areas of the North Western Provinces (modern Uttar Pradesh) the hostility of the peasant-proprietors who has lost their holdings under the British dispensation was an important factor behind the rural uprisings. Similar expressions of discontent, though smaller in scale, surfaced later in the nineteenth century and caused serious concern to the British administration. This was so even though the peasantry, which was ignorant of the techniques of political organization, was unable to give coherent expression to its hostility and often struck blindly at the social classes which appeared to be the proximate instruments of its social misery. The fact of the matter was that no official measure was successful in remedying the distress that flowed from the *raiyatwari* system. The most obvious measure, namely, the imposition of restraints on money-lenders, dried up those sources of credit in the villages which fromed the very basis of agricultural operations. When the British Government went a step further and initiated co-operative credit societies with the objective of creating a new source of credit in the villages, it soon became clear that the beneficiaries of such a measure were those who already controlled a disproportionate share of the wealth and power amongst the peasant-proprietors. It would perhaps be pertinent to remember here that economic theory, outside the realm of socialist theory, had nothing better to offer by way of guidance to a government (like the British Government) which sought to create a prosperous peasant society within the framework of a market economy.

The generation of disaffection among downwardly mobile peasants does not exhaust the list of problems which the *raiyatwari* system presented to the British Government in India. An equally serious matter was the periodic reassessment of the peasant's obligations in tax, which rested upon the Ricardian assumption that the State, as the supreme landlord in the country, had a right to share with the peasant the increasing profits which he drew from the land. This is not the place to discuss the legitimacy of the economic theory upon which the periodic reassessment of the peasant's obligations in tax was based. But it would be pertinent to focus attention on two important consequences of these reassessements. Since the revenue machinery of the British

Government was notoriously corrupt—we have elsewhere defined such corruption as 'socialized' corruption—the burden of any upward revision in the tax was very inequitably distributed between the rich and the poor peasants in a district. But even if the enhanced tax were to be equitably distributed, it would be a measure which the peasantry, ignorant of the subtleties of Ricardian economics, would regard as oppressive and unjustified in the extreme. So long as the peasantry was not properly organized, it reacted to reassessment with primitive fury, often indulging in small-scale jacqueries or migrating in substantial numbers to neighbouring districts. Indeed, the history of reassessments in the *raiyatwari* districts in the nineteenth century shows rural society to be a very turbulent society, though disorganization amongst the peasantry made this turbulence easy to control for the British Government. However, later on in the twentieth century, when modern methods of organization and agitation had spread to the villages, districts which were resettled often erupted into powerful nationalist agitations against the British Raj.

II

Our examination of British attempts at social engineering in rural society and of the tensions which stemmed from such attempts is fully justified by the importance which the rural sector occupied in India. Yet it would be a distortion of reality to neglect the role—in economic productivity, in political organization, or in intellectual creativity—played by urban society during these decades. It would, indeed, be no exaggeration to state that the changes which swept across India in the period under review originated in urban society, even though they ultimately reached out to the villages, to reintegrate social, economic, political and intellectual life in the subcontinent along novel lines.

As in the case of rural society, the changes which the British *imperium* brought about in urban society were complex rather than simple. At the root of these transformations lay some qualitative changes in the manner in which wealth was generated in the cities; in the relationships of exchange between urban and rural society; in the emergence of the market as the hub of the economic order; and in the ties of superordination and and subordination which linked Britain and India in different spheres of social activity.

The most striking feature of British rule over India, so far as urban society was concerned, was the emergence of substantial new cities in the coastal region like Calcutta, Bombay and Madras.[4] These cities owed their origin to the trading activities which the British initiated in the subcontinent during the seventeenth century. But as the British presence on the subcontinent grew in economic and political significance, these cities came to acquire a new importance in the social and economic life of the country. Increasingly, the agricultural produce of India passed through these ports for consumption in the industrial centres of the West; and it was through these ports that the industrial products of the West reached out to the centres of consumption in the Indian hinterland. The vitality of these cities depended upon the two-way system of exchange which marked the transformation of India from a medieval into a colonial economy. But over and above their role as channels of commercial exchange, these cities also served as centres for industrial production : Bombay as a locus for the textile industry and Calcutta as the base for the jute industry.

The social structure of these coastal cities, as well as the quality of their economic creativity, was different from those of the traditional cities of the subcontinent. At the very apex of society in these cities was located a wealthy industrial and commercial bourgeoisie which dominated trade and industry, and controlled the levers of social and economic power in the community. Below them stood a professional class which dominated the bar, or the seats of education, or the vocation of medicine, or the middle rungs of the civil service. Apart from a nondescript petty bourgeoisie, some members of which were shopkeepers while others served as clerks in commercial firms or in government offices, the next significant stratum of society was made up of the industrial working class, which provided the labour necessary for the modern industry that had grown up in these cities. Last but not the least, there thrived substantial lumpen groups of casual workers, or rural migrants, or beggars and mendicants. Finally, it is important to remember that while these cities were undergoing an increase in their prosperity, the growing prosperity was unequally distributed among different social classes. To put it briefly, most of the increasing prosperity of the cities went to the bourgeoisie, industrial, commercial and professional, leaving other classes greatly disaffected at their relative impoverishment in a context of overall prosperity.

When we look at the traditional cities of India, we encounter a situation substantially different from that of the industrial cities. The basic fact about these cities was that they were only marginally affected by industrialization. They were political or commerical centres of greater or lesser importance, and their social structure reflected their role in society. The dominant position in such cities was held by a class of urban notables, who either presided over vast commercial empires which had grown up under the British dispensation, or controlled substantial resources in financial wealth. Next to these notables, and inferior to them in their influence and resources, stood a professional middle class of lawyers, doctors, academics, journalists and civil servants, which was largely the creation of the *Pax Britannica*, but whose appetite for power was growing far too rapidly to be appeased by the British Raj. Apart from this restless middle class, which tapered off into a petty bourgeoisie comprising men on the fringes of business or the professions, the traditional cities also harboured numerous artisans and craftsmen, whose fortunes had declined sharply owing to the displacement of their products by factory-produced goods, and who were, therefore, destined to provide highly combustible material for political movements in the late nineteenth and the twentieth centuries.

The picture which we have presented of the social system in India in the second half of the nineteenth century is a picture which glosses over considerable diversity in order to encompass within in brief essay a very complex organization of society. This is inevitable when we try to generalize on such a scale. But the sectoral division we have carried out in order to facilitate our portrayal of society should not convey the impression that urban and rural societies existed as isolated social fragments; or that the classes within the urban and the rural sectors comprised mutually exclusive social units. Nothing could be further from the turth. This can be readily demonstrated by touching upon the multiplicity of ties which linked rural to urban society, or related different segments of urban and rural society to each other.

The city of Calcutta in the context of its hinterland is a good exemplar of this. As indicated earlier, rural Bengal was dominated by a landed gentry which grew out of the Permanent Settlement that the British Government had imposed upon the region. With the fragmentation of holdings that eventually resulted, this gentry became progressively impoverished, forcing some of its members to migrate to Calcutta to earn their livelihood in the professions. As a result of this, the professional middle class of Calcutta was closely linked through ties of kinship to the landed gentry of Bengal. A similar process was noticeable in Gujarat, where the rural scene was dominated by the landowning caste of the *patidars*. By the close of the nineteenth century these *patidars*, partly as a result of economic pressures but partly also through an extension of their social horizons, were moving in great numbers to the professions in the towns and cities of Gujarat.

The case of those members of the landed classes who flocked to the professions as a result of impoverishment or the extension of opportunities does not exhaust the list of urban-rural linkages in India. An equally significant nexus was the one which ensured the flow of urban credit to rural society and, in exchange, siphoned off a part of the agricultural surplus for consumption in the cities. There exists considerable literature about the role which the moneylender played in the village by extending credit to the cultivator for the payment of taxes, or purchase of seed, or fulfilment of social obligations. But this literature emphasizes inadequately, if at all, the extent to which the village moneylender was the humblest member of a financial hierarchy which was headed by substantial *sowcars* in the cities and whose operations reached out to the villages through a chain of lesser *sowcars* located in the principal centres of districts and *tahsils*. The link between the substantial *sowcars* in the city and the humble cultivator in the village, through a chain of financial intermediaries, served as the channel for a two-way process of exchange. On the one hand, the cultivator secured through this channel the credit which was essential to the business of cultivation; on the other, part of the surplus produced by the cultivator was drawn to the *mandis*, and from there to the retailer, through this network of financial intermediaries.

Yet another linkage between urban and rural society, which acquired increasing importance in the nineteenth century, was the linkages created by the judicial institutions which the British introduced in the country. In the courts located in the provincial capitals, and in the lesser courts based in the district and *tahsil* townships, there thrived clusters of lawyers whose professional work related them, on the one hand, to the landed gentry and the dominant peasant classes and, on the other, to the commercial classes residing in the cities. Here was a relationship that was entirely the creation of the British Raj; a relationship, moreover, which linked the rural classes with individuals whose understanding of the new politics was unrivalled among the educated classes which had grown up under the *Pax Britannica*.

The importance of the linkages between urban and rural society can hardly be overemphasized. Their role in establishing relations of superordination and subordination between different classes is clear from what we have said above. But these linkages also provided a ready-made network to the advocates of nationalist politics when they sought to politicize new classes and disseminate new ideas in the country in the late nineteenth and the twentieth centuries. As has been observed, the professional and commercial classes in the cities were the great driving force behind the movement which sought to create a new unity, a nationalist unity, among different sectors of society in the subcontinent. In their attempt to forge this unity, the professional and commercial classes used their linkages with rural society to great effect. However, as we have seen, the transformation of a professional into a political relationship was by no means a transformation which necessarily favoured the urban classes. It is true that nationalism in India was born in the cities. Yet with the passage of time, the locus of power within nationalist politics shifted from the urban to the rural classes, and the dominance of the latter gave a unique flavour to the economic aspirations as well as the political style of nationalism in India.

III

Our brief survey of the fabric of society in the second half of the nineteenth century provides us with several insights into the relationship between social structure and political process in India. Yet before our explorations take us any further, it may be advantageous to reiterate two points. First, that the social linkages as well as the foci of tension to which we have referred above were responsible for imparting to nationalism its specific characteristics in India. Secondly, that it would be an over-simplification to look upon nationalism, and upon participation in nationalist politics, as phenomena exclusively economic in character, as 'belly politics' pure and simple. As our definition of nationalism indicates, the ideal facets of such a movement—the belief, in particular, that political freedom strengthens the moral fibre and heightens cultural creativity—exercise a powerful influence over individuals and classes caught in its grip, and encourage them to embark upon courses of political action which are difficult to explain purely on the basis of economic motivation. But having voiced such a qualification, let us hasten to add that whatever role ideal factors play in national movements, the overall features of such movements, in India as elsewhere, are shaped by the self-interest of the classes which are drawn into them.

In view of our perception of nationalism, it should occasion no surprise if we leave out of consideration the Uprising of 1857. That this Uprising was informed by a powerful spirit of patriotism; that it embraced vast provinces in northern India; that it involved large sections of the community; that it represented grievances against the British Raj which had grown over half a century—all this is true. Yet the Uprising of 1857 had very little to do with nationalism, as defined here. The leaders of the Uprising were ignorant of the ideology of nationalism, just as they were also ignorant of the principles of organization which inform national movements. If these leaders had been successful, then they would have established a traditional polity in India, a polity based upon the institutions of the Mughal Empire, or some of its successor States, which had been overthrown by the British *imperium*.

To trace the genesis of nationalism in India, it is necessary to go to the decades preceding 1857, when some of the social classes created by the British Raj faced threats to their economic interests, and organized themselves along western lines in defence of these interests.[5] It is significant that the first modern political association in India, the Landholder's Society, came into existence when the great zamindars of the Permanent Settlement faced an attack upon their interests in the shape of the resumption of rent-free lands. This class of zamindars, whose more sophisticated members had absorbed to a substantial degree the political culture of the West, created in the Landholders' Society a body which drew upon modern principles of organization to exercise political pressure on the British Government of India. Even before the creation of the Landholders' Society, the more cultivated zamindars had been active in a variety of fields, which may be called political in an wider sense of the term. The objective of all this activity was to transform Bengal into a bourgeois society tied in bonds of subordination to Britain. Between the opposition which the zamindars offered to the British Government through organizations like the Landholders' Society and the overall identity of interest between the latter and the former, there was no contradiction. For if the social activity of this class reinforced the British connection, then its political activity, too, did not in any way question the overall legitimacy of British control over India. It is, after all, one of the axioms of politics that conflict which does not question the basic principles of a polity reinforces rather than weakens that polity.

The politics of the great zamindars also impinged upon the professional classes, particularly in a province like Bengal, where the close link between the former and the latter has already been touched upon in this essay. The alliance between the landed classes and those members of these classes who had been drawn into liberal vocations constituted the basis of politics in Bengal during the third and the fourth quarter of the nineteenth century. The objectives of this politics were modest: the protection of the interests of the landlords as well as of the middle classes, who sought for themselves secure titles to property and a larger share of jobs in the civil service and in other professions. The pursuit of such modest aims by the alliance of the landlords and the middle classes did not preclude a strategic threat to the British Raj in India. But for the foreseeable future in the nineteenth century, this alliance identified its interests with the interests of the British Government.

The political developments to which we have referred above are well known to scholars of modern Indian history. But equally crucial developments, which are less known, were afoot in other regions of India. In the traditional cities of north India, the establishment of the British Raj gave a great fillip to the commercial classes, whose business activities grew in scale and in volume during the decades under consideration. In these cities, under the patronage of the business magnates, there grew up a professional class which was at home in modern politics, although it had not absorbed the intellectual culture of the West to the extent of its peers in Bengal. In the Urban centres of north India, therefore, political activity which sought to secure for the commerical and the middle classes a larger share of social and economic power was set afoot around the same time as in Bengal.

The foregoing observations about social change and its reflection in nationalist politics do not exhaust the subject under review. For, as already observed, in the *raiyatwari* provinces of the south, the north and the west, although these regions differed from each other, the effect of British economic policies was to create a new affluence among the more substantial cultivators, just as these policies also heightened impoverishment among the poorer cultivators. The upwardly mobile peasants in the *raiyatwari* areas acquired fresh political ambitions as a result of their newly acquired wealth, and either directly, through members of their class who had entered the liberal professions, or indirectly, through lawyers and *sowcars* with whom they had professional links, the ambitions of these rich peasants began to impinge upon the local and regional associations which sprang into life in the last quarter of the nineteenth century.

The interplay between social structure and political activity which is sketched above contributed to the founding of the Indian National Congress in 1885. In referring to this development in nationalist politics, we highlight a theme which is all too familiar to students of modern Indian history. Yet it is a familiar theme which acquires a sharper focus as our perception of our society in the nineteenth century is heightened through new research. Historians no longer look upon the Congress in its first phase as an organization of the the professional middle classes, directly or indirectly supported by the industrial and commercial bourgeoisie. To understand the texture of nationalist politics in this phase, scholars also stress the necessity of examining the new relationships between urban and rural society—between peasants and lawyers, or peasants and *sowcars*, or the landed gentry and the professions—that sprang into life under the British dispensation, and supported the local and regional institutions which underpinned the Indian National Congress. From the very outset, therefore, the Congress rested upon a support base which was intimately linked to the fabric of society, and which reflected the aspirations and the interests of a variety of social classes.

If the foregoing suggests that there was a perfect mesh between social structure and political organization, we must correct such an impression. For a number of developments in nationalist politics during the closing decades of the nineteenth century suggest that despite its far-flung organizational roots, and notwithstanding its broad social base, the Indian National Congress was unable to reflect the full range of social aspirations, or economic discontents, that were afloat in the community. We refer here to a phenomenon which is conventionally described as 'extremist politics', though it should be clear that this term covers a number of distinct phenomena, all of which lay outside the arena of the Congress.

Our contention that extremist politics covered a variety of phenomena is borne out by the most cursory examination of such politics. Take the case of Bengal, in the first instance.[6] In our portrayal of the classes created by the Permanent Settlement, it has been emphasized that this measure caused distress among the lower ranks of the landed gentry, whose strength in numbers prevented them from finding employment in the professions. The frustration of this class could not find satisfaction in the moderate politics of the Congress in its first phase; and it turned to violence against the British Government, such violence being legitimized by a revival of the religious consciousness of the community. Like the *Narodniki* of Czarist Russia, the advocates of violence in Bengal sought to undermine the psychological dominance of the British Raj over its subjects in India through isolated acts of terror, in the hope that such an erosion would trigger off a great populist uprising against the alien rulers of the land. Yet unlike their Russian peers, the terrorists of Bengal refused to subordinate their class interests, the interests of an unpoverished landed gentry, to the interests of the cultivating classes in society. Hence the failure of a movements which rested upon great individual heroism. But perhaps the gulf between the landed gentry of Bengal, which was largely drawn from the upper castes of Hindu society, and the cultivating classes, which comprised low-caste Hindus and Muslims, was too wide to permit the latter to forge an alliance with the former in a movement against the British Government.

While the terrorist movement of Bengal reflected the frustration of an impoverished gentry, extremist politics in the Punjab represented something altogether different.[7] The Punjab was settled along *raiyatwari* lines by the British Government, and we have every reason to believe that a section of the cultivating classes in the province, namely, those who were endowed with some resources in capital and enterprise, prospered under the British dispensation. This was particularly true of the peasant proprietors who were settled in the canal colonies that had grown up under British rule. Yet it was these prosperous cultivators who seethed with discontent in the first decade of the twentieth century, when the British Government added to their financial burdens through enhanced water rates and agricultural taxes. Of course, all this was aggravated by genuine economic distress in the central districts of the Punjab, just as it was also reinforced by the disaffection of the urban classes, Hindu and Muslim, the former because of the Land Alienation Act, and the latter by virtue of the Pan-Islamic movement. Yet the peasant base of political violence in the Punjab gave it a very different complexion from the political violence in Bengal.

The character of violent politics in Maharashtra, to carry our analysis a little further, was qualitatively different from such politics in the north, or in the east, of the country.[8] Although there is reason to believe that some of the advocates of violence in Maharashtra tried to reach out to the villages, the bulk of the recruits to extremism were drawn from impoverished families of high status, who had not learnt to cope with the market society that had come into existence under the British Raj. Like their Bengali peers, the advocates of violence in Maharashtra failed to link up with any substantial section of the community; and like their Bengali peers, they initiated a movement which was soon suppressed by the British Government.

It should be clear from our appreciation of the politics of violence in Bengal, the Punjab and Maharashtra that this phenomenon represented the social frustration of classes which disapproved in the strongest possible terms of the British Raj. It should also be clear why this violence, reflecting as it did the disaffection of fragmented social groups, soon spent itself in futile albeit heroic assaults on the British Government. Yet the significance of these movements for the Indian National Congress, and for nationalist politics, should not escape our notice merely because they failed in their proximate objectives. We have stated earlier that the Congress, when it was launched in 1885, gave expression to the aspirations as well as to the discontent of practically all the politicized classes in society. The outbreak of violence in the closing decade of the nineteenth century clearly indicated that the Congress was unable to play such a role any longer. The social classes behind violent politics—the impoverished gentry of Bengal, the downwardly mobile middle classes of Maharashtra, the peasantry of the Punjab, or the intelligentsia drawn from the Muslim community—were no longer content with a style of politics which rested upon the assumption that nationalist aspirations could be satisfied through a constitutional dialogue with the British Government. All this came to a head in 1907, when the Congress broke up into two fragments which had different perceptions of the relationship between Indian nationalism and British imperialism.

IV

We are now in a position to explore a new phase of nationalist politics in India, a phase dominated by the figure of Gandhi.[9] This phase commenced with the breakup of a united nationalist movement in the manner indicated above. It was also characterized by a new alignment of different classes and communities in India; an alignment which ultimately forced and British Government to dispossess itself of political control over the subcontinent, although all this was achieved at the price of the vivisection of India.

To appreciate this new phase of politics, it is necessary to look beyond those social groups whose aspirations were articulated by the Congress, as it was constituted in 1885. It is also necessary to look beyond those classes which took recourse to violence in the first decade of the twentieth century. A reference has been made earlier in this essay to the growing social differentiation of the peasantry in the *raiyatwari* areas, as also to the changing class character of the landed interests which had been created by the Permanent Settlement in Bengal. It is clear that towards the close of the nineteenth century, the upwardly mobile peasantry in the Punjab, or Maharashtra, or Gujarat, was looking for the means to transform its newly acquired wealth into social and economic power. The restlessness of the peasantry became particularly acute when the British Government tried to enhance its tax obligations through resettlement operations. The occupancy tenants within the villages in the zamindari areas, whose position was comparable to the position of peasant-proprietors in the *raiyatwari* areas, were also chafing at the bonds which tied them to a social order which they increasingly regarded as unjust.

A similar ferment among the lowly classes was in evidence in the urban sector of society, in industrial and traditional cities alike. Cities like Bombay and Calcutta housed rapidly growing working class populations whose relative deprivation made them a fertile recruiting ground for class politics. Below the workers, in the industrial cities, stood the lumpen classes, a shifting, anonymous mass of humanity, seething with discontent and ready to respond to the call of radical politics or communal violence. The situation was equally volatile in the traditional cities. There lived in such cities, in substantial numbers, artisans and craftsmen whose way of life was threatened by the produce of modern industry, whether this industry was based in India or overseas. Because the traditional cities were the locus of such discontented classes, they were veritable powder kegs, ready to explode into political violence at the first opportunity.

It would be legitimate to infer that the tensions located in different sectors of Indian society, rural and urban, constituted the raw material of a great populist upheaval. It is also true that prior to 1919, no institutional means had been devised to channelize these discontents into an organized movement, reflecting popular aspirations, against the British Government.

Gandhi's genius—and we feel obliged to introduce, at this juncture, a political actor of heroic stature—lay in recognizing the discontents which were afloat in different sectors of Indian society, and in giving them organized expression in a revitalized Indian National Congress. When Gandhi returned to India in 1915, he had already developed a unique technique of political agitation, just as he had already given clear evidence of his superb organizational skills, during his sojourn in South Africa. His initial encounter with politics brought him in contact with that middle class restlessness which had been organized in the Indian National Congress, and that petty bourgeois radicalism which was drawn into the Home Rule movement during the First World War. Gandhi came in close contact with such classes during his first year in India, and he sensed to the full their disenchantment with the British Raj. Yet such a perception did not amount to a breakthrough, although few contemporary politicians in India had as sensitive an appreciation of politics on a national scale as Gandhi acquired in a short span of time.

Before long, however, Gandhi was to run headlong into that grassroots restlessness which was so significant a feature of politics in India during the second decade of the twentieth century, even though such restlessness had not registered itself with the established leadership of the day. The manner in which an obscure 'peasant' from Champaran chased Gandhi for a full year before he persuaded him to visit a district that had been repeatedly erupting into violence is well known to students of modern India history. Gandhi discovered similar subterranean discontents at the very doorsteps of his ashram on the banks of the Sabarmati: among the textile workers of Ahmedabad, who sought to persuade the mill-owners of the city to disgorge, in the shape of increased wages, a modest fraction of the enormous profits which they had made during the war; and among the present-proprietors of Kheda, who had reacted very sharply to the enhancement of their taxes through a revision settlement of the district.

The ferment which characterized the peasants of Champaran, the workers of Ahmedabad, or the cultivators of Kheda was qualitatively different from the restlessness which affected the middle classes or the petty bourgeoisie. It was the ferment reaching down to the core of society, and it opened up the most exciting possibilites for nationalist politics. It soon dawned upon Gandhi, who had led small-scale movements among the peasants of Kheda and Champaran and the workers of Ahmedabad with a substantial measure of success, that the true task confronting nationalism was the fusion of two distinct political streams:one consisting of the middle classes and the petty bourgeoisie, and the other drawn from the working classes and the peasantry. At the very moment Gandhi recognized the restlessness of the workers and the peasants he also sensed the social linkages to which we have referred earlier—the bonds between the lawyer and his rural clientele, or the ties between the *sowcar* and the cultivators, or the urban networks of the cultivating classes which had commenced reaching out to the professions. Here lay the raw materials for mounting a powerful populist movement against the British Raj. This task posed the kind of challege which brought about a flowering of Gandhi's political genius.

V

At this point, a brief digression is necessary if we are to appreciate the complexity of politics in India during the first two decades of the twentieth century. We have so far talked of social structure and social differentiation in the terms of the classes,urban and rural, which characterized society in India. Our portrayal of the fabric of society is a very generalized portrayal, if only for reasons of space in a brief essay. Yet even in a brief essay, it is necessary to look at cleavages other than class cleavages if we are to understand the true character of nationalism in India.

It is well known that during the decades under review nearly twenty-five per cent of the population of India subscribed to the religion of Islam. Yet it is a difficult task to assign this great minority its appropriate place in the scheme of urban and rural society which we have portrayed above. We can, however, commence by discarding images of Muslim social structure which bear little relation to reality. It is also legitimate to reject the view that there was a monolithic Muslim society in India. As has been observed by a distinguished scholar, a deep gulf of sensibility and interests separated the landed gentry of the (then) United Provinces from the cultivating classes of Bengal; a similar gulf stood between the commercial groups of the coastal cities, on the one hand, and the artisans and craftmen of the cities in the interior, on the other. There is reason to suggest that Muslims belonging to different classes were torn between two conflicting loyalties: the economic realities of life, their self-interest, prompted them to pursue class politics; yet their allegiance to Islam urged them to seek association with their co-religionists in politics. The tension between a class identity and a religious identity is sensitively reflected in the turbulent currents of Muslim politics in the opening decades of the twentieth century. Yet before this theme is explored any further, it may be relevant to observe that in certain situations, class and religious politics could reinforce each other, with results of great significance to Muslim society in India.[10]

The most significant class in Muslim society consisted of the *Ashraf*, who had migrated from Central Asia or Persia during the centuries of Muslim predominance over India, and had spread as a landowning gentry over the provinces of northern India during this period. While the *Ashraf* monopolized social status and economic power, the strength of numbers lay with the Muslim peasantry, which preponderated in the rural districts of north-west and north-east India, and which had been drawn into the fold of Islam during the medieval centuries. Sandwiched between these two sections of Muslim society were some urban based groups: artisans and craftsmen, who lived in the cities of the interior, and the commercial 'castes', which were concentrated in the industrial cities that had sprung to life under the British Raj.

The standard accounts of Muslim politics point out that the first section of Muslim society to enter modern politics was the landed gentry, whose members linked their political fortune to the British Raj at the same time as they initiated social and intellectual reform within the community. Yet these accounts show insufficient awareness of subterranean currents within Muslim society in India. There is reason to believe that the Muslim artisans and craftsmen in the cities of the interior, whose life style was threatened by the instrusion of industrial products in their traditional markets, were either migrating in substantial numbers to cities like Bombay or Calcutta, or experiencing a serious decline in their standards of living. There is also reason to believe that the Muslim peasantry, which comprised the lower strata of rural society, was going through a comparable process of impoverishment. Both these strata of Muslim society were disorganized and inarticulate.

Yet they could communicate their frustration to the *ulema*, who were the only educated class with whom they had some rapport. The *ulema*, in turn, were linked to some of the principal centres of Islamic theology like Deoband and Firangi Mahal. In Muslim society, therefore, there existed acute distress among the poorer classes in the cities as well as in the villages, and this distress was readily communicated to the *ulema* through their close links with the laity. The *ulema*, on their part, looked upon the British Raj as a threat to the religious values which they cherished; and their apprehensions were sharpened by the impoverishment they saw around themselves amongst the followers of Islam.

Here, then, was an issue agitating wide sections of Muslim society which linked economic with religious grievances in a manner designed to create a sharpened awareness of their identity among the poor and deprived classes of the community. It appears that in the first decade of the twentieth century, the more liberal members of the Muslim landed gentry sensed the storm that was brewing, and tried to harness it to the purpose of political nationalism. But since they did not have any rapport with the poorer classes in their own community, these liberal Muslims were obliged to work though the *ulema* in their bid to launch a crusade against the British Government. Such was the genesis of the Pan-Islamic movement in the country. It was a movement which rested upon the social distress of the poor; it fanned the ideological hostility of the *ulema* to the British Government; it drew upon the intimate link between the *ulema* and the Muslim masses; and it was given organized expression by the liberal Muslims, who felt that the policy of co-operation advocated by their leaders in the past was devoid of any utility in the altered circumstances of the twentieth century. The problem with the Pan-Islamic movement, however, lay in the marginal control which the liberal Muslims exercised over it. The *ulema*, whom they had drawn to the movement, were men of very little faith in constitutional politics as understood by the educated classes, Hindu or Muslim. The impoverished artisans and peasants who followed the *ulema* cared even less for such politics. There was a real danger, therefore, of the Pan-Islamic movement manifesting itself in the form of massive, yet disorganized, violence against the British Government in India.

We have focused upon political ferment in different sectors of society in the first two decades of the twentieth century, because of the significance of this ferment for the new phase of activity which followed Gandhi's entry into nationalist politics. Our analysis also suggests that alone amongst the leaders of stature at that time, Gandhi had a sensitive appreciation of the unrest that was affecting the working classes and the peasantry. There is reason to believe that the explosive feelings abroad in the Muslim community, particularly amongst the *ulema* and the poor, were also a matter of serious concern for him. The situation was pregnant with the most serious consequences. The disaffection which characterized different classes and communities was awesome in its intensity. Yet no leadership was in evidence capable of organizing this disaffection or giving it a creative expression in the form of a movement against the British Government. There was consequently a great likelihood of anarchic violence—what we would like to call urban and rural *jacqueries*—breaking out in body politic. It was clear that such violence would be suppressed by the British Government at great cost to the people. It was also clear that suppression through such means would substantially damage the fabric of society.

Our portrayal of the unrest which characterized society in the period under review provides us with insights into the distinctive character of the great agitations which Gandhi launched against the British Government in the 1920s and the 1930s. The restlessness of the middle classes had even prior to 1919 constituted the basis of many agitations against the British Government. But the question which confronted Gandhi was: how could the disaffection of the middle classes be linked, organizationally and ideologically, with the anarchic violence that was threatening to erupt, on the one hand, among the peasants and the working classes, and on the other, among the poorer sections of the Muslim community? No simple answer could be provided to such a question. However, Gandhi was able to resolve the nationalist dilemma, slowly and tentatively, feeling his way all the while through the intricate maze of politics in India. Like all solutions, Gandhi's solution had its strengths as well as its weaknesses. Yet whatever be these strenghts and weaknesses, the manner in which Gandhi integrated different scheme of politics exercised a decisive influence upon the character of Indian nationalism as well as upon the structure of politics in the decades after 1947.

At this juncture, it would be appropriate to focus upon 'class' and 'communitarian' politics as two contrasting modes of social action available to the political actor in India. The significance of 'class' politics becomes clear when it is observed that the agitations which Gandhi conducted in Champaran, Kheda and Ahmedabad were excellent instances of 'class' politics as defined above: of politics designed to reinforce the economic interests of a particular class in society. It has also been suggested that such agitations gave Gandhi a clear insight into the discontents which were affecting the working classes and the peasantry in India. Similar discontents, so Gandhi was to gather, were at work among the poorer sections of the Muslim community, although, because of a low level of politicization, the frustration of these Muslims found expression in a religious upsurge, the so-called Pan-Islamic movement. The evidence available to us suggests that Gandhi at this juncture came to the conclusion that the pursuit of class politics, though likely to yield beneficial results in agitations confined to specific social groups, would not be an appropriate basis for a united front by different classes and communities against the British Government. In other words, because the interests of the worker were antagonistic to those of the capitalist, or because the interests of the peasant were antagonistic to those of the zamindar, it would be futile to focus upon economic issues as the basis of a nationalist movement in India. The alternative, so Gandhi in effect argued, was to use moral issues to cement a grand alliance of Hindus and Muslims, rich and poor, the middle classes and the petty bourgeoisie, the working class and the industrial magnates, and, last but not the least, the zamindars and the peasants, in a great struggle against the British Government.

The strategy which Gandhi employed to bring about an alliance between different classes and communities, the use of moral issues for creating an anti-imperialist front, becomes clear when we look closely at the large-scale agitations which he organized against the British Raj. The first of these agitations was the Rowlatt Satyagraha in 1919. This Satyagraha, in contrast to the agitations which Gandhi led in Champaran,

Kheda or Ahmedabad, was not linked to the redress of economic grievances. Instead, the agitation of 1919 was directed agaist the 'immorality' of a legislation which threatened to undermine the basic liberties of the citizen in India. Needless to say, the organization of this agitation rested upon concrete discontents which agitated different sections of society: upon the growing political aspirations of the middle classes, or the economic distress of the poor in the cities, or the religious sentiments which were abroad in the Muslim community; but all these discontents were drawn under the umbrella of a moral grievance with which different classes could associate themselves without ceasing to pursue their distinct, or even conflicting, social and economic objectives.[11]

What is true of the Rowlatt Satyagraha of 1919 is also true of non-co-operation in the 1920s, or of civil disobedience in the 1930s. Each of these movements was an integrative movement, calling upon social classes and religious communities with very different economic interests, or social aspirations, or political identities, to forge a united front against the British Government. These classes and communities were drawn into the organizational framework of a restructured Congress; they were also drawn to a common platform under slogans like '*swaraj* within a year' or '*purna swaraj*'; slogans which could mean all things to all men. This does not imply that the agitations of the 1920s and the 1930s were unrelated to the economic discontents which were afloat in the country. On the contrary, recent explorations have made it clear that the classes and communities which flocked to the nationalist standard were motivated by economic distress, or political ambition, or the creative vision of a free polity, and attributed their frustration to the British Government. Nevertheless, we would like to emphasize that economic discontents did not find any clear-cut expression in the slogans which constituted the basis of national unity in opposition to the British Government. The reason for this, as we have already suggested, was Gandhi's belief that the articulation of economic discontents, particularly if sharpened through political struggle, would set class against class, and community against community, and thereby prevent the emergence of a united front against the imperial power. To prevent such disharmony, class interests, class antagonisms, class aspirations and class identities had to be muted in the larger interests of the nation; they had also to be masked in the interests of effective opposition to British rule. This was a political strategy which yielded rich dividends in the shape of massive agitations which ultimately forced the British to quit India. Yet it was a strategy with serious flaws, to the consideration of which we shall turn in the closing paragraphs of this essay.

Even in the 1920s, when Gandhi had tried to draw the Hindu, Muslim and Sikh communities into nationalist politics as communities, critics of his strategy had pointed out that he was widening instead of narrowing religious and communitarian cleavages in Indian society. Gandhi's answer to his critics (over and above the fact that he saw religion as a creative force in politics) was that the strength of religious sentiment in India obliged him to pursue such a strategy. He further believed that the experience of common participation in nationlist agitations would forge enduring political links between different sections of society and, in doing so, lay the basis of nationhood in the country. The strategy adopted by Gandhi, therefore, was a calculated rist. It was also an act of faith and hope that different religious communities, through common struggle against the British Government, would fuse their identities into a new nation held together by certain common objectives and certain shared ideals.

If the political strategy adopted by Gandhi was a calculated risk, then it failed in one of its major objectives, namely, the fusion of different religious communities into a distinct nation, just as it succeeded in its other major objective, namely, the liberation of India from alien rule. Yet in focusing on Gandhi's failure to heal the religious cleavages which bedevilled the country, we would do well to remember the exploitation of these cleavages by the British Government, most blatantly of all through the constitutional devices which it foisted upon India. Perhaps the word failure can be used in respect of Gandhi only if we weigh his stupendous achievements against the formidable objectives which he set for himself. To a very considerable extent, the achievements and failures of nationalism in India are the achievements and failures of Gandhi. Indeed, the Mahatma's achievements no less than his failures continue to determine the structure of politics in contemporary India, three decades after the attainment of independence.

NOTES AND REFERENCES

1. A.D. Smith, *Nationalism : A Trend Report and Bibliography*, The Hague, 1900; H. Kohn, *The Idea of Nationalism*, New York, 1967, and *Nationalism : Its Meaning in History*, Princeton, 1955; F.M. Barnard, *Herder's Social and Political Thought: From Enlightenment to Nationalism*, Oxford, 1965; C.J.H. Hayes, *Eassys on Nationalism*, New York, 1926, and *The Historical Evolution of Modern Nationalism*, New York, 1931; L. Synder, *The New Nationalism*, Ithaca, 1968; E.H. Carr, ed., *Nationalism : A Report*, Oxford, 1939.
2. The Literature on the Permanent Settlement of Bengal is enormous, though most of this literature is directed towards examining British agrarian legislation, and seeks neither to reconstruct social structure or political institutions, nor to assess the changes produced by the legislation. See for instance: R. Guha, *A Rule of Property in Bengal*, Paris, 1963; W.W. Hunter, *Annals of Rural Bengal*, London, 1897; E.T. Stokes, *The English Utilitarians and India*, Oxford, 1957; N.K. Sinha, *Economic History of Bengal*, 3 Vols., Calcutta, 1967, 1970; T. Raychaudhri, *Bengal under Akbar and Jahangir*, Calcutta, 1953; R.K. Mukherjee, *The Dynamics of a Rural Society*, Berlin, 1957; S. Gopal, *The Permanent Settlement in Bengal and Its Results*, London, 1949; *Report of the Land Revenue Commission, Bengal*, Calcutta, 1940; P. Sinha, *Nineteenth Century Bengal: Aspects of Social History*, Calcutta, 1965; C. Palit, *Tensions in Bengal Rural Society*, Calcutta, 1975; J.H. Broomfield, *Elite Conflict in a Plural Society*, Berkeley, 1968; also see P. Sinha, 'Social Change' and B.K. Choudhry 'Agrarian Relations in Bengal, 1859-1885', in N.K. Sinha, ed., *The History of Bengal, 1757-1905*, Calcutta, 1967.
3. Dharma Kumar, *Land and Caste in South India*, Cambridge, 1965; E. Whitcombe, *Agrarian Conditions in Northern India* vol. I, Berkeley, 1972; R.E. Frykenberg, *Guntur District, 1788-1848*, Oxford, 1965; N. Mukherjee, *The Ryotwari System of Madras*, Calcutta, 1962; Sarada Raju, *Economic Conditions in the Madras Presidency between 1800 and 1850*, Madras, 1941; A.V. Raman Rao, *The Economic Development of Andhra Pradesh, 1766-1957*, Bombay, 1965; H.K. Trevaskis, *The Land of the Five Rivers*, Oxford, 1928; R. Kumar, *Western India in the Nineteenth Century*, London,

1968; H. Calvert, *The Wealth and Welfare of the Punjab*, Lahore, 1922; D. Thorner, ed., *The Social Framework of Agriculture*, Bombay, 1967; M.L. Darling, *The Punjab Peasant in Prosperity and Debt*, Oxford, 1925, and his *Wisdom and Waste in the Punjab Village*, New York, 1934; T.G. Kessinger, *Vilayatpur, 1848-1968*, Berkeley, 1974.

4. C. Dobbin, *Urban Leadership in Western India*, Oxford, 1968; D.E. Wacha, *Rise and Growth of Bombay Municipal Government*, Madras, 1913; J.C. Masselos, *Towards Nationalism: Group Affiliations and the Politics of Public Association in 19th Century Western India*, Bombay, 1974; C.A. Bayly, *Local Roots of Indian Politics: Allahabad, 1880-1920*, London, 1975; R. Cashman, *The Legacy of the Lokmanya*, Berkeley, 1974; R. Kumar, *Essays on Gandhian Politics*, Oxford, 1971; K.L. Gillion, *Ahmedabad: A Study in Indian Urban History*, California, 1968; D.W. Ferrell, 'Delhi, 1911-1922', Ph. D. thesis, A.N.U., 1969; A. Ashraf, *The City Government of Calcutta*, Calcutta, 1966; A. Mitra, *Calcutta: India's City*, Calcutta, 1963; F.J. Tysen, *Interest Groups in Calcutta*, Bombay, 1967.

5. S.R. Mehrotra, *The Emergence of the Indian National Congress*, Delhi, 1971; A Seal, *The Emergence of Indian Nationalism*, Cambridge, 1968, and *Locality, Province and Nation*, Cambridge, 1973; Surendranath Banerjea, *A Nation in the Making*, Calcutta, 1945; S.N. Mukherjee, ed., *St. Anthony's Papers, No. 18, South Asia Affairs, No. 2*, Oxford, 1966; D.A. Low, ed., *Soundings in Modern South Asian History*, Berkeley, 1968; C.H. Philips, ed., *Politics and Society in India*, London, 1963; S.A. Wolpert, *Tilak and Gokhale*, Berkeley, 1962.

6. V. Chirol, *Indian Unrest*, London, 1910; A. Tripathi, *The Extremist Challenge*, Calcutta, 1967; M.N. Das, *India under Minto and Morley*, London, 1964; C.H. Heimsath, *Indian Nationalism and Hindu Social Reform*, Princeton, 1964; Lajpat Raj, *The Arya Samaj*, Lahore, 1932; B.B. Majumdar, *Milliant Nationalism in India*, Calcutta, 1966; B.C. Pal, *The Spirit of Indian Nationalism*, London, 1910; S. Sarkar, *The Swadeshi Movement in Bengal, 1903-1908*, New Delhi, 1973; *Sedition Committee Report, 1918*.

7. N.G. Barrier, 'Punjab Politics and the Disturbances of 1907', Ph. D. dissertation, Duke University, 1966; and his 'The Arya Samaj and Congress Politics in the Punjab, 1894-1908', *Journal of Asian Studies*, May 1967; 'The Punjab Disturbances of 1907', *Modern Asian Studies*, December 1967; 'The Punjab Government and Communal Politics,

1870-1908', *Journal of Asian Studies*, May 1968; F.C. Isemonger and J. Slattery, *An Account of the Ghadr Conspiracy, 1913-1915*, Lahore, 1919.

8. D. Keer, *Lokmanya Tilak*, Bombay, 1969; I.M. Reisner and N.M. Goldberg, eds., *Tilak and the Struggle for Indian Freedom*, New Delhi, 1966; G.S. Ghurye, *Gods and Men*, Bombay, 1962; V.S. Joshi, *Vasudev Balwant Phadke*, Bombay, 1959; D.V. Tahmankar, *Lokmanya Tilak*, London, 1956; *Source Materials for a History of the Freedom Movement in India Collected from the Bombay Government Records*, 2 vols.
9. J.M. Brown, *Gandhi's Rise to Power, 1915-1922*, Cambridge, 1972; M.K. Gandhi, *The Collected Works of Mahatma Gandhi*, New Delhi, various dates; A. Ahmad, *Islamic Modernism in India and Pakistan*, London, 1967; J.C. Bondurant, *The Conquest of Violence*, Princeton, 1958; W.C. Smith, *Modern Islam in India*, Lahore, 1963; E. Erikson, *Gandhi's Truth: On the Origins of Militant Non-violence*, London, 1970; R. Iyer, *The Moral and Political Thought of Mahatma Gandhi*, Delhi, 1973.
10. T.N. Madan, ed., *Muslim Communities of South Asia*, New Delhi, 1976; I. Ahmad, ed., *Caste and Social Stratification among the Muslims*, New Delhi, 1973; M. Mujeeb, *The Indian Muslims*, London, 1963.
11. Q. Ahmad, *The Wahabi Movement in India*, Calcutta, 1966; L. Bahadur, *The Muslim League*, Agra, 1954; S.K. Bhatnagar, *History of the M.A.O. College, Aligarh*, Aligarh, 1969; C.F.I. Graham, *The Life and Work of Sir Syed Ahmad Khan*, London, 1909; W.W. Hunter, *The Indian Mussalmans*, London, 1876; M.S. Jain, *The Aligarh Movement: Its Origin and Development, 1858-1906*, Ajmer, 1965; I.H. Qureshi, *The Muslim Community of the Indo-Pakistan Subcontinent, 610-1947*, The Hague, 1962; K.B. Sayeed, *Pakistan: The Formative Phase*, London, 1948.

CHAPTER - XIV

SOCIAL HISTORY OF MODERN INDIA : A TREND REPORT

We propose to begin with a brief survey of the course of development of the discipline of social history in India. This will be followed by an attempt to identify certain dominant paradigms in Indian social historiography. There paradigms have developed, since the end of the last century, in the relatively familiar areas of social history with established and well-trodden lines of research. Beyond these areas new explorations have been made in recent years and such research endeavours are reviewed towards the end of this essay.

Our interpretation of the trends and paradigm changes we have inferred may be open to question. However, such an attempt at interpretation seems to be the only way to arrive at a meaningful over-view of the development of the historiography of Indian society.

It has not been always possible to separate the realms of social history from its neighbouring areas of research, particularly economic history. It is self-evident that this separation is arbitrary and hence a problem of overlapping boundaries. At the same time we had to bear in mind the rubrics laid down by ICSSR. In attempting this survey the emphasis has been mainly on works of historians since, under the ICSSR scheme, research by sociologists and anthropologists in this area has been covered by Prof. A.M. Shah (1974, pp. 432-459). Prof. Shah has, very correctly, confined his survey to sociologists and anthropoligists' approach to social history and ours has been the complementary task of investigating the historians' work, which is larger in volume and goes back further in time. Similarly, Prof. Dharma Kumar and P.C. Joshi have covered some areas of economic history particularly agrarian history in other trend reports for the ICSSR and thus a number of problem areas were excluded from the purview of the present survey. The profits of working under the rubrics and discipline of a joint endeavour had to be balanced against the pleasures of poaching. It has been our aim to prevent overlap: we have not been consistently successful because it is not easy to define the limits of these surveys. However, those readers who may find their particular interests neglected in the present survey may look up these other complementary surveys published by the ICSSR.

It has not been our aim to review all that has been published. The intention was to review the trends of research in the discipline as a whole, to identify problem areas where significant progress has been made, and to suggest thrusts in research efforts in certain areas at the frontiers of our knowledge today. This task is not the same as that of compilation of a bibliography. The task of such a compilation has been partly completed by the excellent. Gokhale Institute publication, *Annotated Bibliography on the Economic History of India 1500-1947*. (1977-1978), particularly Volume IV (1978). In Margaret Case's *South Asian History: 1750-1950: Guide to Periodicals, Dissertations, Newspapers* (1968) and Vimal Rath's *Index of Indian Economic Journals 1915-1965* (1971) there is a great deal one finds useful as regards publications in periodicals. Bernard Cohn's contribution to the Cohn and Singer volume, *Structure and Change in Indian Society* (1968) is at the same time an excellent review and a bibliographic aid. Less specific to social history and covering social and economic history in general are the review essays by Burton Stein and M.D. Morris (1961), T. Roy Chaudhuri (1963), and O.P. Bhatnagar (1964).

Perhaps one should add that ideally a review of this kind should be what Jurgen Habermas has called "the self-reflection of science" (1971, p. vii). What is called for is a social history of social history, an enquiry into the sociology of knowledge. Except for occasional forays, we have not been able to explore that area in this essay. The purpose and limits of a report of this kind had to be kept in mind. The task of confronting social history with itself merits the historians' attention. Lest the few observations we have made on the shaping of our consciousness of social history in the socio-political matrix should be mistaken for a simple relationship (basis-superstructure, etc.). We should also note how the study of social change may itself affect social change. A prominent instance of this is that new caste consciousness was induced by the enquiries into and classification of castes (often in a hierarchical order supposedly justified by tradition) through the various census and survey operations of the British government from the end of the 19th Century. This promoted caste solidarity and led to efforts to establish claims in "caste histories" to higher status in the hierarchy. Dr. Iravati Karve provides another example: during early days of British rule "racial" feelings entered into consciousness as "the unity of the Indo-European language family was discovered. The word 'Arya' was discovered and given a new connotation.... In the same way the British anthropologists, censuses, and the series of books on tribes and castes made people aware of castes called by similar names beyond their own region...... They could not be brought together as inter-marrying groups but became politically conscious entities" (Bhatnagar, ed., p. 37). Again, it is well-known that historical works recording social practices, social evils and reform efforts themselves promoted reform by bringing about a change in the consciousness of the educated. These are instances that show how the observer affects the society observed. However, we have underlined the opposite process chiefly because the awareness of it has attenuated in the study of history more than in any other science. This is the reason why we have found the examination of unstated premises and the implicity accepted paradigms behind social history worthwhile.

DEVELOPMENT OF SOCIAL HISTORIOGRAPHY

The tradition of English historiography have, for better or for worse, strongly influenced the study of Indian history and in England social history as an independent discpline emerged very late. In 1962 a leading English social historian writes: "Judged by the usual criteria of academic disciplines, it can scarcely be said to exist: there are no chairs and, if we omit local history, no University departments, no learned journals, and few if any textbooks" (H.J. Perkin in H.P.R. Finberg ed., 1962, p. 51). This offers a contrast to the flourishing continental tradition in social history. However, this does not mean that the history of English society was an uncultivated and barren field—it was not, till very recently, fenced off as a specialization field. To understand why social history did not develop under British auspices in colonial India one has to turn to other possible explanations.

One major factor was perhaps the fact the British historians, who set the pace, preferred to write not so much about India—nor even about British India—but about the British in India. The emphasis throughout the 19th Century was on the process of British expansion and consolidation and it was the study of administrative structures and policies which provided an incommodious and unaccommodating framework for whatever little work that there was on the indigenous society. The best exemplars of this traditation were the editors and authors of the celebrated *Cambridge History of India* Series (1922-1953). Thus the fifth volume entitled "British India" contained not a single chapter on any social historical theme (H. Dodwell, 1929). As Eric Stokes has pointed out, the British historians' interest was focused on the activities of the British as the actors on the stage of history with India as a shadowy background (Stokes in C.H. Philips, ed., 1961). When the colonial historian turned to social history, he concentrated attention on British social life of India. The early volumes of the first historical journal in India, *Bengal: Past and Present*, are replete with studies in this genre. The most well-known work of this genre is not a history at all but a compilation, *viz.* W.H. Carey's *Good Old Days of John Company* (1882-1887) which contained "curious reminiscences illustrating manners and customs of the British in India" from 1600 to 1858. Some distinguished professional contributions in this area in the 20th Century were H.H. Dodwell's on the nabobs of Madras (1926), T.G.P. Spear's on the nabols in northern India (1951), and Dennis Kincaid's (1938) popular account of British social life in India in the period 1608 to 1937.

While this disinterest in India's social history characterized 19th Century colonial historiography in general (a notable exception was the work of Sir Alfred Lyall, 1882), there existed a prior tradition of a different kind: the late 18th Century 'discovery' of Hinduism through the investigations of

Sir William Jone, N.B. Halhead, J.Z. Holwell, A. Dow, *et. al.* Here was the tradition from which originated Indological studies later to be enriched by Max Muller and others (see R. Thapar *op. cit.* and dumont, 1966). But these early indologists were not actually oriented to what we can call social history despite their interest in the Hindu civilization. As P.J. Marshall (1970) has pointed out, they "did not try to understand what Hinduism meant to millions of Indians. They invariably made a distinction between popular Hinduism which they did not deem worthy of study, and 'Philosopical' Hinduism...". In striking contrast a Frenchman Abbe Jean Antonie Dubois (1816, English ed., 1906) addressed himself to the reality of Indian social life. A year after Dubois' work came James Mill's *History of British India* (1817) and this work, in the tradition of the textual as opposed to the contextual study of Hinduism, was responsible for many of the stereotypes and prejudices which characterized 19th Century British attitude to Indian Society (ef. G.D. Bearce, 1961).

There was however a third tradition, the ethnographic researches, which redeemed to a great extent the poverty of British intellectual response to India's social history. This was mainly a late 19th Century development, though in the socio-economic surveys of Buchanan-Hamilton (R.M. Martin, 1838, Buchanan-Hamilton, 1807, 1833), of Ward and Connor (largely unpublished, MS in IOL) and others and in the early gazetteers of W. Hamilton (1820), and E. Thornton (1854) a beginning had been made. There are broadly speaking three categories of work in this genre. Some investigations were generated in connection with census operations which started in 1872 and in a systematic fashion from 1881. Second, there were various reports not all of which were published, on local socio-economic history generated by revenue settlement operations (Baden-Powell, 1892, provides a magisterial survey). Third, there were the "castes and tribes" series, representing contemporary European interest in ethnography, compiled by Sir Denzil Ibbetson (1883), J.C. Nesfield (1885), H.H. Risley (1891), W. Crooke (1896), E. Thurston (1909), R.V. Russell (1916) *et. al.* It is not our purpose to itemise these ethnographic compilations. While these works suffered, as Barney Cohn (Cohn & Singer, 1968) and A.M. Shah (1974) has pointed out, from the limitations derived from contemporary anthropolotical theories—particularly the "pseudo-history of both the evolutionist and diffusionist varieties" (A.M. Shah *loc. cit.*)—they provide, insofar as they accurately recorded data now irretrievably lost, material for the social historian.

We have confined ourselves till now to the mainstream of Anglo-Indian historiography and its tributaries, the Indological and ethnographic traditions, all fed by the inexhaustible energies of the 19th Century empire builders. What was the extent of Indian participation? Ramakrishna Mukherjee (1977, p. 25 *et. seq.*) has pointed out that the contribution of "proto-socialogists" towards exploration of modern Indian social history was not insignificant. The establishment of the Bengal Social Science Association in 1859—almost contemporaneous with the earliest sociological associations, the British National Association for the Promotion of Social Sciences (1857)—and the various enterprises in Sociological enquiry initiated by a number of voluntary societies, involved substantial Indian participation. This has been recently chronicled by Dutt Gupta (1972, Chapters III-V; she does not however refer to similar enterprises outside Bengal, *e.g.* the Poona Sarvajanik Sabha' Social Surveys and publications). While this was admittedly at an amateur level, there were also Indians professionally committed and employed as such in the ethnographic Survey enterprises: *e.g.*, Hiralal associated with Russell (1916) in his work on Central India, Rangachari associated with Thurston (1909) in the compilation on South India, L.K.A. Iyer (1909-1912) who worked on Cochin tribes and castes. Unfortunately little seems to be known about these pioneers. It was in 1919-1920 that one could say that sociology, or more accurately social anthropology, as a discipline enters the Indian intellectual scene with the foundation of the first Indian department of Sociology in the University of Bombay and the first sociological journal, the Indian *Journal of Sociology* (Baroda). Earlier sociology was being taught in the University of Calcutta, possibly from 1908, and of Bombay, from 1914, but the chan in a department of Sociology, occupied first by Patrick Geddes, marked the beginning of a body of professionals with institutional moorings. In the next quarter of a century a number of Sociologists produced works oriented towards social history, *viz.*, G.S. Ghurye, Benoy Kumar Sarkar,

K.P. Chattopadhyay, D.P. Mukherji *et. al.* Some historians would possibly be of the view that some of the historical investigations of these pioneers can be read with profit even today: *e.g.* B.K. Sarkar's (1917) on folk history and culture which was sadly neglected by professional historians, D.P. Mukherji's (1948) on the Indian elite, G.S. Ghurye's (1962) on old religious symbols and modern politics. Sociologists, however, seem to differ rather strongly in their valuation of this historical interest. A.M. Shah (1974) in a trend report for the ICSSR is highly critical of "the continuing influence of history, including pseudo-history of the evolutionist and diffusionist varieties, in the works of pioneers of sociology and anthropology in India, such as L.K.A. Iyer, S.C. Roy, Brajendranath Seal, Benoy Kumar Sarkar, Radhakamal Mukherjee, D.P. Mukherjee, K.P. Chattopadhyaya and G.S. Ghurye". On the other had, another eminent, sociologist, Ramakrishna Mukherjee (1977), in his trend report for the International Sociological Association, is not at all sacred of the dragon of pseudo-history threatening the muse of Sociology: the report by A.M.Shah "on historical sociology has become fragmentary with hardly any history or sociology in it", for it is vitiated by a "basically a-historical approach", that of the structural-functionalists (R. Mukherjee, 1977, p. 77). Without getting deeper into the quarrels within the sociologists' tribe, it suffices for historians to note that in the 1950s the sociologists begin to turn away from historical questions under the influences of the approach Mukherjee has mentioned. The possibilitiesof·fruitful cooperation between sociologists and historians, particularly in the area of modern Indian history, were allowed to atrophy. This was particularly unfortunate because the Indian historians' interest in social history at this time was confined, by and large, to pre-British India (*e.g.* K.P. Jaysawal, 1930, and A.S. Altekar, 1940). Historians' approach to modern Indian social history consisted of banal eulogies of the so-called renaissance and social reform movements (*e.g.*, H.C.F. Zacharias, 1933; K.K. Datta, 1950) and tangential treatment of "social conditions" as an appendage to works on administrative and economic history (*e.g.* K.K. Datta, 1936; H.R. Ghoshal, 1950; N.K. Sinha, 1950). Up to middle of the century, so far as modern social history is concerned, professional historians were unable to frame their problematic in the manner in which D.P. Mukherjee (1948) A.R. Dasai (1948) or Nirmal Kumar Bose (1949) did within the tradition of sociology.

From the beginning of the 1950s there began on the one hand what we may call the de-historization fo sociologists' interests and on the other a spurt of development in social historiography. The number of such works published between 1950- 1965 was quite impressive. In the area of social policies and ideas Kenneth Ballhatchet (1957) made a detailed study of early 19th Century western India, Eric Stokes (1959) on utilitarian premises of social and economic policies, M.N. Das (1959) on social and economic policies of the pre-Mutiny years, and A.F. Ahmed (1965) on early 19th Century Bengal. In the area of social reform movements, the impact of missionary activities, role of nationalists in social reform, etc. Kenneth Ingham (1956), S. Natarajan (1959), and C.H. Heimsath (1964) contributed on the 19th Century; K.K. Datta (1961) and V.P.S. Raghuvanshi investigated the 18th Century background. Some work was done on education policies and the growth of the educated elite: the earlier work of S. Nurullah and J.P. Naik (1943, 1951) and J.C. Bagal (1944) was followed up by other ones (Bengal, 1956) and B.B. Mishra (1961) provided a wide ranging social history of the "middle class"; a sociologist, E.Shils, published (1961) an extremely influential work on Indian intellectuals laying the conceptual basis of later historical investigations by the Cambridge School. The so-called Bengal renaissance attracted a host of authors: A.C. Gupta (1958) collected some essays reflecting heightened interest in this subject, R.C. Majumdar (1960) and N.S. Bose (1960) published their surveys of 19th Century Bengal, followed by Pradip Sinha (1965) and G. Chattopadhyaya (1965). Finally, the economist D.R. Gadgil (1959) laid the basis of historical study of the sociology of entrepreneurship, an area soon to attract many historians. Above all, a significant sign that social history had finally arrived was the foundation of the *Indian Economic and Social History Review* in 1963, with the declared aim of "representing three disciplines relevant to the study of socio-economic history: history, economics and sociology" (IESHR 1963, editorial statement).

The hyphenation of social and economic history above and the emphasis on an interdisciplinary approach was not without significance.There had occurred in the 1950s'a disjunction between the historians' and sociologists' concerns. According to Saberwal this was in part due to the influence of contemporary British social anthropology which "may fairly be called anti-historical", and in part because the historical interests promoted by the American tradition were confined to species of cultural history which missed out on "historical experience of the middle range: the rise of capitalism, the colonial expansion and its consequences, and the meaning of industrialism—or of a lack thereof" (Saberwel, 1979, p. 247 also see R. Mukherjee, 1977, pp. 44-46). In the late '1960s however, this—a historical style of thinking and the trend of the fifties began to weaken. The exhortation by Dumont (1964) in the pace-setting journal, *Contributions, to Indian Sociology*, to study the 18th and 19th Century history to advance one's understanding of contemporary Indian Society, or the conspicuous cross-disciplinary emphasis in the influential Cohn and Singer (1968) volume, *Structure and Change in Indian Society*, were some straws in the wind. The extent to which in the study of modern Indian social history cross fertization across disciplinary boundaries took place from the '60s will be one of the questions we shall try to answer in the subsequent sections.

DOMINANT PARADIGMS IN SOCIAL HISTORY

At this point an over-view of the development of social history may be attempted. A mere catalogue of titles published or indication of their contents would be of little use as a trend report. In the succeeding sections thematic arrangement has provided a framework to survey some of the main areas of research which have developed in recent years. In the concluding part of this section a survey of the dominant paradigms in the historiography of Indian social history will be our aim.

We use the term paradigm here in preference to the term "model" for the simple reason that the exactitude that model building demands (measurablity of, and predictability of relationship between variables) is unknown in social historiography. The use of the notion of paradigm does not, of course, imply that Thomas Kuhn's well-known thesis applies in detail to the development of a social science discipline. Indeed, one may differ with the Kuhn thesis on a number of issues (what is more, Kuhn has worked under a self-imposed limitation that prevents him from enquiring into the broader changes in the social context and thus leading to "Paradigmatic" revolutions). Kuhn's thesis is relevant here in terms of the questions he raises regarding the so-called cumulative progress of science, rather than in terms of the answers he provides.

The variety of research problems, an aversion to wider questions beyond the immediate empirical limits, and the sheer volume of historians' output make the identification of the central trends over time a difficult task. Social historians in India have generally tended to regard their problems in a discretist fashion—and thus they write monographs on infanticide in British India, or Muslim "manners and customs", or entrepreneurship in a business caste, or urban leadership in a metropolitan city, etc. In works of this genre there is little or no attempt on the part of the historian to locate his individual work in relation to a wider interpretative framework of the historical processes of which a part is under his scrutiny. This of course does not mean that there is no such framework. It is there in the shape of implicit assumptions.

This is not a unique feature of historiography. Most of the writings in social sciences are premised upon assumptions which are unstated. As C.B. Macpherson's study of "possessive individualism" demonstrates, certain assumptions are never explicity formulated because: (a) "when a writer can take it for granted that his readers will share some of his assumptions, he will see no reason to set those out", and (b) "it would be strange indeed if a thinker did not sometimes carry over into his premises some general assumptions about the nature of man and society, shaped by his living in his own society, without being fully aware that he was doing so.... What they leave unformulated may nevertheless pervade their thinking" (Macpherson, 1962, pp. 5-6). These assumption need to be made explicit to make conscious criticism possible. It is useful to recall here Macpherson's caveat that such an exercise—a historical enquiry into the assumptions, the purposes and the audience the writer is addressing—does not necessarily question the adequacy of the writer's substantive argument.

If one takes a long term view of the trends emboided in the works of historians of modern India one begins to see convergent patterns of thinking. Without postulating a conscious choice of an interpretative framework by the individual historians, one may suggest that social historical thinking has not been without certain organizing principles.

The organising principal that held sway throught the last half of the 19th century was the paradigm of progression towards European civil and political society; the guiding hand of the British led India on this path; education combined with "filtration" to the lower orders of society and implantation of such civil and political institutions as the British throught fit to give to India, slowly propelled India on this path to progress. This paradigm of the pupil's progress was not only an integral part of British bureaucratic thinking (enshrined in a statute requiring the Indian Goverment to submit regularly a "Moral and Material Progress Report"), but also of respectable ideological lineage. On the one hand, Benthamite and ultilitarian philosophy ascribed to British role a civilizing mission (cf. Eric Stokes, 1959). On the other hand, the idea of progress leading by stages to the polity and society of the 19th Century Europe was a cornerstone of the outlook of pioneers in sociology, Auguste Comte and Herbert Spencer. Comte emphasized an evolutionary scheme for the historical explication of the emergence of 19th Century European civilization as much as Herbert Spencer. Both were a formative influences in 19th Century of India (S. Bhattacharya, 1974). Spencer difined sociology as a natural history of society concerned with the "history of the transformations through which it has passed". His comparative method led to the view that social evolution was invariably towards the modern complex European society (cf. B. Dutt Gupta, 1972, ch. G.D. Bearce, 1961). Edward Burnett Tylor's evolutionist views also pointed to the same direction. Finally, Sir Henry Maine's contributions in historical jurisprudence underlined a lesson implicit in the evolutionist view, that India's was a stagnant society, which incorporated "great part of our own (European) civilization with its elements .... not yet unfolded" (Maine, 1876, cited Metcalf 1965, p.322). To this trend of thinking Social Darwinism, prevalent in late 19th Century Britain added a racist tinge.

This is the intellectual milieu that gave birth to the "pupil's progress" paradigm. In the early 19th Century James Mill in his celebrated *History of British India* (1817) had, with high

Benthamite fervour, inveighed *ad infinitum* aganist the degenerate and backward Indian society particularly at the point of time when British political authority began to be established; many of the stereotypes which the 19th Century British authors carried in their mind originated with Mill's obiter dicta (frequently ill-informed, as H.H. Wilson painstakingly demonstrated in later editions). In the latter half of the 19th Century the intellectual predilections outlined above were reinforced by Anglo-Indian racial prejudice of the post-Mutiny period. The most typical expression of the new attitude in historical works is to be found in the works of Sir William Hunter, a civil servant who became the editor of the first complete set of Gazetters of India and virtually the recognized official historian. In his first historical work *The Annals of Rural Bengal* (1868) he admirably set out his plan: "My business is with the people". At the same time the "lesson of history" that he underlined was clear: the superior civilization had triumphed and had put the governed raco back on the track of progress." I have depicted the state of rural Bengal when it passed into our hands; and most educated Englishmen know sufficient of its present condition to have some perception of the difference... To any one who questions the benefits of British rule, especially if he be a native of India, I can only say: *Si monumentum quaeries circumspice"* (Hunter, 1868, p.189). The same attitude informed another notable contemporary's work, Sir. Richard Temple's (1881) *India in* 1880, which paid more then usual attention to the social aspects of changes "effected by the plastic touch of western civilization". A few years later a more sirident expression of similar views was provoked by the Ilbert Bill agitation:The British Goverment, wrote Sir Fitijames Stephen, "does not represent the native principles of life or of goverment, and it can never do so until it represent healthenism and barbarism. It represents a belligerent civilization..." (Metcalf, 1965, p. 318). These strident tones of mid-Victorian imperialism get somewhat muted by the end of century (Hunter, 1899). The tutelage was being questioned, the pupils were getting restive. Nevertheless one hears echoes of these tones as late as 1925 in the writings of the first "professor of the history and culture of the British dominions in Asia" in what was then known as School of Oriental Studies, London: for five hundred years the process of "influence and penetration of European ideas" in Indian society has been impeded by "reactive forces" (exemplified by the Mutiny and "Mr. Gandhi's Non-cooperation" movement). "When new influences began to work, when the environment underwent modification, it was long before these could overcome the inertia of so great a mass of humanity as inhabits the sub-continent of India. Even then the great mass has always tended powerfully to relapse into its old posture, like a rock which you try to lift with levers" (Dodwell, 1925, p. 315). One may finally compare with the foregoing L.S.S. O'Malley's survey in 1941 of the interaction of the civilizations of India and the West. "India has reached a point at which she may soon have to decide for herself how far the impact of western civilization is to carry her" [Meston in O'Malley, ed., 1941, p. iv]. A tame end for a belligerent civilization.

In fact an alternative to the paradigm of "pupil's progress" had evolved by the beginning of the 20th Century, that of "national awakening". With the intensification and extension of the nationalist spirit the guiding hand of the rulers was looked upon with suspicion, but the goals themselves remained unquestioned. Thus the alternative paradigm did not constitute a complete break with the Anglo-Indian historiographic tradition which held up progress towards the European model as the goal. That architectonic vision of modern history remained deeply entrenched in the syllabi and every aspect of formal teaching (except for the marginal institutions with ideals of "national education"). On a smaller scale, and research works of necessity are on a smaller scale, the detailed scholarly work by professional historians implicitly accepted and derived their significance from the same vision.

The essential features of the "national awakening" paradigm are that: (1) it presents the recipients of western ideas and institutions as active agents of change rather than as passive recipients (which is how they are viewed in the earlier chronicles of the "pupil's progress"); (2) it compares and often equates a "renaissance" in India, especially Bengal, with the European Renaissance; (3) it links growth of political consciousness to the cultural and social changes in 19th Century India in a way irreconcilable with the "pupil's progress" paradigm.

This new model Indian History developed in the first half of the 20th Century and in its development the 19th Century participants in the so-called Bengal renaissance had no share. For instance, it is interesting to observe that as early as 1880 Bankim Chandra Chattopadhyay uses the term "Renaissance" and consciously makes a comparison between the European renaissance experience and a "renaissance in Bengal"; but by Bengal renaissance he meant something altogether different from the later stereotype. It meant the age of Chaitanya, Raghunath, Raghunandan, Vidyapati, Chandidas, etc. (Chattopadhyay, 1954, p. 339). Or, for instance, M.G. Ranade applied the analogy of Renaissance to the reformation of "Aryan religion, social polity", after recovery from the shock of invasion by "barbarian Scythian conquerors" (Jagirdar, 1963, p. 64). In the early decades of the 20th Century, however, the concept "Renaissance" acquired the new connotation in the Indian context, the connotation familiar to us. C.F. Andrews wrote his well-known work *Renaissance in India* in 1912, Surendranath Banerjea in 1925 paid homage to the poineers of "national awakening" in his *A Nation in Making* (1925), Bipin Chandra Pal wrote a historical account of *The New Age in Bengal* (*Nabajuger Bangla*). H.C.F. Zacharias published *Renascent India* in 1933. By the middle of the century the paradigm of renaissance or awakening passed into the stock of stereotypes of history text books, *e.g.*, K.K. Dutta, *Down of Renascent India* (1950). The quintessential text book by R.C. Majumdar, K.K. Dutta and H.C. Raychaudhury (1946-1950) display all the basic features of the new paradigm replacing the old. While it concedes the role of English education and "liberal ideas of the West" it is emphasized that social change and reform comes about because English rulers "co-operate with advanced Indian reformers" (p. 821). As in Europe the renaissance is said to be the divide between "medieval" and "modern" ages: A "critical outlook on the past and new aspiration for the future maked the new awakening. Reason and judgement took the place of faith and belief; superstition yielded to science; immobility was replaced by progress, and a zeal for reform of proved abuses overpowered age-long apathy and inertia and a complacent acquiscence in whatever was current in society" (p. 812). Finally, again very typically, there is suggested a continuity between the political ideology of the nationalist movement and the consciousness that emerged with the so-called renaissance; *e.g.* "In the field of Indian politics also, Raja Rammohan was the prophet of new age. He laid down the lines for political agitation in constitutional manner which ultimately led to the birth of the Indian National Congress half a century later" (p. 813). Works by R.C. Majumdar (1967), N.S. Bose (1960), B.B. Majumdar (1934), K.K. Dutta (1950), S.R. Mehrotra (1971), particularly emphasized the element of continuity in political consciousness.

The approach outlined above to begin with was a part of the ideological struggle to exercise the colonial hold over the Indian mind. A new definition of national identity was attempted and the writing of history had a major role to play in this process. "The most significant question facing the historian of the time (in British India), namely, the understanding of the historical aspects of the backwardness of the present, tended to be ignored. The ancient period became the golden age..... In order to emphasize the national unity of India since the earliest times, generalizations were made on the history of the subcontinent, essentially from the perspective of the Ganges valley.... Critical opinion on India was sought to be countered by proving that the liberal values in fashion in Britain were all available in the Indian cultural and political past. Thus kingship in ancient India was seen as a kind of constitutional monarchy, forgetting that such an interpretation was anachronistic." Interest in social history tried to justify the caste structure (R. Thapar, pp. 16-17). Ancient Indian historiography in particular was rife with stereotypes which arose "from Indian national sentiments opposed to the nature of imperial rule and seeking justification in the reading of the past.... The more persistent of the stereotypes have dominated not only historical interpretation but have become the foundation of modern politicial ideologies" (Thapar, p.4). So far as the study of modern Indian social history is concerned, the above tendency manifested itself in a shift of emphasis away from the role of indigenous institutions and individual social reformers, away from the evangelical values and Victorian British liberalism which promoted reformism to what was sought to be established as original Hindu values rediscovered, away from the history that ascribed a dependent and loyal role to an English educated elite to the ascription of a politically conscious nationalistic role to an intelligentsia struggling to push forward the nation on social and political and economic fronts. This new approach, initially put forward in the writings of political ideologues and incorporated later in the professional historians' works, had a positive role to play in providing a framework for a reassessment of social and cultural changes in modern times. However, this "national awakening/ renaissance" paradigm did not go far enough in breaking with the tradition of colonial historiography. The 19th Century ideals of progress and enlightenment and reform are carried over and subsumed under the nationalist framework. Ranajit Guha has suggested that the facile criticism of colonial historiography from the supposedly nationalist point of view lacked authenticity. It is true that the imperialistic historiography led to "an obsession with Britian's role in India and to an underestimation of what our own institutions and our own people contributed to the dynamics of political and social change in our country....If any false notion about Indian history originates (with imperialistic attitudes), it is still the Indians themselves clients for Ph. D. degrees, who feed on these without resentment, nurture the lymph carefully in their minds though years of unquestioning application, process the falsehood into dissertational form, and having pocketed the coveted degrees, come back home a carriers.... It is a complicity of elites in a shared fabrication.... This is a vicious circle, and if we have to break out of it at all, we must combine our criticism or British academic attitudes with a good deal of honest soul searching ourselves" (R. Guha, 1969). Guha here anticipates a trend that emerged in the 1970s criticism of the assumptions behind the nationalist "renaissance/national awakening" paradigm (cf. Dipesh Chakravorty, 1972, Barun De, 1973). The substantive contribution that this critique yielded was a reassessment of the ambivalence of the dependent bourgeoisie especially in the early years of the so-called Bengal renaissance (Sumit Sarkar *et. al.* in B.R. Nanda, 1975). The methodological contribution was the demonstration of inadequacies of the renaissance paradigm.

In the meanwhile from the 1950s an alternative paradigm had emerged, "modernization of a traditional society". Even those innocent of any knowledge of its sociological underpinnings found it acceptable. It had the apparent merit of being broad enough to cover the whole range of social change from the abolition of *Sati* to the diffusion of technology. It was such a broad spectrum concept that "modernization" could virtually be a synonym of "change"; conversely continuities could be equally conveniently subsumed under the term "tradition".

The new paradigm of "modernization/westernization", yoked with "Sanskritization", surfaced in historians' works much later than in sociological literature. In 1956 M.N. Srinivas, launched the dual concepts of Westernization-Sanskritization (in *Far Eastern Quarterly*, 1956, included in Srinivas, 1962) later elaborated into a well-developed rubric under which almost all aspects of social change in modern India could be subsumed (*Social Change in Modern India*, 1966). Some of the essential components of this approach were anticipated in a cruder form by historians and British Indian ethnographers. Theus O'Malley (1941) and many other historians employed the concept of "westernization" (and Srinivas draws much of his historical material from O'Malley) and, as Ramakrishna Mukherjee (1977) has pointed out, the historian Sir Alfred Lyall (1882) and the ethnographer H.H. Risley (1891) anticipated Srinivas's concept of Sanskritization. However, in the 1960s the general questions raised by Deniel Lerner's approach to modernization of traditional societies, and the problems specific to Indian social history raised by the retrospective application of the Sanskritization-Westernization model, had some impact on historiography which concerns us here, not the development of the paradigm within the discipline of sociology. However, it may be observed that so far as "westernization" is concerned, what appeared as a discovery to the sociologist was a commonplace to the historian. We should also note that, to the credit of M.N. Srinivas, he entered a caveat that is often ignored; "In the analysis of social and cultural change in India the British model of Westernization is obviously the most important one..... I have treated the British model as a static one, as complete, ready and gift-packed for delivery to India by the middle of the 19th Century. I am aware that such an assumption is historically untenable, but it is heuristically unavoidable" (Srinivas, 1966, 53).

Let us turn to some historical application of the Westernization-Sanskritization paradigm. Srinivas refers to the history of Yadavas' attempt in Bihar to improve their social status through Sanskritization and the violent resistance to that by the upper-castes (Srinivas, 1966, pp. 16-17). Hetukar Jha, (1977), in his detailed study of this phenomenon in the period 1921-1925, (IESHR, 1977) found this model inadequate: "Social-economic oppression by the upper-caste zamindars, led to the attempt of lower-caste peasants for Sanskritization and this brought the two groups face-to-face in violent conflict. Sanskritization implies mobility by gradual accommodation and adjustment and leaves aside conflict which is also a model social process. Considering such a limitation of this concept, I have used another term—contradition—in conjunction with the former for explaining both the phases of the situation discussed in the paper" (H. Jha, 1978). In fact Jha's historical explication is almost entirely in terms of class contradiction and the Sanskritization model survives only as a vestigal tail. It is not surprising that Dr. Leela Dube's criticism was that such situations as the one presented by Jha "cannot be explained by taking recourse to the concept of Sanskritization and trying to refine it by making multi-dimensional. At times we need to forget the concept in order to understand a situation and place it is a proper perspective" (L. Dube, 1978). In Jha's study the Sanskritization attempt is shown to be motivated by "economic and social oppression rather than economic prosperity"; among Hardgrave's Nadars economic prosperity leads to social status through Sanskritization (R.L. Hardgrave Jr., 1960). Jha ovserves correctly that the questions regarding *why* and *where* a caste chooses to Sanskritize itself" is the crucial historical question. "Sanskritization" provides merely a label for a process that may be sometimes an expression of revolt against socio-economic oppression of upward social mobility linked with betterment of economic position. (H. Sanyal, 1974). The model itself yields no hypothesis, it merely helps us recognize and put a name to a phenomenon.

To take another example, the study of the so-called "non-brahmin movement" in Kolhapur under Shahu Maharaj by Chandra Y. Mudaliar (1978) reveals that it was the "decline in power and economic structure" of the Marathas which led to the conflict between them and Brahmin caste groups: "The Marathas attempted to re-establish their claims to the Kshatriya status and generally to Sanskritize themselves. The main idea, especially on the part of Shahu, was to make the Brahmins accept these claims. The Satya Shodhaks, on the other hand, charted their own course of action. They ignored the Brahmin priests altogether, and adopted independent means to Sanskritize themselves. This process continued till 1918 when Shahu and other moderates gave up their earlier stand and established their own competitive religious institutions such as the Maratha priesthood and the Kshatra Jagadguru" (*ibid.*, *p. 17*). This is stretching the term "Sanskritization" considerably: and the author seems to be aware of it when she suggests that this is "one of the modernistic non-Brahmin movement". Does it then mean that here we have a social movement that is simultaneously "Sanskritizing" and "modernizing"? If so, the result is a certain fuzziness and loss of distinction between the two processes the concepts are intended to denote. The historian alone is not to be blamed for this. Srinivas himself, it has been pointed out, defines Sanskritization in at least two different ways and the second difinition diminishes the contradistinction with westernization/modernization to the vanishing point (Y. Singh, 1973, p. 7). The first definition is the one attempted in 1956: "The caste system is far from a rigid system........A low caste was able in a generation or two to rise to a higher position in the hierarchy by adopting vegetarianism, and teetotalism and by Sanskritizing its ritual pantheon. In short, it took over, as far as possible, the customs, rites and beliefs of the Brahmins....." The second attempt to define the process was in 1966: "a process by which a 'low' Hindu caste, on tribal or other group, changes its customs, ritual, ideology, and way of life in the direction of a high, frequently, 'twice born' caste. Generally such changes are followed by a claim to higher position in the caste hierarchy than that traditionally conceded to the claimant caste by the local community". Yogendra Singh has correctly pointed out that "the new connotation of Sanskritization is evidently much broader; it is neither confined to Brahmins as a reference group nor to the imitation of more rituals and religious practices" (Y. Singh 1973, pp. 7-8 citations Srinivas 1962, p. 55; 1966, p. 6). In this sense Mudaliar's use of the term Sanskritization is justified in that Srinivas's authority may be cited in its defence. At the same time the concept loses historical specificity and such a loss is a predictable consequence of Srinivas's later formulations which make "Sanskritization" "an extremely complex and heterogeneous concept. It is even possible that it would be more profitable to treat it as a bundle of concepts than as a single concept" (M.N. Srinivas, 1962, p. 61). Likewise Westernization is also conceived as a cover-all term for a variety of things. "In the political and cultural fields Westernization has given birth not only to nationalism, but also to revivalism, communalism, "casteism", heightened linguistic consciousness, and regionalism" (M.N. Srinivas, 1966, p. 55). Each of these concepts, Westernization and Sanskritization, says Srinivas. "Subsumes mutually antagonistic values." Needless to say historians have often fumbled in applying concept so defined.

In the area of political sociology the westernization/ modernization paradigm has been employed widely. The growth of caste association has been seen as a "modern" adaptation of a "traditional" institution. Lloyd and Susanne Rudolph in particular influenced a new trend of studies of caste associations as agents of "modernity", *i.e.* "how horizontal solidarities and interests latent in the caste system have been used in its structural functional and cultural transformation" (Rudolph and Rudolph, 1969, p. 11). The Rudolphs' research in the sixties was put together in the *Modernity of Tradition* in 1967 and within two years were published R.L. Hardgrave's *The Nadars of Tamilnadu : The Political Culture of a Community in Change* (1969) and L.F. Irschick's *Politics and Social Conflict in South India : The Non-Brahman Movement & Tamil Separatism* (1969). Robin Jeffrey and two other associates have provided a useful comparative survey of the history of several caste associations on which some research has been done. Their most significant conclusion is: "The caste association was a social adapter improvised to connect two sets of social and political forms. It helped to reconcile the values of traditional society with those of the new order by continuing to use caste as the basis for social organization, but at the same time introducing new objectives—education and supra-local political power for example—on the aims of that organization. It tried to relate the traditional geographical units—the marriage networks and the petty chiefdoms—to the wider ones developed by the changing economy, by improved communication and tighter government control. The effective caste association thus constituted a stage on a continuum of development from the local *jati* relationships and village dominant-caste politics towards class relations and the state—or the province—level of political activity (Arnold, Jeffrey, Manor, 1976, p. 372). Thus, it is argued, the blossoming of caste associations was a transitional phenomenon and suffered one of two fates if they were not abandoned altogether—survival as philanthropic agencies or evolution into a party. This picture on the whole appears to correspond closer to historical reality than the "modernization" cum "Sanskritization" model that was fashion in the sixties (Sanskritization schematics fitted South India particularly ill). However, the merit of the Rudolph approach lay in the critique it offered of the conventional and simplistic dichotomy "traditional-modern". "If tradition and modernity are seen as continuous rather than separated by an abyss, if they are dialectically rather than dichotomously related, and if internal variations are attended and taken seriously, then those sectors of traditional society that contain or express potentialities for change from dominant norms or structures become critical for understanding the nature and process of modernisation" (Rudolph and Rudolph, 1969, p. 10). Insofar as this pointed out an analytical lacuna and exposed the misdiagnosis of the so-called traditional society, the Rudolph approach made a positive contribution.

By and large the impact of the paradigm of modernization/westernization and Sanskritization has been marginal in historical literature. It will be presumptuous to assume this to be a measure of the value of the paradigm. The fact is that in historical contexts "Sanskritization" has been applied to such a variety of historical cases of mobility, set in motion by such diverse causes, and ideologised in such multifarious forms, and the term westernization/modernization is used so much as a broad-spectrum concept covering varieties of values, technologies, and institutions—that virtually they have been debased into general notions cannoting respectively endogenous and exogenous sources of social change. Losseness of the initial conceptual scheme is partly to blame for this abuse at the level of marco-level generalizations. What is more important the task of historical explication of social change at the micro-level *e.g.*, caste mobility and caste association activites, often reveals the paradigm to be inadequate and one has to go beyond it towards explanations in terms of class contradiction (H. Jha), position of caste groups in power structure (Mudaliar), transition from jati to class reations (R. Jeffrey), etc.

Similarly in the field of cultural change, to take another example, it has been pointed out that the modernization/ Westernization concept is equally open to such criticism. "The functionalist paradigm was extended to the study of revivalist movement in all major non-Christian traditions. Renaissance experiences in Hindu and Confucian traditions, for example, were discribed and explained in a simple need-fulfilment framework: Impact of the West, impotency of the native tradition, and the nationalist response to a crisis situation... One knows enough about the rapid erosion of Hinduism during the time of Vivekananda creating the objective need for responding though practical Vedanta, and about his fascination for Western methods of organization creating the inner compulsion to duplicate the missionary methods. Once this knowledge is placed in the available framework of the sociology of religion. Vivekananda becomes a prototype of the native response to the Western challenge, leading—depending on one's bias—*to tradition* (Y. Singh) *to modernity* (Srinivas) or to a *tradition modernity* synthesis (A.K. Saran)" (K.G. Gupta, 1974, pp. 27-28). A historian therefore, finds the "modernization of tradition" superficial: "Nothing of the inner structure and dialectics of Hinduism itself remains relevant in this paradigm" viewing as it often does "Vivekananda-type reforms...primarily as transitional vehicles for bringing India closer to a Westernized modernity."

Citation of the above-mentioned historical investigations does not imply here our agreement with their authors on the substantive issues. These are just to illustrate that the critical confrontation of the paradigm "modernization—Sanskritization" with detaile historical data usually reveals the inadequacies of the paradigm. At a higher level of generalization the paradigm has been criticised as not only banal and empty, but misleading. In cultural history it has been condemned as worse than useless (K.N. Panikkar). Again, "modernization" in the socio-economic sense, it has been forcefully argued, is nothing other than colonialization (Bipan Chandra). Why did the modernization of colonial countries fail to provide the fruits of it which the metropolitan advanced capitalist countries enjoyed? Was it the "traditional" elements which blocked economic developments on was it the distorted pattern of "modernization" under imperialist auspices (N. Desai, 1978)? Does the model of modernization raise the relevant questions regarding economic distance between nations and internal social and economic inequalities? These questions inevitably lead to a new organizing principle of thinking in the history of Indian society—one emphasizing the economic structure of imperialist exploitation and the concurrent processes at the levels of culture, social institutions politicization processes and national formation, etc. This would mean rethinking on older paradigms of "progress" (evolution and incorporation into a world capitalist system), "national renaissance awakening" (evolution of national bourgeois hegemony), and "modernization/westernization" (colonialization accompanied by growth of bourgeois class hegemony). Satish Sabarwal's critique of sociologists' lack of sensitivity as well as lack of intellectual response to structural inequalities in Indian society is worth quoting: "our intellectual energies appear to have been more or less fully absorbed in the caste system or, say, in kinship. The wider structures of Indian Society either did not seem to be problematical or, when attention was directed to them.....the digits of discourse were extraneous, they did not emerge from the logic of the structures themselves" (Saberwal, 1979, p. 251). On M.N. Srinivas's, paradigm in *Social Change* in particular: "It presents his most comprehensive interpretation of the wider social processes active in India. The terms "equality" and "inequality" are missing from the index though some related aspects are subsumed under the category "caste".....Perhaps it would not be fair to judge Srinivas's understanding of colonialism in 1966 by todays' standards. Unmistakable, however, is the profound impression made upon him by British humanitarianism, seen to subsume equalitarianism..... To restate the issue more generally, the colonial regime, westernization, etc. came to be mistakenly associated in the sociological mind with a tendency towards equality....(whereas) inequalities common to capitalist societies which have not institutionalised strong and effective redistributive mechanisms, were in colonial India further reinforced by the strategies of colonial governance" (*Ibid.*, p. 244).

These observations of Saberwal lead into the problematic from which a new paradigm may develop. The French historian, Jean Chesneaux, has pointed out a quaint fact: the confucian mandarins referred to rebels and dissidents a *fei*—a negative grammatical expression denoting non-persons,—a denial of their existence in the eyes of history (Chesneaus, 1978, p. 19). Chesneaux has called this "occultation", which is "one of the most widespread practices in the state's system of control over the past.....entire sections of world history have no other existence than what the oppressors permit us to know of them...." Whether it is the paradigm of "pupil's progress" or "national awakening" or "Westernization/modernization"—vast sections of the people have remained *fei*. For example the struggle of the peasantry, the artisans, and the industrial workers vis-a-vis the land controllers, merchant/susury capital, and industrial capital, hardly figured in Indian historical literature till the 1970s'. To the extent they are present in "imperialist" and "nationalist" historiography, they are "objects" in the social thought and action of the colonial bureaucracy and the nationalist leadership. Insofar as "nationalist" history was an ideological effort to define and establish national unity, which was mainly in terms of culture and tradition, it would be difficult to accommodate the question whether such continuity and unity are products of cultural domination; or, let us say, the assertion of national unity in the freedom struggle cutting across classes and communities, would evidently involve the "occultation" of manifestations of class struggle. These phenomena were not a part of the problematic the nationalist historian framed for himself. It was left to those writing in the Marxian framework, such as D.P. Mukherjee (1948) in cultural history, A.R. Desai (1948) in socio-political history, Ramakrishna Mukherjee (1957) in agrarian history, and above all R.P. Dutt and M.N. Roy—to raise broader structural questions which professional historians falled to answer, or even to ask.

It is our contention that the study of the colonialization process in all its dimensions, and the study of structural inequalities in colonial times and since, will yield the organizing principles of new thinking of Indian Social History. The necessary critique of the older conceptual frameworks has not proceeded deep enough. Nor have the historical specificities of the colonial and post-colonial society been investigated with the rigour and craftsmanship one associates with the high tradition of social science. Unless this occurs, the alternative paradigm that is beginning to take shape will be reduced to a set of catch-phrases (Already one senses the danger that an ill-defined *deus ex machina called* "colonization" may be used and debased as an all purpose labour-saving device in the task of historical explication). In the sections below we shall examine the prospects of the emergence of a new paradigm or paradigms which might provide unity in the diversity of problems and methods that will come under our survey. Our interpretation of the trends in this regards as well as the brief sketch of paradigm changes in the past may be questioned by many social historians. We think, however, that what is expected to be a "trend report" will be meaninglesss without such an effort to discern patterns of convergence in the thinking of social historians. By questioning the trends as we have seen them, those who think otherwise are sure to advance our understanding of the unfolding of our consciousness of social history.

Let us not turn to the thematic treatment of major research problems which have engaged historians in the recent past.

SOCIAL MOVEMENTS

In a superficial way it is possible and conventional to distinguish between the following areas of study: (a) history of social reform movements, originating in eastern India in the first decades of the 19th Century and elsewhere in the second half of the 19th Century, accompanied by active State intervention up to 1858 and in more circumspect fashion since then; (2) history of caste movements, often led by caste associations which sometimes developed not only into political interest groups but political parties; (3) history of social ideas, centring around the conflict between the orthodox and reformists in the 19th Century and between the socially disprivilleged and the elite in the later days.

While conventionally such a separation between "fields of study" is accepted, possibly there can be no meaningful study of any of these themes which will not cut across the limits of these fields. For instance, the purely ideological debate called the "*Vedokta* controversy" in Kolhapur in 1900-1901 regarding prescribed rituals and the Maratha attempts to re-establish their calims to *Kshatriya* status and "to Sanskritize themselves" (C.Y. Mudaliar, 1978), the resultant growth of the non-Brahman movement as a political tool of the Kolhapur Raj (Ian Copland, 1973), the role of this movement in reinforcing the patron-client networks controlled by the Maratha aristocrats and jagirdars (D. Attwood, 1974), and the broadening of the movement through the agency of the Satya Shodhak Samaj and Maratha Sangatans and its transformation into an expression of a massbased peasant agitation (Gail Omvedt, 1973)—this complex and multifaceted reality cannot be compartmentalized into history of "social ideas", "caste movement", "social reform", etc. In fact the historiography of social movements is marked by conceptual poverty and fragmented comprehension because of this conventional compartmentalization. Therefore, rather than make a list of research works under the heads "caste movements", "social reform" and so on, we propose to take up some of the important themes and problems which have engaged the attention of social historians.

REFORM "FROM ABOVE" AND "FROM BELOW"

On the so-called social reform movements there has accumulated a substantial literature. We propose to discuss here some of the recent research interests in this area. There has been a good deal of rather stereotyped research on British governmental policies towards the social reform question, particularly in the early half of the 19th Century. Secondly, the reform efforts under Indian sponsorship, often organized through religious bodies like the Brahmo Samaj or the Prarthana Samaj or Arya Samaj, have attracted a good number of historians. Thirdly, we have a fair amount of work on social reform sponsored by caste associations, such as those sponsored by the non-Brahman movement and caste uplift movements in Maharashtra, Tamilnadu, Kerala and other parts of India.

Since O'Malley's influential work on the impact of the West on Indian culture and society, the chronicling or British social policy has been the subject of a number of Ph. D. theses—for the theme lends itself to facile treatment, given a simple "impact-response" framework and masses of easily accessible archival material on British administrative policy and thinking. Some of these works address themselves not to the question of social policy per se, but that of cultural-social interaction between British administration and the natives. One may recall a series of works by K.A. Ballhatchet (1957) on social policy in western India in 1817-1830; by Kenneth Ingham (1956) on reformers in India, 1793-1833; by G.D. Bearce (1961) on British attitude towards India, 1784-1858; by V.A. Narain (1959) on J. Duncan's activities in Banaras and A.T. Embree's (1962) on Charles Grant. Detailed studies of even fairly obscure corners of this area are available in R.S. Vatsa's (1969) work on the Government's social policy towards lepers and the deaf and dumb, or N.K. Barooah's (1969) study of David Scott's brief encounter with the institution of slavery in Assam. A representative example of the approach typical of the School of Oriental and African Studies (London) is Lalita Panigrahi's (1972) well-documented thesis on British Measures to Suppress Female Infanticide in the 19th Century. After a descriptive account of the practice in Bombay, Rajputana, North-Western Provinces, and the Punjab, she describes the streps to suppress the custom culminating in the Act of 1870; the last Chapter deals with the working of this Act. "Thus a century of incessant activity in the field of social legislation was brought to a close. The British Government in India had displayed unparalleled humanitarian zeal and taken scrupulous care to protect human life..... By the time that the measures had become fully effective the passion aroused by the Partition of Bengal was already manifesting itself in other parts of the country. In the heat and passion, India of the early 20th Century paid little attention to the good work done by the alien government" (*ibid*, p. 191). One may compare this work with an illuminating paper on female infanticide written by Viswa Nath (1973) about the same time; it shows that an anthropological study of the totality of the complex institutional framework—hypergamy, polygamy, the lineage system, etc.—can yield a more adequate picture, than masses of quotations from the sanctimonious though well-intentioned writings of English bureaucrats. Unfortunately, there are few studies of this kind. Nor are there many studies of the social philosophy of the Englishmen in decision-making positions which can be classed with that outstanding work by Eric Stokes (1959) on Utilitarians and India. He had set out to explore the motivations behind "the confused surface of events". "The Industrial Revolution and the reversal it brought about in the economic relations of India with Britain were the primary phenomena. A transformation in the purpose of political dominion was the main result..... This transformation of economic purpose carried with it a new expansive and aggressive attitude....... The material and intellectual elements of which it was composed were the three movements.... Free Trade was its solid foundation. Evangelicalism provided its programme of social reform, its force of character, and its missionary zeal. Philosophic radicalism gave it an intellectual basis and supplied it with the science of political economy, law and government" (*ibid.*, pp. xiii-xiv). Although Stokes was concerned mainly with the latter, he provides the most insightful account of the dominant social ideas of the 19th Century policy-makers.

A shortcoming of many of the works cited above was that their analysis of social reform was designed on a simplistic "Stimulus-response" framework and in the execution of that design they fail so far as Indian response was concerned. The Indian response, especially from the second half of the 19th Century, has been a central theme in the writings of the nationalistically inspired chroniclers of the "renaissance" mentioned earlier. In this tradition, authors who specifically address themselves to the history of social reforms are Biman Bihari Majumdar (1934, 1967), C.S. Srinivasachari (1947), and S. Natarajan (1959) of the *Indian Social Reformer*. In the 1960s more research based work was done by C.H. Heimsath (1964) and Sita Ram Singh (1968) on social reform and nationalism, by Amitabha Mukherjee (1968) on the indigenous roots of reform ideas in Bengal, By Salahuddin Ahmed (1965) on the reform era in early 19th Century Bengal, by R.C. Majumdar (1960), Pradip Sinha (1965), Gautam Chattopadhyay (Ed. 1965) on the same period in Bengal. V.A. Narain (1972) provided a somewhat wider all-India perspective, though at a more superficial level.

Since C.F. Andrews (1912) and J.N. Furquahar (1915), social reform and religious movements have been studied in tandem. Many of the early reforms were in fact sponsored by religious bodies in all region: the Brahmo Samaj in Bengal, Prarthana Samaj in Maharasthra, and the Arya Samaj in North India, (Sibnath Sastri, 1911-1912; D.K. Biswas in N.K. Sinha, ed., 19, Jogananda Das in A.C. Gupta, ed., 1958; Chakravarti and Ray, 1933; Lajpat Raj, ed. S.R. Sharma, 1967; Kenneth Jones, 1976). At the same time, there did exist relatively secular impulses towards social reform and this took the form of voluntary associations; from 1887 the National Social Conference began to spearhead a movement inspired by leaders like M.G. Ranade, in the social realm conjointly with that in the political realm under the wide umbrella of Indian National Congress (P.J. Jagirdar, 1963). By the end of the 19th Century, as Heimsath has pointed out, "the all-India social reform movement, reflected in the proceedings of the National Social Conference, had lost most of its drive for centrally-ordained amendments in Hindu Personal Law, which had been the sweeping and hence largely ineffective approach of the major reformers. Of the nationally recognised reformers of the latter half of the Century—such as Karsondas Mulji, Jotiba Phule, Kashinath Telang, Behramji Malabari, Viresalingam Pantulu, Mahadev Ranade,—some had died and others realized that the era of social ādvancement through legislation affecting all Hindu communities had reached an end.... Since the turn of the century caste associations have superseded general religious and social reform movements and the great national personal law reform crusades and have carried the main weight of the Hindu social reform movement (C.H. Heimsath, 1978, pp. 22-23).

We may call this a transition from the era of reform "from above" (initiated by leaders of Western-educated, professional, urban groups organized in religious bodies or elite voluntary associations, backed by discriminating legislative intervention by the State) to reform "from below" (sponsored by caste associations and the like which have primarily the attributes of "ascriptive" groups, but also sometimes display characteristic of a "voluntary" group, and are under a leadership which fragmented the nation-wide reform objectives of the earlier period into caste upliftment/reform programmes). The study of reform from above has become a well-developed area; the second type of reform movements (rituals, marriage practices, education, personal law, etc., of particular castes) have been studied only very recently. In some caste associations the reform aspect is more pronounced than in others. Thus R.L. Hardgrave's (1969) Nadar appear to set store by "reform" in their process of social elevation more than, let us say, Robin Jeffrey's (1976) Nayars and their Service Society. Of course, there was no incompatibility between social reform and political interest-group activities, both being means towards the same end. The same general pattern is observed with monotonous regularity in the Kongu Vellala Sangam of the Gounder caste in Tamil Nadu (D. Arnold, 1974), or the Vokkaliga and Lingayat Associations in Mysore (Arnold, Jeffrey and Manor, 1976), or the S.N.D.P. Yogam of the Iravas of Kerala R. Jeffrey (1974), or the non-Brahman movement and the Satya Shodhak Samaj in Maharashtra (C.Y. Mudaliar, 1978; Ian Gopland, 1973; Gali Omvedt, 1973), or the North Indian Kayastha Conference (L. Carroll, 1975a).

This reform "from below" constitutes a stage only in a qualified sense. Reform from above and from below are two types rather than two stages. The initial inpulse of social reform in Bombay city, for example, may have come from the new educated elite Elphinstone College, but soon after there emerged caste/community founded organizations, like the Parsi Panchayat, which were active in the reform effort simultaneously with the voluntaristic efforts of the former (Christine Dobbin, 1972; on the "ascriptive" caste-based organizations and "voluntaristic" efforts, corresponding to the Weberian "communal" and "associative" relationships see Lloyd Rudolph, 1965; Yogendra Singh, 1973, p. 168). However, by and large, there does seem to be a chronological pattern. By the end of the 19th Century, Heimsath has perceptively noted, the "general social reform associations" and the National Social Conference, the sister organization of the National Congress, were "floating on the tide of the practical transformations in the caste practices all over India, not creating any waves of its own" (C.H. Heimsath, 1978, p. 93).

On the cultural trends in the muslim community there exists an excellent bibliography which makes our task lighter

(Muinuddin Ahmad Khan, 1959). In the Muslim community historian have pointed out trends comparable to those outlined above in respect of the mojority community. The best account of the "modernist" trends in Aziz Ahmad's (1967) celebrated survey covering the period 1857 to 1960s (For the earlier period, see A.R. Mallick, 1961). However, Ahmad's work has not, perhaps, superseded the rather schematic but incisively analytical study of modern Islam by Cantwell Smith (1946). As distinct from the modernistic response, we have contrasting trends studied in the detailed historical works on the Feraidi movement in Bengal by Mulnuddin Ahmad Khan (1965), on the Wahabi movement by Qeyamuddin Ahmad (1966), and on the orthodox Deoband school in relation to the demand for Pakistan (Ziya-ul Hasan Faruqi, 1963). That the so-called modern and conservative trends in both Muslim and Hindu traditions can be subsumed under a common rubric has been well demonstrated by K.P. Karunakaran (1969). This is a useful corrective to the far too common tendency to segregate "minority" history in a special category—reminiscent of the traditions set by "Islamic studies" departments of the Indian universities at one time.

The stereotype of the Muslim community as a monolithic group has often been challenged but the tradition dies hard, (ef. M. Mujeed, 1967). The work of some sociologists has stressed the commonalities in the social organization of both the communities. Among these, two recent studies of historical interest are J.C. Masselos's (in Imtiaz Ahmad, 1978) on the notion of community membership in 19th Century Muslim communities, and Theodore P. Wright's (In Imtiaz Ahmad, 1976) on kinship. In cultural sociology an early historical study was that of Binoy Kumar Sarkar (1917) on Islamic elements in "folk" Hinduism; Tara Chand and other historians have contributed substantially in this area, though this genre really belongs to intellectual history of a kind. Likewise the political interaction between the two communities has been, of course, a perennial subject of research; but the social dimensions have been explored by very few (*e.g.*, Kunneth Mcpherson, 1969; Sumit Sarkar, 1972); this is equally true of the so-called policy studies, *i.e.*, British policy towards the Muslims (cf. Azizur Rahman Mallick, 1961).

One of the interesting aspects of the sociology of religious movements is conversion—especially from Hinduism to Islam in the madiaeval period and to Christianity under the British regime. G.A. Oddie (1969, 1975) in his studies in Christian conversions in Telugu country in the last half of the 19th Century observes a pattern of mass movement noticed by J.W. Pickett earlier (Pickett, 1933). There was tendency of the converts to Christianity to be drawn from similar jatis; Oddie notes that families as one unit were converted quite often and family ties and kinship connections had an important role in the conversion process. The untouchable castes were, of course, most responsive to Christian teaching. Further, "these movements seemed to begin among the more economically independent and to spread to the poorer and more dependent sections of the same community," (pp. 69-70). Responsiveness varied with local power structure and duties/privileges derived by a jati group from the *jajmani* system, "some jati groups in one area having more to loose than those of comparable status in others" (p. 78). In this respect the position of the untouchables varied greatly throughtout South India.

An interesting feature already noticed is the replication of caste-like stratifications in the Muslim community. Hardgrave (1968) has argued that the Christian missionaries' education efforts and propaganda regarding caste disabilities intensified caste solidarity among the Nadars. G.A. Oddie (1970) goes further : "while the missionaries played a part in undermining particular caste observances, in making the system more flexible and in forcing it to change and readapt, they are not as successful as they wished in destroying caste consciousness and feeling." The reformist impact of the Christian missionaries was probably overestimated in earlier works (K. Ingham, 1956; E.D. Potts, 1967). In respect of education they played an important role (M.L. Laird, 1972) and through their propaganda against certain social institutions they facilitated legislative intervention as well as social intervention by the native intelligentsia. But the impact of Christian missionary activities evoked much subtler and more varied responses than a simple "enlightenment" model suggests.

REFORMISM AND REVIVALISM

The term Hindu revivalism has been used to denote that reassertion of religious and communal identity which was associated with the growth of militant nationalism in the early 20th Century. Its distinguishing mark is that, unlike the early social reformers, revivalism did not pursue the path of differentiating itself into an autonomous sphere within Hindu society. Although Heimsath (1964) has not used such a scheme explicitly, this differentiation on the one hand and relationship with nationalism on the other appear to be the basis of his periodisation of the history of social reform. He distinguishes three phases : First, that of individual revolt and reform from the days of Ram Mohan Roy to the 1880s. Second, the phase when social reform movement is elevated to the national plane when the religious bias of the first phase diminishes. Third, the period "in which social reform began to mean a regeneration of the traditional spirit of the nation" conjointly with the "reconstitution of Indian nationalism" by the extremists. This last phase is commonly called the revivalist phase. Sita Ram Singh's (1968) entire book is a long argument with the view, held by Valentine Chirol, among others, that "the new nationalism was socially a reactionary resurgence and as such it retarded the movement for social reforms". Singh rejects the idea that the reassertion of old values was socially reactionary (See also B.B. Majumdar, 1966).

It is by no means a settled question whether revivalist trend in the nationalist mainstream was altogether free of "social reaction". One has to separate here the element of deliberate intention from unintended consequences. The complexities of this question have partly been examined in S. Ghose's study of "social and religious movements which gave rise to the Renaissance as also the revivalistic ideas and trends which later political movements developed" (S. Ghose, 1969; also K.P. Karunakaran, 1969; and Hirendra Nath Mukherjee, 1976, which owes a lost, as other Marxist Studies, to R.P Dutt, 1940). The even subtler complexities of revivalism within the reformist movement or sect is also to be noted. For instance, within Brahmo reformism we have a species of revivalist leaders : David Kopf's (1974) study of the nationalist "Hindu Brahmo" Rajnarain Bose is a case in point At the more trivial level, we have revivalists in the ranks of the Positivists, e.g., Jogendra Chandra Ghosh who "was driven into the camp of the defenders of Hinduism and away from that of social reformers" (G. Forbes, 1974)—a strange fate for a follower of the Comtean Religion of Humanity.

K.K. Gangadharan (1970, Chapter II, III) is one of the few sociologists who have explored the historical aspects of the "Sociology of Revivalism" (cf. A.R. Desai, 1960). Revivalism and its own variety of social reform vitally affected the social organization of tradition (and, consequently, that of Hindu and Muslim communal identities; cf. S. Saberwal, 1980). Krishna Prakash Gupta (1974a) has raised certain methodological problems in analysing Hindu revivalist movements in the framework of conventional sociology of religion. According to him the limitations of this framework originate in "the early bias inherent in the very origin of the sociology of religion which had emerged and evolved in response to the rationalist-positivist and later Marxist-materialist denunciation of the role of religion in Western society" (K.P. Gupta, 1974b). Whatever one may think of this rather novel approach, Gupta's observations merit attention when he criticises the functionalist model widely employed by Western scholars : that paradigm did not treat non-Christian religions "as internally-evolving but merely as anxiety-resolving defence mechanisms used by the people concerned to meet the Western challenge". Thus Gupta has argued, with reference to the Ramakrishna Mission Movement initiated by Vivekananda, that the usual simplistic interpretation has been in terms of "reaffirmation and revitalization of a dying tradition.... Nothing of the inner structure and dialectics of Hinduism itself remains relevant in this paradigm" (K.P. Gupta, 1974b, pp. 26-28). While Gupta is undoubtedly correct in maintaining that sociology of religion has been deeply coloured by Western experience with Christianity, does the interpretation of a non-Christian religion "on its own terms" means this : "To a Hindu society is already fully religious; one cannot theoretically construct it on a new religious basis. Similarly, the problem of rationality is meaningless from a strictly Hindu perspective..., Vivekananda's Ramakrishna Mission is to be viewed in this paradigm. Its precise significance cannot be assessed through its rationality-inducing role as an autonomous sector of Hindu Society" (*ibid.*, p. 48). Perhaps a viable alternative to the existing paradigm is yet to be developed.

It may be contended that revivalism is only a more conspicuous manifestation of a deeper-seated conservatism which has roots extending back far beyond the era of militant nationalism. Sudhir Chandra has argued : "A society impregnated with reformism is the image of 19th Century India that spontaneously conjures up before us. Volumes have been written to delineate, in borrowed terms, the Reformation and the Renaissance that began during this period of national awakening", whereas actually "the key to the understanding of the 19th Century Indian Society is provided by conservatism" (S. Chandra, 1970, p 2003). Perhaps historians have paid little attention to conservatism and its social basis (S. Bhattacharya, 1974). Nor do we have many studies of the bearers of the orthodox tradition and their responses to the reformist challenge. Frank F. Conlon (1971) has provided a detailed and sympathetic account of the leadership of the orthodox sect among Chitrapur Saraswat Brahmins, particularly the role of Pandurangashram Swami (the caste guru at the Chitrapur *Matha*) confronted by the social reformer Narayan Chandravarkar. Conlon's, incidentally, is one of the few historical accounts of a caste group over a long time span, 1700-1935, which is a more meaningful time-frame than that adopted by many sociologists of historians out to "do a caste" for a quick Ph.D. Richard P. Tucker (1970) has studied "the tradition of *Dharmashastra*, the relations of Hindu Law to civil authority, and finally in the late 19th Century the gradual encroachment of political nationalism into the field of social authority". In the 19th Century, on the one hand, the growth of case laws diminished the importance of the *Shastri* and *Qazi* in the British courts of law, and on the other from within the community their position as arbiters of social relations and practices began to be challenged by the reformers and the modern intelligentsia. Christine Dobin (1972) has shown how among the *Shetias* of Bombay a strong orthodox group met the challenge of reformism. S.N. Mukherjee (1970) has made a study of the faction led by Raja Radhakanta Deb of Calcutta and urges deeper study of the phenomenon of conservatism. One is reminded of Louis Dumon's warning that the study of the enduring ideo-structures of a society is the fundamental task while "the study of change answers a strong public demand, and for a part corresponds more to the subjective needs of the student as a member of a modern society than to properly sociological issues" (L. Dumont 1964, p. 12).

MOBILIZATION AND LEADERSHIP IN SOCIAL MOVEMENT

As we have seen above, some time at the turn of the century the baton passed from the social reformers to the caste association leaders. Some of the most interesting studies being done today relate to the caste movements and associated political movements. On their leadership and patterns of mobilization a good deal has been written. Broadly three patterns seem to emerge: (1) the *jajmani* model, *i.e*, the patron-client pattern of relationship; (2) the broker-client group relationship; and (3) the *dal* under a *neta i.e.*, group mobilizer or leader. We have abstracted these models from varieties of historical experiences, but this is warranted by the need to develop a typology. Further, it might serve to identify sources of conceptual models which remain implicit in historians' treatment but are not explicitly acknowledged.

The anthropological studies of *jajmani* in village society, from W.H. Wiser (1936) to more complex variants of present times by Srinivas (1955), Breman (1974) and others are characterized by greater vigour than most historians' works. The model of patron-client relationship has been used widely by the historians of caste politics, or just politics. A recent reviewer of the historiography of modern political movements commented. "In both urban and rural studies, 'connexions' have moved to the centre of the stage in place of communal and caste solidarities which so often claimed the attention of regional historians in the 1960s" (R.K.Ray, 1977). Thus, in place of Brahmin and non-Brahmin rivalry in South Indian politics (E. Irschick, 1969) "there was a shift of emphasis to patron-client linkages in localities irrespective of caste. In this sense, magnates, who dominated and aimed to dominate their localities rallied their dependents to build up factions that straddled both the class and the caste strata of society" (Ray, *op. cit.*, p. 494). Thus D.A. Washbrook (1975,1976) and C.J. Baker (1975,1976) in their study of political movements in Madras Presidency (in 1870-1920) by Washbrook and 1920-1937 by Baker) and C.A. Bayly (1971, 1975) in his study of local roots of politics in Allahabad (in the years 1880-1920) may be cited as exemplars of this new interpretation. One of the consequences of this approach is to shift the focus from the caste associations: unlike Hardgrave (1969), E. Irschick (1969) and R. Jeffrey (1976), Washbrook dismisses the caste associations as "merely another way of building up a constituency in order to raise their (organizers') bargaining power" (Washbrook, 1971 p.282). Washbrook has been criticised on the ground that to ignore the crucial role of caste in politics is to "miss many of the nuances, and some even of the deep tides, of Madras politics" (S. Gopal, 1977) and that this approach goes too far in applying a corrective to the earlier simplistic interpretation attributing to caste associations a homogeneity and political weight which did not correspond to reality (Arnold, Jeffrey and Manor, 1976). As for the patron-client linkages now brought to the fore, that mechanism has for long been observed to be a well-established pattern in economic and political arrangements at the village level in anthropologists' studies. It has also been observed in caste movements. The Maratha non-Brahman movement has been visualized in the patron-client and mobilizer-constituency model by Attwood (1974); this movement has been credibly interpreted as a means of advancing the social and political hold of the Maratha aristocracy, the patrons of local society (Copland, 1973; C.Mudaliar, 1978).

As distinct from the patron in the *jajmani* model, we have the broker or *dalal* stepping into the active role in E. Zelliot's study of the Mahar caste movement in Maharashtra or C.A. Bayly's (1971, 1975) study of Allahabad politics in the late 19th Century. In Allahabad town, according to Bayly, the patrons or local magnates (the *rais*), often with trade and banking interests, depended on the mediation of intermediaries or agents (corresponding to the traditional *vakil*); thus the politicians and publicists are cast in the role of power/influence brokers. Zelliot (1970) in his study of the Mahar movement focuses on the role of "brokers" who serve as links between the caste and institutions of power in society and command channels of communication within the caste group and from the caste to the public. Christine Dobbin's detailed account of voluntary organizations in Bombay city adds up to an analogous picture of Bombay *Shetias* patronizing English-educated publicists and recruiting social support through the members of intelligentsia who in turn were anxious to gain the *Shetia's* financial support for their own ends (Dobbin, 1972). Some historians have employed the term "sub-contractor" to describe the intermediate leadership below the national level leadership (Judith M. Brown, 1972; Ravinder Kumar, ed., 1972).

Both the *jajmani* and the *dalali* (broker) models focus on patron-client vertical linkages. The *dal* under the *dal-neta*, however, is a product of horizontal mobilization independent of, and sometimes running counter to, the traditional superior status of the patron (see Rudolph and Rudolph, 1967). An anthropologist, David Attwood, comments: "To understand the patron we need to understand his competition, the group mobilizer. Data from Western India (Poona district, 1900-1947) reveal that the activities of these two types of political entrepreneurs are closely inter-connected.....The exclusive concentration on the patron-client dyad overlooks the crucial supportive and alternative alliances which the actors must also manipulate" (Attwood, 1974, p. 225). Such a group mobilizer would aim at "connections near the middle or base (instead of the apex) of the local power hierarchy" and the "summation of many similar, individual resources" rather than the interchange of specialized favours which patrons can dispense. "Village studies from all over the country have described efforts by middle peasants or by lower (untouchable) castes to increase their access to vital resources through group mobilization (Cohn, 1955; Gough, 1955; Bailey, 1957; Epstein, 1962; Beteille, 1965). Just as authropologists have abstracted the role of patron from a host of outwardly dissimilar contexts around the world, so I would suggest that there is a basic role strategy for the group mobilizer (in agrarian societies, at least) which could be used to elucidate many of the diverse empirical studies just cited" (Attwood, *op. cit.*, p. 227). This type of group mobilization, leading to the formation of what would be called in north India a *dal* under a *neta*, may involve the use of vertical connections (*e.g.* favour of elite members closer to the power centres or with greater access to resources by virtue of ascriptive status) but the strength of such a formation would depend primarily on the effective aggregation of units in the *dal*. We may note here that S.N. Mukherjee (in Leach and Mukherjee, 1970) has used the term *dal* in a somewhat different context as a synonym for factions: thus he has identified *dals* composed of *grihasthas* or middle class householders led by *abhijats* or aristocrats in 19th Century Calcutta; this type of faction, however, is more appropriately analysed in the patron-client framework. On the other hand, the situation described by Lucy Carroll (1973, 1975a,1975b) fits very well in the *dal* model. The growth of the Kayastha Conference from 1887, its organ *Kayastha Samachar* and its leader Swami Sivaganchand, show how the leader used the Kayastha movement "as a vehicle and constituency" which consisted of "groups which were aware of, and sensitive to, the changing conditions in which they lived and concerned about the issues to which the Conference addressed *i.e.*, with issues of education, employment, and economic security". In fact, although it "appears to be a caste situation" the group mobilized is similar to the groups recruited into the Congress and the Arya Samaj (Carroll, 1975a, p. 315). The line between "social" and "political" movement is thin in this respect. We have many examples of caste networks and a whole cluster of traditional institutions and psychological commitments being used for purposes of political mobilization. Thus, for example, Majid Siddiqi has described the disciplinary role of caste panchayats in the Eka movement in U.P. and the use of caste solidarity as a means of providing cohesion to the peasant movement led by Ram Chandra (Siddiqi, 1978, Ch. II & VI). G.M. Shah's (1974) account of the Bardoli Satyagraha show in detail how in the mobilization of "hetherto apolitical masses" the local leaders "derived their authority from caste and village councils" and used caste sanctions against recalcitrants. Even in the urban context, in the Non-Cooperation Movement the baniyas in north India made use of the solidarity and sanctions system of their community to enforce the boycott programme, *e.g.*, refusal *en bloc* to recognize *hundis* issued by baniyas opposed to the Congress programme (S. Bhattacharya, 1976). Henningham has shown the prominent role of the caste factor in the coalition of social forces against plantations in the Champaran Satyagraha of 1917-1918 (S. Henningham, 1976). In none of these cases there is a caste association.

An interesting question is whether in this typological scheme, ranging from *jajmani* through brokerage to the *dal* model, there is any tendency over time to evolve from purely vertical axes towards increasingly horizontal axes to develop. The Rudolphs (1969) seem to suggest such a linear trend. On the other hand Attwood (1974) argues that these are alternative strategies of alliance building, *i.e.*, that the political entrepreneurs as patron or as group mobilizer are in "complementary role-types". His data on social change and mobilization in Poona district in the early 20th Century suggest that individuals grope among alternative strategies and may use several simultaneously. This is a more complex model than that of F.G. Bailey's in *Tribe, Caste and Nation* (1960) in which competing choices between different affiliations determine the strength of the political system to which the affiliations belong. Attwood's criticism: "In adopting this method of analysis, it is important to avoid the temptation.....to think in terms of choices between complete, self-integrated social structures..... Instead, the facts require us to speak of alternative alliances with overlapping groups as network which can be used for political purposes" (Attwood, 1974).

While it is true that horizontal and vertical alliances may be used simultaneously, the historical accounts of some of the social movements which have been thoroughly studied (*e.g.*, works cited earlier on Tamilnadu and Maharashtra non-Brahman movements) suggest a pattern: the diminution of patron-client type vertical alliances and the increasing salience of horizontal aggregation of the groups being mobilized. Simultaneously, the matrix of the social movement changed from the caste-community polity to the administrative-electoral arenas, and the thrust of the movements moved away from Sanskritic reform/uplift towards power/resources accessible through mobilization.

In a comparative study of five caste associations in western Tamilnadu, Travancore and Mysore in the early 20th Century Jeffrey and others have shown how the early leaders of the caste movements formed an elite, often in non-traditional careers, which stressed a common heritage in the face of increasing occupational diversity and economic disparity. "Externally, the caste association tried to convince outsiders that behind the leaders stood a united community. In the old language and idiom of the people the association proclaimed that the castemen were devout Hindus whose claim to higher status were substantiated by the social and ritual practices. Backed by the devices of modern political agitation.....caste leaders lobbied for concessions" (Arnold, Jeffrey & Manor, 1976, p. 373). The most important point that emerges is that such caste associations constituted a stage in the development from the local jati relationship to cross-caste class relations and from local dominant caste politics to province or State level activities; evolution towards the latter stage meant the obsolescence of the old caste association or their conversion into caste parties. The class dimension on what began as a caste movement has been investigated in the case of a non-Brahman movement of Maharastra by Gali Omvedt (1976).

It will not be germane to our present purpose to elaborate this three-fold typology (the *jajman's,* the broker's, and the *dal neta's* modalities of operation) that emerges from our review. But it should be noted that the vigour of anthropologists' analysis is conspicuously missing in the models implicitly or explicitly employed by historians. Further, the latter, in their use of the patron-client model, show no awareness of the implications of using digits of analysis derived from anthropological studies of diverse societies (such as that of Sicily on Central Italy or the East Arctic—areas where the model has been systematically applied). Hence the historians waffle a bit in relating empirical findings to a general model.

AGENCIES OF "MODERNIZATION"

As we have seen earlier, the tradition-modernization paradigm has been widely employed as a key to understanding social change in the 19th and 20th Centuries. Some of the agencies of this change are technological such as the railways or the printing press and some are institutions set up under colonial auspices; the new legal system, the educational system, the network of communications, etc. To O'Malley (1941) the replacement of the pre-British legal system—which in his view appears to be sometimes arbitrary, often inequitable and always exposed to operational hindrances due to lack of law and order—by the British juridical system was a step towards modernization. The achievements of the British system were the establishment of the principle of equality and the creation of a consciousness of positive rights. This view is not commonly challenged. Thus, for instance, a prominent sociologist writing on the 'modernization of tradition' says, "In the Great Tradition of both Hinduism and Islam, the norms which constituted the foundations of the legal system were an extension of the principle of hierarchy. The *dharmashastras* clearly lay down differential standards to legal rights and administration of justice based on the qualitative-ascriptive status of various castes......With the establishment of the British power in India there came a new turning point in the legal system of the country. Various forums of legal innovations were introduced by the British which were in contradistinction with the traditional Hindu law, and were based on the principles of universalism, rationalism and individualism. Legislation then became an instrument of modernization" (Yogendra Singh, 1973, pp. 95-96). This view is, however, open to question.

The historical aspects of the Sociology of law have attracted very few researchers. J. Duncan M. Derrett's work is mainly directed towards history of juridical ideas and the European efforts to understand and codify Hindu law; yet he throws valuable light on the social impact of the codification of law in the late 18th and 19th Centuries. His evidence suggests that the "Gentoo Code", the interpretations offered by *pundits* and *qazis* in British courts of law, the fumbling attempts of alien judges to understand and standardize traditional laws subject to many local variations,—all this combined to promote the ossification of evolving customary laws into a rigid code (B.S. Cohn, 1959) Marc Gallanter (1966, 1968) in his studies on the changing legal conception of caste has shown textual law and prevailing customs were reinforced by British courts of law which accepted and acted on the notion of caste order in a scheme of articulated prerogatives and disabilities. The British courts recognized and enforced claims of caste groups to the exclusive use of religious premises, awarded damages for purificatory ceremonies necessitated by pollution as a result of trespass to the person of a member of high caste, looked to the position of a caste on the scale relative to other caste groups to ascertain its rights, and conceded the right of caste groups to make rules for themselves and to constitute tribunals to enforce them. Only in the case of exclusionary practices in regard to secular public facilities such as schools or roads judicial support was not available so readily, though caste autonomy in respect of sanctions against outcastes was not interfered with (except regarding property). It is true that there were some conspicuous instances of legislative intervention—often cited in text-books—which were inspired by western liberal outlook and endorsed by leading lights of the bureaucracy and the native intelligentsia. Thus the enactment of the Suttee Law in 1829, Anti-slavery Law of 1843, Hindu Widow Re-marriage Act of 1856, the Native Marriage Act of 1872, and the Age of Consent Act of 1891. On the other hand, as Gallanter has demonstrated the British juridical system, far from introducing equality between one Hindu and another of different castes, adopted and reinforced the hierarchical ranking of caste groups and their privileges and disabilities (Gallanter, 1966).

Further, the principle of equality was not applied without discrimination between members of the subject race and the ruling race. Inequality as a principle was for a long time accepted as a juridical norm: for instance under Act XII of 1865 no "European British Subject" (*i.e.*, a white man) could be tried by a jury of which the majority were coloured. No white man could be tried in the mofussil by a native judicial officer. The reform of the legal system to correct racial discrimination of this kind was overwhelmingly opposed by the British community in India—as the defeat of Ripon's attempt in 1883 indicates. Sudhir Chandra (1975) has shown how formal discrimination under law was as much a part of the system as inequality in the administration of justice in the daily operation of the judicial machinery (For a different view see Uma Dasgupta, 1973). Therefore, to ascribe to the British Legal System a modernizing impact on society on account of its principle of equality, rationality, etc. is to oversimplify a complex situation. In a comparative sense perhaps it can be said that the British judiciary did not go the whole hog in performing the traditional kingly function of enforcing the caste order and other inegalitarian legal traditions. Further, insofar as the pre-colonial legal system was a hindrance to the colonization of the Indian polity and economy, and particular customs were conspicuously at variance with the norms of the British rulers and the native intelligentsia, the colonial regime was motivated to introduce changes. But it will be an error to exaggerate the rupture or to characterise it simply as modernizing in its social consequences.

Unfortunately the interaction between law and society has not been studied in modern India historically, although P.V. Kane's History of the *Dharmshastras* laid down a splendid bridgehead. Lawyers who have written on caste cases in court, for example, have been interested purely in legal aspects as practitioners (*e.g.*, L.T. Kikani, 1912; D.F. Mullah, 1901). The machinery for administration of justice has been studied, but without exception these studies have neglected the social impact of the legal system (*e.g., U.C.* Sarkar, 1958). In particular, the growth of commercial and property laws in relation to the transition from a pre-capitalist economy seems to be an important and neglected area of study. Likewise, socio-historical study of crime remains almost untouched. Dipesh Chakraborty's (1973) study of crime as early industrial protest, and Stewart Gordon's (1969) study of crime in relation to the structure of State power and the process of State formation in the late mediaeval period are two isolated examples.

In the study of the passing of the traditional society or of the process of westernization the influential paradigm builders like D. Lerner or M.N. Srinivas have emphasized the cultural changes emanating from "modern" education. Historians, however, have not addressed themselves to this problem except in an indirect and tangential way. The standard authority, J.P. Naik and S. Nurullah's work (1951), is more a history of the administration and organization of education with little effort to locate education in the context of the social processes. Only in its documentation and detailed treatment it has superseded the earlier works of B.D. Basu (1927) and A.I. Mathew (1926). A major part of the scholarship in history of education in India has been expended on connecting the growth of the education system with the political activities of its products, the "English educated". B.T. McCully (1940) has chronicled the growth of English education and the origin of nationalism till 1885. Aparna Basu's (1974) is the latest work in the field: she has thoroughly covered the period between Curzon's arrival in India in 1898 and the Montagu-Chelmsford Reforms of 1920.

The aim was to show "how differential rates of growth of education affected political development and created tensions within Indian society". However, it is not so much the latter aspect as the political aspect to which attention was devoted. The book is really about education policy, the growth of our English-educated stratum, and "the extent to which education was a determinant of political activity". Anil Seal (1968) and B.B. Misra (1961) have attempted the same task within a wider frame of reference. To begin with a pass at the Education Policy and the growth of the "educated class" seems to be standard foreplay preceding any study of nationalism.

Susanne and Lyoyd Rudolph (1972) have suggested a three-fold pattern of interaction between education and politics: politicization of the educational structure, political influence exercised by the educational structure, and the pursuit of "public interest" in the field of education by the state. This work, mainly concerned with contemporary India, revived some historical questions about the validity of the modernizing role of education. Consider for example educational institutions set up for very particularistic ends by a caste or community, *e.g.*, the experience of sectarian enterprise in education in Mysore. Another important point that emerges is that political "interference" in education—which is commonly assumed to be a post-independence phenomenon—has deeper roots in British Indian education policy itself.

As distinct from the general trend focusing on education policies of the British Government, we have some interesting studies of private, voluntary efforts impired by nationalism: P.M. Limaye (1935) on the Deccan Education Society in Poona and H. and U. Mukherjee (1957) on the National Education Movement in Bengal. It is abundantly clear that to the nationalists the pattern of education introduced by the British appeared to be not modernizing but colonial. In a fragmentary fashion various non-governmental agencies of change in the field of education have been studied: *e.g.* Anglo-Indian institutions in Bengal (Austin D'souza, 1976), the Banaras Hindu University (S.L. Das and Somasundaram, 1966), the M.A.O. at Aligarh (S.K. Bhatnagar, 1969), missionary education establishments in early 19th Century Bengal (M.A.

Laird, 1972), women's educational institutions (Y.B. Mathur, 1973), etc.

By and large, excessive concern with policy and politics has stereotyped historians' approach to the history of education. Thus many important questions do not get answered. For example, even in a well-researched region such as Bengal little is known about indigenous and vernacular education system in the late 18th and early 19th Century. One has still to turn to Francis Buchanan-Hamilton (R.M. Martin, ed., 1838), Adam's Report (1868), and H.A. Stark (1916). How much of the high tradition of scholarship in logic and linguistic and astronomical studies had survived and in what social organization? Again, what were the social strata which formed the catchment area for British sponsored institutions? Except fore stray caste-wise distribution we have no answer to the question in the available authorities. It would be also useful to study the syllabi and content at the higher level of education to understand what kind of ideological influence the pupils were exposed to; there is one such study on social science teaching in the 19th Century (B. Datta Gupta, 1972). We need more detailed study of the growth of science, not merely as an aspect of formal education but as an attitude. If, in the culture of the "English-educated", science was not internalized, how to account for that? The limitations of the non-scientific emphasis in curricula of the Macaulay-Wood vintage are well known. But why the Europeans' scientific endeavour in India was limited to the field sciences, what imperial needs called into existence scientific enterprise within the bureaucracy and native technical personnel, why despite considerable contact with science endeavours the indigenous educated responded tardily—there are some questions to be probed. (The best work on this is by a Physicist, S.N. Sen, 1970). Was there any socio-cultural constraint on the growth of a "Science culture" of the kind that operated, it has been often argued, against technological innovation? (M.D. Morris, 1967; S. Bhattacharya, 1966). It we are to appraise the modernizing impact of education, the growth of science endeavour and scientific attitude and changes in the value system are obvious indicators to be gauged.

Of the so-called agencies of modernization western science and technology brought to India, the Press and Railways clair ı attention most of all. Railways increased physical mobility and the printing press, the diffusion of knowledge and ideas—both potent instruments of cultural change. The modernization of channels of communication may not, however, mean modernization of culture. M.N. Srinivas has perceptively observed that the railway or the postal service not only diffuses "westernization" but also facilitates "traditional" activities such as pilgrimage or caste association organization (Srinivas, 1962, p. 74). The press likewise may be a moderns means of transmitting far from modern messages. William Mc Cormack points out, in his study of communication in Virasaiva religion, how the traditional channels of communications—fairs, devotional recitation, etc.—are reinforced by modern ones, thus inte-grating a religious sect or caste. (Mc. Cormack in M. Singer, ed., 1959). Thus, if one may speculate, there may take place a secondary traditionalization as a result of the introduction of modern communication channels. Unless we attribute a peculiar connotion to the term "modernization", between that process and the growth of new media and communications there is no necessary correlation.

Let us turn to another paradox. One has only to recall the high level of illiteracy and the low circulations of newspapers, to appreciate the constraints on another instrument of "modernization", the press. This fact lends plausibility to the British anti-nationalist opinion that the press did not reflect the opinion of the native masses. Henry Bartle Frere's apothegm is quotable: in India "published opinion is not public opinion" (quoted in S. Battacharya, 1971, p.xxv). And yet, the printing press and the newspaper were evidently instruments of importance to social reformers like Rammohan or Vidyasagar or Ranade who poured forth masses of tracts. The newspaper, till the beginning of the Gandhi era, was virtually the only weapon accessible to the nationalist publicist. And that the British government took the press seriously enough is evident from the efforts to control it from the enactment of the Vernacular Press Act onwards. The key to this paradox lay in the fact that the "public" the Press addressed itself to was admittedly limited in number but, given the role of the intelligentsia in the colonial socio-political transformation, these few mattered. Public opinion was not people's opinion, but the opinion of the relevant minority. Even in the infancy of Indian journalism the editor of *The Hindoo Patriot* was a man to reckon with in political decision making (cf. M. Ghose, ed., 1911). The vernacular press was perhaps less of a political force, but the government kept it under surveillance and one of the by-products of this surveillance system is the series, reports on Native Press, consisting of confidential reports in the Home Department on contents of vernacular papers. Few works are available in the English language on the development of the vernacular press *e.g.*, Pramatha Nath Basu's (1920) on the Bengali papers from 1820, R.R. Bhatnagar's on the Hindi newspapers (1948). The English language newspapers have received more attention. Margrita Barns' (1940) book remains unsurpassed as a comprehensive history of journalism. J. Natarajan (1955) and Uma Dasgupta (1977) are two notable additions to the scanty literature on the subject. The latter addresses herself to the question, how "public opinion" comes into existence. The author reviews the pattern of responses in the Press to some policy issues like the income tax, financial devolution, criminal procedure code, etc. in the period 1870-1880. By the end of this period the Legislation to suppress the vernacular press brings about a strong reaction on a nation-wide scale and thus journalism transcends its local horizon and begins to a determinant of national opinion. On the whole, the political dimensions of journalism are better known, through the above cited works, than the social aspects.

We have seen that, in terms of the paradigm "tradition to modernity", the agencies of change which are commonly identified as critical (in the areas of law, education, communication, etc.) are mainly cultural We have argued earlier that this paradigm is open to question, and we have seen that many of these supposed agencies of modernization may function in a retroactive fashion, preserving or refashioning those components of "tradition" which the colonization process either left unaffected or positively reinforced. When we move to deeper-seated structural changes, the process that first claims attention is urbanization and the growth of new classes.

URBAN HISTORY

Urban history has developed as an area of study more by accident than by design. It has not received its due share of attention, but, entirely incidentally, the historians who have written on the political elite, or the educated middle classes, or social reform movements, etc. have thrown light on the urban locale. We have referred to such works, as well as research on the predominantly urban entrepreneurial groups and the industrial working class elsewhere in this survey. The specific treatment of urban history which derives thematic definition and unity from the coherent and limited entity, the city, has been attempted in very few recent works. Given the wealth of sources in the municipal archives, in the papers of urban business units, family records, voluntary societies and political associations; in the city based newspapers, and in the governmental archives—it is somewhat surprising that urban social history has been neglected in the past. Kenneth Gillion Howard Spodek, Pradip Sinha, Christine Dobbin, Narayani Gupta, Soumen Mukherjee, *et. al.* have published studies specific to an individual city. Some important problems posed by these historians regarding the urban social experience in the 19th and early 20th century may be noted.

A commonly observed phenomenon which has been widely commented upon is the case with which traditional institutions and social mechanisms have dovetailed into the urban context in the colonial period. Vestiges of the guild system and various pre-industrial business institutions and practices, far from being impediments in the "Manchesterization" of Ahmedabad city, played a positive role (Spodek, 1969). Likewise, Milton Singer has found traditional mechanisms and traditional business communities in Madras perfectly attuned to the demands of British-sponsored "modernization" (Singer, 1972). This has also been observed in mid-19th Century Bombay City by C. Dobbin (1972). As we have noticed elsewhere in this essay, the recent explorations in the sociology of entrepreneurship have exploded the notion of "traditional" values and culture as long-term impediments to social adjustment to economic transformation (M.D. Morris; 1967). The findings of Spodek, Dobbin and Singer confirm that conclusion and enlarge own understanding of the complex process of adjustment to—not perhaps "modernization" as they would have it,—but the colonial transformation of the economy and the place of the city in that process.

An interesting question of common concern to urban historians is : what is the catchment area for the recruitment of the new urban middle-classes and what determines different groups' induction into urban role ? Pradip Sinha (1965, 1978) and C. Dobbin (1972) have provided some answers. "Bombay city provides an interesting case study in one of the main themes of modern Indian history, the speed and variability with which different communities in the Indian sub-continent espoused the new opportunities and new ideas which were the concomitant of foreign rule. In particular the question arises whether the possibilities for trade and commerce furnished by the city in the 19th Century led to the rise of a new class of commercial magnates; whether British educational endeavour produced a new elite of learning : or whether both the merchant princes and the English-educated intelligentsia of the city were linked to the traditional commercial and intellectual elite of the area....." (p. vii). Dobbin concludes that the answer to the first question is in the negative; "castes and communities whose livelihood was traditionally gained from commerce continued to engage in commercial pursuits.... Similarly, those whose livelihood was traditionally won by the pen, particularly in the service of the state, continued to wield it in the service of the new masters" (p. 259). Thus in Maharashtra the Chipavan Brahmans (Masselos, 1974), in Guntur the Desasthas (Frykenburg, 1965) continued to serve the bureaucracy. On the other hand, we have evidence of another kind : a substantial number of the comprador merchants of Calcutta in the early 19th Century were Kayasthas and Brahmans (N.K. Sinha, 1962). The most successful exploiters of new business opportunities in Bombay city were new entrants into commerce and the big city (A.V. Desai, 1968).

Dobbin's explanation, that the Parsis were "adaptable enough to be able to succeed", appears to be inadequate and tautologous. Part of the explanation may be seen in the pre-colonial urban scene (cf. Saberwal, 1977). The varying opportunities for accumulation of capital, relation between urban merchants and artisans, pattern of rural-urban exchange, and the political composition of the pre-colonial urban scene (cf. Saberwal, 1977). The varying opportunities for accumulation of capital, relation between urban merchants and artisans, pattern of rural-urban exchange, and the political composition of the pre-colonial city might have determined access of different groups to resources and skills while the uneven development, inter-regional disparities varying demand for administrative personnel, and salience of foreign capitalist control in the colonial period were other determinants of success in the process of induction into the colonial urban context. There are in this context a number of economic factors which lie beyond the limits of the urban history specialist.

In fact this is a general problem with urban history, even of the most comprehensive kind (*e.g.*, Gillion, 1968). Urban history has not generated as analytical framework to locate the individual experience of the city in the context of the general experience of the society of which it is a part. H. Spodek (1976) and S. Saberwal (1977) have made some attempts in this direction. Spodek focuses on the role of the city in relation to regional economic development. He underlines the need to develop a comprehensive outlook incorporating the approaches of geographers and economists and planners as well as that of historians. However, his study of the Saurashtra region in 1800-1960—a region which has been urbanized for a long period—demonstrates the importance of political structures, regional economic pattern, and historical traditions in determining the role of the city in relation to its region. The methodological point he makes is well taken, but his wide-ranging survey of the various models of urban-rural integration in regional development does not quite match with his sparse empirical data on what was actually happening in Saurashtra. Unlike Spodek's, Saberwal's is more limited exercise intended to "develop a perspective for interpreting urban social phenomena in India". In doing this Saberwal's strategy seems to be, first, to proceed from a historical approach towards entry into the present sociologically, and, second, to focus on the inter-urban spread and not on particular urban centres. "I have deemed it economical to begin by looking for the process which may be expected to act over the widest range; and this analytical primacy has in this essay gone to the process of industrialization" (Saberwal, 1976, p. 16). To historians this approach may not be startlingly novel. But, through the skilful deployment of historians' data, Saberwal has substantiated one important hypothesis : "the supra-local caste group continues to be important for many urbanites; but the processes of depression and decompression have tended to pull caste groups generally out of shape. These are often cross-cut, furthermore, by other sorts of identity, other frames of reference...." From this point of departure Saberwal enters into the stratification and structural position of the modern urban groups in the industrial capitalist milieu. The concept of "decompression" is useful in analysing the enlargement of social horizons and the scattering and mingling of the "traditional social groups". (*ibid*., p. 5).

Finally, among the studies in urban history which have yielded patterns of a high order of generalizability, one must mention Milton Singer's "orthogenetic-heterogenetic" thesis. It has been suggested that one can analytically distinguish between primary urbanization (leading to fashioning of a "Great Tradition" by the professional literati of the orthogenetic centres, from elements in local folk cultures or "Little Tradition") and secondary urbanization (leading to a heterogenetic transformation of Great Tradition in colonial cities where a new intelligentsia mediated the interaction between indigenous and an alien culture). (Redford and Singer, 1956: Singer, 1959). While in the colonial city the heterogenetic transformation undoubtedly destroyed and refashioned indigenous traditions, Singer reminds us that it was a complex interaction between different civilizations which was characterized not by a sharp break but by many funda-mental continuities. An interesting application of this model to the social order and social geography of a colonial city is Patrick Roche's (1975) study of caste in Madras city, 1639-1749. Roche has "studied the possibility of the British being agents not only of change but also of the continuance of such traditional features as caste. In doing so we eschewed two stereotyped approaches—namely, the over-emphasis on change by Indian urbanists, and the presumption that Indian conservatism and traditionalism alone have been responsible for such continuity... British values and commercial interests were the motivating factors behind regulations that established and redefined caste demarcations—both spatial and social" (Roche, 1975, pp. 405-406).

The comparative study of the social geography of other British colonial cities, including some in South East Asia, also suggests a similar role of colonial administration in the preservation and demarcation of various groups. Thus the familiar Black Town and White Town. It is also remarkable how strongly did caste identities persist, *e.g.*, that of the left and right hand castes in colonial Madras which has been chronicled in detail recently (A. Appadorai, 1974). It is interesting to see that in anti-British protest movements caste *Panchayats* played a leading role in Varanasi city in the early 19th Century (R. Heitler, 1972) and caste links continue to be important in the political context in commercially more advanced Allahabad in the late 19th Century (C. Bayly, 1971).

SOCIOLOGY OF ENTREPRENEURSHIP

The sociology of entrepreneurship has attracted many scholars since the 1960s. In part this might have been due to the growing interest abroad, especially in the U.S., in entrepreneurial studies. In the 1960s the works of A.H. Cole (1959), Clifford Geerts (1963), Everett E. Hagen (1962), David C. MacClelland (1961, 1969) *et. al.* and the studies published in the second series of the journal *Exploration in Entrepreneurial History*, marked this as a major growth area in America. At the same time the interest in engineering economic development on capitalistic lines in underdeveloped countries channelled funds into the study of entrepreneurship in such countries.

The result was a series of studies in the sixties and seventies in Indian entrepreneurial history. Some of these works do not have any historical depth, *e.g.* James J. Berna (1960) on Madras industrialists or Leighton Hazleherst's (1968), on merchant caste and enterprise in Punjab. On the other hand the works of Milton Singer, Howard Spodek, Blair Kling, J. Kennedy and Tom Timberg in U.S.A. and R.S. Rungta, D. Tripathi, Raman Mahadevan, A.V. Desai, A.K. Bagchi, etc.

in India throw light on the historical aspects of entrepreneurship in India.

We need not discuss here the purely biographical works on individual entrepreneurs for they fail to raise explicitly issues of social history. This is as much true of an old biography like that of J.N. Tata by F.R. Harris (1938) as of more recent ones, *e.g.* biographies of Sir Purshottamdas Thakurdas by Frank Moraes (1957), of Sir R.N. Mookerjee by K.C. Mahindra (1962), of Shri Ram by Khushwant Singh and Arun Joshi (1968). Some of these also happened to be commissioned works—and thus subject to obvious limitations.

A more fruitful enquiry was initiated along social historical lines by D.R. Gadgil in 1951 : his work was never printed but circulated widely in its mimeographed from. About the same time Helen Lamb began to publish a series of essays on Indian business communities, beginning with a paper in *Pacific Affairs* (1955). Both Gadgil and Lamb were interested in the 18th and 19th Century background of modern Indian business communities. An important question that arises is the appropriateness of studying enterprise in the framework of "community" rather than "class". Gadgil was probably more justified in doing so since he was studying an early period when the "class-ness" was not pronounced : further, the distinctive social characteristics of each community and the inter-regional differences might have demanded the study of business communities in that framework. Nevertheless, the validity of "community" as a category begins to be dubious in the later decades of the 19th Century for purposes of supralocal generalizations. Helen Lamb seems to be aware of this (1955; 1959). Categories other than "community" are found more useful by some analysts of entrepreneurial activity : for example D.P. Pandit (1957) gives primacy to the type of activity and region of origin rather than the communal entity. However, many observers find it convenient to use communal categories—Bohra or Marawari or Armenian or Chettiar. This includes Soviet historians (*e.g.*, V.I. Pavlov, 1964). A justification offered for the preference for the category "community, rather than regional or sectorial or class categories, has been that "behaviour patterns are common to whole communities" (T. Timeberg, 1978, p. 7). Perhaps communal boundaries are relevant in entrepreneurial activity in the early stages of capitalist development but with the progressive unification of internal market and the homogenization of institutional structures in regions exposed to the world capitalist system, the communal categories became increasingly irrelevant. The formerly distinct communities merge into heterogeneous regional business elites, get differentiated in terms of mercantile interests, industrial interests, etc., and display such a wide range of behaviour patterns as to make the category "community" less and less meaningful. This is true insofar as economic behaviour is concerned; on the other hand, historians with other questions in mind—kinship or affinal connections or family structure—may find the category useful irrespective of the above changes.

A question of common concern to most entrepreneurial historians has been the role of social and cultural values in inhibiting enterprise in underdeveloped, and usually colonial or semi-colonial, countries. This role has been emphasized in William Kapp (1963) and Vikas Mishra's (1962) interpretation of Hindu culture and Indian development. Respectable lineage is claimed for this interpretation, *viz.*, Max Weber's sociology of religion; especially his analysis of the religions of India (1958 Tr.). The thesis that non-Western religious traditions were dysfunctional to capitalist progress was latest in Weber's celebrated work on the Protestant ethic and the rise of capitalism (1948 Tr.). This was elaborated with reference to the "irrational" and "other-worldly" nature of Hindu ethos and the elaboration included a special theory explaining successful enterprise by some Hindu sects in terms of the values inculcated in Jainism or the Vallabhacharya sect of Vaishnavism. Fundamentally the same approach characterizes explanation of successful entrepreneurship in India in terms of the value system of a successful community like the Parsis. This is the thesis of Robert Kennedy (1962). An obvious weakness of this approach is that it is based on a textual rather than a contextual study of a religion. The *Manu-Samhita* or the *Zendavesta* are not the best sources of information on religion as it is actually practised and believed. Moreover, simplistic correlations between religious belief-systems and economic behaviour fail to explain significant intersect and intra-sect variations within the fold of Hinduism. Finally, the subtleties of Max Weber's methodology—especially his use of the "archetype"—has not been, perhaps, appreciated by latter-day Weberians and hence certain crudities in the elaboration of his ideas.

Empirical studies of business enterprise tend to undermine the pseudo-Weberian theory. Thus, for instance, Ashok V. Desai (1968) does not suggest that the values of belief system of the Parsis hand anything to do with their business success : it is to be explained in the light of the specific economic position Parsis occupied in relation to the British in Bombay in the 19th Century (Also A. Guha, 1970). Bagchi emphasizes the regional economic variations produced by the uneven impact and tenure of British rule as the factor determining the structure of opportunities for indigenous entrepreneurs (Bagchi, in Leach and Mukherjee, 1970; 1972). Raman Mahadevan's empirical findings support his approach with reference to Tamilnadu. (R. Mahadevan, 1978; also see M. Singer, 1958 and 1972, for a somewhat different approach). D.Tripathi (1971) rejects the thesis that religious values, inculcated in Jainism for instance, are causally related to business success. He generalizes that "the behaviour of businessmen throughout the world justifies the impression that their business ethics and values do not necessarily conform to their personal ethics or religious values". The case for the pseudo-Weberian approach was already lost wen M.D. Morris wrote its obituary in 1667 in an essay on the insignificance of "values as an obstacle to economic growth".

Another debate—which has not really developed—is on the role of "traditional" institutions in "modern" enterprise. N.K. Sinha (1965) has lent his authority to the view that social factors played a crucial role in inhibiting Bengali business enterprise : the structure of the joint family, the complications of the *dayabhagwa* laws of succession, the wasteful litigation and division of business capital into small portions, the conspicuous consumption practised by the Bengali rich, the wasteful expenditure of the new rich businessmen on religious rituals to acquire prestige, etc. However, many of these social features were pre-19th Century and did it constrain entrepreneurship earlier? Blaire Kling's (1966) study of Dwarkanath

Tagore does not suggest that these are critical factors in enterprise building. R.S. Rungta (1969) has shown how a new institutional framework of corporate business was available, from the last half of the 19th Century, to bypass some of the pitfalls Sinha emphasizes. Moreover, non-Bengali business communities with a similar family structure, joint Hindu undivided family, have, far from feeling it a limitation, made it a vehicle of enterprise. Shoji Ito and Singer have observed such adaptation of the Chettiar joint family to the demand of modern business and industry (Singer, 1968). Tom Timberg (1971, 1978) has profusely documented the analogous experience of Marwari joint families running business; one of his major points is the continuity and adaptability of "traditional" arrangements to the challenge of new opportunities in the 19th and 20th Centuries. Likewise H. Spodek (1965 and 1969) has argued that traditional institutions like the guild and client relationships developed by the Ahmedabad *bania* community aided successful and modern enterprise in the colonial period. Thus we have many examples of the so-called traditional institutions, far from being a constraint on entrepreneurship, playing a positive role.

To conclude, the debate on the role of "tradition" in the development of capitalism under colonialism is continuing. The tendency today is to move away from explanations which are based on the supposed characteristics of the Hindu ethos. At the same time, it is curious to find that values of social ethos of the British in India have attracted attention as factors influencing their business activity in India. For instance, Amartya Kumar Sen (1965) argues that no economic explanation can account for the commodity pattern of British investments in 19th Century India : it was their social ethos which prevented them from investing in areas, *e.g.*, cotton textiles, where they would make a profit but would be compelled to compete with "home" industries. Again, when one looks at British society in India and the channels of association and lobbying and pressure-group activities—one realizes the importance of an ethos commonly shared by the British businessmen and administrators in securing for these pressure-groups access to and influence over crucial areas of policy of the colonial state (A.K. Bagchi, 1972 : S. Bhattacharya,

1971). In short, it will be foolish to dismiss social ethos, values etc.—they do play a role within limits defined by the economic structure—but to posit a simplistic dichotomy between "traditional" and "modern" in this context is an error. They very terms in which this debate is cast is not likely to help in the analysis of entrepreneurship and economic development.

LABOUR HISTORY

Labour history is one of the newly developing areas of social history. On the purely economic aspects a beginning has been made in the works of M.D. Morris (1965). V.B. Singh (1963), K. Mukherjee (1959, 1967), S.A. Palekar (1962), etc. but labour history in its wider connotation remains virtually unexplored. The social and cultural world of the industrial working class remains unknown till now partly because the kind of sources which are available to the historian of let us say the European working class—on account of the literature generated by the literate artisan and skilled workers and petty-bourgeois radicals—do not exist in India. Moreover, the academic historians' dependence on "official" sources, *i.e.*, those to be found in government archives, has until recently, excluded from their notice whatever data that there may exist in the private papers of labour leaders, trade union organizations, industrialists, social workers, etc.

In this area the problem which has attracted most attention till now is the recruitment and social composition of the labour force. P.S. Gupta (1974), Ranajit Dasgupta (1976), Beniprasanna Misra (1975), and Lalita Chakravorty (1978) have been concerned mainly with this problem. The latter has made a significant contribution to the development of an analytical framework to study labour migration in a "dual economy". Contrary to the premises of many labour economists writing on third world countries (*e.g.*, marginal calculations involving free choice by migrant labourers) and distinct from the Arthur Lewis type models (with income-differential between the subsistence level in agriculture and the wage rate for coolie labour at growth poles as the migration motivator in a labour surplus agrarian scene), Chakravarty develops an explanatory scheme which recognizes spatially differentiated subsistence level, resting upon the operation of "agricultural involution"—a concept derived from Clifford Geertz (1963). The merit of this scheme lies in its ability to recognize and accommodate geographical and historical specificities in the development of labour catchment areas and rhythm patterns of migration. The essential point here, the predominant role of the push factor in subsistence agriculture in determining inland and overseas migration, is, of course, a part of the perennial explanations of rural-urban migration. In capturing the historical specificities of the Indian scene and in constructing a generalizable model from out of that the author's achievement is substantial.

P.S. Gupta's (1974) study of the labour supply question led him to the hypothesis "that labour migration followed a well-observed pattern of moving in stages of relatively short-distance migration from village to small-town in the first instance, and from there to the big industrial towns in the second. Reluctance to venture into the uncertainties of construction work or plantation labour in a distant region undoubtedly limited the area of mobility. Apart from this, the migrant labourer had no inhibitions in moving in quest of better economic opportunities" (*ibid.*, 422). Among the several questions raised by Gupta is that of caste origins of migrants: he tends to agree with Morris that deindustrialization and the dislodgement of handicraftsmen from traditional occupations had nothing to do with migration of craft-castes to factory employment. His data, however, are rather thin. Ranajit Das Gupta (1976) has shown that a "especially notable aspect (of migration of labour to cities) was industrial migration in the sense of the flow of weavers, carpenters, and other such artisans which had been distressed or displaced from traditional craft industries" (*ibid.*, p. 326). R. Das Gupta provides a good deal of evidence which runs counter to another of Morris's contentions. Morris (1965) had argued, on the basis of the TISCO and Bombay textile mill data, that there was no evidence that members of economically and socially depressed groups, *e.g.* the untouchables, showed a greater tendency to migrate to industrial employment. Das Gupta on the contrary found that in eastern India these groups "not only constituted a very substantial proportion of the jute labour force but also showed a high propensity to enter the jute mills". (Das Gupta, *op. cit.*, p. 321). On these and other issues Das Gupta has successfully related the specifics of Indian labour history with the general structure of the colonial society and economy.

This task demands very careful use of scarce data. One of the examples of methodologically unsound and speculative generalization is B. Misra's (1975) research based on evidence presented before the Factory Commission of 1890. Misra treats the statements made by workers before the Commissions "as so many case studies of factory workers". While his procedure may be considered dubious in itself, what he proceeds to do with these evidences is erroneous beyond doubt. For instance, classification of these "accidental" samples by "sources of origin" leads him to the conclusion that 50 per cent were from the category he calls "lumpens, including beggars, criminal tribes and widows" (Misra, 1975, p. 216). On the other hand, only 25 per cent are from agricultural occupations, according to Misra. He goes on to remark that "the total labour force demand from the manufacturing sector bore such a small proportion to the total population that there was possibly no need to release people by revolutionizing agriculture. Moreover.... India had a large supply of "people" from other categories, *viz.*, "superstructural classes" (sic.), manufacturing, and the so-called "lumpens". The "superstructural classes", it may be explained, means in this context "priests, barbers, washermen, etc.". Equally astonishing is the author's conclusion that of the factory workers "56 per cent had no link with village and agriculture" in 1890. Although the size of the sample is so small—11 workers in Ahmedabad and 13 in Kanpur—on that basis Misra makes the following generalization : "It is also remarkable that in Ahmedabad 10 out of 11 workers, and in Kanpur 8 out of 13 had no ties with villages. Compared to Bombay or Calcutta, Ahmedabad and Kanpur were both smaller urban centres, but the proportion of workers without any link with the villages is on the high side. Thus, it appears that at this stage of development, there is no appreciable relation between the growth of urban centres and the extent of proletarianization" (*ibid.*, p. 214). (For criticism of Misra on other grounds see W. Mersch, 1977).

A lot of recent research in labour history has been in the area of recruitment and composition of the labour force. The other subject that has attracted attention is the labour movement. But the works of V.B Karnik (1966), G.K. Sharma

(1963), A.S. and J. Mathur (1961), S.C. Jha (1970), Sukomal Sen (1978), *et. al.*, do not address themselves to questions germane to social history. The social history of labour protest remains to be written. One exception is the series of papers published by Dipesh Chakrabarty. His study (1976) of crime and protest in labour consciousness and behaviour among early railwaymen in India throws light on the "instinctive responses of the first groups of men coming into the situation of industrial work, their instincts developing out of an interaction between their new work-situation, and the different alternative modes of behaviour that this traditional culture offered to them". The crime of train-wrecking is seen by Chakrabarty as a mode of reaction, of a basically pre-industrial people, which is "midway between 'crime' and 'protest' ".

Another in-depth socio-historical study of labour protest and organization is by E.D. Murphy (1977, part of Ph.D. thesis, "Labour Organization in the Cotton Mills of Tamilnadu, 1918-1939", University of W. Australia, 1976). Murphy poses the question whether and how ascriptive differences divided the Madras Textile Workers in the early stages of unionization in 1918-1921, and more broadly speaking, the degree to which social influences of caste and community inhibited class consciousness and unity. The concept of class consciousness is employed here in the restricted sense of what Lenin called trade-union consciousness, and community is so defined as to restrict its denotation to caste Hindus, Muslims and untouchables among Madras workers. The most general conclusion Murphy arrives at is that "caste and community by no means necessarily seriously inhibit the development of class consciousness in India", but "they cannot as yet be ignored". More specifically, Murphy shows that primordial of community and caste have contributed to disunity in the period under study and that during periods of economic and political tension such ascriptive differences surface. This conclusion does not conform to E.A. Ramaswamy's (1976, 1977) : he analyses the Coimbatore textile workers' perception of their Union today to conclude that traditional social loyalities, including caste links, have little influence on loyalty to the trade union. That Murphy finds such ascriptive differences important and Ramaswamy does not, may be a measure of the growth of trade union consciousness over the last half a century. More important, the complex interaction between communal loyalities and class consciousness is subject to wide regional variations (see *e.g.*, Gail Omvedt, 1973, on Bombay labour) and fluctuations over time determined by various exogenous factors. This impression is strengthened by the very perceptive study of the role of jute mill workers in communal riots in the environs of Calcutta in the 1890s by Dipesh Chakrabarty (1976). Chakrabarty traces the growth of a "community consciousness" which on occasion expressed itself through Hindu-Muslim riots, through purely Muslim grievances on other occasions, and .... (through) the expression of pan-Islamism. Factors such as the large scale immigration of upcountry workers into jute mills in this period, "carrying with them a community consciousness from their place of origin", and the presence of a group of leaders among the wealthy Muslims of Calcutta who encou-raged the workers' communal loyalities, reinforced tendencies inherent in the conditions engendered by the quality and organization of life, in jute mill areas. Chakrabarty assembles this picture with admirable craftsmanship. However, it is possible that he has been led by his sources of information to emphasize "community consciousness" among Muslim workers more than in the other community. Communal leadership and ideology in the minority community certainly assumes a more explicit and visible form : this may misled us into neglecting its less visible mirror image in the majority community, *i.e.*, into neglecting the "community consciousness" immanent in the larger society of which the Muslim workers from a part. Ranajit Das Gupta (1979) offers a more fundamental criticism from a different viewpoint : he finds the term "community consciousness" inappropriate to describe the complex aspirations, identity consciousness, and striving of the working class. For example, he differs from Chakrabarty's inter-pretation of workers' demand for Muslim festival holidays as a manifestation of communalism : "this demand mirrored a resistance at the passing away of the traditional way of life, loss of traditional forms of joy and festivities", in short,· relief from a drab existence that the Hindu workers reacted against as much as the Muslim workers. (For an extended critique of Chakrabarty, see Das Gupta, 1979; both have worked on the same area and analogous problems).

The study of "mentalities", the culture of the "common people", popular perceptions and beliefs, ideas behind collective action of the masses, etc. is yet to begin. This is why the explorations of Omvedt or Das Gupt or Chakrabarty are virtually important. The latter has also contributed to our understanding of the cultural world of the Bhadraloks and their perception of the industrial workers' existence conditions and struggle : beginning with a biographical study of Sasipada Banerjee, a philanthropist in the Victorial mould and the editor of the first Bengali journal for workers, Chakrabarty (1975) has gone deeper into the social and ideological context in which occurred this "first contact of the Bengali Bhadralok with the working class of Bengal".

Finally, let us turn to the neglected area of social existence conditions of the industrial workers in the 19th and early 20th Centuries. While the purely economic indices of workers' level of living are a little better known (cf. J. Kucznski, 1965; K. Mukherjee, 1967; S. Palekar, 1962; V.B. Singh, 1963), and likewise our knowledge of the work force and labour process and organization has now been extended by recent researches (cf. R.K. Newman, 1979; Kuiman, C.P. Simmons, 1976; R. Das Gupta, 1979)—many aspects directly germane to social history remain unexplored. For instance, we know very little yet about the working class family and the women workers, or of the rural links maintained by the urban industrial worker, as of the socio-political vocabulary and conceptual grasp of the members of the working class (*e.g.*, their idea of "exploitation" or "just wages") over processes in which they are participants. There are these and other gaps. However, the rather simplistic generalizations made by sociologists upto the sixties (cf. Oscar Ornati, 1955; C.A. Myers, 1958, 1959; B.F. Hoselitz in W.E. Moore and A.S. Feldman, 1960; R.D. Lambert, 1963) which provided bridge-heads into the unknown area of labour history initially, have now been definitely left behind by the recent researches in that area.

THE "INTELLIGENTSIA"

In the history of modern India the centrality of the role of the "English-educated" professionals or the urban "middle classes" is one of the common places of modern historiography. Sometimes this group is called the "intelligentsia" (vide

Christine Dobbin, 1972, on the counterpoint between the traditional and modern ideas, between the conservative Shetias and the reformist enthusiasts from Elphinstone College); sometimes this social group is called the "modern intellectuals" (Edward Shils, 1960, 1961); and some historians prefer the terms "Elite" (Broomfield, 1968; A. Seal, 1968) or plain "middle class" (B.B. Misra, 1961). Since these concepts have been widely used in the exposition of social and political history of colonial India, a systematic critique of these concepts and the associated stereotypes is one of our tasks.

Edward Shils is perhaps the most eminent among sociologists who have addressed themselves specifically to the problem. His work on Indian intellectuals, facing in Janus-fashion, "tradition and modernity", has been extremely influential. For instance, it is not surprising to find a distinguished Indian sociologist's essay on "the new elite" consisting exclusively of citations of Shils' work (I.P. Desai, 1965). Shils considers the role of the "modern intellectual", before the new States (of Asia and Africa) acquired sovereignty and since then, highly important in "civil politics" (Shils, 1960). He poses the question, "what is an intellectual ?" in under-developed countries. He excludes the "traditional intellectuals, largely religious in their political concerns" while not denying their influence in political life. The intellectuals are "all persons with an advanced Western education and the intellectual concerns and skills ordinarily associated with it" (*ibid.*, p. 198). Thus, only the products of the British Indian education system are recognized as modern intellectuals, for they alone have undergone "a partial transformation of the self and a changed relationship to the authority of the dead and the living". Obviously the stress is on the culture of this group which is described as a "class". The boundary is defined in terms of self-perception by its members and of perception by others. Shils' definition is defended by him with reference to the fact that modern education is the "means of identification employed in the new states by the intellectuals themselves and by others". Shils also feels the need to justify the fact that he makes no distinctions between "intellectuals" and the general body of the educated : "the present definition of intellectuals is a less selective or discriminating one than we would use to designate the intellectuals in the more advanced countries. This is in no way condescension towards the new states. It is only an acknowledgment of the smaller degree of internal differentiation which has until now prevailed within the educated class in the new states, and the greater disjunction which marks that class off from the other sections of the society".

It is perhaps not unfair to translate the first part of this statement as follows : in under-developed countries, among the educated there are too few intellectuals, in comparison to those of advanced countries, to make a distinction worth-while. The second part of the sentence is difficult to interpret for it is difficult to see how the "disjunction" of a subset from a set would hinder recognition of divisions within the subset.

To give him his due, Shils is basically concerned not so much with the social context as with the "moral structure" of political movements and the "modern intellectual's personality". He is mainly concerned with what he calls "a special calling from within" which explains the commitment of the intellectuals to politics. The other part of his projected explanation, "positive impetus from without", gets very little attention. Thus, the general approach is subjectivist. When he occasionally turns to objective factors, his observations are rather unsatisfying: *e.g.*, "in most underdeveloped countries during the colonial period, the unemployed intellectual was always a worry to the foreign ruler and to constitutional politicians, and a grievance to the leaders of the independence movement" (*ibid.*, p. 204). We shall later see how this figure of the "educated malcontent" appears over and over again in the writings of modern elite theorists like Seal (1968), Broomfield (1968) or B.B. Misra (1961). In Shils' explanatory framework, however, such objective factors have less weight than the moral and attitudinal factors. In this sense, Shils operates on a more sophisticated and rarefied level, but the link with elite theorists is not to be missed.

In the 1950s and the 1960s, the United States produced a large crop of literature based on elite-role analysis in the new Afro-Asian states. This was, perhaps in part, in response to the necessity of the United States to get acquainted with the background of the current leadership of the newly independent countries with whom the United States would have to deal in the international arenas, political and economic. Such an effort was necessary more for the U.S.A. than for the European powers with a more "glorious" imperialistic past. Furthermore, more than the latter, it was the U.S. which would be involved in shoring up the dominance of such elites in some of these countries, sometimes with success, sometimes without. In part, this crop of literature was the product of organized research efforts to apply, at a cross-national comparative level, grand theories in political science and the sociology of politics fashioned in the 'fifties and sixties' by top academicians (the name of David Apter, Robert Dahl, A. Kaplan, H.D. Lasswell and Arnold Rose readily come to mind).

Under such influence, a special variant of the pluralist theory, applicable to "underdeveloped countries", was developed. The elaboration and the extrapolation of this approach to the study of the modern history of colonial countries began in the 'sixties'. Among political scientists, those who made empirically oriented micro-studies often drifted away from grand theories. The author of a very significant work of this type, David B. Rosenthal (1970), noted the "failure of comparative politics to come fully to grips with cross-polity studies at a subsystem level" (p. 2). Others who worked on a grander scale, covering the national political arena—Myron Weiner is a case in point—developed a paradigm of "elite plurality" and inter-elite or intra-elite conflicts as an explanatory framework for the politics of the new states.

The work of J.H. Broomfield, *Elite Conflict in a Plural Society* (1968), deserves special attention because it is one of the few historical works which elaborately defines and systematically applies the "elite" concept. He begins with the equation of the term *elite* with a local term of indigenous origin and known only in Bengal : "Bengali rural and urban society differed in many fundamental respects, yet they shared at least one feature : a common, dominant elite .... who claimed and were accorded recognition as superior in social status to the mass of their fellows. These were the *bhadralok*, literally, the "respectable men", the "gentle men" (1968, p. 5). Broomfield uses this term "as an analytical category" (*ibid*., p. 13) and defines it as "a socially privileged and consciously superior group, economically dependent upon landed rents and professional and clerical employment; keeping its distance from the masses by its acceptance of high-caste prescriptions and its command over education, sharing a pride in its language, its literate culture and its history; and maintaining its communal integration through a fairly complex institutional structure that it had proved remarkably ready to adapt and augment to extend its social powers and political opportunities" (*ibid.*, pp. 12-13).

Since the term *bhadralok* is peculiar, to the Bengal region, Broomfield has to abandon this category and resort to other concepts whenever he makes cross-regional comparative statements or cross-national generalizations: *e.g.*, "In Bengal, as in most other parts of 20th Century Asia and Africa, there was a great problem of communication between the small westernized intelligentsia, eager to build a nation free from European imperialism, and the rural populace, traditionalist and illiterate" (p. 33). The *bhadralok* is, in this view, a species within the genus "intelligentsia". But Broomfield rejects an occupational definition, which is the usual way of defining the intelligentsia as a social group : "The use of the word underlines the cardinal fact that this was a status group (in Max Weber's sense of the term) not an economic or occupational class" (pp. 13-14). Yet Broomfield uses occupation as one of the differentia in defining the group and, what is more important, posits occupation as the *only* factor in the process of differentiation within this group. A weakness in this conceptual framework is that, while the characterization of the *bhadralok* emphasizes the *status* aspect, when it comes to processes or changes over time, Broomfield depends on the *economic* aspects for an explanation. Thus, the changes in the fortunes of the *bhadralok* group, the growth of a class within it, which he calls "lower class *bhadralok*" (a "class" which is included in a category that is not a class), is entirely in terms of occupational distribution. It is as if he felt the explanatory inadequacy of a treatment in terms of status categories and is compelled to resort to economic categories.

The term used by Broomfield, *bhadralok,* is indigenous and that is almost its only merit. It is of late 19th Century origin—not to be found in early dictionaries of the Bengali language. It is, in part, the "gentleman" reincarnated in the tropics and thus, a neologism was called for. It is useful in comprehending the sociology of culture of colonial Bengal. But to make it an "analytical category", applicable to the political economy of Bengal, is to mistake an epiphenomenon for the real thing. The fact that Broomfield has to invent a term, "lower-class *bhadralok*", for which there is no corresponding indigenous term, shows the inadequacy of his initial analytical category. The "lower-class *bhadralok*" share, with their superiors, all the status traits : high caste, access to education, abstention from manual labour, etc. Where they differ from their superiors is in occupation/income. In fact, it might be argued that the other "status" traits are merely dependent variables, with the exception of caste. And, as regards caste, Broomfield shows that low caste was no barrier to entry into the *bhadralok* world, provided the criterion of appropriate occupation (and its pre-condition, appropriate education) was satisfied (*ibid.*, p. 9). It is, of course, quite true that the *bhadralok* do not constitute a class, but that does not mean that we cannot locate them in a class framework.

Anil Seal (1968) also shares a preference for a non-class conceptual scheme with Broomfield.

> The political arithmetic of India during the 1970s or 1980s, when the (nationalist) movement was taking shape, shows that it was not formed through the promptings of any class's demands or through the consequence of any sharp change in the structure of the economy. India had been developed little and efforts at development have brought about a new unevenness in the social and economic structure of the country. There were internal rivalries, but these were between caste and caste, community and community, not between class and class. Moreover, these groups, which felt a similarity of interest, were themselves more the product of bureaucratic initiative than of economic change. Since these groups can be largely identified with the men whose hopes and fears went into the building of the new associations that emerged as the Indian National Congress, a conceptual system based on elites, rather than on classes, would seem more promising (1968, p. 34).

We shall ignore for the present many other interesting aspects of Seal's approach (it has marginally changed in subsequent works), and concentrate on this concept of the elite presented in his first and most influential work. The elite is identified with "Indians educated in the western mode" (p. xiii). Given the period Seal is interested in, it is understandable that he is concerned almost exclusively with this group. But the economics bases—the colonization of the economy and factors in the creations of such a stratum—are dismissed as a whole, since no "sharp changes in the structure of the economy" are discernible in the 1870s and 1880s. A lot depends on what one means by "sharp changes". Granting that exactly in these twenty years no dramatic change took place, the question remains whether this is a sufficient time span for any serious attempt to relate structural changes and class formation with the rise of nationalism. In place of such an effort, crude Economism is applied to explain the behaviours of this category of people, "western educated". "In large part the answer to the question why modern Indians politics began when they did, depends on defining the period when the (British) regime was no longer able to satisfy enough of these competing aspirations" (p. 344-345). The educated malcontents, the job-hungry *babus*, dominate this scenario.

One feature of this scenario is too obvious to be missed: it is that ideology is assigned a marginal role in the explication of nationalist politics. Does this retrospective deideologization of nationalism offer an adequate explanation of what made men in leading positions, of "elite status" if you prefer, jeopardies their individual fortunes in a struggle against heavy odds ? If the answer is "interest" then the question arises, whose interest ? The individual's or that of the "group", the caste or community or whatever ? Is there a congruence between the interests of the individual, say a leader of the "group" and those of the group he leads ? Is the interest of any such group just the aggregation of the individuals comprising the group ? If the answer is "no", then Seal's use of the category group-interest is unwarranted; if the answer is "yes" why deny the aggregation of interests in the form of national interest ? And finally, "interest" in what sense, subjectively perceived, or objective interest ? How is subjective agreement or what common interests are brought about except through ideology ? Is it possible to identify the short-term goals of individuals or groups with their objective interest in the long run ? These questions are not faced squarely in Seal's work. The explanatory adequacy of this conceptual scheme is judged here in terms of the implicit theory of (a) motivation; (b) aggregation of interests; (c) perceived and objective interests. In these respects the poverty of the theoretical framework is perhaps due to an unconscious acceptance of premises of a dominant trend of thinking in the 1960s, the theory of pluralism. Pluralist theories might have had some limited validity in the micro-level studies, especially urban politics, in the U.S.A., but extrapolated on the Indian scene it fails to contain in its framework the Indian nationalist, altogether a different kind of political animal in a different kind of habitat.

While one can argue about the success or failure of the above three variants of a conceptual-theoretical framework, the problem is the absence of such a framework in the other major work concerning the Indian intelligentsia. B.B. Mishra's *Indian Middle Class* (1961). He shows like many Indian academics a tendency to look upon the intelligentsia just as a sub-set of the category "middle-class". Perhaps this is in part the result of the revival of interest in Britain and U.S.A., since the 1950s, in the "middle class". The works of G.D.H. Cole (1955), Roy Lewis and Augus Maude (1950) and David Riesman (1950) are representative of a trend which had an impact on India; Misra specifically mentions Lewis and Maude's work as a formative influence.

"From the circumstances of their growth the members of the educated profession, such as government servants and lawyers, college teachers and doctors constitute the bulk of the Indian middle class" (*ibid.*, p. 12). They also dominated the Indian National Congress and entered Legislative Council as Congressmen (p. 352) and the reason was their thwarted aspirations of entry into the bureaucracy (p. 357). In a section on the "unemployed malcontents" (p. 371 *et. seq.*) this thesis is elaborated—an earlier and less sophisticated version of the theory of Seal and Broomfield in this respect. One feature of this work is the recognition of the new relationship between "the literary and the business class"; "the middle classes in general advocated indigenous capitalist development....It tended to effect a radical change in the traditional relationship of the literary and business classes. The intellectual and the plutocrat, who had in the past pulled in opposite directions were under the British drawn closer together...." (pp. 356-357). The explanation offered is startlingly simple : the business classes were denied tariff protection and the "educated middle classes" denied jobs, hence their alliance.

Misra, Seal and Broomfield are historians and one might expect greater theoretical richness in the sociologists' approach to the question. In the sociological studies of intelligentsia the stress has been mainly on structure and recruitment of the so-called bureaucratic and professional elites (H. Tinker, 1966), the occupational structure and "ethos" of the educated professionals, a la Shills (cf. T.B. Bottomore, 1965), and the role of the political elite in contemporary India (R.S. Khare, 1970, and D.B. Rosenthal, 1970). The model usually consists of a plurality of elites, jostling each other for furtherance of their particular interests, and the boundary of each of these elites—bureaucratic, professional, intellectual, etc.—is defined in terms of occupation. Insofar as there is any attempt to define relationships with the rest of society, it is in terms of simple elite-mass dichotomy. There has been no attempt to locate these numerous and ubiquitous elites in the over-all class framework, nor is there the historical depth required to investigate the continuity and change in the elite role of the intelligentsia in political and civil society from colonial times onwards.

To sum up, there is a family resemblance between the conceptual frameworks of both historical and sociological studies of the role of the intelligentsia in colonial or excolonial societies for they are derived from, not so much Pareto or Mosca, but the dominant trend of thinking in American Social Sciences in the sixties and seventies which is based on a "discretist" theory of groups and plurality of elites, a theory that obscures the relationship between such groups and social classes. As a Marxist political scientist has pointed out recently, this approach is vitiated by a "narrow subjectivist interpretation of interests"; and this approach is accompanied by "a crypto-functionalist theory of conflict which is unable to produce explanations of most long range social changes, and hence leads its adherents to piecemealism" (Frank Cunningham,

1976). We have referred to studies in South Asia but a similar theoretical framework is apparently employed in the study of many other colonial or ex-colonial countries ranging from Malaya (William R. Roff, 1967, a study of "three new elite groups", since mid-nineteenth Century, the Arabic-educated, the Malay-educated, and the English-educated !) to tropical Africa (Tom Kersteins, 1966, "A Comparative Study of India and Ghana" P.C. Lloyd, 1966, H.H. Smythe and M.M. Smythe, 1960).

METHODOLOGY AND THE CONCEPT OF SOCIAL HISTORY

Some problems of methodology have been posed earlier with reference to substantive research issues. Only a few more observations are called for. From the point of view of methodology progress in social historiography has been rather slow. This impression is unavoidable if one compares, for instance, Pramatha Nath Bose's work published in 1894, *A History of Hindu Civilization during British Rule*, with a recent work conceived on a similar scale, Kali Kinkar Datta's A *Social History of Modern India* (1975). At the same time one must concede that in detailed micro-level studies, often in the form of doctoral thesis, historians have excelled, as is evident in the pages of *Indian Economic and Social History Review* or *Contributions to Indian Sociology* and other journals. While we have not undertaken a survey of agrarian history in this essay, since it has been covered in two trends reports for the ICSSR by Professors P.C. Joshi and Dharma Kumar, one notices significant advance in that area. Agrarian studies have a longer tradition. Consider for instance the value of studies over a long span of time of a single village, *e.g.*, the study of the village Lonikand in Maharashtra in 1819 by Coats (1823) and by Ghurye (1960) in 1954; or the survey of a single Gujarat taluka, Matar by J.C. Kumarappa (1931) followed up by a similar study twenty-five years later (V. Shah & S.H. Shah, 1974); or the study of a Bengal village, Kanchanpur, at three points of time, 1872, 1933 and 1958 (Tarakrishna Basu, 1962). Comparison of these studies, separated by a century or more in some instances, help us appraise not only change in the object of study but also the methodological advance. One forms a similar impression if one compares the early literature on agrarian disturbances with the rapidly growing mass of writings on protest movements (vide bibliography by Amit K. Gupta, 1979).

However, to go beyond the micro-level studies, to get an integrated view of social processes in the subcontinent over a long time span, the historian needs a conceptual framework which can accommodate larger social aggregates than the micro-studies are accustomed to handle. Cahnman and Boskoff (1964, p. 565) have suggested that the generalizability of the historians' findings depend on the implicit or explicit use of concepts developed by the sociologist : "Data with a time perspective (either in the contemporary or distant past) are inherently attractive and necessary for sociologists. In the same way, the recurrent search for means of establishing continuity in data and clearly ascertainable variations or changes in specific institutions appears to result in the implicit or explicit use of sociological concepts and generalizations by historians." Leaving aside the question whether these latter constructs are "sociological" in the sense of being the sociologists' creation, the fact is that historians use these constructs usually in an implicit rather than in an explicit way. Often this leads to a fuzziness in the definition and application of constructs so imported without being declared; on the conceptual structure, as Butterfield has put it quite neatly, the historian usually devotes only the kind of thinking that is done in asides. We have cited an example earlier on in this essay : the use of the anthropologists' model of patron-clients relationship in certain historians' study of political leadership in the Indian national movement.

In economic history two important developments in recent times are the growth of quantitative history and, second, the diversification of sources beyond the limits of conventional archival sources. In the writing of Indian social history quantitative methods have not yet been used on a wide scale. Except in demographic history, statistical sources are, if used on any scale at all, merely reproduced without any analysis of the crude data. Thus one may have statistics of the incidence of infanticide, estimate of educated manpower and the like reproduced from standard sources. While it would be a mistake to make a fetish of the quantitative methods in the manner of the school of "new" economic history, the obvious advantages of quantification in its appropriate context need to be propagated and appreciated in social historiography.

One of the encouraging developments in recent years has been the diversification of sources. The concentration of interest in social policy, education policy, social reform movements, etc. till the 1960s meant a heavy dependence on government archives and printed material such as newspapers, pamphlets and journals. The Indian Historical Records Commission, a government agency, was also concerned exclusively with the governmental archives till the '70s. In the last decade or so the historians' range of sources has suddenly expanded. This is partly because the archives and some non-government agencies began to receive collections of private papers of Indians in positions of leadership in politics, social work, trade unions, journalism, etc. The use of governmental archives in conjunction with such private papers has made of possible to look at history in the round. However, these private papers tell us mainly about the top of the elite—the people who would make it to the "Who's Who" so to speak. For history nearer the ground we have to turn to other sources.

For example, reconstruction of family histories has been attempted by Ronald Inden and Maureen L. Patterson (1968) on the basis of *kula vrittantas*. The history of prominent Chitpavan Brahman families of Maharashtra from early 18th Century has been traced to analyse the changing pattern of occupation (Patterson, 1970). Records kept by priests in centres of pilgrimages have been skillfully deployed by the art historian B.N. Goswamy (1966). Papers of caste associations have been extensively used, but much of this material remains unexplored. V.D. Divekar has pointed out that there were about 200 caste journals published by seventy castes and sub-castes in the Marathi language alone between 1860 and 1950 (Divekar, 1978). Timberg (1977), S. Chandrashekhar (1980) and Raman Mahadevan (1978) have effectively used caste histories together with genealogies and business papers in their studies of Marwari and Nattukottai Chettiar entrepreneurship. Among others, A.M. Shah (1963) and Tom G. Kessinger (1970) have used village records and oral traditions in Gujarat and the Punjab. Village records of various sorts have been, of course, a standard source for a long time : it was part of the routine of the land revenue settlement operations to consult these records (particularly in areas under temporary settlement). Their utility was brought home to the sociologists rather recently : M.N. Srinivas records how in the fifties his interest in rural caste disputes led him to explore old documents in the possession of caste and village headmen and since then some of his pupils have utilized such records extensively (Srinivas, 1959; A.M. Shah, 1964).

A major constraint on the use of sources other than records in the English language—usually belonging to the middle and upper ranges of administration and available in the central (union) and provincial archives (state level)—has been the inability of many researchers to handle sources in local languages. With a solitary exception, Indian universities do not require language courses as a part of research training. The consequence has been that either local language material remain unutilized or research is limited to the linguistic region to which the researcher belongs (to the detriment of a larger and comparative perspective).

The innovative use of the sources of the kind mentioned above marks a break from the older historiographic tradition. This is not just a result of new sources being available. More fundamentally the impulse comes from changes in the conception of social history. Let us turn to that question.

Social history seems to be in need of a definition, unlike, let us say, political or economic history. Social historians are plagued with this problem more than others partly because the discipline has arrived late on the scene and there is, indeed, a view shared by a good number of historians that it is not an independent discipline or field of study. Even those social scientists who operationally concede its existence as a field of study, tend far too often to treat it as residual category. That is to say, it assumed that what is left over after political and economic historians have staked their claims is the preserve of the social historian. This was at one time a feature of the British historiographic tradition which has had an overwhelming influence on Indian historical studies. Thus, G.M. Trevelyan offered a definition which may now be considered obsolete but was widely accepted for a generation: Social history is the "history of a people with the politics left out" (Trevelyan, 1944, p. vii). Till the 1950s the majority of Indian historians, interested primarily in "political history", would consider their job well-done if they appended to their monograph a penultimate chapter on "social conditions" which would cover diverse topics such as manners, customs, food and drinks, costume, caste order, education system, position of women, daily life etc. While these and other subjects subsumed under "Social History" were not trivial in themselves, it is their discretist treatment in isolation which trivialized them. Even this concession to "history with politics left out" was commoner in works of ancient and mediaeval history than in works on the modern or British period. (We have used here this conventional tripartite division, despite the obvious inadequacies of such periodization, in the interest of certain intellectual economies in the adoption of a convention widely in use and implicitly accepted in the design of the ICSSR trend report plans on history).

In contrast, economic history, especially of the modern period, developed much earlier. Hobsbawm has pointed out that "social history" began its career in Europe in combination with economic history and "the economic half was overwhelmingly preponderant. There were hardly any social histories of equivalent calibre to set beside the numerous volumes devoted to economic history", till the 1950s (Hobsbawm, 1971). This is also true of India, though for reasons altogether different. It was not so much, in our opinion, autonomous developments within the disciplines concerned, nor the earlier acceptance of history, economics and economic history (as "Indian economics") as subjects taught in Indian universities—though these factors did play a role. The early birth of economic history as an intellectual concern was due to the fact that the historical context of Indian economic problems, *viz.*, the colonial pattern contrasting the advanced capitalist metropolis, could not be ignored. M.G. Ranade is the best exemplar of this. "The political domination of one country by another attracts far more attention than the more formidable, though unfelt domination which the capital, enterprise, and skill of one country exercise over the trade and manufactures of another." (Ranade, 1893 : 1916, p. 92) Ranade suggested that along with this domination, there is an intellectual domination, that of the ideas of "political economy" evolved in England which pretended to offer "one set of general principles (which) hold good every where for all times and places" (Ranade, 1892 : 1916, p. 4). Ranade, therefore, looked towards another intellectual tradition, that of the Historical Economists, especially those of Germany. He refers to Auguste Comte ("the first who denied the name of science to the doctrines taught by the deductive school" and to elaborate "the historical method of research"); Ranade also cited the contemporary German economists like "Raw, Knies, Roscher, Hildebrand, Wanger and others" who elaborated "the historical view" (*ibid.*, p. 20). "The method to be followed is not the deductive but the historical method, which takes account of the past in its forecast of the future; and relativity, and not absoluteness, characterizes the conclusions of economical science" (*op. cit.*, p. 21). In general, economic nationalism nurtured an interest in the questions of growth and backwardness in the context of colonial-metropolitan relations, which raised basically historical questions contrary to the inclinations of the neo-classic school (cf. Bipan Chandra, 1966; B.N. Ganguli, 1974). This continued to be a trend in Indian economic thinking, even if the digits of discourse were different, after the growth of a body of professional economists in the first half of the 20th Century. On the other hand, professional sociologists arrived late on the intellectual scene. In the nationalist phase of Indian intellectual development their presence was not conspicuous. Further, social anthropology as it was first introduced in India was in a sense a part of the ideological apparatus that was linked with a colonization process. J.P.S. Uberoi in his mani-festo for Swaraj in science cites a very preceptive comment of Levi-Strauss that anthropology has been the outcome of a historical process that made the large part of the mankind subservient : "Anthropology is daughter to this era of violence". (Levi-Strauss, 1966, cited in Uberoi, 1968). Uberoi also points to a colonialism in the realm of ideas and cites Nirmal Kumar Bose : "The position of Indian anthropology has, on the whole, been colonial in relation to schools which have dominated the European and American scene from time to time" (Bose, 1963, cited in Uberoi, 1968). A.K. Saran and Ramkrishna Mukherjee have also underscored this dependency as a feature of sociology in India. (Saran, 1958; Mukherjee, 1977; Mukherjee, *op. cit.*, p. 42, finds that only the first generation of Indian sociologists "did not indulge in repetition of the so-called western theoretical formulations" and, as we have seen above, their work did show a sense of the historical in contrast to the sociology since the 'fifties). All sociologists may not agree with these views. But then very little of what elicits universal agreement is worth recording. It is sufficient to note that the economic history of modern India had developed well before, "social history" appeared on the scene as a discipline.

In Europe, Hobsbawm points out, the study of "socio-economic" history, the dominant partner being the economic historian, had not "produced a specialized academic field of social history until the 1950s, though at one time the famous *Annales* of Lucien Febvre and Marc Bloch dropped the economic half of its subtitle and proclaimed itself purely social. However, this was a temporary diversion of the war years, and the title by which this great journal has now been known, *Annales : economies, societies, civilizations*—as well as the nature of its contents, reflect the original and essentially global and comprehensive aims of its founders" (Hobsabawm, 1971). Concurrently with the increasing acceptance of social history as a field of study, there occurred a broadening of the conception of social history (cf. Lewis Namier, 1952; J.H. Hexter, 1955, R. Williams, 1958, H. Perkins, 1962). Its best practitioners "felt uncomfortable with the term (social history) itself. They have either...., preferred to describe themselves simply as historians and their aim as 'total' or 'global' history, as men who sought to integrate all relevant social sciences in history rather than to exemplify any one of them" (Hobsbawm, 1971). One recalls Lucien Febvre's oft-quoted statement that there is no such thing as economic or social history—there is just history.

Though this broader conception of social history as the history of society did not have an impact on Indian studies, there began the 1950s a steady flow of works on some aspects of modern Indian social history. As we shall see later, the areas of interest initially were : social policies of the government, education and cultural history, ideas and movements in "social reform", growth of the so-called "middle class" local rural history, social origins of entrepreneurship, etc. Admittedly in the post-independence years national intellectual energies were concentrated in the areas of technology, science and economics. At the root of it was the concern with techno-economic development but this itself raised certain questions regarding economic development and "modernization"—the social and institutional framework, the value system, the origins of entrepreneurship, continuities and changes in village India, etc. Often, despite their conceptual anchorage in a contrary tradition (*e.g.*, structural-functionalism), social scientists were compelled to turn to certain historical dimensions. The detailed village studies, for example, compelled researchers to go into the past. Perhaps, as E. Le Roy Ladurie has put it, the compelling reason may be the "stratigraphic character" of rural society : 'the specific contribution it receives from every century, or group of centuries, is not wiped out but merely overlaid.... One has, therefore, even before it becomes possible to understand their structural arrangements, to read the sum of these contributions as if they were laid bare by a geological section...." (Ladurie, 1979, p. 80). The historical perspective could not be ignored even by those working as field anthropologists (Srinivas, 1962, pp. 136-147; Cohn, 1960 and 1961; and Srinivas and Shah, 1960). Similarly, in all social sciences some historical questions regarding the long-term dynamics of economic and social change were bound to be raised. It is true that "the social historians" were not fully equipped to respond to the challenge the new problems posed. It is also possible to argue that the entire problematic of "modernization" was misconceived and, as Gunder Frank has put it, the new sociology of underdevelopment exposed the "underdevelopment of sociology" (Frank, 1969, p. 21). Nevertheless, the 'sixties and the 'seventies saw the opening up of new research areas, problematics, and methods as a result of the re-thinking process forced upon all social scientists. Social history could not be trivialized into a study of "manners and customs", its concerns could no longer be divorced from the larger problematic of history.

The task of redefining social history is not for us to take up here. It is being defined continually by its practitioners. The agenda for the student of society in history has been boldly outlined by Lucien Goldman : "Every social fact is a historical fact and *vice versa*. It follows that history and sociology study the same phenomena and that each of them grasps some real aspect of these phenomena; but the image which each discipline gives of them will necessarily be partial and abstract insofar as it is not completed and qualified by the findings of the other... sociology cannot be concrete unless it is historical, just as history, if it wishes to go beyond the mere recording of fact must necessarily become explicative, that is to say, more or less sociological". Goldman, 1969, p. 23 : this is one of the best critiques of the tradition of a historical sociology). If social history must live up to such claims it becomes not a specialization but an approach to the totality of history. It may study the system of relationship between the parts and the whole of society in all human activities including economic, cultural and political (cf. Jacques Le Goff, 1971). However, in practice the study of such relationships in their social aspects usually takes as datum what is explicandum for the political or economic historians. It is only by the definition of what is "given" and what is to be explained, that the social historian may continue to demarcate his concern from that of neighbouring disciplines.

—S. BHATTACHARYA

CHAPTER - XV

NEW SOCIAL PATTERNS: VOLUNTARY COMMUNITY ACTION

Independent India has as its objectives not only the creation of a political democracy, based on a synthesis of Indian and English ideas and practices, and of a mixed socialist economy. It is also determined to create at the same time a "good society," not by government fiat and coercion, but through voluntary community action. This third objective, like the first two, is an integral part of the 1950 constitution, which spells it out in detail in what might be called a bill of Social Rights.

The character and scope of the social revolution which was to be carried out after independence had been clearly stated by Gandhi. In the Mahatma's opinion, political independence (*swaraj*, or self-rule) was part and parcel of the struggle for social and economic equality. "The two things," he said, "social re-ordering and the fight for political swaraj, must go hand in hand; there can be no question of precedence." Swaraj was not to be merely the substitution of an Indian government for a British administration, but "the poor man's swaraj," with full economic freedom for the "starving toiling millions."

"Economic equality," Gandhi said, "is the master key to non-violent independence... A non-violent system of government is clearly an impossibility so long as the wide gulf between the rich and the hungry millions persists. The contrast between the places of New Delhi and the miserable hovels of the power laboring classes cannot last one day in a free India in which the poor will enjoy the same [political] power as the richest in the land. A violent and bloody revolution is a certainty one day unless there is a voluntary abdication of riches and the power that riches give and sharing them for the common good."

Gandhi urged the city people to go to the villages and there come in "living touch" with the poor by "working for them in their midst, sharing their sorrows, understanding their difficulties, anticipating their wants." He contended that "whether the British remain or not, it is our duty always to wipe out unemployment, to bridge the gulf between rich and poor, to banish communal strife, to exercise the demon of untouchability... If crores [millions] of people do not take a living interest in this nation-building work, freedom must remain a dream and unattainable either by violence or non-violence." He enjoined the ancient Hindu principle of trusteeship on the big landlords, the princes, and other rich people, reminding them that wealth is held in trust to share with and serve the interests of the poor.

At the same time, in contrast to the Marxists, who argue that the end justifies the means, Gandhi declared that the new social order he envisaged should be achieved by non-violent means. For Gandhi "means are everything; as the means, so the end." Force to accomplish a purpose, no matter how worthy it might be, was repugnant to him. "The spirit of democracy cannot be imposed. It has to come from within."

"A new social order cannot be forced; that would be a remedy worse that the disease. I am an impatient reformer. I am all for thorough-going, radical social re-ordering, but it must be an organic growth, not a violent superimposition... What is needed is not extinction of landlords and capitalists but a transformation of the existing relationship between them and the masses into something healthier and purer... In India a class war is not only not inevitable but it is avoidable if we have understood the message of non-violence...

"Let us not be obsessed with catchwords and seductive slogans imported from the West. Have we not our own distinct Eastern tradition ? Are we not capable of finding our own solution to the question of capital and labor... ? It is surely wrong to presume that Western socialism or communism is the last word on the question of mass poverty."

The pattern of an egalitarian society where justice is assured to all—a "socialist pattern of society"—includes, according to the Indian constitution, a wide range of rights of a kind not explicitly stated in the American constitution, but found in two such diverse documents as the 1936 constitution of the U.S.S.R. and the 1946 constitution of the Fourth Republic in France. The Indian constitution, in the section on fundamental rights, provides for equality before the law and for equality of opportunity in public employment. It prohibits discrimination on grounds of religion, race, caste, sex, or place of birth, and abolishes untouchability, forbidding its practice in any form—thus striking a double blow at the caste system.

In Part IV of the constitution, on directive principles for the policies of the state, it is provided (Article 38) that "the State shall strive to promote the welfare of the people by securing and protecting as effectively as it may a social order in which justice, social, economic and political, shall inform all the institutions of the national life." Equal pay for equal work is to be assured for both men and women (Article 39). The state is to "make effective provision for securing the right to work, to education, old age, sickness and disablement, etc.," foreshadowing some form of social security. The state is also to "make provision for securing just and humane conditions of work and for maternity relief" (Article 42), fore-shadowing labor legislation. The State "shall endeavor to provide, within a period of ten years from the commencement of this Constitution, for free and compulsory education for all children until they complete the age of fourteen years" (Article 45). And Article 47 emphasizes that it is the duty of the state to raise the level of nutrition and the standard of living and to improve public health.

This article also provides for the introduction of prohibition, which was close to the heart of Gandhi who believed that excessive drinking was demoralizing, particularly for the poor, who would be tempted to fritter away their meager earnings on drink. So far, complete prohibition has been introduced in a few states—Andhra, Bombay, and Madras, with a progressive system of prohibition in New Delhi which is slowly strangling the social life of the capital. Other states, although paying lip service to Gandhi's principles, have hitherto preferred to maintain a business which brings substantial revenue, but agitation for the extension of prohibition is growing. Moreover, it has been found that, where prohibition is in force, the rich circumvent it, as Americans did under similar circumstances, by obtaining liquor for "medicinal" purposes, or through smugglers, while the poor continue to suffer from inebriation by manufacturing their own potations, the best-known of which is toddy, made out of fermented coconut juice.

It would be easy to say, as come critics do, that the constitution's Bill of Social Rights is but a list of pious hopes, which the government can hardly expect to fulfill in the lifetime of this, or even a subsequent, generation. Leaving aside the only partial, and mostly ineffectual, realization of Gandhi's ideal about prohibition, it is admitted that the harsh realities of an underdeveloped country make it extremely difficult to implement the admirable social principles enunciated in the constitution. The official abolition of untouchability has not yet closed the economic and social gap between the four castes on the one hand, and between the castes and the out-castes on the other, nor has the prohibition of discrimination on grounds of religion, race, caste, sex, or place of birth, brought about equality. Provisions about equality of opportunity in matters of public employment and equal pay for equal work for men and women are challenged every day in a country where a population which increases by five million a year is faced with underemployment, as well as unemployment, and two million new workers come into the labor market annually, with little hope of obtaining stable work.

In a country where capital resources for minimal economic development are in short supply, provisions about free and compulsory education for all children until the age of fourteen, and for protection against old age, sickness, and disablement, are blocked by lack of funds. And recurring shortages of basic goods, while food consumers continue to multiply, make the task of raising the level of nutrition and the improvement of public health and Herculean undertaking.

For India is trying to do something that has never before been attempted in history. It is trying to provide, on however modest a scale, measures of social welfare regarded as essential by Western nations in the twentieth century, but within the framework of an economy which, except for a few industries, is approximately at the level at which the West was in the fifteenth century—and to do this without resort to force and violence.

Critics might say that, given this vast gap between ideals and realities, the Indian government would be well-advised not to arouse the hope, which may prove illusory, that improvement can be expected by people now living, for fear that when the illusion becomes apparent, the masses may rise up in revolt and seek alleviation of their ills in some form of political extremism—whether reactionary communalism or communism. But, the leaders of India are confronted with two ineluctable facts. First, the people, exposed to information about the economic and social improvement that have taken place not only in the West, but also in Russia, will not be put off by pleas that nothing can be accomplished for them at this stage of the country's development. And, second, Gandhi and Nehru and their associates could not have failed to try to implement their promises, without betraying the very cause for which they had fought during the struggle for independence. True, available facts and figures inevitably raise the question whether the government has not "oversold" social advancement in a backward country. But, there is one element in the picture which, while it can neither be weighed nor measured scientifically, may prove to be the unpredictable yet decisive factor in the forging of a new society in India.

This element, which in tables of statistics appears only in terms of depressingly rising population figures, or discouraging numbers of more mouths to feed, more children to be educated, more men and women to be given some sort of work, is the Indian people itself. As is so often the case in countries with vast population figures, the numerically staggering millions, seen in impoverished villages and crowded city slums, appeared to the British, and still appear to Western visitors and to their own fellow-citizens who dwell comfortably in cities, as "masses," a term which conveys an impression of hordes of human beings, faceless and voiceless, who press relentlessly on the resources of the land but have no ideas or initiatives of their own. For decades, the British, and many Indians as well, thought of India's millions of peasants as human beings who had humbly accepted the station in life to which God, and the caste system, had called them, who bowed their heads to natural disasters such as drought or flood, who produced innumerable children with no heed for their health, nutrition, or education, and who could never be expected to stir out of their fatalism and apathy.

The signal achievement of Gandhi and other leaders of the independence movement is that they recognized the human being in the face of the peasant, that they sensed his potential capacity for enterprise, for self-discipline, and for sacrifice on behalf of his children, and of the community in which he lives. These qualities, they believed, were like veins of ore that had never been mined, but that would produce great riches once they had been probed. Fatalism and apathy, as they saw it, were not ineradicable features of the Indian's outlook on life, nor were they an inevitable product of his Hindu faith which, as we saw, dictates a life of action where action is the result of careful meditation about the deeds that are to be performed. Nor did they believe, as some Westerners had assumed, that the Indian lacks the gifts of business acumen, thrift, and acquisitiveness which Western experts often attribute to the Protestant ethic, yet which are frequently displayed by Indian merchants not only in their own country, but in the countries to which they have emigrated—Ceylon and Malaya, Kenya and South Africa. What was necessary, in their opinion, was to find the key to unlock the storehouse of initiative which, they believed, was latent in the Indian peasants. This key has been provided by voluntary community action.

The government encourages active self-help and participation by villagers in a wide range of projects through the community development program, which was launched on October 2, 1952, the anniversary of Gandhi's birthday. "The community projects," Mr. Nehru has said, "are of vital importance not only for the material achievements they will bring about, but much more so because they seek to build up the community and the individual, and to make the latter a builder not only of his own village centre but in a larger sense of India."

This program, which started in 1952 in 25,000 villages, by the end of the first Five-Year Plan in April 1956 was reaching 123,000 villages containing 80 million people, or about a fourth of all the country's villages. It is hoped that, by the end of the second Five-Year Plan in 1963 (the date originally set was 1961), the program will cover all of India. The two extra years were asked by the Committee on Plan Projects, appointed by Parliament, which in November 1957 urged better training of rural workers at all levels to man the projects.

Community development is carried out through the national rural extension service which was founded in 1953. This service is based both on the experiences of India's own rural workers, stimulated by Gandhi and the poet Rabindranath Tagore before independence, and on the agricultural extension systems used in the United States and Japan. As the Indian Planning Commission has stated in its book, *The New India*, the essential method of the community development program is "education and persuasion; never coercion and dictation. Its incentive is the advancement both of the individual and the community."

The government, in effect, proposes reforms in the village areas, but it is the village community that disposes. The representative of the government is the multipurpose village extension worker—a young man, or, less frequently, a young woman (the ratio of men to women village level workers is ten men and two women per block of one hundred villages)—with high-school education or better who has been specially trained in rural extension work. He, or she, goes from village to village, from farmer to farmer, introducing techniques with which we are familiar in American extension work—field demonstrations, individual talks, and group discussions, audio-visual teaching, and other ways of arousing the interest of the villagers. The multipurpose worker gives help and information on improved methods of cultivation, on health care and sanitation, on cattle diseases and their prevention, and so on. He encourages not only the individual farmer, but the village as a whole, to start new enterprises—a dam, a latrine, a school, a hospital. The government provides technical advice and advances part of the funds, but the decision to build a school, for example, must be made by the village, and the villagers must pay a share of the cost in cash, labor, or materials.

As a result of this democratic process of voluntary participation in a community undertaking, the villagers acquire the habit of working with their neighbours, as well as with other villagers in the area covered by the multipurpose village worker. The rapid expansion of the community development program has roused the Indian peasants to see what can be accomplished by pooled efforts to improve living conditions. It is a heartening experience to visit villages where community development projects are under way, and to see the interest of men and women in taking steps, modest as they may seem to a Westerner, toward a better life for their children for whom the Indians have a deep affection.

They listen avidly, with respect and even reverence, to those who bring expert knowledge to the village—the multipurpose worker, the school teacher, the veterinary, the mid-wife—and show endless ingenuity, with the limited resources of tools and knowledge at their disposal, in carrying out suggestions they regard as practicable. If animals have been sharing the one-room mud house with the family, and the villagers are told this is not a hygienic way to live, they will take the animals out and arrange to tether them in the village square. After watching the teacher intently as he or she instructs their children under a tree, for lack of a schoolhouse, in the mysteries of the alphabet and the operations of addition and division, they want eventually to build a school, providing the land, the building materials (usually local stone, or bricks they make themselves), and the labor. Almost always the plot of land set aside for the school is well situated, open to the sun, and great care and pride go into the construction work. The adults, when they know that their children are beginning to become literate, want to follow suit, and welcome help from the teacher in training themselves, after the men return from the fields at night, or after the women are through with their morning chores, so that they in turn can form classes to teach others. They will put together their few annas to buy a newspaper, so that there will be something to read—and later perhaps try to get a few books. They adorn their homes, not only with the beautiful traditional copper vessels and the designs women paint on the floor and on walls, but with added amenities purchased from local craftsmen or in the bazaar of the neighbouring town on an infrequent visit there.

The moment hospital facilities, to use Asoka's phrase, "for man and beast," become available, they flock to see the doctor—often a "lady doctor"—and the women, with time, when they find out about planned parenthood clinics, go in for consultations, while the men bring in their sick animals to be looked at by the veterinarian. New ideas for improvement of agricultural production are eagerly seized upon, as the government discovered after it had established just one fertilizer plant, thinking the peasants would be slow to make use of the new product, only to be swamped with orders. They are eager to have electricity brought into their villages. These peasants, who had once been considered as unwilling or unable to change, who often know hunger and thirst, are hungry and thirsty for knowledge, and look forward to a better life for their children.

It is easy, in the glow of a deep longing for improvement, however modest, of the Indian peasant's miserable lot, to be carried away by overoptimistic expectations about the impact of the community development projects on India's long-stagnant villages. An outside observer, who would like nothing better than to share this glow, must admit that some of India's administrators as well as Western visitors have allowed themselves to be carried away by overoptimism, and to confuse the goal with the actual performance. There is a constant danger that the sparks started by government initiative will die out after a brief period of activity, and that the villages stirred by new ideas will relapse into lethargy for lack of sustained effort.

Many peasants are afraid of change of any kind. This is more true of men than of women, and of the very poor than of those who have some resources of their own. Many, too, are suspicious of all government, and look askance at any undertaking in which they have to deal with officials. The multipurpose village workers, for their part, must not only be skilled in the tasks they are called upon to perform, but must have a sympathetic concern with the villagers without falling into a "lady-bountiful" bathos; must be willing to start with small improvements which are within the peasant's reach rater than with large schemes that may frighten him off; and must have a sense of the equality of human beings, irrespective of wealth or poverty, of caste or religion. This is a strenuous assignment for any young man or woman—yet it is perhaps the most important assignment an Indian citizen can undertake today in a land of villages.

The poignant mixture of hope and apprehension one feels during visit to the villages has been vividly described by Margaret Parton, the most perceptive American journalist to write about India, in her book *The Leaf and the Flame*, when she says: "And as we drove away over the rutted earth, I found myself with hands clasped in lap, praying in a sort of way that they would keep up the zeal even when the illustrious leaders had left, that they would build their road to the future, that they would not relapse into a 'pathetic contentment,' which in India is another phrase for stagnation and sometimes for death. But they must do it themselves; they must understand that they must do it themselves, for the government is too harassed, too financially burdened, too lacking in trained personnel to do it—to build the roads to the outside world which are a key to so many village problems."

The same point has been made by a distinguished American rural sociologist, Dr. Carl Taylor, in his article, "Two Major Evils," published in the January 26, 1959 issue of *Kurukshetra*, the monthly journal of the Community Development Ministry. Dr. Taylor, who had seen the start of the Community Development Program, which he regards as "excellently designed and soundly launched," believes, after studying it in operation, that corrections are needed both at the village level and in the "administrative assembly line." He contends that administrators doubted the villagers were clearly and keenly aware of their needs, and assumed they would have "to be baited to work at the improvement of their own life." As a result, "an undue and unwise amount of material and financial assistance was given "to motivate the people." This, in turn, caused the program to become more and more an administrators' program and less and less a "community development—extension" program. The remedy he recommends is as follows: "The development of the people, the development of unpaid local leaders, the maximum possible contributions of village level workers, who work with the people and the people's chosen leaders and self-created groups, are the very essence and genius of community development." It is hoped in India that the newly adopted "democratic decentralization" of the villages, through the creation of the Block Committees described in Chapter 6, will help to make community development, as Dr. Taylor suggests, a "people's program instead of what it has been so far, a government program."

But if the overoptimists are to be deprecated so are the overpessimists—and no Westerner can be as critical of India's conditions as are some of its most thoughtful critics—who contend that the community development program has proved a complete failure. For in spite of mistakes, disappointments, and setbacks, thought and action are stimulated by two important factors. First, independence, although it has brought many new difficulties, has given the peasants a sense they had not had for centuries—the sense of working for themselves in their own country, not under foreign rule. The electrifying effect of independence cannot be overestimated in the non-Western countries which have known colonial rule. First, even if the native rulers prove unsatisfactory, the Indian peasants know that they have the right "to throw the rascals out"—a right they did not enjoy while the British were there. And, second, the government has tried to make clear that it is not directing the peasants' decisions. What the government workers do is to ask the peasants: "What do you want ? We are here to help you in every way we can, but it is you who must choose." This attitude of respect for the individual and for the community of which he is a member gives the peasants a feeling of dignity they had not enjoyed before. And as the individual becomes involved in improving his village, then his community, then the surrounding area, he also starts to think in terms of building the nation as a whole. In this respect, the community development program acts as a cement to hold the disparate elements of a vast subcontinent together.

But the program does more than that. It also creates new needs, which must be filled if the program is to succeed. There must be more and more trained personnel capable of handling community development projects—more multipurpose workers, teachers, doctors, midwives, home economists, veterinarians, public health experts, engineers. It is estimated that under the second Five-Year Plan 200,000 new workers will be needed at all levels, whose training will require 61 training centers and 95 agricultural schools.

But as plans are made for obtaining these trained people, new ideas arise about the kind of education India should have. It becomes evident that, by modeling its schools and colleges and universities on the British experience, India has produced vast numbers of white-collar workers and intellectuals who, literally, have no place to go at the present stage of economic development, when most of the available jobs are in government, and industry, as it becomes more specialized, needs men and women trained in science and technology, not in the humanities—as do the community development.

And yet, encouraged by the promise made in the constitution of free and compulsory education for all, more and more young people every year hammer at the doors of educational institutions, which are short of funds, of buildings, of library facilities and, most important, of trained teachers in practically all fields of knowledge. The thirst for knowledge, released by independence and by the start India has made on modernizing its social and economic system, cannot be readily slaked. Desperate educators, confronted with a tidal wave of students, are busy trying to rethink the purpose and methods of education for vast masses of people, still 85 per cent illiterate, who must be prepared as soon as possible to man, not only government offices and newspapers and law offices and hospitals, as was done in the past, but also primary and secondary schools, and the multifarious activities of community development projects.

New Methods are being studied, on the basis of information about general education in the United States, of American agricultural extension schools, of the training the Russians give in science and technology to a people who only forty years ago were at approximately the same educational level as the Indians. New textbooks must be written and published. But the Indians are so poor that hard-cover books would be accessible only to a few—so paperbacks are being published not only in English, spoken by but 10 to 15 percent of the population, or in the official language, Hindi, which is not yet familiar to many of the people who speak other languages, but also in the various major tongues of India—Marathi, Gujerati, Telugu, Bengali, and so on.

And still another question arises—should instruction be given in English, as it was under British rule, or should the government bow to nationalist sentiment, exclude English, and insist on having all instruction given in Hindi, the newly proclaimed official language, along with the local or regional language ? The argument made in favour of the adoption of Hindi as the language to be spoken by all officials was that, first, it would provide a common tongue for the nation as a whole, replacing English, the language of the ousted foreign ruler; and, second, that it was the language of the largest language group in India.

While the first argument carried great weight during the years of the nationalist struggle against Britain, the second argument, once independence had been achieve, aroused fear in the non-Hindi areas of the country that the Hindi-speaking regions of the north would attempt to dominate the rest of the new nation in more than linguistic terms—particularly since Hindi was being pushed by the extremist Hindu religious groups. At the All-India Languages Conference held in Calcutta in 1958, Master Tara Singh expressed this fear vigorously when he said: "The conquering Muslims imposed Persian and Arabic on us and the conquering British imposed English. Now, the Hindi-speaking people are trying to impose their language because they are more numerous than any other language-group in the country." And, Chakravarti Rajagopalachari, former Chief Minister of Madras state in the South, where Tamil is the prevailing language and the opposition of the predominantly Dravidian population had taken dramatic forms, such as the use of passive resistance and the destruction of Hindi railway signs, declared: "God alone knows what will happen if Hindi was pushed like that !" Bearing in mind the agitation for Hindi, backed by violent demonstrations, which had occurred in the state of Punjab in the north, Rajiji, as this elder statesman is affectionately called, also said that a secular state should have a secular language as its official language. These mutual denunciations by supporters and opponents of Hindi seemed to justify Mr. Nehru's earlier warning that, "Language is both a binding force and a separating one and we have to be very careful in the matter of languages in India lest in our enthusiasm we might encourage disruption."

This issue, which threatened to assume dangerous proportions in 1957, has gradually been eased as responsible leaders have pointed out that English is not merely the tongue of a former colonial power. but a medium of expression essential for work in scientific and technical fields, not to speak of diplomacy, the press, and other media of contact with the outside world. C.D. Deshmukh, former Finance Minister and now president of the University Grants Commission, strongly pressed the case of retention of English at a conference on the problems of teaching English held in New Delhi in 1958. He described English as "the main gateway of learning," and contended that development of the mind would be impossible without extensive and reinforced resort to the English language which opened "the doors to us of at least two-thirds of the current scientific and technological literature and 'belles-lettres.'"

The mere thought of having to find substitutes, in Hindi and other languages, for the terms used in nuclear physics, which is of such importance to India, conscious of the possibilities of atomic energy for peacetime use, has caused even nationalists to reconsider their opposition to the use of English. The compromise that will probably prove workable is to teach students Hindi, the official language for all of India, and the local language through the primary school, and to introduce English, the language used by the literate minority for 300 years, for study during the seven or eight years at the secondary level, continuing with it in colleges and universities. To those who have protested that the process of learning more than one language would be too arduous for the young, Mr. Nehru pointed out in 1958 that, in the Low Countries and the Scandinavian countries he had just visited, children thought nothing of speaking two or three languages; and he particularly singled out the example of Finland where, he reported, children speak five languages—Finnish, German, English, Swedish, and that of their neighbour Russia. Thus, the needs of modern education seem to assure that India will remain a multilingual country from which English, even if it is not taught as well as when the British were there, will at least not be excluded, as at one time seemed possible. This seems to be assured by the government's decision to establish an English-language Training Institute.

As the villagers begin to improve their living conditions, they become eager to start saving through the rural credit system, and begin to have new wants which before they had either not experienced or had no hope of satisfying. Where once they could walk on foot in their villages, now they need bicycles to get around the community development area. The men want an extra shirt, the women an extra sari. They begin to look for leather sandals. Perhaps new pots and pans are coveted by the housewife. Radios and sewing machines may be seen, and dreamed about for the future. Slates and chalk and pencils and paper have to be obtained for the schools. If the house is enlarged by the addition of another room, new furniture may be required. Slowly, imperceptibly, but in a way that eventually makes itself felt, the peasants turn to nearby sources of modest industrial goods.

The government, following Gandhi's injunction to try to take industries to the villages, instead of villagers to the industrial towns, has encouraged the growth and modernization of the traditional and "cottage industries," which still form an intimate part of Indian village life and economy, and of the towns as well. These industries include handloom (cloth hand woven from mill-made yarn), *khadi* (handspun yarn, and cloth hand woven from homespun yarn); silk; handicrafts, such as art metalwork, toys, ivory carving, ceramics; and the manufacturing of raw sugar, matches, and leather footwear.

Thus, slowly—much too slowly not only from the point of view of Western critics but also of the more impatient Indians—ancient ways of life are being changed, old customs are being replaced by new, and the individual gets a glimpse of the wider horizons of the modern world without having to tear up his, and his nation's, past by the roots. The gains achieved by these gradual methods seem modest, even pitifully so, compared with the spectacular victories reported by the Russians and the Chinese from industrial and agricultural battlefronts. But the Indian leaders believe that by building without haste they are laying solid foundations for the country's future, and that the preservation of human values—of life, and liberty, and a sense of personal dignity in a mass society—is in the long run more important than sudden transformations of an existing order, no matter how dramatic or, in the short run, desirable from a practical point of view. India accepts mechanization, and collective effort, and the latest contributions of science and technology, including atomic energy for peacetime purposes—but it regards them not as ends, but as means to achieve the end it has set for its people: and that is the welfare of society as a whole, with as close an approximation to equality of rights, opportunities, and well-being as its resources and level of economic development permit.

A similar approach has been made to the task of reorganizing the social order since independence. This, too, —except for the initial Muslim-Hindu riots—has been accomplished with little or no violence, and with a striking degree of mutual respect between social groups which in other counties at a comparable stage of economic growth have clashed in bloody political strife or brutal class warfare. Instead of eliminating some groups by force, on the "we or they" principle, the Indians, without fanfare, have readjusted themselves to new circumstances, have averted potential clashes, have sought accommodation and reconciliation rather than clear-cut victories for one section of the population over another.

Within a decade, the princely heads of 561 states, instead of trying to overthrow the central government by revolution, or nursing grievances in exile, have for the most part accepted their new status with good grace, and have not been above seeking lucrative employment in business or political responsibilities as members of parliament. Some, like the Maharajah of Jaipur, have transformed their palaces into attractive hostelries for tourists. Others, for example, the Maharajah of Patiala, who heads Coca Cola in India, have gone into business enterprises. Still others, entering electoral contests alongside commoners, have garnered the votes of their former subjects who, far from being hostile to dethroned rulers, are ready to choose them as their representatives in a democracy, provided they display the necessary qualifications. A readjustment which, in a country like France required the 1789 revolution, followed by Napoleon's seizure of power and by several restorations of the monarchy before the country settled down to being a republic, has been carried out smoothly, leaving no significant residue to ill-feeling on either side.

Similarly, while the Indians are still suspicious of the private entrepreneur, fearing that he may be ready to sacrifice public weal for private gain, the government, as already pointed out, far from making martyrs of businessmen, has encouraged private enterprise, has welcomed wealthy leaders of commerce and industry to the ranks of the ruling Congress party, and has operated on the theory that partnership between government and business is far more beneficial for the country than the suppression of merchant, banker, and investor. The business community, for its part, although often critical of specific governmental policies, has not been alienated, realizes that it would be unable to win enough votes in the country to form a viable opposition party, acknowledges the need for state initiatives in some basic sectors of the economy, and does not hesitate to turn to the state in obtaining financial assistance at home and abroad. And, while labour conditions in India leave much to be desired, particularly in some of the textile mills of Bombay and Allahabad, industry does not question the freedom to form unions, and the government, often acting as mediator, tries to maintain a balance between the interests of capital, labour, and consumer.

Nor has India's predisposition toward egalitarianism spared even the group which, in another society, might have assumed the role played elsewhere by monarchy or aristocracy—the civil servants. These men, usually educated in England, and nurtured in the traditions of British administration and justice, might have aspired to the role once played by British rulers; or, alternatively, their past association with the foreign ruler might have made them unacceptable to the new political leaders, who had suffered imprisonment and repression at the hands of the British.

Yet, neither of these alternatives occurred. The government of independent India made effective use of the civil servants it inherited from Britain, integrating them into the new system, but did not set them up on a pedestal. On the contrary, the civil servants soon discovered that they were responsible not only to the executive, as in the past, but also to the representatives of the people, as chosen by the vote s for service in Parliament. This was not always an eay adjustment to make for men who had no experience with parliamentary democracy, and who still often look with distaste, even contempt, on legislators who may not be their equals in education, *savoir-faire*, and knowledge of the world—even though they are much closer to the hopes and fears of the average citizens. But, here again, although there have been some important instances in which civil servants have received what they understandably regard as unfair treatment at the hands of politicians appointed to the top cabinet posts, and even at the hands of Mr. Nehru, the balance of power and interests between political leaders and administrative technicians who today must master the intricacies not only of government operations but also of state industrial enterprises, is being gradually adjusted without revolt on either side.

There is one problem, however, which will require greater clarification than it has so far received. The ruling Congress Party has indicated on a number of occasions—and Mr. Nehru himself has publicly made this point—that members of the civil service should not be "neutral" and should come out of their "ivory tower." The implication of these remarks is that the civil servants are too aloof from the political ideas of the Congress party—particularly from its socialist plans—and fail to achieve an emotional integration with the government's policies. It has even been suggested that the concept of the British civil service as a group of trained administrators uncommitted to any given political course but ready to serve every government, whatever its policy, is not a good example for India to follow. Critics of the government—notably *The Eastern Economist*—have pointed out that if civil servants are today to associate themselves with a given political party simply because it happens to be in power, they will be obliged to become equally associated tomorrow with a different party which may subsequently take the helm. Thus the civil service would become a weathervane, turning with every political wind. On the contrary, critics say, if the civil service is not to be recruited solely from the ranks of "yes" men careful to avoid taking the initiative, they should be encouraged to exercise detachment and independence and, through fearless criticism of the proposals made by politician-Ministers, produce a creative "cross-fertilization" of ideas which would enrich the country's administrative development. This issue—whether, as claimed by some government and Congress par.y spokesmen, the civil service is becoming as ossified bureaucracy, incapable of adapting itself to the country's new economic and social needs, or, as critics of Nehru contend, is being forced to bow to the will of politicians—will have to be resolved if the growing requirements of an expanding economy and an increasingly complex administrative system are to be adequately met with both imagination and integrity.

The armed forces, which in some underdeveloped countries have either assumed, or been forced by lack of other strong leadership to assume responsibility for government—as in Egypt and Iraq, Pakistan, and some of the Latin American countries—have so far remained completely aloof from politics. They have displayed a discipline, loyalty, sense of public service, and intellectual qualities which are not only respected by their own people, but have impressed observers abroad wherever Indian troops have performed military assignments, as in the repatriation of prisoners at the end of the Korean war, or in the United Nations Emergency Force in Sinai after the Suez crisis.

Thus, without mobilizing the entire population for national tasks, without subordinating the individual to the state, without trying to brainwash citizens into excluding all private thought and feeling, the Indian government, in spite of the appalling problems with which it has been confronted since independence, has succeeded in maintaining an orderly society, based on voluntary cooperation by a wide variety of religious, linguistic, economic, and social groups, and guided, through their own decisions, by objectives common to a majority. Purists might argue that the Indian system is not a true democracy in the Western sense, since it is ruled by a single-party government, under the leadership of an individual who exercises vast personal authority. Yet, under the conditions of an underdeveloped economy only now emerging from the Middle Ages, and of a social order faced by the strains of adaptation to technology at home and of cold-war tensions abroad, India's multiracial, multireligious, multilingual society, animated by a drive toward egalitarianism and dedicated to voluntary cooperation, cannot but be regarded as evolving new patterns of democracy. These patterns may not be properly comparable with those of the West, but they hold rich promise as an example to other non-Western countries—provided, of course, they can be maintained in the future. Whether or not India succeeds in pursuing a democratic way of life, or is forced to follow the road taken by Russia or China, will depend not only on its own resourcefulness and sense of dedication but also on the understanding and support it may receive from the advanced Western democracies.

■■■■